Canadian Cataloguing in Publication Data
Davis, M. Dale, 1947–
  Civilizations in history

For use in high schools.
Bibliography: p.393
Includes index.
ISBN 0-19-540526-9

1. Civilization. 2. Europe–History. 3. World history. 4. History.
I. Title.

D21.D38 1986   909   C85-090847-7

DESIGNER: Geraldine Kikuta
COVER DESIGN: Stan Godzisz
ILLUSTRATORS: Susan Calverley, Christine Alexiou, Helen Fox
ASSEMBLY: Christine Alexiou
EDITOR: Geraldine Kikuta
EDITORIAL ASSISTANTS: Elspeth Staniland, Sandra Richmond, Maryjean Lancefield
COMPOSITOR: Compeer Typographic Services Limited

Printed and bound in Canada by The Bryant Press Limited

2 3 4 5 6 7 8 9 BP 90 89 88 87

Civilizations
in
History

A Thinking Skills Approach to the Study
of Human Development

M. Dale Davis

Oxford University Press

Contents

Acknowledgements

The completion of *Civilizations in History* represents the combined efforts of several people. A special thank you is extended to Tilly Crawley of Oxford University Press for having faith in the original manuscript and in the author. While many publishers were hesitant about producing new books on the eve of changing ministry guidelines, Tilly was supportive and willing to make a firm commitment.

A debt of equal importance is owed to Drs. Len Popp and Jim Love of Brock University for the success achieved in adapting a problem-solving approach to the study of history and related disciplines. Their expertise and guidance were essential to my understanding of the importance of process as a focal point in a learning sequence.

Similarly, the contribution of Woodland's teachers Campbell Coulter and Brian Lorimer was of major significance as they kindly consented to use this and earlier drafts of the manuscript in their classrooms. The suggestions that sprang from their experience have greatly improved the organization and usefulness of the book for both student and teacher.

An additional improvement came from the pen of illustrator Alfie Gould, whose diagrams submitted with the original manuscript brought to life many images that would have otherwise remained lifeless on a page.

Only the author can appreciate the value of an extremely talented editor. Geraldine Kikuta's unfailing good humour, energy, insightful judgement, and organizational wizardry consistently augmented and maximized the total impact of the book. Her approach made it fun for everyone.

My deepest debt of gratitude must go to my wife, Renate. Her assistance with the technical aspects of the book and as a proofreader was professional. Her patience with, love and understanding of the author and his task were vital. It is to Renate, the centre of my life, that I dedicate this book.

Introduction

The fascinating paths of human development have never been completely traced. We, in the twentieth century, are blessed and burdened with a quantity of information that is too large for any individual to know or comprehend. As we peer farther back towards the remote era of our origin, evidence of human activity or even presence becomes rare indeed. Yet the task of understanding remains the same: We must be able to select and arrange the information at our disposal–no matter how much or how little–to paint the most accurate picture possible of what really happened.

All too often history is presented in a way that provides too many answers and asks too few questions. These answers, particularly when based on extensive research and much hard work, become engrained in our minds and can lead us to be less creative, to make fewer comparisons, and to fail to look for answers of our own. At the other extreme, we often quickly accept ideas about the past that seem glamorous and exciting even when there is little evidence to support them. Careful examination of all sources, whether serious or fanciful, is essential if our past is to be better understood. The educational nature of history lies in seeking answers by asking intelligent questions rather than merely accepting prepackaged ideas or popular notions.

When questions are omitted, it begins to look as if all of history was somehow inevitable. This attitude, when carried into everyday life, can leave the impression that there is little that can be done to turn the tides of political, economic, and social events. Only by raising questions, however, and studying their long- and short-term effects, can the choices that were present in every historical situation be used to reconstruct the past and relate it to the present and future.

This book attempts to look at the past in a series of studies that present real choices about major historical issues. Each chapter provides background information that outlines why an issue exists and then presents the issue as a unit question, or problem, that becomes the focal point of study. Only two contrasting viewpoints on the issue in question are studied in the first chapter. This serves to introduce students to the method of examining alternatives to answer a problem question.

For each subsequent chapter, three contrasting opinions, ranging from traditional explanations to wishful thinking and speculation, have been adapted as possible answers. A section entitled "Answering the Problem Question" then guides students in their analysis of the alternatives, explaining the factors to be considered before a reasoned conclusion can be reached. No definitive answer is given. It is left to the students to apply the suggestions that are offered or to develop additional, creative approaches.

A descriptive account of developments and events that lead to the next problem is then presented for chronological continuity. At the end of each chapter, a comment is made to clarify the present state of opinion about the topic, pose unanswered questions, identify future trends and consequences, or relate general ideas of historical importance.

As the study proceeds from chapter to chapter, the sentence structure, type of question, choice of criteria, and depth of material increase slightly in level of difficulty. This is intended to provide an opportunity for intellectual enhancement and growth.

By studying a variety of choices for each issue, intellectual instincts to question rather than to accept are encouraged in an honest and positive direction.

Geologic Period	Millions of Years Ago	Event
Precambrian (earliest era)	4500	Creation of the earth
	4000	Formation of primordial sea
	3500	First signs of life, single-celled algae and bacteria, appear in water
	900	First oxygen-breathing animals appear
Paleozoic (ancient life)	500	First fish with backbones appear
	400	Small amphibians venture onto land
	225	Age of dinosaurs
Mesozoic (middle life)	65	Prosimians, the earliest primates, develop in trees
Cenozoic (recent life)	40	Monkeys appear in South America and Africa
	30	Apes appear in Africa only
Lower Pleistocene (oldest period of most recent epoch)	3.5	"Lucy"–earliest human ancestor (?) appears
	2.5	First stone tools used
	1.8	Homo habilis, first true human, emerges in Africa
	1.6	Homo erectus emerges
	1.4	First use of fire
	.3	Homo sapiens emerges
	.04	Homo sapiens sapiens emerges

1

The Origin of Humans

BACKGROUND

The Issue Emerges

4004 B.C.! That, proclaimed Archbishop James Ussher in 1650, was the actual year of human creation as described in the Book of Genesis. Dr. John Lightfoot, Master of St. Catherine's College, Cambridge, soon after declared the precise day and time to be 23 October at exactly 9:00 in the morning! These statements were accepted by many for generations.

By the mid-nineteenth century, however, more and more people began to question these claims. Scientists were puzzled by the discovery of animal imprints and bones reproduced in stones known as fossils. Many of these fossil-animals were extinct. Although some existing animals resembled the fossils, there were clear differences that were hard to explain.

A young naturalist, Charles Darwin, took up the problem on a five-year, around-the-world voyage aboard the H.M.S. *Beagle*. He carefully studied living animals and birds in South America and the Galapagos Islands. He also studied fossils found at these locations. The results of Darwin's work were published in 1859 in *On the Origin of Species*.

In his book, Darwin explained how new types of animals developed. He argued that animals changed gradually over long periods of time, as did the world around them. Through the centuries, climates warmed and cooled affecting the animals' habitats. When these changes were lasting, the animals either adapted to the new conditions or died. The fittest were those who survived and adapted. Those that could not change eventually became extinct. This was the process of **natural selection**. The small physical changes created stronger animals that could live successfully in the new conditions. With enough small changes over a long period of time, the survivors would eventually become different from their ancestors. Darwin's theory of gradual change became popularly known as evolution.

Darwin's ideas caused an outrage in a world that was very religious. Although he had not discussed humans in his book, the implications were clear. If Darwin was right, humans were much, much older than the six thousand years ascribed to them by the Church. The notion that humans might have evolved from a lower life form to their present position of dominance on the planet was still a remote and frightening idea.

Darwin's idea of gradual change has been slightly modified by some of today's scientists. New ideas have suggested that evolution can, at times, take place in quicker steps than Darwin realized. Nevertheless, a basic question is still often asked. Was Darwin on the right track in tracing the path of human development?

The Fossil Record

FOSSIL FORMATION

The major source of evidence for evolution is the fossil record. To create a fossil, an animal's dead body must lie undisturbed. The ideal location is at the edge of a river or lake. There, if enough rain falls to raise the water level and cover the skeleton with silt and mud, the bones are protected and preserved. Gradually, the space occupied by the bones is replaced by minerals in the water. This process duplicates in stone the exact imprint of the skeleton.

Unfortunately, fossils are rare. Usually, when an animal dies its bones are moved about by scavengers or passing herds. Hot weather and wind quickly break up the remaining pieces of bone leaving nothing to fossilize.

HOMO ERECTUS

After the publication of Darwin's book, several fossil finds suggested that humans were much older than was previously thought. Locations as far apart as Java, China, Germany, Spain, Hungary, and Africa yielded fossils of a short, muscular, heavyset human relative. It was eventually given a scientific name –Homo (man) erectus (upright)–based on its ability to walk on two legs like present-day humans. Scientists guessed that Homo erectus was about five hundred thousand years old! At the time, however, there was no way to prove such a claim.

Where did Homo erectus originate? A possible answer to that question burst into the scientific world in 1924. The tiny skull of a six-year-old child was found near Taung, South Africa. This creature appeared to have walked in an upright position and had large teeth that were shaped like those of a human. Nevertheless, its brain was smaller than the brain of Homo erectus. In fact it was closer in size to that of an ape. Although close, it was not quite human,

AUSTRALOPITHECUS

and scientists gave it a separate Latin name–Australopithecus (southern ape). Adult versions of the Taung child and even different types of Australopithecus were found during the 1930s, 1940s, and 1950s.

RELATIVE DATING

The age of Australopithecus was estimated at well over a million years, but again there was no way to prove this. A technique known as **relative dating** could prove that fossils found in rock layers deep in the ground were older than fossils found in layers near the surface, but it could not give a date in years. In any case, the importance of Australopithecus was long overshadowed by another find that took place just after the turn of the century.

1. When a creature dies near a lake or swamp the flesh and soft parts of the body rot quickly.

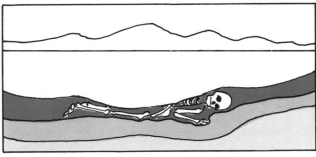

2. All that is left are the bones and teeth which are covered with mud and sand during the flood season of the first year.

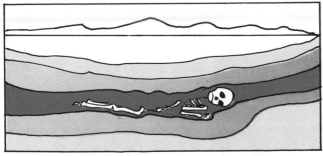

3. The bones turn into minerals. More and more layers of mud and sand pile on top of the skeleton.

4. Later the earth's movements lift the land up above the sea. Wind and rain wear the rocks away. In time a fossil appears.

Piltdown Man: An Embarrassing Setback

How Fossils Form.

The great industrial advances that took place in the late nineteenth and early twentieth centuries were attributed to the brain and intelligence–the main features that make us human. Most of the early human fossils, however, had smaller brains by comparison. How, then, did humans evolve to their present cranial capacity? Was there still fossil evidence missing?

In 1912, an amateur archaeologist, Charles Dawson, made a startling discovery in a gravel pit at Piltdown, Sussex. Dawson found a braincase, comparable in size to that of a contemporary human, with a primitive, ape-like jaw and ground-down teeth.

The fact that this remarkable discovery was made in England at a time when England was a major world power gave the new find unwarranted credibility. Even though their requests to study the original Piltdown fossils were refused, most leading British scientists eagerly accepted the Piltdown Man into the family of human ancestors. In the 1920s, many of these same scientists scoffed at the suggestion that Australopithecus, with its small brain, was a human ancestor.

CHARLES DAWSON

PILTDOWN MAN

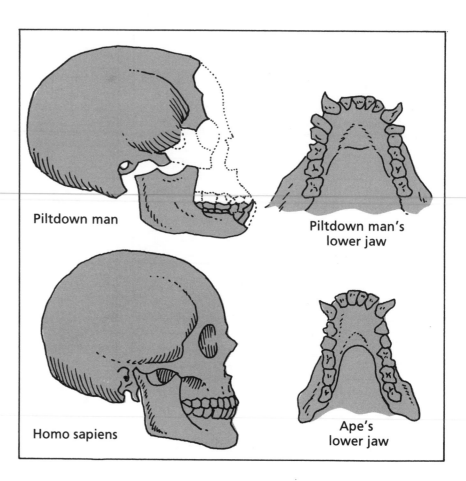

Piltdown man

Piltdown man's
lower jaw

Homo sapiens

Ape's
lower jaw

The Piltdown Forgery.

Modern fluorine tests released by the British Museum in 1953, however, showed that Piltdown Man was a fake. The bones of a modern man and an orangutan had been chemically treated to give the appearance of fossils. It has been suggested that university students did it as a prank to fool their professors. However, it was most likely Dawson who manufactured the deception.

IMPACT OF THE FORGERY

He died in 1937 without changing his story. Nevertheless, the fact remained that the scientific community had been fooled for a very long time.

Once the forgery was revealed, the role of Australopithecus as a probable human ancestor was fully recognized by the scientific community. Yet, could the public, who had witnessed the entire Piltdown story in the newspapers, now be expected to believe these same scientists who had apparently been fooled for four decades?

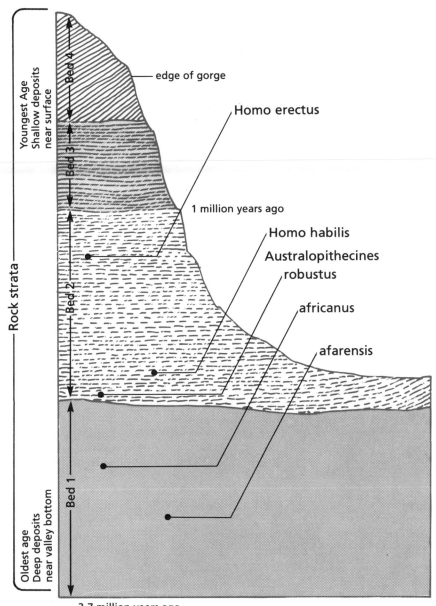

edge of gorge

Homo erectus

1 million years ago

Homo habilis

Australopithecines

robustus

africanus

afarensis

Rock strata

Youngest Age
Shallow deposits
near surface

Bed 4

Bed 3

Bed 2

Bed 1

Oldest age
Deep deposits
near valley bottom

3.7 million years ago

Profile of Relative Dating at Field Site.

The Pattern of Primate Evolution

What can scientists tell us about the pattern of primate evolution? Many gaps still exist in the fossil record, but a general line of development has emerged.

The discovery of new dating methods has helped verify the pattern of primate evolution. Until the 1950s, only relative dating was possible. However, now a more precise date of age can be established by testing the volcanic rock in the vicinity of the fossil discovery for radioactive elements. Using the known rate of decay for radioactive elements, scientists can determine the age of the rock in years. If the rock samples are pure and not severely weathered, a fairly accurate date can be established. This is known as **absolute dating**.

ABSOLUTE DATING

THE PRIMATE ORDER

The primate order, which includes prosimians, monkeys, apes, and humans, slowly began to appear after the decline of the dinosaurs 65 million years ago. At first the prosimians, small, tree-dwelling creatures, developed features common to all primates. They had clutching hands and binocular vision to distinguish depth and colour. Their descendants still live in the remote jungles of the world.

PROSIMIANS

Between 40 and 30 million years ago, monkeys evolved from some of the prosimian lines into more than one hundred fifty different types. Their mastery of the tree tops ensured their survival. In Africa and southern Asia, monkeys continued to change in response to their environment into at least three types of prehistoric apes between 30 and 20 million years ago. It is from this evolutionary stage that scientists have intensely debated human origin.

COMMON ANCESTOR

Darwin did not argue, as some people claim, that humans descended from modern apes. His basic argument was that humans and living apes had had a common ancestor at some time in the distant past. It has since been estimated, from the fossil records and biochemistry, that separate development of humans and apes began between 17 million and 4 million years ago.

Differences Between Ape and Human Jaws.

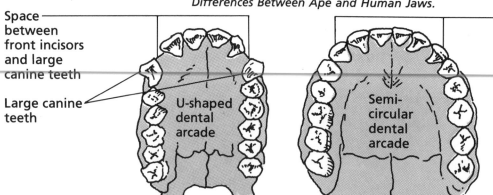

Space between front incisors and large canine teeth

Large canine teeth

U-shaped dental arcade

Semi-circular dental arcade

Small canine teeth same size as front incisors and molars

No space between canine and front incisors

Male Ape Jaw   Human Jaw

Differences in Shape and Orientation Between Ape and Human Pelvises.

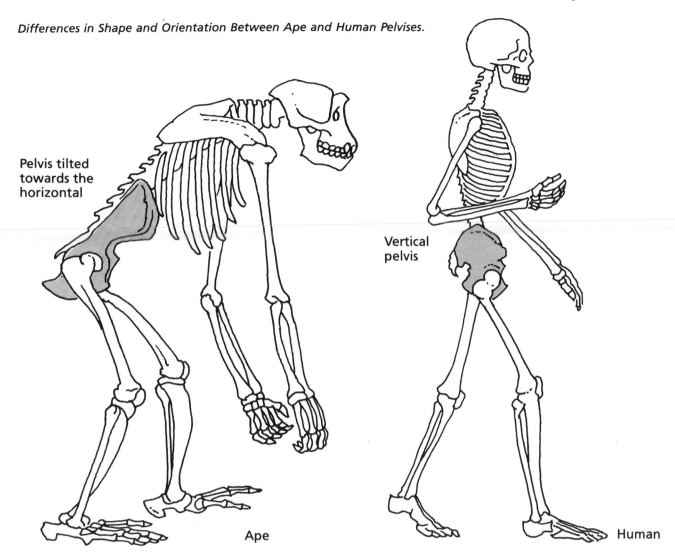

Pelvis tilted towards the horizontal

Vertical pelvis

Ape

Human

   To determine when this point of departure took place, the key differences between humans and apes had to be established. The major characteristics that separates humans from apes–indeed from all other land mammals–is the ability to walk upright on two legs. Although apes often appear to walk on two legs, this is only for brief periods. They always return to a four-legged posture because their knee and hip bones are not suited to an upright stance. Human ancestors, however, have been walking upright for at least 4 million years. Scientists have suggested that the survival practices of peering over tall grass on open ground, having to carry food, and even manufacturing and using tools may have caused upright development.

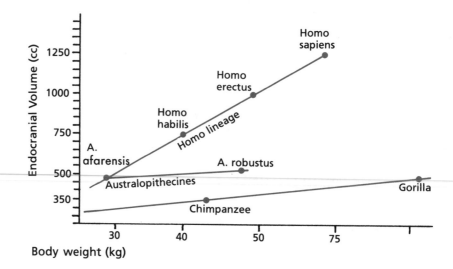

What distinguishes the Homo line from Australopithecines and Pongides (apes)?

HUMAN CHARACTERISTICS

Humans are also distinguished by their large brains. The largest among all primates, it is about three times the size of the brain of a chimpanzee. Humans began to develop larger brains about 2 million years ago. These early humans had a precision grip made possible by a thumb set across from the fingers of the hand. This large brain/precision grip combination enabled humans to make and use stone, and probably wooden, tools and weapons. Thus, superior intelligence became the means for human survival.

In the last decade, a remarkable series of fossil discoveries relating to human origins have surfaced. The search has been focussed in the Great Rift Valley of Africa where fossil-forming conditions in the distant past were excellent. Richard Leakey's now famous "Skull 1470" and Don Johanson's "Lucy" and "First Family" discoveries have added greatly to scientific knowledge of human origin. Has our way of looking at our prehistoric past been placed on the right track, or have the experts been fooled again?

PROBLEM QUESTION

What can scientists tell us about the origin of humans?

ALTERNATIVE ONE

Lucy and the First Family–Based on *Lucy* by Donald Johanson and Maitland Edey, 1981

In 1974, Don Johanson and his expedition set out to find fossil evidence of early humans in the Afar region of Ethiopia. By chance they discovered the fossil of a new type of Australopithecus. The night of the discovery the Beatles' song "Lucy in the Sky with Diamonds" was playing on the tape deck in camp. Johanson's team agreed to call the new fossil "Lucy."

Lucy was something special and different from anything found before. Johanson felt that Lucy might provide a possible answer to the question of human origin.

Reconstruction done by Johanson and his team produced these results. The skeleton, which was 40 percent complete, indicated that Lucy was only 1.1 m tall. The shape of the wide pelvis, designed for childbearing, established her gender. Although only a small fragment of the skull remained, the brain-case appeared to be about the size of a softball.

Lucy's jaw was small and V-shaped, rather than the bowed or semicircular shape of an early human jaw. However, when it was placed in order with other fossil jaws, Lucy's fit the pattern according to size. It differed only in its narrowness. Although too primitive to be called human, Lucy was clearly an earlier ancestor. Of critical importance was Lucy's knee. Its shape enabled her to walk upright. This factor clearly placed her in the human family.

Partly-worn wisdom teeth indicated Lucy was fully grown and between twenty-five and thirty years of age when she died. By using the radioactive decay principle and by comparing her with other fossils, Johanson decided Lucy was 3.5 million years old.

Johanson made a second discovery in the same region, in 1975. At a site numbered 333 near Hadar, the remains of thirteen human-like creatures were found. Nicknamed "The First Family," they had apparently drowned in a narrow ravine hit by a flash flood. Johanson's tests indicated they were about the same age as Lucy.

A year later, another anthropologist, Mary Leakey, made yet another discovery in the region. Her fossil and fossil footprints were reported to be those of upright-walking primates about 3.75 million years old.

Don Johanson believes these discoveries are evidence of a new pattern of human evolution. According to Johanson, 8 million years ago on the shores of Africa, the prehistoric ape, Ramapithecus, slowly changed into an Australopithecine—Lucy and the First Family. At the 3 million year mark, the Australopithecine evolved in two directions. One line produced new types of Australopithecus. These continued to adapt until they became extinct about a million years ago. The second line, the true Homo line according to Johanson, produced Homo habilis—handy man—2 million years ago. By 1.6 million years ago, Homo habilis had become Homo erectus. The descendants of Homo erectus eventually evolved into Homo sapiens.

Questions

1. a) Where did Johanson search for fossils of early humans in 1974?
   b) What fossil did he discover and how did the fossil get its name?
2. Describe the size, appearance, and age of Lucy.

3. What important fossil finds were made in 1975 and 1976?
4. What are the stages—different types of creatures—that Johanson now feels are part of human evolution?

ALTERNATIVE TWO

The Making of Humans—Based on *The Making of Mankind* by Richard Leakey, 1982

The noted anthropologist, Richard Leakey, has a different theory about the origin of humans. According to him, tests done on two complete skulls discovered by Dr. David Pilbeam in 1980 indicate that Ramapithecus was the ancestor of the orangutan. This suggests that another creature, possibly a derivative of the Ramapithecines, formed a common ancestor for all higher primates. These higher primates included humans, Australopithecines, chimpanzees, and gorillas. Sometime between 8 and 5 million years ago, the chimpanzees and gorillas evolved from this common ancestor into the familiar creatures of today.

The puzzle is to establish what happened in between Ramapithecus and Australopithecus and humans. Contrary to Johanson, Leakey feels there is not enough evidence to establish just when humans and Australopithecus evolved in separate lines. He places the common ancestor at about 5 million years. This is much older than the 3.5 million years suggested by Johanson. Leakey bases his argument on the difference in brain sizes between Lucy and Homo habilis, as illustrated by Skull 1470. Too little time had passed between the existence of the two—1.5 million years—for such an increase in size to have evolved.

Leakey also disagrees with Johanson's belief that Lucy and the First Family represent a type of Australopithecus that was the root stock of all Australopithecines and humans. Johanson had identified the larger individuals in the discovery as males and the smaller ones as females. However, Leakey challenges this explanation. The difference in size is so great that the males would have been almost twice the size of females.

According to Leakey, it is more likely that the size differences represent two different types of creatures. The smaller fossils probably produced the Australopithecine line that eventually became extinct. The larger creatures, in all likelihood, led to the true Homo line as we now know it.

To date, too few fossils of any primates between 8 and 4 million years old have been found. As far as Leakey is concerned, the real pattern of human origin will remain a mystery until new discoveries from this period are made.

Questions

1. When did chimpanzees and gorillas evolve in a separate path from humans and Australopithecus?

These fossilized hominid footprints were found by Mary Leakey (shown here) and her team at Laetoli.

2. Don Johanson has a collection of small and large fossils that date to about 3.5 million years.
   a) How does Johanson explain the difference in size?
   b) How does Richard Leakey explain the difference in the size of the fossils?
3. Johanson argues that Homo and Australopithecus evolved along separate lines about 3.5 to 3 million years ago. When does Richard Leakey feel that the separate lines began?
4. What evidence does Leakey have to support this view?

ANSWERING THE PROBLEM QUESTION

Once you understand the views of each author, compare them to see which is the most convincing. Where they agree, there is a good chance that the information is reliable. Where they disagree, we must develop a way to see which one is on the right track.

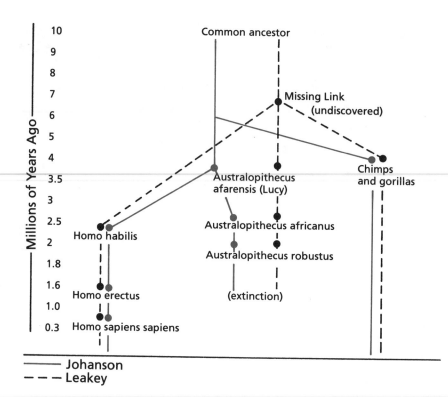

10
9
8
7
6
5
4
3.5
3
2.5
2
1.8
1.6
1.0
0.3

Millions of Years Ago

Common ancestor

Missing Link
(undiscovered)

Chimps
and gorillas

Australopithecus
afarensis (Lucy)

Australopithecus africanus

Homo habilis

Australopithecus robustus

Homo erectus

(extinction)

Homo sapiens sapiens

—— Johanson
– – – Leakey

Johanson's and Leakey's Views of Human Evolution.

MAN'S FIRST
TOOLS

The problem question focusses on the scientific view of human origin. Scientists use one factor above all others to identify humans–the ability to walk upright on two legs. This is the first human feature to emerge on the path of evolution. It separates us from all other land mammals. How can this criterion–the ability to walk upright–be applied to the question about human origin answered in slightly different ways by Johanson and Leakey?

THE STORY CONTINUES . . .

Homo erectus

Homo habilis (man handy) slowly evolved into Homo erectus by about 1.6 million years ago. It was Homo erectus who thrived on vegetation-rich African rivers and lakeshores, and who eventually spread into Europe and Asia.

Probably the most important influence in the development of Homo erectus was fire. The earliest use has been dated at 1.4 million years ago, in Kenya. Homo erectus learned to save and use the coals left by lightning storms and lava flows. This led to both physical and cultural changes. As cooked meat was added to the diet, for example, the large molars once needed to grind coarse

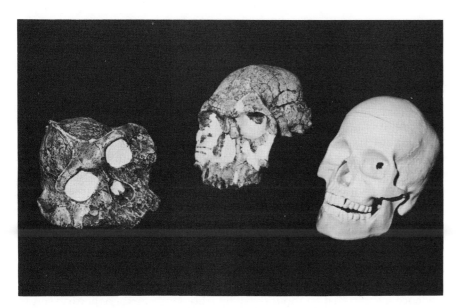

L. to r., replicas of Australopithecus robustus, Homo habilis (Skull 1470), and Homo sapiens sapiens. What features suggest that Australopithecus robustus was most primitive?

THE IMPORTANCE OF FIRE

food were gradually reduced in size. Fire also increased the creature's mobility. Its warmth now meant that Homo erectus could live in parts of the world once considered too cold and harsh. It also provided a new sense of security. By lighting up the darkness, fire was an effective weapon to fend off wild animals.

The use of fire at a temporary campsite, whether in a cave or a crude shelter made of branches, encouraged a division of labour and family-oriented life. At first, the men probably had limited success as hunters of even small animals, but large-scale elephant hunts were staged in Europe about five hundred thousand years ago. Women, children, and the elderly remained at the campsite, continuously tending the fire and gathering the fruits, nuts, and vegetables that were really the essential parts of the group's diet and survival. When the hunters returned to the camp, they could cook their food, fashion weapons and tools, and, finally, relax. Although physically capable of making only slow and clumsy speech, the gathering of the group probably led to the desire to verbalize their experiences, thus beginning the critical development of language.

As hundreds, thousands, and hundreds of thousands of years passed, the physical and cultural evolution of human beings continued. Their superior brains, which had been not much larger than those of apes before Homo erectus, increased in size and complexity. The technology of toolmaking in stone and probably wood (wood decays rapidly and hence cannot be found by paleoanthropologists) had been developed as far back as 2.5 million years ago. These tools gave the early humans additional control over the way they lived by enabling them to build small shelters, hunt, and skin wild animals. Tempered over a fire to harden, the quality of tools and weapons produced by Homo erectus improved, as did their ability to use them in an increasing number of ways.

This process, repeated over thousands of generations, encouraged the physical and mental development of the brain as the demands placed on it became greater and greater.

Homo sapiens

Somewhere between four hundred thousand and one hundred thousand years ago, Homo erectus gradually evolved into Homo sapiens (man the wise). In turn, about forty thousand years ago, Homo sapiens evolved into Homo sapiens sapiens, our present subspecies. Many of the fossils found during this time show transitional features. These include a rounded braincase, high forehead, and reduced, if any, browridges. When Neanderthal Man was discovered in 1856, scientists were not impressed. Today, however, Neanderthal Man is considered a Homo sapiens who probably merged with the first true Homo sapiens sapiens about thirty-one thousand years ago.

The first modern humans, Homo sapiens sapiens, were named Cro-Magnon after the caves in southwestern France where they were first discovered. Cro-Magnon represents a high point in the development of the Stone Age. Evidence suggests that by about thirty-five thousand years ago they had spread into all areas of the globe, except Antarctic, crossing a land-bridge from Siberia to North America and reaching as far south as Australia.

Homo erectus and Homo sapiens had become good hunters. Cro-Magnon, however, invented better weapons and became the finest hunter of all. The spearthrower, a wooden or bone extension of the arm, was first used about fourteen thousand years ago. Australian Aborigines still use the spearthrower today. Drawings on caves and rocks suggest that Cro-Magnon used the bow and arrow at about the same time. Rawhide snares were used to trap foxes, three-pronged spears to catch fish, dugout canoes for travel, and animal leather was sewn together to provide warm clothing. The gathering of plants was very well organized, stopping just short of seed planting.

Of key importance is the fact that Cro-Magnon was the first to develop fine art. Cro-Magnon drawings have been found in over one hundred European caves. They usually show deer, horses, and animals that are now extinct. Even more intriguing are the figurines of clay, ivory, and stone found from France to Russia. They are called Venus figurines because of the exaggerated curves used to show the female body. Some date to about 30 000 B.C. Experts suspect they may represent fertility symbols of a mother goddess.

Spiritual developments can be traced to Neanderthal times, but more advanced practices are found with Cro-Magnon. The skeletons of two boys who died twenty-three thousand years ago have been found laid head-to-head in a grave in Sungir, Russia. Finely made spears and daggers of mammoth tusks, beads, and ivory jewellery were found with the bodies. This suggests they were laid to rest according to some ritual, perhaps with a view to an afterlife.

These advances marked the end of the prehistoric era and set the stage for rapid cultural development.

Venus of Willendorf, 27 000 years old.

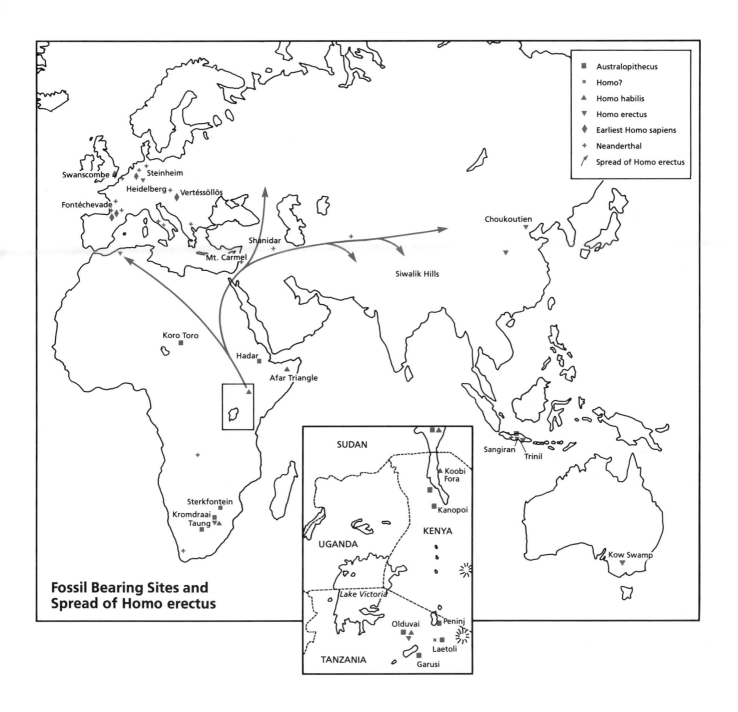

Fossil Bearing Sites and Spread of Homo erectus

Legend:
- Australopithecus
- Homo?
- Homo habilis
- Homo erectus
- Earliest Homo sapiens
- Neanderthal
- Spread of Homo erectus

Swanscombe
Steinheim
Heidelberg
Vertéssöllös
Fontéchevade
Shanidar
Mt. Carmel
Choukoutien
Siwalik Hills
Koro Toro
Hadar
Afar Triangle
Sangiran
Trinil
Sterkfontein
Kromdraai
Taung
Kow Swamp

Inset map:
SUDAN
UGANDA
KENYA
TANZANIA
Lake Victoria
Koobi Fora
Kanopoi
Olduvai
Peninj
Laetoli
Garusi

COMMENT

The fossil record and scientific studies clearly support the notion of evolution. To scientists, the only real issues are the mechanisms that cause these changes and the stages of development that can be identified. For example, suppose tests prove "Lucy" is younger than the 3.5 million years Johanson claims. This will not disprove the theory of evolution. It will simply mean that scientists will have to reorganize the pattern of change based on the most recent and accurate information.

Adjustments to the evolutionary pattern are not new to the scientific community. From the first explanation to the present, many changes have occurred. Charles Darwin tried to explain the origin of new species by describing a process of natural selection in which only the fittest specimens survived. These changes would have occurred gradually over long periods of time, perhaps millions of years. In Darwin's time, the fossil record was fragmented. However, he felt that the transitional forms between species would appear as additional fossils were discovered.

Today, we believe that the major species in the pattern of evolution have been discovered. However, most of the expected transitional forms have not been, and probably will not be, found. How do scientists account for this?

One view suggests that evolution occurs through a series of rapid changes followed by long periods of no change. The origin of a new species, according to this view, occurs among groups that are geographically isolated from their main populations. These creatures must adapt rapidly to their new environment if they are to survive. These changes give them a better chance of surviving in other regions as well. As the new, fully developed species spreads, it quickly dominates each new area. This means that there would be no transition shown in the fossil record. This explains the sudden steps forward and the gradual adaptations that are found in the fossil record.

While adjustments to the pattern of evolution continue, so, too, does the controversy over the theory itself. The religious community of Darwin's day raised the first objections, but the famous "Scopes Trial" of 1925 marked the turning point. While Scopes lost the battle, he won the war. John Scopes was fined $100 for teaching evolution instead of the story of divine creation. But the brilliant defence of his lawyer, Clarence Darrow, made a laughing stock of the prosecution. The trial symbolized the decline of public acceptance of the biblical version of human origin.

In the decades that followed, most Christian churches adopted some aspects of the theory of evolution into their teaching. Indeed, many scientists were devout Christians who easily accepted the role of a divine hand controlling the changes found in the fossil record. Others just as easily accepted the idea of random chance causing the same pattern of development.

During the 1970s, however, the California-based Creation-Science Research

Center issued a new legal challenge to the teaching of evolution. The Creationists, as they are called, publicly revived the idea that a single divine act can explain human origin. They argued that their view should receive equal time in the public school system. In a 1980 campaign speech, presidential candidate Ronald Reagan supported this position.

Whatever political success the Creationists might enjoy, their approach cannot be considered a scientific one. In science, evidence is gathered and studied before conclusions are suggested. These are then subjected to additional tests for accuracy. The Creationists start with the conclusion–human origin was a single act of divine creation–and offer very little evidence to illustrate the conclusion. Instead, they focus on the weaknesses of the evolutionary theory.

The debate will no doubt continue, but it appears that the evolutionists have the edge. They have solid evidence to support much of their claim. The Creationists, on the other hand, offer much speculation and little evidence. It is the objective analysis of solid evidence, not speculation, however, that will continue to shed light on human origin.

Date	Event
B.C.	
400 000–100 000	Homo erectus evolves into Homo sapiens
100 000–40 000	Homo sapiens evolves into Homo sapiens sapiens–Cro-Magnon
16 000	Earliest agriculture occurs in the Nile Valley
10 000	Rapid extensive flooding occurs in Gulf of Mexico from glacial meltwater
9 500	Earliest domestication of cattle occurs in southern Europe and Egypt
8 000	Jericho emerges as a settlement of at least two thousand people
5 000	Megalithic cultures begin in Europe
4 800	Oldest-known massive stone monument built in Brittany
3 800	First city-states develop in Sumer Use of cylinder seals as identification marks begins in Middle East
3 400	Wheel originates in Sumer Earliest-known pictographic writing appears in Sumer
3 000	Approximate date for Noah's flood according to Creationist writers
2 800	Sumerian writing evolves into cuneiform script Stonehenge I
2 600	Plough developed in Middle East Variety of gods and heroes glorified in *The Epic of Gilgamesh* in Middle East Groups of menhirs erected at Avebury and Carnac
2 400	Stonehenge II
2 000	Earliest occupation of Mystery Hill Stonehenge III

2

Noah's Ark

BACKGROUND

The First Cities

Cro-Magnon had more control over the environment than their ancestors had had. They ate far better, and had better clothes and tools. Dwellings made of wood, animal bones, and skins meant that they could stay in one place for weeks or even months. Yet, despite these improvements, their lives were still basically nomadic. Because they depended on a diet of meat, they had to follow the animals as they migrated.

As modern humans, Homo sapiens sapiens, learned to develop agriculture, domesticate animals, and engage in trade, they were able to establish more permanent settlements. The first city was built at Jericho, in Mesopotamia, between 8000 and 7000 B.C. There, humans could depend on having a food surplus rather than merely subsisting. Between 8000 B.C. and 1500 B.C., thirty-one cities flourished over distances from the eastern Mediterranean to India. This marked the end of 3 million years of nomadic life.

Cities did not develop at the same rate or for the same reasons in every part of the ancient world. Not all cities followed the pattern from agriculture to village to a city of industry. At Shanidar in Iraq, for example, the use of metal was highly developed before people domesticated plants. In Mexico, however, ten types of food plants had been raised by 5000 B.C., yet people did not settle in towns for another thirty-five hundred years. Instead, they chose to live a seminomadic existence.

Archaeologists have found that trade, in general, and trade in obsidian, in particular, were crucial factors in the origin of cities. **Obsidian**, a volcanic glass, was fashioned into razor-sharp tools and weapons, and was used as mirrors and to make fine works of art. It was one of the most valued materials traded among the widespread towns of the prehistoric Middle East.

Since there was no money, trade worked on a barter system. City dwellers living near obsidian-producing volcanoes probably stockpiled obsidian to exchange for farm produce.

By tracing the obsidian found in objects to their source areas, archaeologists have been able to establish four trade routes. These overlap in time and area. Other minerals–salt, iron ore, copper, and soapstone–accelerated trade around 8000 B.C. This may well explain the sudden growth in the number of cities from then on.

The First Civilization

CIVILIZATION

While villages and towns spread rapidly, the seeds of true civilization began to grow. The word "civilization" refers to societies that share many common features. By 4000 B.C., urban societies included not only farmers and herders, but merchants, artisans, priests, slaves, debtors, creditors, and leaders. Daily interaction had become increasingly complex.

THE SUMERIANS

The earliest formal organization emerged in Mesopotamia's Fertile Crescent. Here, after centuries of Neolithic (New Stone Age) settlement, the Sumerians formed the first city-state at Sumer. A central authority controlled an army of officials, tax collectors, and workers who built dams and canals to tame the flood waters of the rivers.

ZIGGURATS

Their building skills enabled the Sumerians to construct large temples called ziggurats. These became the focal point of religious ceremonies in each of the cities. Made of sun-dried mud bricks that eroded easily, few of these temples have survived the ravages of time. Only the still-imposing ziggurat at Ur hints at the past grandeur of the region.

CUNEIFORM

As affairs became more and more detailed, the need to recall transactions, ideas, and techniques became clear. By about 2800 B.C., the first true writing had evolved into a script called **cuneiform**. This consisted of wedge-shaped marks engraved on tablets of wet clay with a special stylus or pen. Life no longer depended on memory. It could be recorded.

Cultural Tradition of a Great Flood

It is from the prehistoric era, before the birth of writing, that stories emerge from peoples all over the world about a Great Deluge or flood. Estimates suggest there have been as many as two hundred cultural accounts of a great flood.

The Epic of Gilgamesh, a Sumerian cuneiform text written during the reign of Hammurabi, tells of a flood long ago that is similar to the Hebrew flood legend of Noah. In the Sumerian version, the rain preceding the flood lasted only seven days and nights, and a man named Utnapishtim floated the ark.

FLOOD LEGENDS

Although they differ in detail, the worldwide flood stories have a general set of common characteristics: one man is warned of the approaching catastrophe; others disregard the warning; the flood destroys civilization with the exception of the chosen man and his family; animals provide information about conditions after the flood; and the survivors always land on a mountain to start afresh. Does the general consistency in stories from far-flung cultures prove that there is an important kernel of truth behind the flood legends?

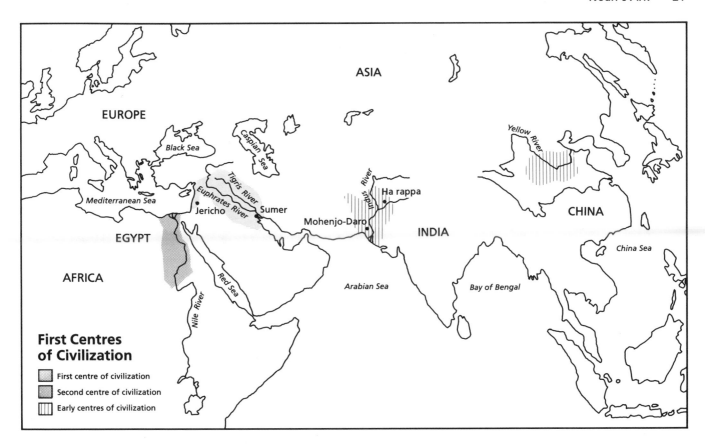

First Centres of Civilization

- ▨ First centre of civilization
- ▨ Second centre of civilization
- ▥ Early centres of civilization

Standard geologic research has, for the most part, failed to support the idea of a Great Deluge, but has supported the idea of severe local flood damage. In 1928–1929, Sir Leonard Wooley found a layer of clean clay 3.7 m thick deposited under the ancient city of Ur in lower Mesopotamia. The deposit, dated at 3500 B.C., seemed to support the story that a great flood had occurred. Digging in four other pits in different parts of the city, however, revealed that only one contained deposits of water-borne debris. This indicated that only part of the city had been affected. Other evidence showed that part of the city had been continuously settled. This would not have been the case if a universal flood had struck the region. Similar patterns have been found in other locations in the Middle East.

Later, geologists indicated that local floods are not unusual. From a scientific viewpoint, regional floods are still common all over the world. However, only a **tsunami** or tidal wave is capable of flooding vast areas and distances at the same time, and even its effects last for a much shorter period than most flood legends suggest.

The most familiar flood legend in Western culture is the biblical description of Noah's ark. Is this simply an appealing story like numerous other myths, or is there a factual basis on which the legend was founded? Let's look at three contemporary points of view.

PROBLEM QUESTION

What can Balsiger and Sellier, Morris, and McGowan tell us about the existence of Noah's ark on Mount Ararat?

ALTERNATIVE ONE

Noah's Ark and the Great Flood–Based on *In Search of Noah's Ark* by David Balsiger and Charles Sellier, 1976

The Bible, and especially the Book of Genesis, has proven to be a remarkable historic document, according to Dave Balsiger and Charles Sellier, Jr. In their book, *In Search of Noah's Ark*, they make some interesting observations to verify the authenticity of the Bible.

Archaeologists who have used the Bible as a guide book have been handsomely rewarded. More importantly, many of their discoveries support biblical passages that were previously questioned. Many scholars, for example, doubted that Moses could have written any of the Bible. Egyptian hieroglyphics, they argued, would have been far too difficult for such a mammoth task. However, a stone tablet discovered in 1906 on the Sinai Peninsula indicates that an alphabetic system of script existed as early as 1600 B.C.–some one hundred fifty years before Moses.

Other biblical passages challenged by scholars refer to camels in Abraham's time and lions in Daniel's. In both cases, statues showing the animals mentioned have been found by archaeologists; in both cases, dating proved their existence at the time indicated in the Bible.

Could the Tower of Babel possibly be the multistoried ziggurat that evidence suggests occupied the Mesopotamian Valley near ancient Babylon? Archaeologists believe it is.

Balsiger and Sellier believe that the same standard of biblical accuracy proven by archaeological finds would apply to the reporting of the flood and Noah's ark. Indeed, evidence exists for this, too. Fossils found in Wyoming, the Baltic region, and Germany, for example, contain a mix of fish, insects, and animals that originated in different parts of the globe. A flood of universal proportion would explain their presence in the same areas.

Similarly, fossils of fish and shells found atop Everest and other mountains indicate that these mountains were once covered with water. On Ararat, where the search for remnants of the ark has focussed, crystalline deposits of salt have been found. Is this the residue left by receding flood waters?

But what of the flood itself? Is there a scientific explanation for this catastrophe? Balsiger and Sellier offer this theory, which is supported by many scholars.

Prior to the flood, the climate of the earth was much more uniform than it is now. There is evidence of broad-leaved forests near Cairo and in the semiarid American West. Admiral Richard Byrd found petrified forests 160 km from the South Pole, and it is known that Australian and South American deserts once had swampy conditions. All of this can be explained, according to Balsiger and Sellier, by the presence of a canopy of water vapour, perhaps 1 km thick, that covered the earth.

This canopy created a greenhouse effect that kept daytime temperatures at about 21°C and evening temperatures only one or two degrees cooler. The canopy and increased amounts of carbon dioxide kept the heat in and radiation out, increasing the life span of people and animals. Little, if any, rain fell because the small cooling change from day to night provided enough moisture to water the plant life.

Dr. Brandenburger of Laval University in Québec has calculated that the earth's axis shifted significantly in 2345 B.C., which is about the time of the flood. This shift may have been caused by the close passage of, or a collision with, a large meteorite. The impact caused seabeds to rise, earthquakes to spread, volcanoes to form, and water to emerge from beneath the crust. The collapse of the water canopy then produced the forty days and nights of rain associated with the global flood.

Without the water canopy as protection, the effects of radiation reduced life spans, and wind and rain produced the variety of climates, from deserts to tropics, that we live in today.

Balsiger and Sellier can verify that the ark could have withstood such an ordeal. When the biblical figures are converted, the ark would have measured approximately 137 m × 23 m × 14 m. Laboratory tests show that this would have been stable enough to handle waves of 60 m. In fact, measurements of the same ratio were used to design the U.S.S. *Oregon* which was considered the most stable battleship in the United States Navy.

While the building task facing Noah was certainly enormous, it was not impossible. As evidence, Balsiger and Sellier point out that present-day workers, using four-thousand-year-old stone tools, have been able to clear 500 m² of forest in four hours. Noah had both metal and stone tools.

Is it possible that hard physical evidence of the ark's existence could be found on Ararat? The mountain has a glacier-covered summit rising 5200 m, and is lined with deep crevasses. Blizzards, thunderstorms, and ice slides are common. A person speaking can trigger an avalanche. Nevertheless, 200 people in twenty-three sightings have claimed they have seen the ark.

Several sightings occurred in the nineteenth century after Ararat was first climbed in 1829. One of the most famous sightings in the twentieth century took place in 1916. A Russian aviator, flying a test mission at 4200 m, reported

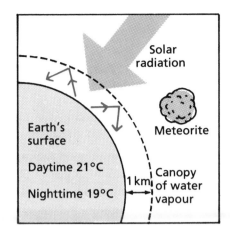

Balsiger and Sellier's Water Vapour Canopy. The canopy would moderate the climate much like a greenhouse does. Temperatures would change by only 2° from day to night, providing the moisture necessary for plant growth through condensation. There is no evidence that such a canopy existed in 3000 B.C. or that a meteorite of sufficient size passed the earth at that time.

U.S.S. Oregon, *July 1898.*

seeing a strange ship. Records of the follow-up mission sent out by the tsar were lost during the Russian Revolution.

Perhaps the most significant evidence was provided by Fernand Navarra. After unsuccessful climbs in 1952 and 1953, Navarra found what he felt was the ark just below the 4000 m mark. He removed a 1.5 m wooden section from the glaciated mountain side. Apparently, part of the ark had fallen during a storm or snow slide from its previous position at 4200 m. An expedition led by Navarra in 1969 found additional wood fragments on the ice-covered slopes of Ararat. Carbon 14 dating tests indicated that the wood was somewhat younger than the usual dates given for the flood. Recently, however, the accuracy of this testing method has been challenged. Other scientific tests on the wood gave dates that were close to the flood date. Circumstantial evidence clearly points to Navarra's wood as physical proof that the ark exists and that the story of Noah is true.

Questions

1. a) What evidence does Balsiger provide to illustrate his claim that the Bible is an accurate source-book for archaeologists?

    b) Explain why you think the evidence he presents is convincing, partly convincing, or basically misleading.

2. a) What "scientific" proof does Balsiger present to show that a universal flood had occurred?

    b) Are the conclusions reached or implied by Balsiger the only reasonable ones that could be made from the material he presents? Explain your answer.

3. Describe the role of the water canopy in the flood theory.
4. a) How does Balsiger try to prove that the ark was a seaworthy craft?
   b) To what extent does it seem probable that Noah and his family could have built an ark of the size outlined in the Bible? Give evidence to support your view.
5. Do the expeditions of Navarra provide enough circumstantial evidence to prove that Noah's ark did come to rest on Mount Ararat? Explain your answer.

ALTERNATIVE TWO

The Flood of Noah—Based on "Scientific Creationism" by H.M. Morris, 1974

H.M. Morris, a Creationist, supports the biblical story. The flood was a violent, worldwide catastrophe that began with forty days and nights of rain and surges of pressure from the earth's interior. Everything that was not carried in the ark was destroyed by the flood, which lasted for about ten months. Then, the ark came to rest on Mount Ararat. This means that the floodwaters were at least 5000 m deep, judging from the present elevation of the mountain.

According to Morris, the practical aspects aboard the ark, such as space and feeding, would not have been a problem. The ark had a capacity of about 522 railway freight cars. This would have been large enough to accommodate two of every species of land animal. Feeding them might appear to have been a difficult task for only eight people. It seems likely, however, that the flood experience might have created an atmosphere of hibernation during which most of the animals slept. This would reduce the amount of food needed and lighten the task of feeding.

Morris points to the fossil record as scientific evidence for a worldwide flood. The Creationists believe that prior to the flood, all creatures now found in the fossil record existed at the same time. All, including humans, were the result of God's perfect act of Creation ten thousand years ago, and no new species have since appeared.

The fossils and geologic formations that we study today do not represent a sequence of time stretching back 4.5 billion years, according to Morris. They simply show the impact of the single, devastating event that occurred about five thousand years ago. With the chaos caused by the flood, the bodies of the victims sank, became covered with sediment, and eventually fossilized. Their position in the fossil record depended on where they drowned, their ability to swim, and their shape and weight. Thus, the deepest sediments would contain simple organisms whose spherical shape caused them to settle first. The next layer would be marine animals without backbones—invertebrates—who lived near the bottom of the sea. The vertebrates would be found next because they would escape burial, for a time, by swimming. Above these fish would be the

Earth's surface

Better swimmers	Humans always found near surface
	Mammals always found above reptiles
	Reptiles always found above amphibians
	Amphibians always found above fish
	Fish with backbones (vertebrates) always found above invertebrates
	Marine animals without backbones (invertebrates)
	Simple spherical-shaped organisms shape and weight
Poorer swimmers	Deepest Sediments

The fossil locations suggested by the Creationists' Column are based on the results of the Great Flood in 3000 B.C. However, there is no scientific evidence of a flood, nor do the fossil locations shown correspond to the actual locations of geologic discoveries.

amphibians and reptiles who lived at the boundary of water and land. Because of their herding instincts, the higher forms of land animals would be found in large numbers in the upper layers of the fossil record. Few humans and birds would be found, owing to their mobility. For the people who escaped burial, their bodies would be exposed on the ground and would decompose after the flood receded.

Following the flood, Noah's family and the animals that were saved formed the bases of all present-day human and animal populations. Physically and mentally, humans have always been humans. The fossil record shows no transitional forms. Morris suggests that it is more likely that fossils such as Homo erectus were the negative results of inbreeding, poor diets, and a hostile environment rather than a stage in human development.

Questions

1. a) According to Morris, what creatures lived at the same time before the flood?
   b) Again according to Morris, what is the age of the earth?
   c) What was the extent and depth of the flood?
   d) Is any scientific evidence presented to support Morris's claims?
2. a) How could the problem of accommodating and feeding the animals on the ark be overcome?
   b) Explain why you agree or disagree with the solution presented by Morris.
3. a) According to Morris, what do the geologic column and fossil record show?
   b) Explain why a scientist would disagree with Morris's view.
4. a) What factors determine a creature's position in the geologic column?
   b) Explain why you agree or disagree with this view.
5. Morris argues that Noah's family provided the basis for today's human population. To what extent does this claim seem possible?
6. Morris also argues that the fossil record shows no transitional human forms. Would a scientist agree with this statement? Explain your answer.

ALTERNATIVE THREE

Noah's Ark: Fact or Fable?–Based on *In the Beginning . . .* by Dr. Chris McGowan, 1983

In his book, *In the Beginning . . .*, Dr. Chris McGowan challenges Dr. Morris's view and the Creationists' story of Noah's ark by pointing out a number of interesting problems that Noah would have encountered.

According to Dr. McGowan, it is unlikely that the size of the ark, as described in the Bible, would have been large enough to hold all of the animals. However, assuming that it was ,where would Noah have stored the food required for the journey? In one day, an African elephant eats about 160

kg of food. In ten months, the duration of the flood according to Dr. Morris, a pair of elephants would consume 96 t. And this is only one type of animal. Multiply this by the number of different pairs and the various types of food they would have required. Imagine the storage space Noah would have needed! And how would Noah have kept the meat fresh for the carnivorous pairs before the days of refrigeration? And, of course, what goes in must come out. Noah and his family must have been kept very busy shovelling fertilizer.

Another problem would have been the supply of drinking water. Dr. McGowan points out that the floodwaters would have been contaminated with dead bodies and, therefore, not drinkable. The ark must have been equipped with freshwater storage tanks. This would have taken up even more space.

Although the Bible makes no mention of taking sea life aboard, Dr. McGowan suggests that the 5000 m of fresh floodwater would have killed most of these saltwater inhabitants. Since they exist today, Noah must have included them on the passenger list. The size and cleaning of the tanks for whales, sea lions, walruses, and others would have added to the space problem.

The end of the flood raises even more questions. Where, for example, did all the water go after the flood? It could not have become locked in polar ice-caps because they only account for about 2 percent of the world's water, both fresh and salt. If all the ice were to melt today, the sea level would only rise about 40 m. This is a lot less water than would have been required to cover the highest mountain peak.

Food would have been another problem. Since all the plants and animals were destroyed by the flood, what would those on the ark eat while new crops were growing? Another puzzling question is the location of animals today. How did animals like the kangaroo and the panda get from Mount Ararat to Australia and China? These are only a few of the interesting questions Dr. McGowan raises.

The Creationists refer to the fossil record as evidence that a great flood occurred. They argue that a creature's position in the fossil record relates to its swimming ability. Dr. McGowan points out that, in fact, this is contrary to scientific evidence. Relative and absolute dating techniques show that the fossil record covers millions and billions of years. The appearance of simple sea creatures at the bottom, or of fish, amphibians, reptiles, and mammals at higher levels represent only their *first* appearances as life. They are also found at later times in younger rock layers because they continued to live long after their first appearances.

As for humans, their fossils are rare, not because people were good swimmers, but because they did not live and die in fossil-forming locations. Even so, Dr. McGowan argues, in the past decade fossils have been discovered that support the transitional stages idea of human development from Australopithecus to Homo erectus to Homo sapiens.

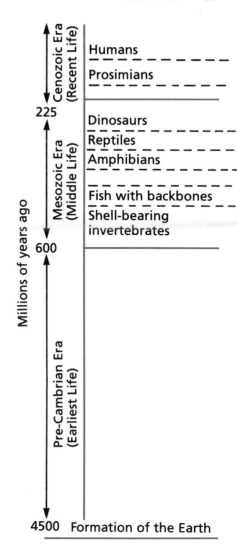

Fossil Locations on the Geologic Column. Only the first appearance of each creature is shown on this geologic column which covers 4.5 billion years. Fossils of each type have also been discovered at higher levels.

Questions

1. Does McGowan accept the Creationist argument that the flood of Noah is supported by scientific evidence?
2. What problems are raised by the vast quantity of water necessary for a global flood 5000 m deep?
3. a) What made it possible to feed and care for the animals according to Morris's explanation?
   b) What problems does McGowan see in caring for and feeding the animals?
4. What problems did the animals and Noah face after the ark landed on Mount Ararat?
5. Morris argues that the geologic column of fossils and rocks is evidence of a single, devastating, worldwide flood. McGowan, in contrast, argues that the geologic column illustrates the story of the earth and animal development over the past 4.5 billion years. Which argument is more convincing? Explain your answer with evidence.
6. Morris and McGowan both believe that human fossils are rare. Indicate which author provides the best arguments for his conclusions and justify your choice.

ANSWERING THE PROBLEM QUESTION

For some Christians, the criterion needed to solve the problem is simple–faith in the word of God. This eliminates all other factors since the Bible is not to be questioned.

If reason is applied to the problem, the story must be verified by specific evidence. Three major areas must be considered: evidence for the size, date, and duration of the flood based on geologic analysis; direct physical evidence of the ark itself; and indirect eyewitness sightings of the ark, transferred by word of mouth.

You must decide, based on what you have read, which of these criteria is the most important in solving the issue. How, then, can these factors be applied in determining which viewpoint presents the best explanation for the possible existence of Noah's ark on Mount Ararat?

THE STORY CONTINUES . . .

The Megalithic Builders of Western Europe

MEGALITHS

Before and after the proposed date of 3000 B.C. for Noah's flood, western Europe became dotted with over fifty thousand unusual stone constructions. These structures, called **megaliths**, consist of single boulders or groups of boulders placed in a pattern. They are usually found within 100 km to 200 km of the ocean. The oldest megaliths date back to before 5000 B.C., while the youngest were constructed as recently as 1500 B.C. The building then came to an abrupt end for unknown reasons.

"Come along, dear, we're off now."

For centuries people were puzzled by the randomly spaced stones, but recent archaeological work has resulted in three major classifications. The first, a monument of a single, upright stone, is called a **menhir**. It can be as small as .5 m tall or as large as the Grand Menhir Brise at Locmariaquer in France that once stood at 21 m and weighed 303.5 t. The second classification refers to groups of menhirs. These can be arranged in circles, semicircles, or in stretches of parade-like ranks, as long as 6.5 km. In Britain, stone and timber circles are found surrounded by ditches and banks and have been called **henges**. The final category is identified as **dolmens** or roofed structures. Scattered tools, ornaments, and bones have been found inside some dolmens, suggesting that most were used as tombs.

Many **megalithic tombs** have survived along the coastal areas of Sweden, Britain, Ireland, France, Spain, Portugal, and Italy. Most of these are covered by mounds of earth and are known as **barrows**. The largest prehistoric mound is Silbury Hill in Britain which measures 163 m wide at the base. The flat-topped peak is over 38 m high.

Perhaps the most ambitious builders were the temple builders of Malta. They had completed thirty monuments by 3000 B.C. Their multiroomed tombs had chambers measuring 30 m across in complex, clover-leaf arrangements. These contained burial catacombs for as many as seven thousand people at a single site.

Over the centuries, megalithic monuments have suffered a common fate. As they were abandoned, the natural processes weathered and eroded them.

MENHIRS

HENGES
DOLMENS

MEGALITHIC TOMBS

Christians often dismantled their arrangements in the belief that they were destroying pagan monuments. Farmers, too, moved the stones as they cleared the land, and villagers claimed the material for local construction. Still, it is clear that these monument builders were creating impressive structures in stone, while the people in the Nile Valley were still using sun-dried bricks.

Stonehenge

The most famous of all the megalithic monuments is Stonehenge. It is located on Salisbury Plain in southern England. An outer ditch with a bank immediately inside surrounds the monument and forms a circle that is 95 m across. As visitors approach the site, however, it is the stand of 45-t megaliths mixed with the tumble of fallen stone that catches the eye.

STONEHENGE I

AUBREY HOLES

Stonehenge was built in at least three major stages, and several minor ones, over a period of thirteen hundred years. The first stage, Stonehenge I, was built by a tribal people who lived by farming different crops and trading in stone axes. Their tombs were collective graves in which no one received special consideration. These people laid out the fifty-six Aubrey Holes (named after the person who discovered them) that were evenly spaced about 5 m apart just inside the ditch. On the outside of the site, they placed the Heel Stone, a 31-t megalith, in a very precise position.

STONEHENGE II

Stonehenge II was built in 2400 B.C. by the Beaker People. They were named after the shape of the cups they produced. Like the earliest tribes, the Beaker People farmed the land. However, they were influenced by a class of warriors, which prompted changes in their burial practices.

STONEHENGE III

The final phase, that produced Stonehenge as it is known today, was completed around 1500 B.C. Stonehenge III was built by the Battle Axe Folk. Their warrior class was dominated by a chief whose leadership was associated with trade in metal axes. He lived in a heroic style like the heroes of a later period in Greek history.

Stonehenge is a very complex structure. The precise positioning of the stones has caused great debate. When one stands in the very centre of the monument facing the entrance, the straight line of vision overlooks four additional upright stones at and beyond the outer circle and focusses on the all-important Heel Stone. The view along this axis is aligned with the sunrise over the Heel Stone on 21 June.

THE HEEL STONE

Many modern-day investigators have argued that the placing of the Heel Stone is so exact that it reflected an advanced understanding of astronomy and mathematics. What is strange about this possibility is that these people could neither read nor write. Nevertheless, when viewed from the centre of the monument, the fifty-six Aubrey Holes appear to mark the fifty-six-year cycle of the moon as it rises and sets at different points over the horizon. This meant that eclipses of the sun and the moon could be predicted.

Was this structure the design of an ancient astronomer or priest who used it to predict the disappearance and return of the sun and moon gods? Or was it,

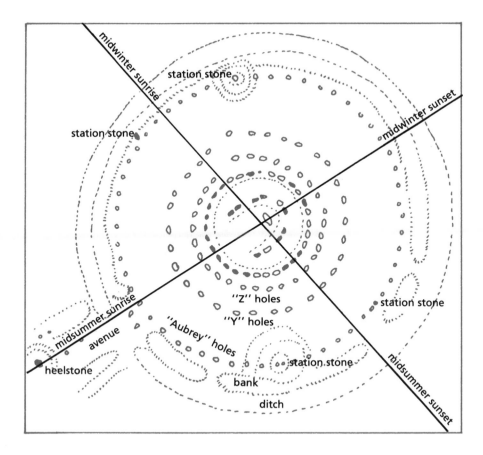

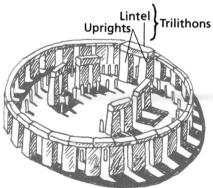

Stonehenge. The final form of Stonehenge was a complex structure. Inside the original ditch and chalk embankments were fifty-six Aubrey holes (named after their discoverer) forming an inner circle 87.78 m across that was overgrown by the final phase. Four station posts were positioned within these holes on opposite sides. Two additional circles of holes surrounded a 29.56 m-ring of large Sarsen posts and crossbeams called lintels. Inside this ring was still another circle of smaller bluestones. Huge trilithons made of two stone posts and one lintel were then arranged inside in a horseshoe pattern along with a final group of bluestones.

as others have argued, built to show the changing of the seasons for planting and harvesting in an agricultural society?

A firm conclusion about the purpose of Stonehenge has still not been reached. For centuries, Stonehenge had been associated with the Druid priests of the fourth century B.C. In fact, Stonehenge was in ruins for almost a thousand years before the Druids arrived! At the very least, Stonehenge is a monument that reflects the building skills and perhaps the religious beliefs of the many cultures that helped in its construction.

Mystery Hill

An 8-ha site an ocean away in North Salem, New Hampshire offers a potential historical connection to the megalithic culture of western Europe. Somewhat overstated as America's Stonehenge, Mystery Hill is a complex of stone-slab chambers surrounded by henges and rock walls, and highlighted by triangular-shaped stones. These stones mark seasonal change by pinpointing the position

AMERICA'S STONEHENGE

of the rising or setting sun at the vernal equinox on 21 March, the autumnal equinox on 21 September, and the winter and summer solstices on or about 21 December and 21 June, respectively.

Although the stones used are much smaller, the chambers and walls of Mystery Hill strongly resemble the type of construction at several European megalithic sites. Of key importance are the charcoal remains at the oldest part of the site which, when carbon dated and cross-checked with Bristle Cone pine tree ring growth, indicate that Mystery Hill was occupied as early as 2000 B.C. This overlaps with the final building stage at Stonehenge and suggests that megalithic builders might have crossed the Atlantic over three thousand years before Columbus! In addition, inscriptions found on the site suggest that such transoceanic contact might have been at least intermittent, if not continuous. The astronomical calendar, based on a division into eight half seasons, reflects certain reforms made at the time of Julius Caesar in 45 B.C.

DATING MYSTERY HILL

In 1975, the first of many markings was found and identified as a type of Celtic script which made reference to the Phoenician god Baal. It is thus possible that the Celtic astronomers, or Druids, as they have been identified by ancient European writers, were once active in New England.

CELTIC CONNECTION?

In more recent times, Mystery Hill was occupied by North American natives and pioneering settlers. During the nineteenth century, as much as 40 percent of the stone was removed by contractors to build dams, roads, and bridges. As a result, researchers now find it difficult to piece together the puzzle of construction. Many archaeologists believe that the stones only fit together in a limited number of ways, and were therefore probably used by eastern tribes to build the sites which are only now under serious investigation. Any apparent similarity to European megaliths would be coincidental. Perhaps studies currently in progress will determine if the transatlantic link is valid.

NATIVES AND PIONEERS?

COMMENT

At the time of the worldwide flood, usually given as 3000 B.C., the human population would have been reduced to the eight members of Noah's family, and would have remained relatively small for generations. Yet, the work of the megalithic builders of western Europe and the blossoming of the first civilization in Mesopotamia, among other cultures, show no such universal, or even local, break in population at or near the flood date.

As for the flood, the depth of water is often given as the approximate height of Mount Ararat. This is slightly higher than 5000 m, a vast quantity of water to be sure. Yet, the Bible gives the flood depth as 15 cubits (about 7 m) above the highest peak. Mount Everest is actually the world's tallest mountain at about 8800 m. This would make the floodwaters around the globe higher than sixteen CN Towers placed on top of one another. It is hard to imagine this much water.

It is more conceivable that regional floods covering hundreds of kilometres, common then and now in some river valleys the world over, might have seemed large enough to cover the then-known world. This would account for the flood legends of isolated cultures on different continents, each of which had a local mountain as a resting place for the ark. The retelling of the event through several generations before it was actually written down might account for added details that exaggerate the original story.

Eyewitness accounts of any event can be helpful and valuable sources of information. In the case of the ark, however, there is a nagging doubt about this testimony owing to the lack of physical evidence. The wood found by Navarra on the upper slopes of Mount Ararat just might be this evidence. Yet, small pieces of hand-hewn, partly petrified wood found above the tree line do not prove that the ark existed. Granted, the ice-bound mountain is difficult to climb, but many generations have searched the area in question. This makes it hard to accept that only a 1.5-m plank could be salvaged from a ship supposedly over 130 m long. It seems likely that much more of such a large structure would have been preserved, and thus identified and retrieved by the many expeditions that have made the attempt.

The biblical description was not written for a scientific audience. Many Christians believe that the appeal and impact of the ark's voyage is in no way affected by a literal, step-by-step analysis of its accuracy. Even though the search for the ark continues, it is probable that the relevance and importance of the biblical story will survive any effort to establish its basis in fact.

Period	Date B.C.	Event
Prehistoric	16 000	Earliest agriculture occurs in the Nile Valley
	4 500	Isolated agricultural communities emerge along the Nile Mud-brick buildings first constructed
Archaic	3 100	Upper and Lower Egypt united by Narmer First Dynasty established with capital at Memphis Trade begins with Mediterranean and Red Sea areas via boat, and with Nubia and African coastal settlements overland
	3 000	Approximate date for Noah's flood
	2 700	Third Dynasty
Old Kingdom	2 686	Pyramid Age
	c.2 570–2 500	Great Pyramid of Cheops (Khufu in Egyptian)
	2 200	Seventh Dynasty
First Intermediate	2 100	Disunity begins, pharaohs lose authority while nobles, priests, and officials gain power
Middle Kingdom	1 991	Eleventh Dynasty Central authority is restored
Second Intermediate	1 650	''Hyksos'' enter delta and slowly gain control of Egypt Decay of central authority
New Kingdom	1 558	Eighteenth Dynasty Thutmose III expands Egyptian Empire to Euphrates River Amenhotep IV becomes Akhenaten and orders all Egyptians to worship the sungod, Aten
	1 347	Tutankhamun ends radical changes of Akhenaten
	1 287–1 220	Ramses II builds the great temple at Thebes, the rock-cut temple at Abu Simbel, and hypostyle hall at Karnak
	1 100	Twenty-first Dynasty
Late Dynastic	525	Persians conquer and rule Egypt
	332	Alexander the Great gains control of Egypt
Ptolemaic	30	Rome conquers Egypt

3

Puzzle of the Pyramids

BACKGROUND

Egypt and the Nile

Shortly after the rise of Mesopotamia, the civilization of ancient Egypt developed along the Nile River. The Nile was Egypt's lifeblood. It flowed through vast stretches of scorching desert forming a narrow band of fertile ground 1.5 to 22 km wide. Each year, between June and September, the river flooded up to 16 m above its level. This provided some of the richest soil in the world for Egyptian farmers, who had practised agriculture in the valley as early as 16 000 B.C. The fertile river banks could support three crops a year.

THE NILE AND AGRICULTURE

Like their counterparts in Mesopotamia, most of the private homes in Egypt were built of mud brick. This material was well-suited to a dry climate and lasted a surprising length of time in a region that received little rain. As tribal groups developed, fighting occurred over the valued strips of river land. Eventually, the entire Nile Valley in its lower 1200-km course became divided into provinces called **nomes** by the Greeks.

HOMES

Two main kingdoms developed. Upper Egypt stretched from Cairo to the south, while Lower Egypt encompassed the delta region. In 3100 B.C., Narmer, the chief of Upper Egypt, swept north with his armies. He captured the delta region and, for the first time, the Nile Valley was unified under a single ruler. Narmer established the first of thirty dynasties that would last for three thousand years as sources of power and culture, despite periods of decline.

NARMER

The Nile continued to play a central role. On either side of the river, the desert was so vast that it could not be crossed. This protected Egypt from foreign invasion. The Nile provided water for the growing of grain from which the bread staple was baked. A type of paper came from the papyrus reed that grew in the river. Written records were kept on this material in Egypt's own picture-script known as **hieroglyphics**. The reeds also served as tough, buoyant material for building a variety of barges and boats that were used on this natural roadway. Transportation upstream was helped by the wind blowing against the current. A downstream drift gave river craft even greater speed.

THE NILE AND EGYPTIAN LIFE

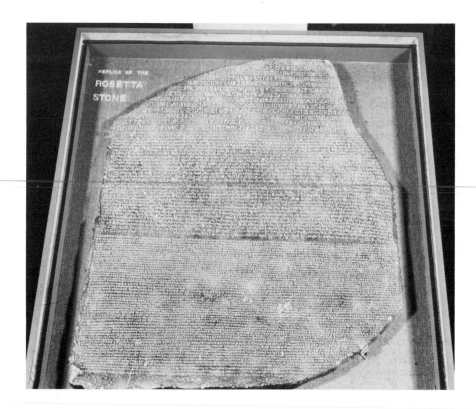

Unearthed during Napoleon's Egyptian campaign of 1799, the Rosetta Stone was deciphered by Jean-François Champollion in 1822. By matching the Greek message at the bottom with the hieroglyphics shown on the top, he was able to decode the Egyptian inscription and identify the symbols.

Regular geometric surveys were made over the flooded land in the delta. This ensured that land was properly distributed among the farmers. Columns known as **Nilometers** stood at the river's edge. Their notched surfaces indicated when the flood waters would arrive and leave so that planting and surveying could be planned. The pictures on several monuments show water being pumped by an oxen-powered water wheel and a shaduf. The **shaduf**, which is still common in many Third World countries, is a pivoted pole with a bucket hung from one end and a stone weight on the other. It is raised and lowered to move water from one level to another. These simple tools made land reclamation and irrigation possible and ensured that the water of the Nile would continue to guide the course of Egyptian history.

Religion

GODS AND GODDESSES

The Egyptians lived in both fear and awe of nature. As local villages grew, each town created its own gods and goddesses in animal form. Over two thousand creatures were worshipped. The list included Sobek, the crocodile-god of sun, earth, and water; and Bast, a cat-goddess of joy and love. These animals were often mummified like humans were when they died.

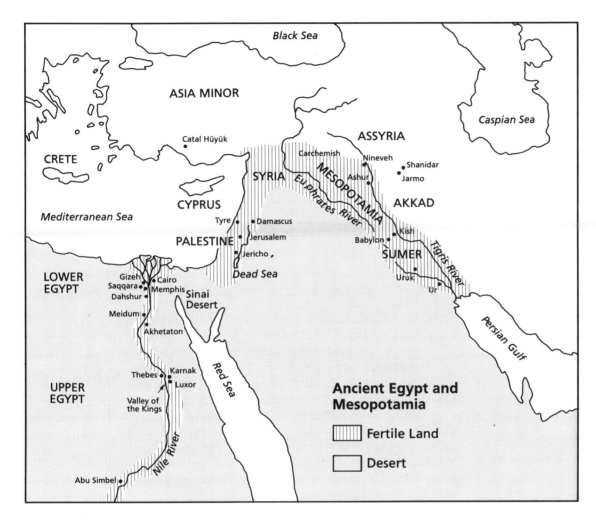

As people gained confidence in their environment, the idea of gods having human form gradually emerged. Annubis, a jackal-headed guardian of the tomb, and Horus, the falcon-headed god with whom the pharaohs associated themselves, had human bodies. Osiris, the father of Horus, who represented the yearly life cycle of the Nile, was shown entirely as a human image.

The dominant fact of nature in Egypt was the sun. Its importance was clearly shown in the worship of the sungod "Ra." This was the first god to gain acceptance by every village along the Nile. During the Pyramid Age, the pharaoh came to be regarded as the all-powerful "son of Ra" here on earth. Throughout his lifetime, the pharaoh, like every other Egyptian, prepared for death.

RA

The pharaoh's ba *hovers over his body.*

The afterlife was thought to be an extension of earthly existence. At the moment of death, the inner power that determines the nature of personality, the *ba*, was thought to leave the body. If the pharaoh's body was preserved intact, the well-being of the *ba* was ensured. Usually represented as a human-headed bird, the *ba* was a spirit of the night that supposedly moved about the stars. A second spiritual entity, the *ka*, variously described as the vital life force, soul, conscience or "other self," stayed with the pharaoh in death as it had throughout life. The Egyptians sometimes referred to their tombs as the "houses of the *ka*." It was believed that the *ka* remained in the tomb and it was for the *ka* that offerings were left on behalf of the body. Even Stone Age graves contained small objects that could only have been intended for use by the dead. The humblest peasant in Egypt followed the practice with a grave that was nothing more than a hole in the ground covered with dirt. The pharaoh's preparations, of course, were much more elaborate!

Mummification

THE HEAVENLY BOAT

At first, eternal life after death was limited to only the pharaoh and his family. The solar cult believed that the spirit of the dead pharaoh boarded the sun's heavenly boat and travelled across the sky each day in the company of Ra. Boats buried near the largest tombs are evidence of this belief.

PREPARATION OF THE BODY

Egyptians practised mummification to preserve the bodies of the deceased. In the most elaborate types of mummification, the internal organs were removed, dried, and wrapped separately. They were stored in what were known as **canopic jars**. Although the brain was removed (usually through the nose!), the heart was left as it was regarded as the source of intelligence. The body was then soaked in a bath of salt or natron for seventy days. Then, the body was removed, pads were placed under the skin to achieve a lifelike appearance, and the corpse was wrapped in linen. For a royal mummy, jewellery was placed under the wrappings. This explains why later tomb robbers recklessly stripped the mummies when their coffins were found in burial chambers. Working in combination with the dry and hot Egyptian climate, this and other methods of mummification preserved even Stone Age corpses to a remarkable degree. The three-thousand-year-old mummy of Ramses II in the Cairo Museum still has dried skin, hair, and teeth intact.

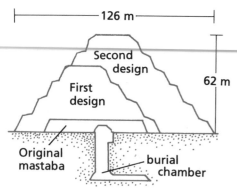

The Step Pyramid at Saqqara (c. 2682).

Pyramids of the Old Kingdom

Their religious beliefs and building skills inspired the Egyptians to erect spectacular monuments. The first pharaohs were buried in stone-lined, mud-brick structures called **mastabas**. Mastabas contained many chambers where material for use in the afterlife could be stored. The burial chamber itself was always well below ground level.

About 2686 B.C., in the reign of Pharaoh Zoser, the architect Imhotep made a great breakthrough. Based on the idea of a mastaba, he designed a pyramid built in six stages as if one mastaba was placed on top of another. The result was a steplike appearance. The bricks used were small, but the stepped pyramid of Saqqara was the world's first building made completely of stone. A massive wall enclosed a large complex of buildings and courtyards. They were used for ceremonies relating to the afterlife. The centrepiece was the stepped pyramid that rose over 62 m above the desert sand.

Soon after, in about 2600 B.C., Pharaoh Seneferu began an even grander project. At least two pyramids were under construction at the same time. Unfortunately, the angle of the pyramid at Meidum was too steep and the pyramid collapsed. To avoid the same fate, the angle of the second pyramid at Dahshur was changed, creating the Bent Pyramid which stands to this day. The nearby Red Pyramid was the first to achieve true pyramid shape. The gentle angle is the same as the reduced slope at the top of the Bent Pyramid.

The greatest pyramid building was achieved under the rule of Pharaoh Cheops in about 2570 B.C. At Gizeh just outside Cairo, the Great Pyramid was better built, larger, and made with bigger blocks than any pyramid before or since. The square base of the Great Pyramid is aligned almost exactly with the main points of the compass. It reached 147 m into the sky and contained 2.3 million blocks of limestone averaging 2 t each. Blocks of granite weighing 53.5 t were moved from Aswan, some 950 km away, to line the burial chamber. Unlike other pyramids, Cheops's burial chamber was located above ground in the centre of the pyramid and was reached by a complicated series of passages. This included the 9-m high Grand Gallery that ran at a steep angle of twenty-six degrees. Originally, the entire outer casing was finished in highly polished limestone blocks. They were fitted together without mortar within millimeters of each other. Today, only a few casing stones remain at the edge of the base.

Strangely, of the eighty pyramids built on the west bank of the Nile, not a single body has been found in any of them. Most, including the Great Pyramid, contain a granite **sarcophagus**–the outer casing of the coffin–but empty they remain. Tomb robbers may have removed the bodies in some cases, but in the first entry into the King's Chamber of the Great Pyramid, recorded by Arab historians in A.D. 820, the impression is left that either the body of Cheops (Khufu in Egyptian) was never placed in the sarcophagus or it was spirited away! Possibly the threat of grave robbers prompted Egyptian priests to remove the pharaoh's body after the burial ceremony and place it in less pretentious surroundings that did not draw anyone's attention.

How could such an enormous monument be built so long ago? Clearly, it was an effort that involved a major commitment of a religious nature. Egyptians were free labourers, working the land for wealthy officials. During the flood season, when no seeds could be planted, farmers were called upon to provide labour for the pharaoh's construction projects, including pyramid building. Egypt at the time of Cheops was rich, united, and at peace with its neighbours.

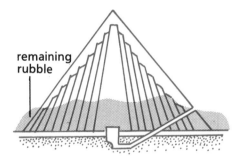

Collapsed Pyramid at Meidum (Seneferu) (c. 2600).

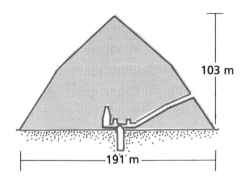

Bent Pyramid at Dahshur (c. 2600).

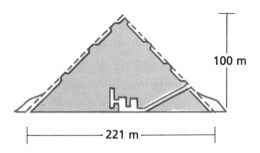

Red Pyramid at Dahshur (c. 2600).

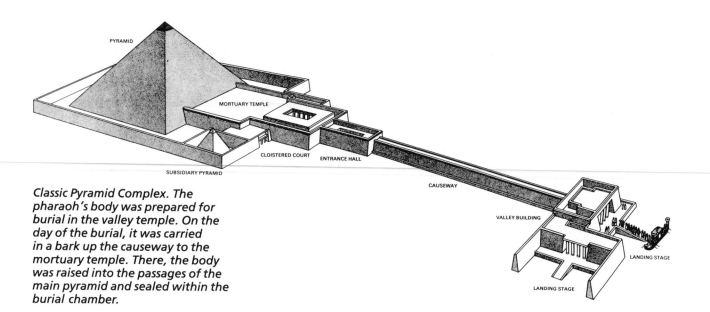

PYRAMID

MORTUARY TEMPLE

CLOISTERED COURT — ENTRANCE HALL

SUBSIDIARY PYRAMID

CAUSEWAY

VALLEY BUILDING

LANDING STAGE

LANDING STAGE

Classic Pyramid Complex. The pharaoh's body was prepared for burial in the valley temple. On the day of the burial, it was carried in a bark up the causeway to the mortuary temple. There, the body was raised into the passages of the main pyramid and sealed within the burial chamber.

In 2686 B.C., the Old Kingdom was growing rapidly in material wealth, with Egyptian trading vessels sailing the waters of the Mediterranean and Red seas, while Nile cities were enriched with trade from Nubia, to the south, and the African kingdoms on the coast. Under these conditions, most Egyptologists have argued that well-organized labour, using a heave-ho, hauling technique, completed the pyramids. The Egyptians had already refined construction methods for over three centuries as they built bigger and bigger mastabas. After the completion of Zoser's stepped pyramid at Saqqara, it took more than another century of trial and error before pyramid building reached its peak under Pharaoh Cheops. Experience seemed to be the best teacher.

Challenge of the Great Pyramid

The Great Pyramid still seems unexplainable to people today. Many theories have been advanced to account for the actual construction process. Erich von Däniken has suggested that the earth was visited by astronauts from outer space who begot the human race as it is known today before leaving for the stars with a promise to return at a later, unspecified date. Primitive people remembered them as "gods" who possessed exceptional knowledge and skills that were left with the ancients here on earth. These abilities accounted for the breathtaking achievements of many early societies from Easter Island, Mexico, and South America to ancient Egypt–in particular, the Great Pyramid.

More recently, Joseph Davidovits proposed the idea that an advanced knowledge of chemistry, using little technology, would have allowed the Egyp-

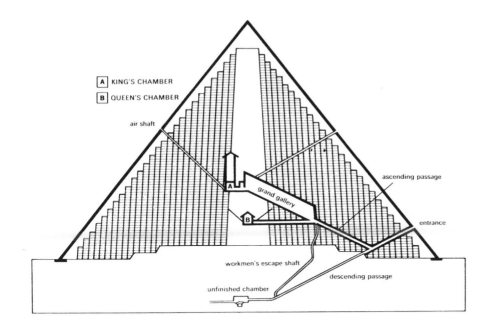

A KING'S CHAMBER
B QUEEN'S CHAMBER

air shaft

ascending passage

grand gallery

entrance

A

B

workmen's escape shaft

descending passage

unfinished chamber

The Great Pyramid is the only one with the burial chamber in the heart of the structure above ground level.

tians to cast the large blocks of stone from moulds on the building site. This would have eliminated the apparent difficulty of transporting huge blocks over long distances. Is there any substance to either of these radical views, or is the more traditional, heave-ho explanation a better solution to the problem?

PROBLEM QUESTION

In what ways are the arguments put forward by von Däniken to explain the construction of the Great Pyramid more or less convincing than the views expressed by Wilson and Davidovits?

ALTERNATIVE ONE

Chariots of the Gods–Based on *Chariots of the Gods* by Erich von Däniken, 1968

If we meekly accept the neat package of knowledge that the Egyptologists serve up to us, ancient Egypt appears suddenly and without transition with a fantastic ready-made civilization. Great cities and enormous temples, colossal statues with tremendous expressive power, splendid streets flanked by magnificent sculptures, perfect drainage systems, luxurious tombs carved out of the rock, pyramids of overwhelming size–these and many other wonderful things shot out of the ground, so to speak. Genuine miracles in a country that is suddenly capable of such achievements without recognizable prehistory!

Mycerinus's pyramid at Gizeh.

Painted and gilded cartonnage mummy case of the musician-priestess of Amun, Djed-maat-es-ankh, ninth century B.C.

Fertile agricultural land exists only on the Nile Delta and on small strips to the left and right of the river. Yet experts now estimate the number of inhabitants at the time of the building of the Great Pyramid at 50,000,000. (A figure, incidentally, that flagrantly contradicts the 20,000,000 considered to be the total population of the world in 3000 B.C.!)

With such enormous estimates, a couple of million more or less does not matter. But one thing is clear—they all had to be fed. There were not only a host of construction workers, stonemasons, engineers, and sailors; there were not only hundreds of thousands of slaves; but also a well-equipped army, a large and pampered priesthood, countless merchants, farmers, officials, and last but not least the Pharaonic household living on the fat of the land. Could they all have lived on the scanty yields of agriculture in the Nile Delta?

I shall be told that the stone blocks used for building the temple were moved on rollers. In other words, wooden rollers! But the Egyptians could scarcely have felled and turned into rollers the few trees, mainly date palms, that then (as now) grew in Egypt, because the dates from the palms were urgently needed for food and the trunks and fronds were the only things giving shade to the dried-up ground. But there must have been wooden rollers, otherwise there would not be even the feeblest technical explanation of the building of the pyramids. Did the Egyptians import wood? In order to import wood there must have been a sizeable fleet, and even after it had been landed in Alexandria the wood would have to be transported up the Nile to Cairo. Since the Egyptians did not have horses and carts at the time of the building of the Great Pyramid, there was no other possibility. The horse-and-cart was not introduced until the seventeenth dynasty, about 1600 B.C. Of course the scholars say that wooden rollers were needed. . . .

It is well known that the ancient Egyptians practised a solar religion. Their sun god, Ra, traveled through the heavens in a bark. Pyramid texts of the Old Kingdom even describe heavenly journeys by the king, obviously made with the help of the gods and their boats. So the gods and kings of the Egyptians were also involved with flying. . . .

Is it really a coincidence that the height of the pyramid of Cheops multiplied by a thousand million—98,000,000 miles (157 711 400 km)—corresponds approximately to the distance between the earth and the sun? Is it a coincidence that a meridian running through the pyramids divides continents and oceans into two exactly equal halves? Is it coincidence that the area of the base of the pyramid divided by twice its height gives the celebrated figure, 3.14159? Is it coincidence that calculations of the weight of the earth were found and is it also coincidence that the rocky ground on which the structure stands is carefully and accurately levelled?

There is not a single clue to explain why the builder of the pyramid of Cheops, the Pharaoh Khufu, chose that particular rocky terrain in the desert as the site for his edifice. . . . it would certainly have been more practical to locate the building site nearer the eastern quarries in order to shorten transport distances . . . Since there is so much to be said against the textbook explanations of the choice of site, one might reasonably ask whether the "gods" did not have their say here, too, even if it was by way of the priesthood. For the pyramid not only divides continents and oceans into two equal halves; it also lies at the center of gravity of the continents. If the facts noted are not coincidences—and it seems extremely difficult to believe that they are—then the building site was chosen by beings who knew all about the spherical shape of the earth and the distribution of continents and seas.

Today, in the twentieth century, no architect could build a copy of the pyramid of Cheops, even if the technical resources of every continent were at his disposal.

2,600,000 gigantic blocks were cut out of the quarries, dressed and transported, and fitted together on the building site to the nearest thousandth of an inch. And deep down inside, in the galleries, the walls were painted in colors.

The site of the pyramid was a whim of the pharaoh.

The unparalleled 'classical' dimensions of the pyramid occurred to the master builder by chance.

Several hundred thousand workers pushed and pulled blocks weighing twelve tons (10.9 tonnes) up a ramp with (non-existent) ropes on (non-existent) rollers.

The host of workers lived on (non-existent) grain.

They slept in (non-existent) huts which the pharaoh built outside his summer palace.

The workers were urged on by an encouraging "Heave-ho" over a (non-existent) loudspeaker, and so the twelve-ton blocks were pushed skyward.

If the industrious workers had achieved the extraordinary daily rate of ten blocks piled up on top of each other, they would have assembled the 2,600,000 stone blocks into the magnificent stone pyramid in about 250,000 days—664 years. Yes, and don't forget that the whole thing came into being at the whim of an eccentric king who never lived to see the completion of the edifice he had inspired.

We know next to nothing about the how, why, and when of the building of the pyramid. An artificial mountain, some 490 feet (149.4 m) high and weighing 6,500,000 tons, (5 896 761 tonnes), stands there as evidence of an incredible achievement, and this monument is supposed to be nothing more than the burial place of an extravagant king! Anyone who can believe that explanation is welcome to it. . . .

From Erich von Däniken, *Chariots of The Gods*, pp. 74–80, by permission from Souvenir Press of London.

Questions

1. What is the picture of ancient Egypt described by Egyptologists, according to von Däniken?
2. Why does von Däniken ask the question, "Could they all have lived on the scanty yields of agriculture in the Nile Delta?"
3. What problem does von Däniken see with the possibility that wooden rollers were used in constructing buildings and pyramids in ancient Egypt?
4. a) What technique does von Däniken use when he mentions a series of so-called "coincidences" about the Great Pyramid of Cheops?
   b) Who, according to von Däniken, chose the building site of the Great Pyramid?
   c) Is von Däniken's writing technique convincing? Explain your answer.
5. a) What is the traditional explanation of how the Great Pyramid was built?
   b) What objections does von Däniken have about this explanation?
6. Who, according to von Däniken, gave the Egyptians the knowledge and technology to build the pyramids?

ALTERNATIVE TWO

Building the Great Pyramid–Based on *The Chariots Still Crash* by Clifford Wilson, 1975

Clifford Wilson believes that the heave-ho theory of pyramid building is a more convincing argument than the one offered by Erich von Däniken. In his book, *The Chariots Still Crash*, Wilson uses the construction of the Great Pyramid to respond to the issues von Däniken raises and to explain his own viewpoint.

Both granite and limestone were used in the construction. The former would have been brought down the Nile on rafts from Aswan, and hauled on wooden sleds to the building site. Troyu, across the Nile, would have been the source of the huge amount of limestone required. Although, as von Däniken points out, it would have been more practical to build closer to the quarries, practicality was not the Egyptians' main concern in choosing a site. Their choice was influenced by their religious belief that the setting sun in the west was the dwelling place of the dead. According to Wilson, this was the reason they chose the west bank of the Nile.

As for the construction itself, Wilson disagrees with many of the points von Däniken makes. How were the huge blocks moved on wooden rollers, rafts, and sleds, when the only available trees were needed for the food and shade they provided? According to von Däniken, importing the wood would have been too difficult. In fact, counters Wilson, the Egyptians did just that. As support, he refers to Professor J. Pritchard's text that describes the importation of coniferous timber from Phoenicia at the time of Senefru.

Another source, *The Pyramids of Egypt*, by I.E.S. Edwards, is cited as more evidence that the Egyptians did use wood extensively for sleds, scaffolding, and balks in the construction process.

While the average stones weighed 2.2 t, some weighed as much as 11 t. How were such massive blocks lifted into place without machinery, unless astronaut help was available? In fact, says Wilson, the Egyptians have left their own record of how such achievements were accomplished. A picture from the tomb of Djehutihotep shows a huge statue of Djehutihotep being moved on a wooden sled by 172 men. The picture shows a liquid being poured along the route, no doubt to lessen the friction for the 53.5 t load. If it was possible to move a statue of this size with this number of workers, then, Wilson suggests, it would have been even easier to move the blocks into place. Using pulleys and ropes, workers could drag the stones up embankments. Made of earth, the height of these embankments could be increased as the height of the pyramid increased. Once the project was complete, the earth could simply be removed.

As for von Däniken's claim that rope was nonexistent, this too is incorrect. According to Wilson, rope was used in Egypt even before Pharaoh Zoser's step pyramid was built. This was about seventy years before construction of the Great Pyramid.

Wilson believes the accounts of the precision fit of the 2.5 million blocks that were used are exaggerated. It was only the outer limestone blocks that were so accurately fitted that the blade of a knife could scarcely be fitted between them. This fit was accomplished by trimming the blocks before they were hauled into place. In all probability, according to Wilson, the stonemasons would have cleaned and smoothed the outer limestone surfaces once the structure was complete and the earthen ramp was removed.

Based on an average of ten blocks a day, von Däniken estimates it would have taken 664 years to complete the Great Pyramid. Wilson considers this nonsense. Herodotus, a historian who lived about two centuries after the pyramid was built, has written that one hundred thousand workers completed the Great Pyramid in twenty years. Even this, Wilson contends, is probably an exaggeration, since modern calculations indicate it could have been completed in less than ten years.

Wilson cannot accept von Däniken's argument that the pyramid stones could not have been moved using the heave-ho method. At Karnak, Wilson has seen workers, using a single rope and simple pulley, move huge stones as the foreman chants out instructions. If a method as simple as this works now, then why not in 2550 B.C.?

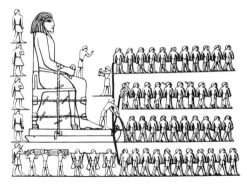

Djehutihotep.

Questions

1. a) In what way does Wilson agree with von Däniken about the number and construction of the blocks used to build the pyramid of Cheops?
   b) In what way does Wilson differ with the claim that all blocks of the pyramid were fitted very precisely?

2. Where did the Egyptians acquire the limestone and granite to build the pyramid?
3. Explain how Wilson counters von Däniken's argument that wood was not available to be used as wooden rollers in constructing the pyramid of Cheops.
4. Describe the picture on the tomb of Djehutihotep. What is the significance of that picture with respect to the way the pyramid of Cheops could have been built?
5. Why does Wilson claim that the Great Pyramid was constructed in much less than 664 years?
6. Why does Wilson support the heave-ho method? Is this explanation convincing? Explain your answer.

ALTERNATIVE THREE

Pouring a Pyramid?– Based on a theory of Joseph Davidovits outlined in "Plastic Megaliths" by Douglas Starr, 1983

In 1974, Joseph Davidovits, a French chemist, announced a radical new theory. What if, instead of being cut and hauled, the pyramid blocks were simply cast on the spot?

When Davidovits discovered a simple chemical process that turned a putty mixture into stone, he began to wonder if perhaps it had also been discovered earlier. This would explain the mystery surrounding the construction of the Great Pyramid of Cheops at Gizeh. It would also explain why there are no murals of the time showing the ramps and sleds that were supposedly used to move the blocks. The earliest known relief showing a statue being dragged is dated eight hundred years after the Great Pyramid was finished.

The idea of using ramps has always been a puzzling one. How could the early Egyptians have made ramps with a gentle enough slope to enable the workers to drag the huge limestone blocks? A ramp with such a slight angle would have been more massive than the pyramid itself.

The probable answer is that Davidovits's almost-primitive process for stone casting was available. Common clay contains loosely bound silicon and aluminum. When the right amount of alkali (salts) is added, this loose material binds together to form stone. Natron (sodium carbonate) is the chemical used to make artificial stone. Experiments in the laboratory, mixing these materials with granite powder, produced a rock that only experts can distinguish from the natural.

In early Egypt, natron was used for everything from embalming to brushing one's teeth. The aluminum and silicon binder was also available in the silt of the Nile River. Suppose the workers mixed these ingredients with limestone rubble and poured the mixture from buckets into a wooden mould. In a few hours, the heat from the desert sun would have dried the mixture into a block of rock. This block would become part of the mould for the next block, which explains how they were laid so close to one another.

Tests done on natural limestone found in France reveal small shells about 1 cm long. These are arranged in neat layers, as though they had settled to the bottom. Although similar shells have been found in the limestone blocks used in the interior of the Great Pyramid, they are scattered throughout. This suggests that the pyramid stone could be artificial. When Davidovits tested pieces of pyramid casing block with x ray analysis, the visual patterns were identical to those of the artificial lime brick he had produced in the laboratory. This convinced him that the casing stone of the Great Pyramid was, indeed, artificial.

According to Davidovits, the late Stone Age and early Copper Age were really the golden ages of alchemy. Certainly, the Egyptians had enough knowledge to perform the process. We know that they had the technology to make wine, beer, and vinegar, not to mention their expertise in mummification. Perhaps they learned to cast stone in wooden moulds as well. Indeed, people in other parts of the world may also have taken clues from their environment. This would explain some other ancient mysteries, such as the huge statues on Easter Island.

What happened to this golden age of geological science? According to Davidovits, when people developed metallurgy and the wheel, it made them masters of the stone environment, but less attentive to its uses. The knowledge, therefore, was lost.

Questions

1. What problems exist with the traditional explanation of how the Great Pyramid was built?
2. How does Davidovits believe the construction of the Great Pyramid was accomplished?
3. Does Davidovits produce enough evidence to prove that the stone in the pyramid was manufactured? Explain your answer.
4. If Davidovits is correct, what problems does the ability to pour rock into moulds solve when examining the process of construction for the Great Pyramid?
5. Is there more evidence to support the heave-ho method of pyramid building as outlined by Wilson or more evidence to support the new ideas advanced by Davidovits? Again, explain your answer.

ANSWERING THE PROBLEM QUESTION

The very existence and magnitude of the Great Pyramid instantly challenges the mind to imagine how it was built so long ago. Von Däniken questions several traditional assumptions about pyramid construction. In some cases, the facts he cites differ from those given by Wilson. When you encounter a situation where there is disagreement about basic information, other views should be consulted to determine which of the original claims is accurate.

Many have argued that the builders of Stonehenge must have had an advanced understanding of mathematics and astronomy. Von Däniken holds the same belief about the builders of the pyramids. Are all of the calculations mentioned by von Däniken precise enough to have any meaning? Does logical speculation indicate that a) the presence of these relationships is more than a coincidence? b) that any structure may contain numerical patterns that were not necessary for construction? c) that the Egyptians could not have mastered these ideas? or d) that such concepts could only have come from ancient astronauts who visited the earth and left their knowledge and skills long before the emergence of Egyptian civilization?

In examining the more practical side of pyramid building, the material and process of construction must be considered. How were the large amounts of limestone shipped across the Nile, and how were the enormous granite blocks transported from Aswan? Or, was the burden of transportation greatly reduced by the ability to pour a mixture into a wooden mould and produce the stone right on the spot? Were the tools of Egyptian technology and labour organization advanced enough during the Old Kingdom to have quarried, transported, shaped, and polished the finished product? How coud ramps have been used to move heavy stone upward as the height of the pyramid soared? Or were the ramps needed at all!?

An absolute answer to all of these questions will probably never be found. Nevertheless, based on what you have read, how can the criteria be ranked and applied to determine the best explanation for the construction of the Great Pyramid?

THE STORY CONTINUES . . .

The Middle Kingdom (1991–1633 B.C.)

Great as the wealth and system of labour was, the colossal task of building the pyramids exhausted each resource by the end of the Old Kingdom in the twenty-first century B.C. The pharaoh lost much of his power and prestige as priests, nobles, and officials gained local loyalties when organizing work crews for public construction. The decline that followed the breakdown of central authority was reversed when the Theban pharaoh Mentuhotep II reunited the country by 1950 B.C. The Middle Kingdom was stabilized after almost two hundred years of Indo-European invasion and strife.

During the Twelfth Dynasty, the increased power of the pharaoh led to a new era of commercial expansion, backed by the creation of a permanent army. The awe-inspiring prestige of the pharaohs of the Old Kingdom, however, was never recovered. The Theban god ''Amun'' was merged with the Old Kingdom divinity ''Ra'' to become the sungod ''Amun-Ra.'' The royal privilege of

MENTUHOTEP II

AMUN-RA

Queen Hatshepsut (1503–1482 B.C.) was the most powerful female pharaoh in Egyptian history. During her reign, defence was strengthened, trade was bolstered, and the country prospered. This is her mortuary temple.

immortality was now transferred to all Egyptians, who were assured of survival after death by virtue of their faith in the religion of Osiris. Although some class distinctions remained, every Egyptian enjoyed equality before the law.

Despite superficial unity, the Thirteenth Dynasty ushered in a series of weak pharaohs who could not maintain a firm grip on the many people spread along the reaches of the Nile. The expansion of the Hittite Empire in the eastern Mediterranean again pressured Indo-European groups to spread into the delta region of Egypt in large numbers by about 1650 B.C. Earlier arrivals, between 1900 and 1800 B.C., had been kept under control by a firm central government. The later "Hyksos" or "rulers of foreign lands" seemed to infiltrate and conquer the country by sheer force of numbers, without striking a blow. The Hyksos adopted almost every aspect of Egyptian culture, from administration to hieroglyphic writing, but foreigners they remained and their presence was resented by native Egyptians.

THE HYKSOS

The New Kingdom (1558–1085 B.C.)

A national resistance movement, again under Theban leadership, struggled for decades against the Hyksos intruders. They were finally successful and established the Eighteenth Dynasty in 1558 B.C. This marked the beginning of Egypt's final hour of greatness. The "New Kingdom" as the era was called, saw strong pharaohs, like Thutmose III (1490–1436 B.C.) and Ramses II (1287–1220 B.C.), use the superior bow-and-horse chariot introduced by the Hyksos to help create the first Egyptian Empire outside of the Nile Valley.

THE "HERETIC" PHARAOH

Religious life briefly took an unusual turn under the "heretic" pharaoh, Amenhotep IV. He insisted that the sungod was more important than all other deities and dedicated a new city to Aten at the site of Amarna, halfway between the ancient capital of Memphis and the later centre of Thebes. To Amenhotep, the purest form of worship was the sun itself which, as represented by the winged disc of Aten, was the creator of the world and the source of all life. In honour of the sun, Amenhotep changed his name to Akhen*aten* and that of the city Amarna to Akhet*aten*. All competing temples to other gods were closed. The name of the previous sungod, Amun, was removed from the face of all public buildings. With Akhenaten's death in 1347 B.C., the religious revolution that he and his wife, Nefertiti, had imposed quickly collapsed.

Akhenaten's successor was a boy-king whose tomb was discovered only after years of expensive and patient searching. By virtue of their size, the pyramids of the Old Kingdom had been open invitations to grave robbers to steal anything the dead pharaoh might not use! Hence, from the Middle Kingdom onward, attempts were made to hide the burial place of the pharaoh. Cham-

THE VALLEY OF THE KINGS

bers were cut into the solid rock of a desolate location, across the Nile from Luxor and Karnak, called the Valley of the Kings. With sealed entrances covered and disguised by debris, the high priests of the burial hoped to keep the pharaoh's resting place a secret. Most tombs, however, were broken into and looted soon after they were closed.

By the end of the nineteenth century, many excavators were convinced that the Valley of the Kings had been fully explored. Nevertheless, Lord Carnarvon, a wealthy English sportsman, sponsored a patient and determined

HOWARD CARTER

archaeologist named Howard Carter to search for an undiscovered tomb. Clay jars with seal impressions bearing the name of Tutankhamun, that had been discarded after a funeral ceremony, had been recovered by a previous excavation in 1907. Carter felt that the real tomb was still to be found, but excavations from 1917 to 1921 yielded nothing. Only after serious pleading by Carter, who pointed out the need to excavate a small, unchecked area below the tomb of Ramses VI, did Carnarvon reluctantly agree to finance the digging for one more season.

On 5 November 1922, Carter's team found the first of sixteen steps that led to a tomb entrance. In the days, weeks, and, eventually, ten years of work

TUTANKHAMUN'S TOMB

that followed, the world became familiar and fascinated with "Tut's tomb," as Tutankhamun's resting place was popularly dubbed in the press. Travellers from every continent came to witness the process, much to the annoyance of Carter, who hated the publicity almost as much as the administrative difficulties he endured with the Egyptian government.

The fabulous treasure, of over five thousand items found in the cramped space of the tomb, dazzled the imagination. The exquisite thrones of inlaid gold, sculptures of alabaster, and jewellery of precious and semiprecious stones reflected the supremely artistic craft of the artisans. This storehouse of knowl-

The Great Pyramid stands to the right of the Sphinx. Chephren's pyramid, to the left, still has a layer of casing stones near the peak.

edge about Egyptian life was highlighted by the inner coffin, made of over 100 kg of solid gold, and the death mask that rested on the head of the mummy itself.

TUTANKHAMUN, THE BOY-KING

Surprisingly little is known about Tutankhamun himself. It seems that he reversed the religious revolution started by Akhenaten and reopened the temples dedicated to other gods. He moved the capital from Amarna to Thebes, and changed his name, which had been Tutankh*aten*, to Tutankh*amun* in honour of an earlier sungod.

After a nine-year reign, Tutankhamun died at the age of eighteen. The magnificent burial of this otherwise insignificant pharaoh staggers the mind that tries to visualize the riches that must have been associated with more important leaders, like Ramses II and his imposing temple-tomb at Abu Simbel. Although Tutankhamun's tomb had been broken into by thieves, it was still largely intact when discovered by Carter. It is this fact that gives Tutankhamun's name the kind of immortality that the ancient Egyptians cherished.

THE DECLINE OF EGYPT

The New Kingdom lasted until the eleventh century B.C., but internal and external pressure resulted in its gradual decline. A new capital, built at Tanis in the Nile Delta, seemed to represent the power of the pharaoh. In practice, however, control was taken over by the high priests who dominated the weaker successors of Ramses II. The arrival of the Iron Age in Europe and in the Aegean saw military power spread northwest as Egypt eventually fell to a series of better-equipped and better-trained armies. The domination of Persia in the fifth century B.C., of Alexander the Great in the third century B.C., and of the Romans in the first century B.C. brought a rude end to a classic age of civilization and achievement.

COMMENT

The daring success of the United States space program in the late 1960s represented one of our greatest technological triumphs. It was in this emotionally charged atmosphere that Erich von Däniken introduced his ideas about ancient astronauts visiting the earth and founding the modern human race as it is known today. Von Däniken's many books have been translated into several languages and have been reprinted through numerous editions. This illustrates the widespread and consistent appeal of his dramatic story to a worldwide audience well acquainted with the excitement of space travel. Since we have now ventured into space, it is easy to imagine that somewhere in the almost-limitless expanse of the galaxy another planet might have conquered space much earlier, and possibly travelled to the earth.

Public attention to glamorous possibilities is a frequent phenomenon that often confuses the issue at hand and the facts involved. The year after Howard Carter discovered Tutankhamun's tomb, Lord Carnarvon was bitten by a mosquito, and became infected. Although he recovered, he soon caught pneumonia and died within a month. During the next five years, Georges Benedite of the Louvre and Arthur Mace of the excavation team, both of whom were associated with the discovery, also died of natural causes. These deaths and rumours that the lights in Cairo went out at critical moments (as they still do today) gave rise to the popular notion of the ''Mummy's Curse,'' which has been the subject of several movies. Overlooked was the obvious fact that Howard Carter, who had tabulated and analyzed the mummy, survived the ordeal in good health, as did his distinguished photographers.

Similarly, the popular press has often expressed a ''Star Trek'' enthusiasm that relishes the idea of a visitation from an ancient astronaut without examining the evidence presented by von Däniken to see if his ideas merit serious consideration. Von Däniken's style is interesting to read as it poses a series of questions that challenge traditional interpretations. This is also a valuable exercise, since theories should be tested for accuracy as new evidence is produced. Although von Däniken questions expert opinion, he implies, without specifically stating, that each time a gap exists in the heave-ho theory of pyramid construction, the answer lies with the technology passed on to earthlings by ancient space travellers. No specific evidence is advanced to prove that extraterrestrial visitations really occurred.

In contrast, there is evidence in wall paintings that the heave-ho method of pyramid building *was* practised, even though the wall paintings follow the Pyramid Age itself. Rope and wooden sleds that von Däniken claims did not exist have been found at pyramid sites. The use of such technology did not require the knowledge and assistance of an ancient astronaut. This type of oversight is common throughout von Däniken's writings, and casts doubt on the credibility of his entire argument.

The startling opinion expressed by Joseph Davidovits, that suggests the Egyptians manufactured the rock for the pyramids on the construction site, also seems extreme. Although even his critics admire his chemistry, Davidovits has never actually seen the monuments whose building structure he describes. His tests were performed only on laboratory samples of the temple stone that were submitted for examination.

Many of the blocks used in the Great Pyramid were marked with practical instructions such as "this side up" while others named the quarry team–"Vigorous Gang" or "Enduring Gang." Some crews demonstrated a sense of humour, found throughout Egyptian art, by inscribing the message "How drunk is the king"! The quarries across the Nile still contain unfinished limestone blocks the same size and shape as those used in the Great Pyramid. When viewed in connection with the copper saws, chisels, and dolerite hammers that the Egyptians were known to possess, it appears more likely that manual labour rather than chemical wizardry supplied the necessary stone.

Modern estimates have calculated that between twenty-five hundred and four thousand labourers organized into gangs of eighteen or twenty workers could have constructed the Great Pyramid within twenty years. Most authorities accept the idea that ramps around one, two, or three sides were used to haul blocks to increasingly high elevations. Did the Egyptians build ramps for such a purpose? If so, how were the ramps that would be larger than the volume of the pyramid itself at maximum height be constructed and dismantled without leaving a clear trace of their presence? Unanswered questions such as these will continue to tantalize those who feel that the real story of pyramid construction has yet to be told.

Archeological Time Period	Date	Event
		B.C.
Paleolithic (Old Stone Age)	2 500 000	Earliest use of stone tools
	9 600	Plato's date for Atlantis
Neolithic (New Stone Age)	9 000	
	7 000	Neolithic farmers on Crete
Copper Age	5 000	
	3 100	Unification of Upper and Lower Egypt
Bronze Age	3 000	Proposed approximate date for Noah's flood
	2 600	Outsiders from Cyclades arrive on Crete Trade, pottery making, and metalworking flourish
	2 000	Old palace period on Crete
	1 700	All palaces destroyed by earthquake and rebuilt
	c.1 500	Volcanic eruption on Thera ends Minoan civilization. This may be the actual date for Atlantis.
	1 450	Knossos inhabited by Mycenaen "squatters"
	1 380	Knossos destroyed for last time
	1 347	Tutankhamun rules in Egypt
	1 300	Fortified citadel at Mycenae becomes the most powerful of Mycenaean palace states in the Aegean
Iron Age	1 100	Sea peoples destroy and sack all Mycenaean palace states
	750	Homer composes *Iliad* and *Odyssey*
	600	Solon visits Egypt and hears story of lost civilization
	355	Plato write *Critias* and *Timaeus*
		A.D.
	1 900	Arthur Evans excavates Knossos

4
Atlantis

BACKGROUND

Dating Periods of Human Development

Dates separating periods of human development are really guideposts that help us to classify time for convenience and study. One era does not simply end while another begins like the switching off and on of a light. Characteristics from a previous period are usually partially preserved, forgotten, altered, and then added to as change gradually takes place with the passage of time.

GUIDEPOSTS IN TIME

Often the names given to the major divisions reflect the type of technology that has survived and been discovered by archaeologists. For example, Paleolithic refers to the Old Stone Age, when crude stone tools were in use, while Neolithic refers to the New Stone Age, when stone was finely crafted into tools and artifacts; the Copper Age identifies the period when work was done with one particular metal, while the Bronze Age marks the stage when copper and tin were mixed through a more advanced process of metallurgy.

TECHNOLOGY AND TIME PERIODS

Although one part of a society may utilize the new material or invention of an age, other parts of the society may continue with previous technology, and competing societies may take generations to reach the same stage of development. Today, for example, world powers have entered the computer-dominated space age, while Third World countries struggle to industrialize and some Australian aborigines still live in the Stone Age!

Discovery of a Lost Age

One era of remarkable accomplishment that was lost to history for over twenty-five hundred years was the Bronze Age of the Aegean which paralleled the development of ancient Egypt from about 3000 to 1100 B.C. It survived only as a shadowy legend passed on by word of mouth until Homer recorded it some four or five centuries later. Most people regarded references to this period as entertaining stories that were not to be taken seriously. In the late nineteenth and early twentieth centuries, however, spectacular finds by amateur archaeologist Heinrich Schliemann and–of direct interest to us here–Sir Arthur Evans opened up striking details of a missing civilization.

BRONZE AGE OF THE AEGEAN

Evans's pioneering efforts on the Aegean island of Crete, in combination with recent archaeological work, have provided a surprisingly clear, though somewhat incomplete, picture of the growth of an independent cultural tradition. Peopled originally by Neolithic farmers from coastal Mediterranean societies, settlement began in mud huts and caves. By 2800 B.C., when the builders of Stonehenge I were outlining their circle on Salisbury Plain, building skills in the Aegean had improved to the point where boulders were used to construct rough, circular, multiple graves called **tholoi**. About 2600 B.C., when the Pyramid Age flowered in Egypt, a brilliant Bronze Age culture quickly emerged with better technology in stone and metal, and a unique tradition of pottery and art for which Crete is famous. It seems likely that a new wave of settlers with advanced abilities entered the island, probably travelling by boat from the Cyclades–the numerous Greek islands of the Aegean. These recent arrivals had developed their own culture, but found themselves limited by the few resources and small size of the islands on which they had lived. Products from Crete during this period have been found throughout the Middle East, Egypt, and the Cyclades, indicating that a vigorous trading system established itself in a relatively short time.

The demands for food, and social and religious organization in a thriving community, led to the growth of many small villages during the next five hundred years. By 2000 B.C., however, the political power of the island became concentrated in eight centres, each with an impressive palace, the largest of which was Knossos.

According to a famous Greek myth, Theseus, son of Aegeus of Athens (which was under tribute to King Minos of Crete), volunteered to be one of seven youths sent each year to be sacrificed to a half-man, half-bull monster known as the Minotaur. The Minotaur lived in the twisting, turning passages of the labyrinth beneath the palace of King Minos from which escape was most difficult. The daughter of the king, Ariadne, fell in love with Theseus and wanted to save his life. She talked to Daedalus, the builder of the labyrinth, who suggested that Theseus take a ball of thread and lay it out behind him as he passed through the confusing network of tunnels. Theseus took this advice, slew the Minotaur, and followed the life-saving thread back to the entrance.

The Flowering of Minoan Civilization

Whether the palace at Knossos was the source of the Minos legend remains an open question. In any case, Arthur Evans, who excavated the palace at the turn of the century, called the civilization on Crete Minoan.

Knossos does contain a complicated series of inner passages, but, more importantly, facilities were available to accommodate over four hundred jars called **pithoi** that were often taller than a person and had a large storage capacity for grain and oil. This indicated that the palace served as a distribution centre for the accumulated agricultural produce.

Pithoi jars were storage containers of the ancient world.

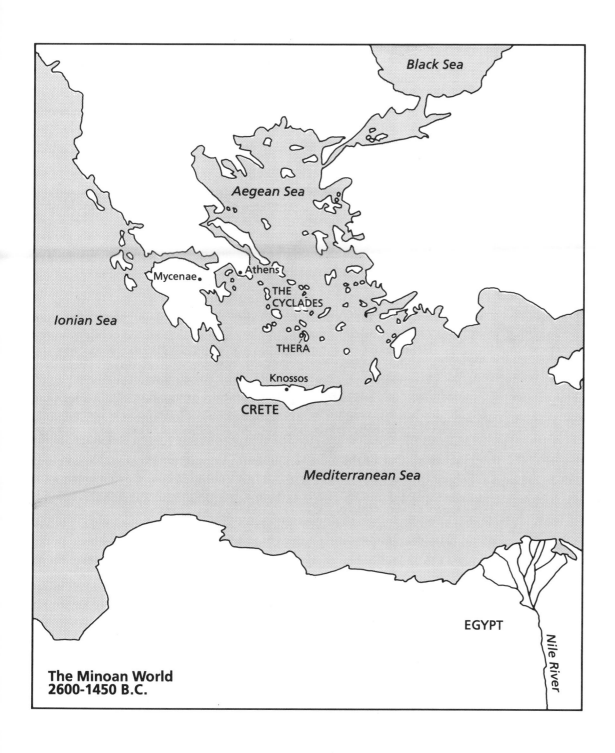

Black Sea

Aegean Sea

Ionian Sea

Mycenae

Athens

THE
CYCLADES

THERA

Knossos

CRETE

Mediterranean Sea

EGYPT

Nile River

**The Minoan World
2600-1450 B.C.**

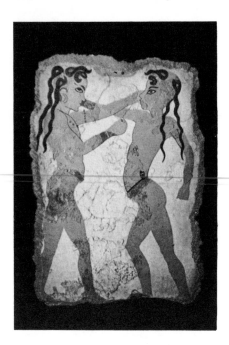

Replica of the Boxing Children, *a Theran fresco, c. 1500 B.C.*

THE BULL

MALES AND FEMALES

ART

The overall plan of the palace focussed on a central courtyard surrounded by a maze of hundreds of rooms. Here, chambers for royalty, administrators, civil servants, and artisans were provided. Many of the buildings were several stories high and finely finished with closely hewn masonry and superbly engineered drainage systems. Water was brought to Knossos through terracotta pipes extending 15 km. Within the palace, a series of open and closed channels directed water flow, and each rain gutter was designed with right-angled turns and baffles to reduce the speed of the water as it drained.

Although the Minoans developed a system of writing, history meant little to them. There is no record of individual personalities and dates as in ancient Egypt, or any indication of their system of government. Based on the illustrations in frescoes, the numerous altars at palace sites, and the evidence of control over the store of wealth and the redistribution of food, the general population was probably ruled by a small elite dominated by a priest-king. The system certainly seems to have been effective. There were few squabbles among Minoan palaces because of the need to work together to obtain maximum output from the land. The lack of palace fortifications suggests that the dominating strength of the Minoan navy in the Aegean left them little to fear from their neighbours.

The religious significance of the palaces and the priest-king appears to be tied in with the almost universal presence of double-headed axes. These were found as artifacts in themselves, and depicted on pottery and in what appear to be shrines. Just as the cross would later have deep meaning for Christianity, the double-headed axe seems to have symbolized something special to the Minoans.

Of equal interest is the respect granted to the bull. Their horns were represented in architecture, while the animal itself was depicted in a variety of activities. One of the most famous frescoes found by Evans shows male and female youths somersaulting over a large, charging bull. Archaeologists have suggested this was either a ritual for all youths or perhaps a demonstration by a special class of athletes.

Frescoes indicate that the Minoans saw or idealized themselves as a graceful, slender people with long hair that curled as it hung down the back. Males are traditionally shown with red skin and females with white throughout Minoan art. The society seems to have given women a free and prominent role. Many statuettes and frescoes, like the *Ladies in Blue*, show females in elegant dress. Many of the deities at shrines were either female or accompanied by female figurines which suggests that goddesses were as important as gods. Animals, and possibly humans, were sacrificed to both as a matter of reverence.

Most of the art in Minoan culture was miniature in size, rather than the monumental work done in Egypt and Mesopotamia. The gem and seal markings on beads and finger-sized cylinders, and the elaborate engravings on gold and silver jewellery and gold vases and cups, often depict with amazing skill the same kinds of pictures found on the larger wall paintings. Again, in contrast to the Egyptians, not a single piece of writing is found on palace walls or in tombs.

Bull vaulting, as shown in this fresco, was either a ritual activity or a Minoan sport.

The End of Minoan Civilization

This advanced and prosperous Bronze Age civilization suffered a wide-scale catastrophe in 1700 B.C., when all Minoan palaces on Crete were destroyed simultaneously. Walls were toppled, pithoi jars fell through floors, and the unique narrow-based, wide-crowned columns were charred and broken. Most archaeologists have concluded that the disaster was the result of an earthquake. Despite this setback, Minoan civilization recovered quickly and built even larger palaces on the old site, incorporating and improving upon earlier achievements in art and architecture. At Akrotiri, on the island of Thera, archaeologist Spyridon Marinatos unearthed from volcanic ash a Minoan community that dates to the same time period as the reconstructed palaces on Crete. Continued excavation, which is expected to last into the twenty-first century, may push the origin of this site even further into the past.

Tragically, Minoan civilization came to an abrupt end when another cataclysm struck between 1500 and 1470 B.C. An enormous volcanic eruption on the island of Thera sent tsunamis and spread volcanic ash across much of the Aegean, including a large part of the island of Crete. Only Knossos, largest of the Minoan palaces, escaped general destruction. By 1450 B.C., only Knossos was occupied. "Squatters," as Evans called them, had replaced the Minoan builders. The palace itself was finally destroyed for the last time in 1380 B.C., possibly by outsiders from the mainland or by the rebellious Cretans who resented foreign occupation of their soil. What is clear is that Minoan civilization had ended about a century before the boy-king Tutankhamun came to the throne of Egypt.

CATASTROPHE AND REBIRTH

U-shaped horns, the symbol of Knossos.

Ladies in Blue. *The elegance in female dress, illustrated in this fresco, suggests a prosperous and cultured Minoan society.*

PLATO

ATLANTIS

The Source of the Legend

Writing over one thousand years later, the Greek philosopher Plato left a puzzle that often appears to jump across several time periods that are traditionally accepted by archaeologists as the general sequence of development. Writing as though he was a pupil listening to Socrates discuss issues with a group of friends, Plato produced two dialogues called *Timaeus* and *Critias*. Atlantis, a lost paradise, was mentioned briefly in the former and in detail in the latter.

Plato's Atlantis was an earthly paradise that existed nine thousand years before Solon, a Greek lawgiver who lived around 600 B.C. As was usual in ancient histories, Atlantis was given a legendary beginning when Poseidon, the god of the sea, begot ten sons of a mortal woman. The eldest son, Atlas, was given control of the empire of Atlantis, which was ruled thereafter by the descendants of the ten kings. The original small island became the metropolis of the empire and was the site of the temple of Poseidon.

The metropolis itself was a circular city 25 km in diameter, ringed with walls and canals. One enormous canal connected it to an irrigated, agriculturally rich plain some 368 by 544 km in size. The central hill supplied hot and cold springs for the city, and kings, and private men and women bathed in warm baths during the winter. Walls were made from red, white, and black stones quarried locally, and the inner enclosure, focussing on the royal palace, was lined with valuable metals. In addition to the worship of Poseidon, a bull was sacrificed every five or six years for religious purposes. Beyond the city,

*View overlooking the caldera of
Santorini, ancient Thera. The homes
are typical of the Cycladic buildings
of the Minoan period.*

Atlantis used its military power of ten thousand chariots and twelve hundred
ships to control the island and coastal empire beyond the Pillars of Hercules.

**THE SOURCES OF PLATO'S
INFORMATION**

Over ten thousand books and articles have sprung from Plato's description. Nevertheless, it is Plato's information, which clearly states four times in
the dialogues that the story is true, that is of critical relevance. In both dialogues, all comment on Atlantis comes from Critias who was, in fact, a real
person. He received his information from his grandfather, Critias the Elder, and
from lost documents once in his family's possession. These documents, in turn,
were based on what the statesman Solon had learned from Egyptian priests.
Solon did travel the Mediterranean about 600 B.C. and the Roman historian
Plutarch later quoted a fragment of his poetry that describes the Nile. It therefore seems likely that the story told to Solon, and any written sources he was
given, represented a genuine Egyptian tradition.

One important element in Plato's writing has captured popular imagination. Atlantis, as a great sea power, launched an attack on Athens and Egypt
when suddenly,

THE DISAPPEARANCE OF ATLANTIS

> there occurred violent earthquakes and floods; and in a single day
> and night of misfortune the island of Atlantis disappeared in the
> depths of the sea.[1]

Was this possible? As mentioned earlier, Plato had located Atlantis "beyond
the Pillars of Hercules," which most observers have taken to mean beyond the
Strait of Gibraltar in the Atlantic Ocean. Others, including Plato's student Aristotle, felt that Plato simply made up the entire story. Recent investigators have
tried to link Atlantis to the Minoan civilization on Crete and Thera.

1. Francis Hitching, *The World Atlas of Mysteries* (London: William Collins Sons and Co. Ltd.,
1978) p. 137.

Caldera Formation on Thera.

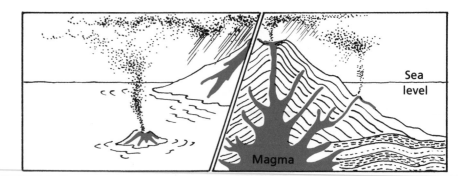

Stage 1: Mild explosions–magma fills inner chambers

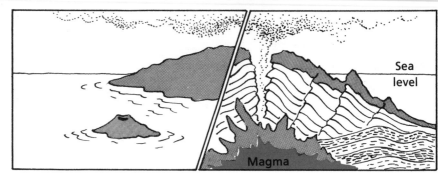

Stage 2: Increasingly violent explosions produce great eruption of pumice. Magma level drops and roof begins to crack.

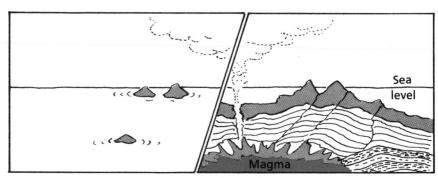

Stage 3: Cone collapses forming a hollow chamber that quickly fills with sea water and produces a colossal explosion.

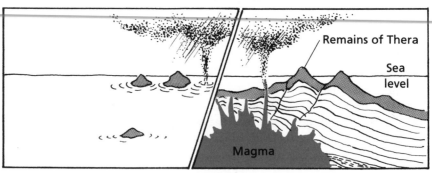

Stage 4: New cones appear after a period of silence.

PROBLEM QUESTION

In what way is the question about the existence of Atlantis best answered–as a continent in the Atlantic, as a myth invented by Plato, or as the story of Minoan civilization?

ALTERNATIVE ONE

The Secret of Atlantis–Based on *The Secret of Atlantis* by Otto Muck, 1976

Otto Muck is one person who believes that Plato's story in the dialogues is true, and he explains why in *The Secret of Atlantis*. If by the Pillars of Hercules Plato meant the Strait of Gibraltar, then Atlantis would have been about 1200 km west of Europe in the vicinity of the Azores. Indeed, crude pottery and weapons discovered on these islands suggest that the area was once inhabited by Neanderthal Man, the precursor of Cro-Magnon.

In France and Spain, archaeologists have uncovered weapons, artifacts, and cave paintings of red-skinned people which they credit to Cro-Magnon. They have not discovered the origin of this more advanced culture, however. It seems possible to Otto Muck that Cro-Magnon travelled from the west up rivers from the Atlantic, and that these European discoveries provide evidence of the existence of Atlantean colonies.

There is also evidence to suggest connections between Atlantis and other parts of the world. The striking similarities between the Egyptian pyramids and those of Central and South America are puzzling. But even more fascinating, according to Muck, is the connection between the Basques of Spain and the Mayan Indians.

In Guatemala, an early Basque missionary was surprised to discover that an isolated tribe of pure Mayans understood his unique language. Other similarities included their hooked-nose appearance, the digging sticks both used to loosen the earth for planting, and a sport known to Basques as pelota. This game, played with a small, hard ball and wicker rackets fastened to the players' hands, is practically identical to one that was played by Mexican natives at the time of the Spanish conquest.

Otto Muck points to nature to support his belief in the physical presence of the continent itself. European eels born in the Sargasso Sea, southwest of the Azores, follow a dangerous mating pattern. For three years they float with the Gulf Stream to Europe where they make their way up freshwater rivers and streams. When they are ready to mate, ten to fifteen years later, they return to the Sargasso.

According to Muck, this journey to the safety of freshwater rivers is instinctive, but was first formed around the freshwater rivers of Atlantis, a short distance away. Although the continent has disappeared, the eel's instincts continue to guide them along the Gulf Stream until they reach freshwater.

For more support, Muck refers to the oceanography of the Atlantic. The floor of the ocean is divided by a ridge 2800 m high. This ridge runs from Iceland almost to the Antarctic Shelf. In the area that Muck claims Atlantis once occupied, there is a massive bulge almost 1100 km long and 400 km wide. Known as the Azores Plateau, it has submarine volcanic peaks that break the ocean surface. According to Muck, the size and shape of this plateau are amazingly similar to Plato's description of Atlantis.

Muck thinks it is possible that the same phenomenon that created the two enormous gouges on the ocean floor, known as the Puerto Rico Trench, might also have contributed to the disappearance of Atlantis.

Plato refers to a "deviation in the courses of the stars, and the destruction by fire of everything on earth." This deviant star, according to Muck, was an asteroid from the Adonis group. Judging from the immense scars on the ocean floor, he estimates its diameter to have been about 10 km.

Muck describes the catastrophe this way:

> At a height of about 400 km, the asteroid began to be surrounded by the red . . . hydrogen light. The hotter the asteroid became, the whiter and more brilliant was the light. . . . Its gaseous tail became immense. . . . After entering the densest part of the atmosphere . . . it burst.[2]

At this point two enormous pieces plunged into the ocean; one creating the Puerto Rico Trench, the other penetrating the earth's crust and starting a chain reaction of volcanic eruptions and earthquakes. In the vicinity of Atlantis, these were stupendous. Huge clouds of steam and ash rose from the red-hot magma that swelled from the earth's crust into the Atlantic. This erupting magma created a depression into which Atlantis began to sink. In twenty-four hours, just as Plato reported, the island continent had completely vanished. All that remained, according to Muck, were the lava-covered peaks that we now call the Azores.

The effects of the asteroid's impact were not confined to the vicinity of Atlantis. The destruction was widespread. Each catastrophe triggered another around the globe. One of the most devastating effects was a deadly gas that took its toll wherever the wind carried it. The disappearance of tens of thousands of Siberian mammoths is evidence of its pervasive effects.

Vegetation found in the stomachs of these animals indicates that Siberia was then an ice-free environment. It was only when the impact of the asteroid tilted the earth that the climate abruptly changed.

The catastrophe was also responsible for the Great Deluge mentioned in the Bible. According to Muck, water condensed from the enormous clouds of steam and ash, creating the flood conditions. The magnitude of the destruc-

2. Otto Muck, *The Secret of Atlantis* (Toronto: William Collins Sons and Co. Ltd., 1976), p. 167.

tion, Muck explains, is why the memory of Atlantis was lost. Those who survived the catastrophe and their descendants struggled to live under an immense cloud of volcanic ash that hovered over northern Europe. It took about three thousand years before even the rudiments of civilization were acquired. By this time, 4000 B.C., the name "Atlantis" was all that had survived.

Questions

1. Why does Muck feel that Atlantis was located in the Atlantic Ocean?
2. a) What evidence does Muck present to prove that the Cro-Magnon were from Atlantis?
   b) Did Cro-Magnon develop the kind of Bronze Age civilization that the people of Atlantis supposedly possessed (see "The Origin of Humans," p. 14)? Explain your answer.
3. How does Muck use the flow of the Gulf Stream and the mating habits of European eels to illustrate the existence of Atlantis in the Atlantic?
4. a) What connections can be found between cultures on both sides of the Atlantic that suggest Atlantis may have provided a link between the Old World and the New?
   b) Is this evidence convincing? Explain your answer.
5. What evidence does Muck present to suggest that the area surrounding the Azores may have been the former site of the Atlantean continent?
6. a) How does the argument about a large asteroid striking the earth relate to the disappearance of Atlantis in a single day and night, as described by Plato?
   b) The asteroid described by Muck seems to be similar to the Creationist description of the meteorite that started the flood of Noah. Compare the date, extent, and impact of the Great Deluge as described by Muck with the account given by the Creationists (see "Noah's Ark," pp. 25–26).
   c) Does either explanation seem feasible? Give reasons for your answer.
7. When Muck explains other mysteries, such as the disappearance of the Siberian mammoths, is the case for Atlantis weakened or strengthened? Explain your answer.
8. Why, according to Muck, was Atlantis forgotten for such a long time?

ALTERNATIVE TWO

Atlantis—Based on "Appendix on Atlantis" by Desmond Lee, 1977

In an "Appendix on Atlantis" in his translation of *Plato Timaeus and Critias*, Desmond Lee addresses two questions: Could Minoan Crete have been overwhelmed by earthquakes and volcanic explosions? Could any inkling of this catastrophe have reached Plato?

The eruption that Lee has in mind is similar to the 1883 explosion in Krakatoa, but on an even grander scale. Because the Krakatoa explosion occurred in the recent past, we know a lot about it. For six or seven years prior to the explosion, several earthquakes had occurred in the area. Finally, the underground accumulation of volcanic matter or magma blew a great hole in the earth. Most of Krakatoa disappeared.

The effects were almost beyond belief. The explosion was heard 5000 km away in Western Australia. Clouds of volcanic ash literally turned day into night within a 250-km area. The massive tidal wave had a reach of 80 km where waves averaged 15 m high. It was so powerful it sent a small warship, anchored in the harbour, 3 km inland.

Thera, like Krakatoa, lies on a major fault line. According to Lee, there is no doubt that a similar explosion occurred there in the last half of the fifteenth century B.C. The difference is that it is more difficult to assess events prior to and following the explosion. There seems to be a connection between the explosion and the destruction of Minoan sites in Crete in the latter part of the fifteenth century B.C., however.

The size of the crater at Thera is four times larger than the one at Krakatoa. This suggests that the distribution of volcanic ash and the size and extent of tidal waves would increase accordingly. Indeed, Lee tells us that cores taken from the seabed show widespread distribution of ash. The average depth of 20 cm found in central and eastern Crete would have destroyed all vegetation and made the area uninhabitable. The size and extent of the tidal wave can only be estimated. But, as Lee points out, it would have damaged ships and harbours, at the very least.

The explosion at Thera was, in all likelihood, associated with earthquakes. Similarly, the destruction in Crete—the collapse of buildings followed by fire—was the type caused by earthquakes. Desmond Lee suggests that the earthquake that damaged Crete was the same major earthquake that was associated with the explosion. This being the case, the answer to the first question is "Yes."

The destruction of Atlantis, according to Plato, occurred nine thousand years before Solon. Lee points out, however, that if Plato had misunderstood the original figures in a multiplication by ten, then the destruction actually would have occurred during the same period as the eruption on Thera.

If the Solon story is possible, then, according to Lee, it is equally possible that it mentioned the destruction of a highly civilized island to the west. Communication between Egypt and Crete would probably have relayed the Thera catastrophe. Indeed, Egypt was close enough to Thera to have experienced some of the effects firsthand.

Desmond Lee feels that if Plato used the story at all, it was for the catastrophe alone. There are no other similarities between Atlantis and Minoan Crete.

Plato's concern in the *Critias*, as well as in most of his other works, was the conflict between appearance and reality, between what things should be like and the way things actually are. According to Lee, Atlantis was a byproduct of this framework.

Indeed, Lee suggests that the *Critias* could be considered the first essay of science fiction. Science fiction has two motives, according to Lee: One is to peer into the future to see what humans are capable of achieving; the other is to escape from reality.

Although Atlantis was a civilization of the past, it was an advanced society rich in human achievement. By choosing a lost civilization of the past, Plato was also indulging in escapism. According to Lee, it could as easily have been a society of the future.

Questions

1. Why does Lee compare the volcanic explosions on Krakatoa and Thera?
2. Why does Lee feel that the eruption of Thera and the end of Atlantis could have happened about the same time?
3. How, according to Lee, did the ash, tidal wave(s), and earthquake affect Crete?
4. What was the end result of the Thera explosion for Minoan civilization?
5. a) What evidence does Lee provide to prove that Plato could have known about the Thera explosion?
   b) What was Plato's purpose in using Atlantis in his writing?
   c) What was Plato's main concern in the dialogues of *Timaeus* and *Critias* and in his other scholarly work?
6. a) How does Lee regard the Atlantis story?
   b) Is his argument convincing? Explain your answer.

ALTERNATIVE THREE

Atlantis: The Truth Behind the Legend—Based on "Atlantis" by Edward Bacon, 1974

Atlantis is exceptionally rich and fertile, with level plains and well-wooded mountains, producing two crops a year with the aid of hot and cold springs, protected against cold winds and intensively cultivated. Politically, it is a federation of ten kings, led by the descendants of Atlas, meeting in the ancient metropolis for conference, consultation and a ritual bull-game. Technologically, it is extremely advanced with written laws, a knowledge of metalworking including the use of gold, silver, and bronze, and an exceptional grasp of engineering and architecture involved in the construction of temples, walls, long canals, tunnels, and harbour works. The inhabitants worship a number of gods, of whom Poseidon is the chief, and they also practise a bull cult. Socially there is considerable stress on the good life, with public gardens and baths not only for men and women but also for horses.

All of this is consistent up to a point; and that point is that the empire collapsed in a single day and night. That is the account given by the Egyptian priests 9000 years before the date of their conversation with Solon, which means about 9600 B.C. This is a glaring impossibility. For example, in 9600 B.C., there were no Athenians to oppose Atlantis; the Mycenaean city of Athens existed not much before the 16th century and metal-working had not been discovered anywhere in the world. The first and simplest farming communities date from, at the earliest, 7000 B.C. Horses were unknown in Europe until the Bronze Age and were previously confined to Central Asia. The earliest monumental architecture can be dated to not before 4000 B.C. In brief, Atlantis as described by Plato is so impossible that his younger contemporary, Aristotle, assumed that Atlantis was a myth, an imaginary kingdom thought up by Plato to illustrate certain political theories.

But this explanation of Aristotle is not really satisfactory. Plato's Atlantis is not a consistent myth; it illustrates no particular theory and is full of curious detail, very like a historical report, very unlike a political allegory. The characters in Plato's dialogue find the story baffling and apparently incredible, but continue on the basis that, strange though it seems, it is indeed true historical fact.

For some years now it has been apparent to scholars that the Atlantis described by Plato was very like what archaeology has uncovered of the High Bronze Age civilizations of the Aegean and the Near East, such as the Minoans, the Mycenaeans, the Hittites, the Egyptians, and the Babylonians, between about 2500 and 1200 B.C. Was there then something wrong with Plato's date? Had the Egyptian priests or Solon confused 900 with 9000 years? If so the date of the disaster would be 1500 B.C. instead of 9600 B.C.

This idea immediately makes the Atlantean civilization credible. Again if there is a mistake with the power of ten here, it could apply equally to the large dimensions given for the empire of Atlantis. If so, the dimensions for the Royal City of Atlantis shrink to something very closely approximating the central plain of Crete, the heartland of Minoan civilization. The time would then approximate the collapse of the Minoan Empire following a series of disasters which led to the Mycenaean takeover. Furthermore, Minoan Crete was a prosperous power in close contact with Athens and Egypt, both of which were then in existence.

Thera today consists of three islands. These lie around a great expanse of water in the center of which rise two relatively modern volcanic islets. The great expanse of water is about 11 km from north to south and close to 8 km from east to west while the depth ranges between 300 and 400 m. It is in fact a gigantic volcanic crater known as a caldera formed by a colossal explosion.

The most striking recent example of such a disaster is the explosion of Krakatoa in Indonesia in 1883. This explosion was heard nearly 5000 km away, some 295 towns in Java and Sumatra were wholly or partially destroyed,

36 000 people perished, and the sound-waves travelled around the world three times. Tidal waves crossed the entire Pacific and were still strong enough to break anchor chains in Valparaiso, Chile. Volcanic dust rose to a height of 8 km and some of it fell in Japan.

Now the effects of such an eruption can be calculated on the basis of the size of the caldera. The caldera of Thera had a volume about five times that of Krakatoa; and the violence of its explosion must be assumed to have been something like five times as great. Its effects in the landlocked and island-studded Aegean and its wider effects in the whole eastern Mediterranean must have been catastrophic beyond imagination. It caused the disappearance of the greater part of the previously circular island which it had already rendered uninhabitable with deposits of pumice and ash, which are still nearly 60 m deep in places. It also produced tidal waves which must have swept many kilometres inland in nearby Crete with wholesale destruction and loss of life.

We are therefore left with two curiously similar accounts, one of which is Plato's. The other, the sum of the discoveries of geophysicists and archaeologists, tells us that the great empire of Minoan Crete suffered a series of natural disasters in the late 16th century B.C. and that these disasters were caused by fires, earthquakes, and floods which brought about the end of civilization; and that around 1500 B.C. a fertile island, some 100 km north of Crete blew up in almost total destruction and caused widespread devastation throughout the Aegean and eastern Mediterranean.

These two accounts of unparalleled disaster are so similar in nature, location, and date that they must be different accounts of the same disaster. And when an archaeological expedition, led by Professor Marinatos of Athens in 1967, uncovered Minoan remains deep under the pumice of Thera, the final link was added. The identification of Thera with the ancient metropolis of Atlantis, and of Minoan Crete with the Royal City and empire of the Atlanteans, thus became virtually inevitable.

Questions

1. Does Bacon's description of Atlantis appear to be a civilization of the Stone Age, the Copper Age, the Bronze Age, or the Iron Age? Explain your answer.
2. a) Why does Plato's date of 9600 B.C. for Atlantis seem impossible to Bacon?
   b) Does Lee agree with Bacon's conclusion about the date?
   c) How would Muck react to the conclusions of Bacon and Lee about the date for Atlantis?
   d) Which argument would be the most convincing?
3. How does Bacon's argument about a mistake in the power of ten (nine thousand to nine hundred) relate to the size of Atlantis and the size of the central plain of Crete?

4. Identify the similarities and differences in the descriptions of a volcanic explosion given by Lee and Bacon in the case of the eruption of Thera in the fifteenth century B.C.
5. a) What is Bacon's overall conclusion about the existence of Atlantis?
   b) Suggest why Lee, a literary critic who was aware of the geological work done on Thera and Crete, reached a different conclusion about the existence of Atlantis than Bacon, a writer who worked closely with Greek archaeologists studying the Aegean.

ANSWERING THE PROBLEM QUESTION

In selecting the best explanation about the existence of Plato's Atlantis, several factors must be considered. For example, the apparent sequence of indirect evidence passed by word of mouth and by written translations from Egyptian priests to Solon, from Solon to Critias the Elder, and from Critias the Elder to Critias and Plato, poses a problem in credibility. If the pattern is correct and if the story is based on a real event, how many changes in the original version were made by exaggeration or accident before it reached Plato? There is also the problem of the conventions of classical literature. Once Plato heard the story, did he simply use this tale as the framework for yet another example of his lifelong preoccupation with the gap between the ideal and the real world?

One of the most fascinating aspects of the issue is trying to determine the exact location of Atlantis. Taken literally, Plato's reference to beyond the Pillars of Hercules would seem to place Atlantis in the Atlantic Ocean. Geologic evidence, however, must be seriously examined. Is the argument presented by Muck about the impact of an asteroid and the subsequent sinking of the land surrounding the Azores convincing? Or was Plato misleading us about the location? If he was, perhaps the argument about the extent of the damage from the Thera explosion could be more relevant. What are the characteristics of such volcanic eruptions and what were the precise effects of the Thera explosion on the Aegean world?

In addition, can it be arbitrarily assumed that an error was made in the power of ten during the original translation of the story? If there was, then the date for the Thera explosion closely matches the time period of Atlantis, and the size of the city and empire of Atlantis approach that of Thera and Crete. Could the catastrophe of the fifteenth century B.C. on Thera have destroyed Atlantis in a day and a night, or should Plato not be taken literally on this point? If some of these ideas are found to be persuasive, then the work of archaeologists in identifying Atlantis and Minoan civilization as Bronze Age cultures should be closely studied.

How, then, can these criteria be evaluated, ranked, and applied to the problem about the existence of Atlantis?

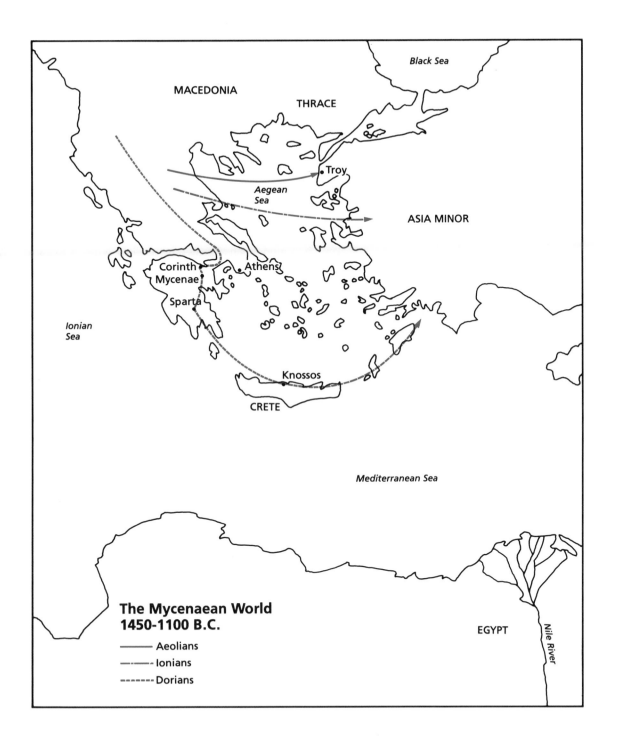

Black Sea

MACEDONIA

THRACE

• Troy

Aegean
Sea

ASIA MINOR

Corinth
Mycenae

Athens

Sparta

Ionian
Sea

Knossos

CRETE

Mediterranean Sea

EGYPT

Nile River

**The Mycenaean World
1450-1100 B.C.**

———— Aeolians
—·—·— Ionians
------- Dorians

THE STORY CONTINUES . . .

The Rise of the Mycenaeans

While the Minoan civilization of Crete dominated and flourished in a relatively peaceful Aegean community, another group of people, known as the Mycenaeans, began to develop small, independent kingdoms on the mainland. Although the explosion on Thera threw havoc into the Minoan world, civilization clung to life until 1450 B.C., when Knossos was finally abandoned. Most likely, it took thirty to fifty years for the smothering volcanic ash to destroy agricultural production. At this time it seems as though at least one group of Mycenaeans (the squatters Evans referred to) occupied Knossos and exploited its fading role for what they could.

Why the palace at Knossos was destroyed in 1380 B.C. remains a mystery. By then, the small Mycenaean kingdoms had grown into palace states at Pylos, Mycenae, Athens, Thebes, and Tiryns but, unlike the peaceful Minoans, the new powers often competed against each other and conflict ensued. Possibly the destrucion of Knossos was the result of a battle among Mycenaean palace states for more territorial control or larger spheres of trading influence.

MYCENAE

Mycenaean strength replaced the Minoans as the prime influence in the Aegean and beyond. In addition to effective control over the Cyclades, colonies were established in Rhodes, Miletus, and Cyprus. Trading posts were set up in Asia Minor, and travel extended from Troy to Egypt. Based on the crowding in grave sites by the year 1300 B.C., it seems possible that the population approached that of the Golden Age of Athens some nine hundred years later.

The focal point of power was Mycenae, a location that possessed several advantages. In a region where mountains made arable land scarce, the fertile plain of Argos provided space for a hinterland of villages, labour, and farm produce for its citizens. The development of crafts in the working of ivory imported from Syria, the manufacture of weapons in bronze, and the production of fine pottery further enriched this thriving community.

THE CITADEL

Crowning a hilltop that overlooked the area was the citadel. Its massive stone blocks were so impressive that later classical Greeks thought it was the work of giants, or Cyclops, as Homer described them in the *Odyssey*. The Lion Gate, a triangular-shaped stone that rests over the entrance to the citadel, reveals a carving of two lions on the base of a column slightly tapered in the Minoan style. The entrance can only be reached on an inclined slope that would have made any attack on the fortress extremely difficult. Indeed, most tourists making a leisurely climb to the citadel summit are usually winded by the steepness of the slope.

MYCENAEAN GRAVES

Inside the walls, fourteen graves contained twenty-four unnamed royal corpses. Not far from the citadel a number of circular-shaped tombs, much larger and more finely built than those on Crete, can be found. The largest of these, the Treasury of Atreus, is entered through a corridor banked by sides

The tomb of Agamemnon is indicative of the burial chambers of Homeric heroes.

sloping upward towards an enormous gateway, inside which the tomb rises in the shape of a beehive to a height of about 14 m.

The Collapse

Although Mycenae was at its zenith of power, the extensive, thick-walled fortifications suggest that the Aegean world was still unstable and insecure. As it turned out, these fears were fully justified. All of the great Mycenaean palace states were burned, pillaged, and destroyed over the course of a century from 1250 to 1150 B.C. Why did this happen? Again, the answer is not clear.

Some indication may be found, however, by comparing the fate of the Mycenaeans with other empires that collapsed about the same time. During the last five hundred years of the Bronze Age, a powerful empire grew on the Anatolia Plateau in modern-day Turkey that was controlled by the Hittites. Their main rival to the south was a revitalized Egypt of the New Kingdom. In 1288 B.C., under Pharaoh Ramses II, the Egyptians marched north with thirty-five hundred war chariots to fight the Hittites for control of the Lebanese coast. The battle, at Kadesh, was inconclusive and exhausting. Both the Hittites and the Egyptians withdrew from the disputed area. By 1200 B.C., the Hittite Empire had been sacked and burned, and the Egyptian Empire greatly weakened from attacks by a mysterious group referred to as the ''peoples of the sea'' in Egyptian inscriptions.

Initially, the vacuum of power was exploited by the warlike Mycenaeans, who set up trading posts in the now-open Lebanese coastal region. It is quite possible that some Mycenaeans had actually joined various groups of sea peoples on their increasing number of raids. This would have created much of the

CONFLICT IN THE AEGEAN

THE "PEOPLES OF THE SEA"

Mycenaean Chronology

B.C.

1450	Mycenaeans occupy Knossos after Minoan collapse
1380	Palace of Knossos destroyed for last time, possibly as result of conflict among Mycenaeans
1300	Fortified citadel at Mycenae becomes the most powerful of Mycenaean palace states in the Aegean
1288	Kadesh: Hittite and Egyptian empires fight an inconclusive and exhausting battle
1250	Mycenaeans move into trading areas vacated by Hittites and Egyptians in eastern Mediterranean
1200	Sea peoples end Hittite empire
1100	Sea peoples destroy and sack all Mycenaean palace states during past century

HOMER

HEINRICH SCHLIEMANN

END OF THE AEGEAN ERA

uncertainty and tension reflected in the extensive fortifications of many palace states. Although Homer's epic poetry must be sifted with care in separating fact from fiction, the basic story tends to support this idea.

In the *Iliad*, Homer describes a combined force of Greeks from the Mycenaean world, which included men from Mycenae, led by Agamemnon, and the men of Pylos, led by Nestor, attacking Troy, a powerful and wealthy city on the northwest coast of Asia Minor. Heinrich Schliemann, a wealthy German industrialist and amateur archaeologist, took Homer literally. In 1876, he believed he had discovered Troy, a city that had been regarded as purely mythical. Critics pointed out that, despite the wealth of artifacts and fabulous treasures of gold and silver vases and jewellery, the city was only one of nine stacked on top of each other, and that Schliemann had picked the wrong one as the city of the Trojan Wars. Undaunted, Schliemann again took Homer as a literal source and again found an incredible amount of gold and bronze objects at five royal grave sites, this time at the citadel of Mycenae. He labelled one gold mask the death mask of Agamemnon. This, he claimed, illustrated that Homer should be taken literally. Archaeology has since proven that the mask predates the era of Troy. Despite his shortcomings, Schliemann's work suggests there is at least some truth behind the legend.

Other details in the *Iliad* suggest that Homer was describing the Aegean world in Mycenaean times. In Homer's day, four centuries later, Sparta, Athens, and Corinth were of prime importance. Mycenae was a backward community and Pylos had disappeared. Homer glorified the latter rather than the former to preserve the stories of a previous age that had been handed down by word of mouth. Homer's mention of tower shields shaped in figure eights, in contrast to the small shields of the eighth-century-B.C. warrior, and his description of chariots in varying capacities were references to weapons and vehicles he had never seen. They were already obsolete, but having heard of their appearance and use, he passed on the information.

Although the origin of the sea peoples is clouded in generalities, their impact on Aegean and Mediterranean civilization is clear. Neither the Hittites nor the Egyptians were a sea-going people, beyond using basic river transportation. In wartime, they recruited navies from surrounding coastal centres. Eventually, these sea peoples turned on their former allies, usually joining the side that seemed most likely to succeed. Finally, they disposed of the major powers of the land-based empires. As the strength of the sea peoples increased, they disrupted the trade in goods and grain on which the Mycenaean world depended. Eventually, the sea peoples, playing no favourites, sacked Mycenaean palace states. There is no archaeological evidence to indicate that they occupied the areas for any length of time. It seems that they were content to strike, loot, and leave.

By 1000 B.C., the Mycenaean culture had disappeared and mainland Greece was gradually infiltrated by an illiterate, less-advanced group called the Dorians. Their feudal society, dominated by a king and tribal council, achieved little. In fact, their presence marked the beginning of a three-hundred year period known as the "Dark Ages" through which no records of the once-flowering Mycenaean culture remained. Only the stories written by the blind poet Homer, regarded as legends for over twenty-five hundred years, hinted at an age that was long lost in history.

THE DARK AGES

Comment

The image of Atlantis as a lost paradise from an ancient golden age has been so vividly portrayed by authors and filmmakers that many have simply assumed that there must be some truth behind the popular myth. Schliemann's success in the discovery of Troy, which focussed on a literal interpretation of Homer's epic poetry, does provide some justification for this romantic and adventuresome approach. The same logic is also applicable to Atlantis. The word-of-mouth passage of information to Plato paralleled the verbal stories of the poets who passed on knowledge of the Trojan Wars to Homer. Taking Plato seriously could thus be the key to the search for Atlantis. A literal interpretation does have limits, however. Many of the details in Homer's work were added to improve the appeal of the story and in any word-of-mouth process, changes are made, either intentionally or unintentionally. Plato's work is no exception. The problem really focusses on determining if *enough important parallels exist* between the source of the information and the available evidence to justify the claim that Atlantis was once a real and thriving civilization.

Otto Muck uses Schliemann's idea in stressing that the original source, Plato, must be taken literally. Many of his arguments, however, are based on half-truths about Cro-Magnon, irrelevant facts about European eels, and faulty geology that overlooks the fact that no large Atlantic landmass has been exposed above sea level during the time of humans. Indeed, by suggesting that an asteroid caused the flood of Noah (about sixty-six hundred years before the Creationist meteorite!), Muck is trying to prove one legend with another when the scientific foundation for both is questionable. Just as von Däniken used unrelated coincidences about pyramid construction to suggest that ancient astronauts visited the earth, Muck introduces the disappearance of mammoths to indirectly illustrate that Atlantis existed. The parallel development among populations on both sides of the Atlantic is not really that close when carefully examined. Nonetheless, the similarities might be better explained through isolated contact with pre-Columbian Phoenician voyages than by a mid-oceanic cultural exchange with Atlantis.

Desmond Lee outlines the present state of geologic evidence that might explain the disappearance of Atlantis in the Aegean, but he concludes that the story of Atlantis represented the first essay in science fiction. His role as a literary critic rather than a scientist might account for his emphasis on Plato's philosophical considerations. By arguing that Atlantis was a mythical creation, Lee offers a reasonable and likely explanation, but his claim that Plato's *Critias* was the first essay in science fiction is as much speculation as the ideas presented by Muck.

Edward Bacon also takes Plato literally. His emphasis, however, is on the many parallels between the Bronze Age civilization of the Minoans and the characteristics of Plato's Atlantis. The high standard of living, the bull cult, the existence of Egypt and Athens, the architectural achievements, the metallurgy, and the sudden catastrophic end are some of the many similarities found between the Minoans and the Atlanteans. Clearly, the parallels suggest that the Minoan Empire could have been the source of the legend. Whether Plato consciously used the story as fact, as he claimed in his dialogues, will probably remain uncertain.

Bacon's account relies on a translation error in the multiplication by ten to adjust the date and size of Atlantis to fit the Minoan situation during the Bronze Age. The apparent location of Atlantis beyond the Pillars of Hercules would also have to be overlooked. These adjustments can be done with some justification, particularly since the Atlantic was not familiar to either Plato or the earlier Egyptians who carried the legend, but they do remain assumptions that cannot be proven.

The interest in Atlantis has continued to increase since Plato wrote his dialogues in the fourth century B.C. The ultimate truth about the existence might never be known and, ironically, may not have been known by Plato! His choice of a lost continent could have been a whim, or a literary vehicle, just as easily as a historical description. Any claims about the reality of Atlantis must be filtered to identify solid evidence from exciting, but wishful, speculation. The importance of the story may lie not in the final solution to the problem but in the effort to discover and explain the image that Atlantis has produced.

Sir Arthur Evans's excavation of the palace at Knossos.

Date B.C.	Event
1100	Sea peoples destroy and sack all Mycenaean palace states Dark Ages begin
800	Greek city-states emerge
776	First Olympics are held
750	Homer composes *Iliad* and *Odyssey*
650	Age of Tyrants in city-state government
620	Sparta suppresses the Messenian Rebellion and develops the best army in Greece
520	Persian Empire dominates vast region from the Indus River to the eastern Aegean
490	Greeks defeat Persia at Marathon
480	Three hundred Spartans fight bravely to the death against Persia at Thermopylae Athenian navy defeats the Persians at Salamis
479	Sparta defeats Persians at Plataea
477	Delian League formed to protect Greek city-states from Persian attacks
465	Greeks defeat Persians again Athens turns Delian League into an Athenian Empire
447	Construction of Parthenon begins
445	The Thirty Years' Peace is declared between Athens and Sparta
431	Peloponnesian War begins between Sparta and Athens
429	Pericles dies during plague
416	Athenians massacre Melians
404	Sparta wins Peloponnesian War and occupies Athens Sparta demolishes the Long Walls from Athens to the port of Piraieus
399	Socrates, tried and condemned to death, drinks hemlock
377	Second, more democratic, Athenian League is formed
376	Athens defeats Spartan navy at Naxos
371	Thebes defeats Spartan army at Leuctra using new military tactics
338	Philip II of Macedonia defeats Athens and Thebes at Chaeronea Philip II imposes a unity on Greek city-states
336	Philip II is assassinated Alexander assumes his father's role

5

The Ideals of Sparta and Athens

BACKGROUND

The Rise of City-States

Geography played a major role in shaping the characteristics of Greek development. Most of Greece has little space for agriculture. The mountainous interior often extends to an irregular coastline, leaving only separate pockets of ground. During the Dark Ages, a series of individual towns, called city-states, emerged in these isolated pockets. Most of these settlements had populations of less than fifteen thousand.

The early Greeks had an intense loyalty to their individual communities. As the source and focus of their political, economic, and cultural life, each city-state was regarded as the *only* city by its residents. The city-state, which included small, defensible sections of arable land, became a separate political unit called a **polis**. At the centre of the polis was the **agora** or marketplace, where men gathered to gossip, discuss affairs of the day, and shop. Usually, a fortified hilltop called an **acropolis** provided sanctuary during an attack.

The major drawback to this system was that the extreme loyalties to local cities prevented any large-scale co-operation throughout Greece. In fact, many city-states squabbled and fought among themselves. The only forces of unity centered on universal religious or athletic festivals held at Delos, Delphi, or Olympia. As conflict continued between city-states, neighbours conquered neighbours. This meant that the victors had additional mouths to feed which strained already-inadequate supplies of food.

By 750 B.C., the apparent solution, reached in combination with newly developed skills as seafarers and a sense of adventure, was to colonize fertile areas beyond mainland Greece. Over the next two hundred years, colonization took place on an unprecedented scale. Greek colonies spread from the Black Sea and the Dardanelles to the coastal areas of what are now Italy, France, and Spain. The solution was only temporary as economic pressures continued to grow along with the population, but it did represent the first age of progress since the Mycenaean downfall.

The Parthenon on the Acropolis (shown at the top) is seen from the agora, the marketplace and social centre of the ancient city-state of Athens.

CHANGES IN GOVERNMENT

Oligarchy versus Democracy

Government also changed during this period of expansion. Kings were gradually replaced by influential landowners and aristocrats, who could afford to buy equipment to defend the city. Ordinary farmers, however, were usually deeply in debt and, as many lost their land, cries for reform greatly increased. As battle tactics came to require large armies of infantry or hoplites, heavily armed with spears, swords, and shields, the warrior class and the merchants who financed it demanded a greater say in affairs.

To replace government by city-state aristocrats, the Greeks turned to rule by one individual known as a tyrant, a word that did not have the evil tone associated with it today. During the Age of Tyrants, from 650 to 500 B.C., those who ruled codified laws, developed industry and commerce, and even broke up large estates to be divided among the peasants! Although some Greek states remained under this system, others were either ruled by a small group, a system known as an oligarchy, or by the many, a system called democracy. The best example of oligarchic government was developed by the Spartans. Unlike their neighbours who colonized beyond the mainland, the Spartans secured more land in the Peloponnesus by enslaving fellow Greeks in their own province of Laconia and in the bordering province of Messenia. Because twenty-five thousand Spartans had to control a mainland empire of two hundred fifty thousand Greeks, they trained and maintained an army of the best foot soldiers in all of the Aegean world. The Spartan ideal became selfless devotion to the common good of the state at any expense.

OLIGARCHY

DEMOCRACY

GREEK GOVERNMENT

Sparta: Oligarchy
Rule by the few

2 KINGS

Priestly and judicial functions
Elected by the Assembly

5 EPHORS (overseers)

Presided over the Senate and the Assembly
Put legislation before the Assembly: ''Yes'' or
''No'' vote decided by the loudest yell as judged
by the ephors
Had the most political power
Elected annually by the Assembly

SENATE

Elected by the Assembly for life
Prepared legislation for the Assembly and advised
the kings

ASSEMBLY

Free male citizens over thirty
Elected kings, ephors, and Senate
Voted on legislation but could not initiate it

Athens: Democracy
Rule by the many

COUNCIL OF FIVE HUNDRED

Chosen by lot from citizens over thirty
Divided into ten groups of fifty
Carried on day-to-day business and prepared legis-
lation and topics for Assembly discussion
New president elected every day

BOARD OF TEN GENERALS

Elected by the Assembly for one year

JURY OF SIX THOUSAND

Selected by lot from free citizens over thirty

JUDICIAL BOARD OF NINE ARCHONS

ASSEMBLY

All male citizens over eighteen
Open meetings, public discussion of all issues
Passed all laws, determined foreign policy, and
directed military operations
Decision of majority was final
Three obels paid for attendance

Most of what is known about Sparta comes from written sources left by its chief rival, the city-state of Athens, located on the peninsula of Attica. In contrast to Sparta, Athens adopted a type of democratic government and was in constant contact with outlying colonies and city-states, depending as it did on trade and commerce passing through the port of Piraieus. Nevertheless, some Athenians, including Plato, admired the order and self-discipline achieved by Sparta, while others, such as Aristotle and Socrates, were critical of the chaos and instability in their own democratic system.

The extreme differences in political, economic, and social attitudes between Sparta and Athens were typical of the individuality of every Greek city-state. Only the threat of a common enemy would unite them, and then only temporarily.

The Persian Wars

PERSIA

While the Greek city-states were completing their colonization, the greatest empire the world had yet seen burst from obscurity after 559 B.C. Cyrus II of Persia established the actual imperial structure, but it was during the reign of Darius I, beginning in 522 B.C., that Persian dominance was pushed to its limit. This 4000-km expanse, from the Indus River to the eastern Aegean, had a total population of ten million. A powerful community, it had a common language, used a standard coinage, and recognized a single ruler. The Persians borrowed heavily from each of their subject peoples in art and architecture and were flexible in recognizing local laws and traditions, but they also maintained a great pride in their own homeland bordering the Persian Gulf. To the Persians, the Greek city-states were barbarian outposts on the fringe of their immense civilization.

IONIAN REVOLT

Conquest had been the key to Persian expansion and, in 546 B.C., the need for naval bases and trading centres led to the inclusion of Greek outposts on the Ionian coast within the Persian Empire. In 499 B.C., Athens and Eretria supported the Ionian cities in a revolt against Persia, but the enterprise was brutally crushed. Persia looked to the Greek mainland for punishment and perhaps additional conquest. Given the past divisions that had existed among Greek city-states, the chances of victory for the apparently invincible Persian army appeared great indeed.

MARATHON

The Persians, under Darius, first struck in 490 B.C., easily taking the Eretrian force of about forty thousand, and then landing at Marathon, about 40 km north of Athens. There, only ten thousand Athenians and about one thousand Plataeans were left to face the Persians. Sparta claimed that it was in the middle of a religious festival and could not send troops. Despite the odds against them, the Greeks attacked at dawn, catching the Persians off guard and without their cavalry. The brilliant victory, in which 6400 Persians were killed, while only 192 Greeks were lost, changed the course of Greek history by showing that Persia could be defeated and by raising city-state unity to unprecedented heights.

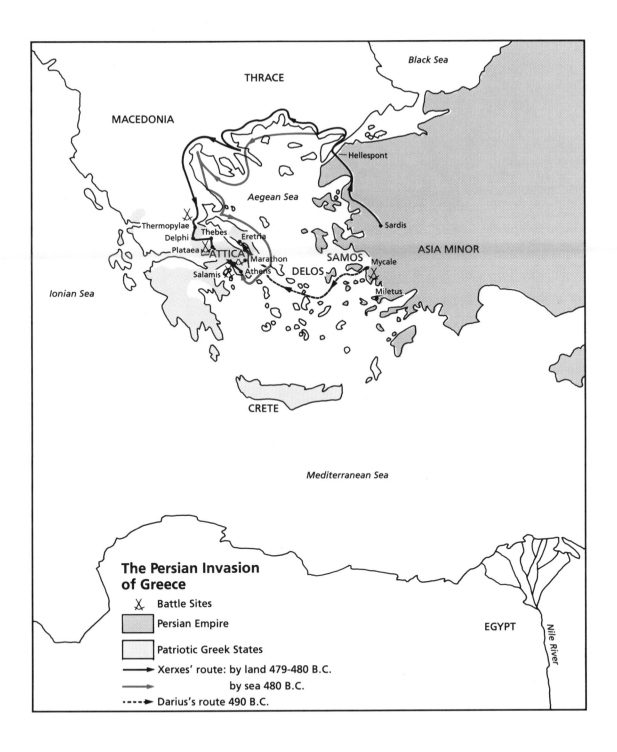

Black Sea

THRACE

MACEDONIA

Hellespont

Aegean Sea

Sardis

ASIA MINOR

Thermopylae
Delphi   Thebes
Plataea   Eretria
        ATTICA
            Marathon
Salamis   Athens   SAMOS   Mycale
                  DELOS
                              Miletus

Ionian Sea

CRETE

Mediterranean Sea

The Persian Invasion
of Greece

⚔ Battle Sites

▨ Persian Empire

▢ Patriotic Greek States

——▶ Xerxes' route: by land 479-480 B.C.

——▶   by sea 480 B.C.

----▶ Darius's route 490 B.C.

EGYPT

Nile River

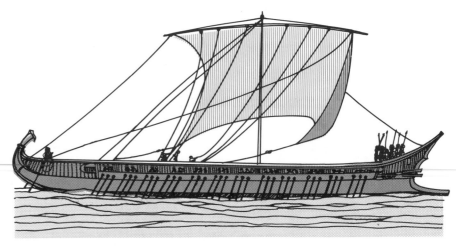

The Greek Trireme. This type of manoeuvrable ship was very successful against the awkward craft of Xerxes' Persian fleet at Salamis. The men on board included 170 rowers, 30 crew members, and 18 soldiers who used metal-tipped rams to puncture and sink enemy ships. Two eyes were painted on the bow of the trireme so the vessel could "see" its way.

THERMOPYLAE

A decade later Darius's son, Xerxes, organized an expedition of one hundred fifty thousand men and five hundred warships to seek revenge. The Greeks, including the Spartans, stood firm at the narrow pass of Thermopylae until a traitor showed the Persians a secret road by which the Greeks could be attacked from the rear. Left to defend the pass, three hundred Spartans, who represented the best fighting soldiers in all Greece, along with seven hundred Thespians fought bravely to the death. Their gallant sacrifice gave the main Greek force time to prepare a battle plan. Athens had to be abandoned to the Persians who sacked and burned the city. The oracle at Delphi, chief centre of prophecy, advised Athenians to put their faith in the "wooden wall," which many interpreted as the ships of the fleet. In the bay off the island of Salamis, the Athenian navy, with its disciplined and manoeuvrable fleet of triremes, defeated the Persian navy in a decisive, hard-fought battle. Shortly thereafter, the Spartans again proved themselves to be the finest troops in the civilized world when they defeated the Persians at Plataea.

SALAMIS

PLATAEA

THE DELIAN LEAGUE

Although Sparta retreated to the Peloponnesus after the war, the fact that a group of tiny city-states defeated the might of the Persian Empire added to an overall sense of Greek unity. A new confederacy, known as the Delian League, was organized under Athenian leadership to protect against attacks from the Persians. Initially, membership was voluntary, with each state contributing money which Athens used to build a strong navy, but the three hundred members of the Aegean community soon fell under Athenian domination.

The League did prove its value when another Persian military thrust against Greece was soundly defeated in 465 B.C. Nevertheless, the organization itself became an Athenian Empire, with Athenian officials and troops "defending" many of the smaller city-states that were now forced to provide money and men for the glorification and strengthening of Athens.

Black Sea

THRACE

Byzantium

Sea of
Marmara

MACEDONIA

Apollonia

Methone

AEGOSPOTAMI

Lampsacus

Potidaea

Abydos

Hellespont

EPIRUS

Aegean
Sea

Troy

Corcyra

THESSALY

LESBOS

MYSIA

CORCYRA

Mytilene

Ambracia

Leucas

Thermopylae

ASIA MINOR

LEUCAS

AETOLIA

LOCRIS

Delphi

PHOCIS

CHIOS

LYDIA

CEPHALONIA

Naupactus

BOEOTIA

EUBOEA

IONIA

Plataea

ATTICA

Ionian
Sea

ACHAEA

Megara

Athens

Corinth

Piraeus

SAMOS

Argos

Epidaurus

SALAMIS

Miletus

DELOS

CARIA

PELOPONNESUS

NAXOS

Sparta

MELOS

THERA

RHODES

CRETE

Mediterranean Sea

**Greece in
the Golden Age**

Athenian Alliance

Spartan Alliance

Neutral States

The Parthenon is a classic example of the visual harmony of Greek architecture.

The Golden Age of Athens

PERICLES

The threat of additional expansion by Athens, and the contrast between Athenian democracy and Spartan oligarchy led to several military clashes between the two city-states until an uneasy Thirty Year Truce was declared in 445 B.C. Under the inspirational leadership of Pericles, the greatest of all Greek orators, Athens consolidated the financial benefits of an empire to build a lasting monument to past victories, present peace, and the value of democracy as the Athenians understood it.

THE PARTHENON

The Acropolis of Athens, inhabited since Neolithic times, had been the site of two temples dedicated to the goddess Athena. These had been destroyed during the Persian occupation. Pericles wanted a new, special temple erected there for Athena, who was to be represented by an 11-m gold and ivory statue. Phidias, a sculptor and personal friend of Pericles, was commissioned to direct the work. The final product was the Parthenon, an achievement of unmatched harmony and classical beauty.

Construction lasted from 447 to 438 B.C., with an additional six years needed to complete the sculpturing on the ends. Precision and skill in the planning and execution were so exceptional that allowance was made for the fact that straight lines, when seen at a distance, appear to be curved. To compensate for this optical illusion, the foundation was slightly curved towards the middle on each side and the Doric columns were inclined. Thus, from a distance, the entire building appears to be made of absolutely straight lines. Because

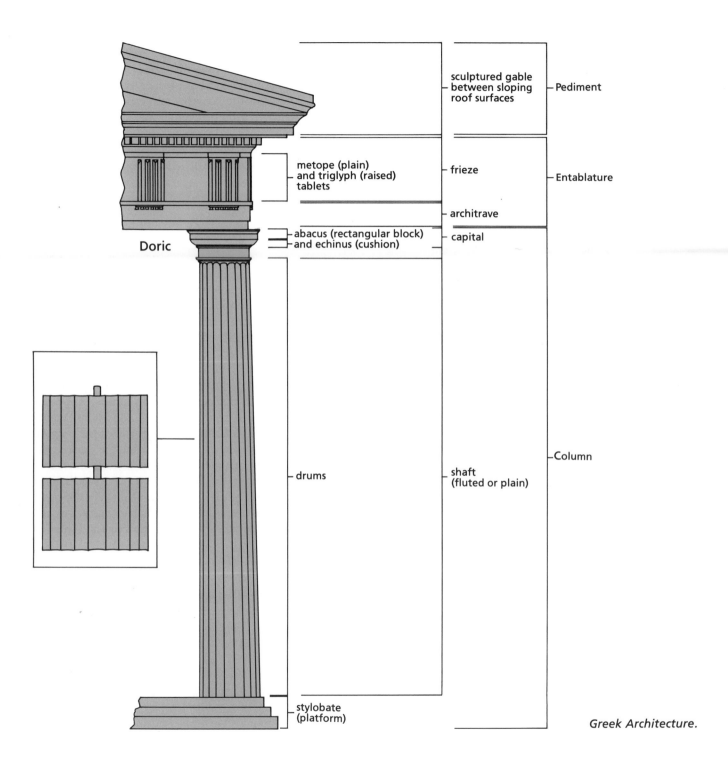

Doric

sculptured gable
between sloping
roof surfaces — Pediment

metope (plain)
and triglyph (raised)
tablets

— frieze

— architrave

— Entablature

abacus (rectangular block)
and echinus (cushion) — capital

— drums

— shaft
(fluted or plain)

— Column

— stylobate
(platform)

Greek Architecture.

Ionic

Greek Columns.

Corinthian

of the actual curve required to give a horizontal plane, every piece of marble had to be made to an individual size and fitted into place.

Clearly, this was appropriate for the goddess of their beloved city. Every four years a summer festival, known as the Panathenaea, was held with special splendour. Celebrations consisted of athletic events, musical and oratorical contests, and a culminating Panathenaic Procession along the Sacred Way to the Parthenon. Here, in one of the two large interior rooms, Athena, represented by her magnificent statue, was presented with a new robe from her people.

The Peloponnesian War

The prosperity of the Golden Age was short-lived. When a bitter trading rival, Corinth, appealed to Sparta, Thebes, and other allies to attack the wealthy Athenian Empire, the Greek world was thrown into a bitter struggle from which it never fully recovered. In 431 B.C., Greece was divided into two armed camps, with those city-states supporting Athens and its ideals in conflict with Sparta and city-states that resented Athenian domination. The Peloponnesian War, as it was called, lasted for twenty-seven years with a record of atrocities by Sparta on land and by Athens at sea that betrayed the high standards of Greek civilization.

Inspired by Pericles, in his famous ''Funeral Oration,'' which outlined the virtues of democratic life, Athens developed a war strategy of coastal raids on the Peloponnesus followed by naval blockades of food supplies. As people flooded into the city for protection against an attack by land, conditions became crowded and a plague broke out that killed almost one-quarter of the population, Pericles among them. Athenian morale was devastated and the war became an endurance struggle between evenly matched opponents, with neither side capable of a final victory. When Athens gradually weakened as the war dragged on, Sparta betrayed its fellow Greeks by borrowing money from Persia to build a fleet of its own. The Athenians were overwhelmed in a surprise attack by the Spartan navy in 405 B.C., and surrendered all foreign possessions and ships to Sparta in a peace treaty the following year.

Sparta, though victorious on the battlefield, failed, like Athens before her, to find a common ground to unite Greek city-states in a lasting relationship. Could other ways of life have brought a more fitting conclusion to the Golden Age of Greece? Or were the choices made the only realistic options?

PROBLEM QUESTION

To what extent were the interests of the Greek people better served by the oligarchy of Sparta or the democracy of Athens?

ALTERNATIVE ONE

Sparta—Based on "Greece The Golden Age" (*Life Educational Reprint #66*), 1963

Spartans were not always the rigid, self-denying people that they eventually became. In their Golden Age they enjoyed the good life with music and dancing. Then, in 620 B.C., the enslaved Messenians rebelled. Although the Spartans crushed the revolt, it took all their strength to do so. The experience taught them a valuable lesson. If they were to successfully control their empire and defend it against their enemies, they must sacrifice their comfort and culture for a more rigid and disciplined armed camp. They must forge themselves into a ruthless fighting machine.

Although the Spartan fighting force was never more than eight thousand strong, their reputation for being unbeatable and their bloodcurdling war cry and disciplined attack terrified their enemies. The Spartan simplicity, straightforwardness, and fanatical dedication, which the other Greeks envied, were rooted in the Spartan constitution. The state was everything, the individual was nothing. All Spartans were taught that goodness was simply strength plus bravery, and their lives were dedicated to serving this ideal. In fact, newborn infants were literally examined for defects and weaknesses by state inspectors. Those who failed to pass were left to die on Mount Taygetus.

Military training began at the age of seven. Young boys were taken from their homes and placed in schools where they were repeatedly bullied and brutalized to toughen them for combat. They were taught that to cry out in pain was an unforgivable sin. To test their physical endurance, an annual ceremony was performed at the altar of the goddess Artemis. The boys selected were whipped until the altar stones were flecked with blood. Throughout the beating their parents urged them not to flinch or cry out. It was not unusual for a boy to die rather than show weakness. Besides physical endurance, they learned unthinking obedience and self-discipline.

Another important lesson was training in self-sufficiency. A soldier's survival often depended on his ability to forage for food. Boys were even encouraged to steal, providing they did so without being caught. The Spartan courage and endurance are illustrated in the famous legend of the boy caught stealing a live fox. To conceal his theft, the boy hid the fox under his tunic. As the animal gnawed away at the boy's internal organs, he stood firm.

The years between the ages of twenty and thirty were spent in military barracks. There, life was raw and rough. Indeed, it was virtually opposite to the sophistication and grace of Athenian life. What little conversation there was was gruff and terse. The food was unappetizing and almost inedible.

Only at age thirty, when his military service was complete, did the Spartan male become a citizen. Then he was allowed to participate in the Assembly. His involvement, however, amounted to nothing more than listening to proposals and shouting out his vote en masse. The loudest shout won.

The legislation that was put before the Assembly was prepared by a council of elders and two kings. But the real power was held by a group of five men called *ephors*. Elected annually, they had command over all. The ephors controlled education and both public and private moral conduct. They enforced the laws through a secret police force. One of the laws they enforced was the offence of celibacy.

Every Spartan had an obligation to breed new generations of soldiers, and it was towards this end that Spartan females were groomed. They were taught to be proud of their bodies, and their young years were spent in rigorous training to develop them for healthy childbearing. After a certain age, those who remained spinsters were paired off with bachelors, a system considered just as acceptable as marrying for love.

Spartan women enjoyed far more freedom than any other Greek women. In fact, they had equal rights with Spartan men in everything except voting. Active military duty and the requirement that males under thirty live in military barracks gave their wives complete authority over the households. The state lightened their load by taking care of most of the child-rearing responsibilities.

The criticisms of Plutarch, the Athenian, were indicative of the way other Greeks saw Spartan women. He described them as being "bold, masculine, overbearing to their husbands . . . and speaking openly on even the most important subjects."

Spartan citizens, male and female, were freed of many responsibilities by enslaved workers like the native Laconians and Messenians. These *helots*, or serfs, who worked the land on a sharecropping basis, were kept in check by the secret police. For good measure, the ephors declared war on them every year. In spite of these precautions, the Spartans frequently had to suppress helot revolts.

Another subjugated class, the *Perioeci*, acted as shopkeepers and trades-men. Sparta's economy was frugal and self-sufficient and transactions were completed with cumbersome iron bars as currency. These factors made it extremely difficult for the Perioeci to gain any power.

The Spartans were rigid, narrow-minded people. They were suspicious of anything foreign, including trade, and they resisted change of any kind. Periodi-cally they even deported foreigners lest they spread new ideas. This attitude, which was partially responsible for Sparta's downfall, was reinforced through their educational system. Mindless obedience destroys imagination and with it the ability to adapt to change.

The Spartan victory over the Athenians proved their military supremacy. However, leadership over all the Greek city-states was a different story. Corruption among the Spartan leaders grew rampant as gold was introduced into the country. One general, Pausanias, even offered to betray Sparta itself for the right price.

Spartan Warrior.

Perhaps the Spartans had been right to resist change, for it was a change that eventually undermined their strength. New land inheritance laws meant that traditionally small lots became absorbed into large estates. As a result, many Spartans, who were left landless and without citizenship, emigrated. The Spartan army gradually grew smaller and Sparta's power dwindled. By the fourth century B.C., Sparta was no longer a major power in Greece.

Questions

1. How did Sparta change after the Messenian rebellion in 620 B.C.?
2. a) How large was the Spartan army at its peak?
   b) Describe the reputation this army earned.
3. a) Briefly describe the training given all Spartan men from birth to the age of thirty.
   b) In what way did the ceremony for the goddess Artemis and the story of the boy stealing a fox reveal the self-discipline expected from all Spartans?
4. Explain the origin of the word ''laconic.''
5. a) What were the requirements needed to become a member of the Spartan Assembly?
   b) Who prepared legislation for the Assembly?
   c) How was the decision made to accept or reject the legislation?
6. a) Why has it been said that the ephors were the real power in Sparta?
   b) Explain how the ephors' control over private life extended to marriage and childbirth.
7. What kind of lives were led by the women of Sparta?
8. a) Who were the Perioeci?
   b) Why were the Spartans suspicious of foreigners?
   c) Why were Spartans considered narrow-minded?
9. What was the major cause of Sparta's downfall?

The Greek Phalanx. This method of warfare was developed by the Spartans and improved upon by Philip and Alexander.

ALTERNATIVE TWO

**Pericles' Funeral Oration—Based on *History of the Peloponnesian War*
by Thucydides, c. 410 B.C.**

Our constitution is called a democracy because power is in the hands not of a
minority but of the whole people. When it is a question of settling private
disputes, everyone is equal before the law; when it is a question of putting one
person before another in positions of public responsibility, what counts is not
membership of a particular class, but the acutal ability which the man
possesses. No one, so long as he has it in him to be of service to the state, is
kept in political obscurity because of poverty. And, just as our political life is
free and open, so is our day-to-day life. . . . We are free and tolerant in our
private lives; but in public affairs we keep to the law. This is because it
commands our deep respect.

   We give our obedience to those whom we put in positions of authority,
and we obey the laws themselves, especially those which are for the protection of the oppressed, and those unwritten laws which it is acknowledged to
break.

   And here is another point. When our work is over, we are in a position to
enjoy all kinds of recreation for our spirits. There are various kinds of contests
and sacrifices regularly throughout the year; in our own homes we find a
beauty and a good taste which delight us every day and which drive away our
cares. Then the greatness of our city brings it about that all the good things
from all over the world flow in to us, so that to us it seems just as natural to
enjoy foreign goods as our own local products. . . . . Our city is open to the
world, and we have no periodical deportations in order to prevent people
observing or finding out secrets which might be of military advantage to the
enemy. This is because we rely, not on secret weapons, but on our own real
courage and loyalty. There are certain advantages, I think, in our way of
meeting danger voluntarily, with natural rather than with state-induced
courage.

   Our love of what is beautiful does not lead to extravagance; our love of
the things of the mind does not make us soft. We regard wealth as something
to be properly used, rather than as something to boast about. As for poverty,
no one need be ashamed to admit it: the real shame is in not taking practical
measures to escape from it. In our city each individual is interested not only in
his own affairs but in the affairs of the state as well. . . . We do not say that a
man who takes no interest in politics is a man who minds his own business; we
say that he has no business here at all. . . . And this is another point where we
differ from other people. We are capable at the same time of taking risks and
of estimating them beforehand. Others are brave out of ignorance; and, when
they stop to think, they begin to fear. But the man who can most truly be
accounted brave is he who best knows the meaning of what is sweet in life and

of what is terrible, and then goes out undeterred to meet what is to come
. . . . Taking everything together then, I declare that our city is an education to
Greece, and I declare that in my opinion each single one of our citizens is able
to show himself the rightful lord and owner of his own person. . . . And to
show that this is no empty boasting, . . . you have only to consider the power
which our city possesses and which has been won by those very qualities
which I have mentioned. . . . Mighty indeed are the marks and monuments of
our empire which we have left. Future ages will wonder at us, as the present
age wonders at us now.

From Thucydides, *History of the Peloponnesian War.* Translation copyright © Rex Warner,
1954, by permission from Penguin Books Ltd.

Questions

1. Thucydides recorded Pericles' tribute to those Athenians who died in the
   first year of the Peloponnesian War with Sparta, that began in 431 B.C.
   How would you expect Pericles to describe Athenian society in that situation? Explain your answer.
2. a) Where did the power lie in Athenian democracy, according to Pericles?
   b) How did this compare with Spartan society?
   c) Could a person be held back in Athenian society if he was poor or a
      member of a lower class? Explain your answer.
3. a) When work was completed, what kind of life could Athenians enjoy?
   b) How did this compare with life in Sparta?
4. a) When Pericles spoke of "state-induced courage," to what society was
      he referring?
   b) Why did Pericles feel the Athenian system was superior?
5. a) How important was politics in Athenian society?
   b) How important is politics to Canadians today? Explain why you feel our
      present attitudes towards politics are different or similar to the attitudes
      expressed by the ancient Athenians.
6. What did Pericles mean when he said "Future ages will wonder at us, as the
   present age wonders at us now"?

ALTERNATIVE THREE

Athenian Democracy–Based on *What Democracy Meant to the Greeks* by W.R. Agard, 1965

Just how democratic was Athenian democracy? In *What Democracy Meant
to the Greeks*, W.R. Agard examines the composition of Athenian society, its
political system, and some of the advantages and disadvantages associated
with it.

   In 430 B.C., according to Agard, only about 10 percent of the total
Athenian population had political rights. These forty thousand voters were all
male, over eighteen years of age, and born of Athenian citizen-class parents.

*Klepsydra (water-clock). The jars, of
which those shown here are replicas,
contained two choes, "XX," about
27 l of water. Speakers in a lawsuit
were allowed so many water-clocks
of time–about six minutes each–with
jars of this type.*

The remaining 90 percent of the population comprised about twenty-four thousand aliens or *metics*, who had settled in Athens for business purposes, one hundred thousand enslaved war captives, and the women and children. The restriction was based on the belief that only those who were experienced and had a permanent stake in the city's welfare should be allowed to determine policy.

Although limited to citizens, the electorate was not limited by class. According to Agard, country gentlemen and businessmen participated in government alongside the farmers, day workers, and artisans who made up the majority of the membership. Indeed, all citizens formulated every policy.

Participants in the Council of Five Hundred and the Jury of Six Thousand were selected annually, by lot, from a list of citizens over thirty years of age. Even the chairman of the council was chosen by lot, but on a daily basis. Only the members of the Board of Ten Generals were elected, since these positions required a knowledge of military and naval strategy not familiar to all citizens. Agard suggests that every citizen would have engaged in public service at some point in his life span.

To perform their public-service duties, citizens had to take time from their normal work schedule. This decreased their earning power. Since the majority of the members were already from the lower economic class, this worsened their situation. In compensation, council members and jurors were paid for their services. In the fourth century B.C., this was extended to include payment for attendance at the Assembly.

There were some disadvantages to the system. According to Agard there was often inconsistency between the adoption and execution of a policy. A persuasive speaker might well sway the Assembly to adopt his policy but he had no further responsibility once it was approved. The execution was left to other men who were not always in favour of the action.

Another disadvantage was a built-in safeguard known as *ostracism*. If one person became too powerful as a speaker in the Assembly, he could be expelled from the country simply by a majority vote of the Assembly. This privilege was seldom exercised wisely. Agard tells the story of one farmer who voted for the expulsion of Aristides the Just simply because he was tired of hearing him referred to as "the Just."

In spite of the disadvantages, the Athenian democracy controlled the city-state during the century of its greatest achievement. This included cultural, economic, and political development of the approximately two hundred fifty states within the Athenian Empire.

A democracy in which there are slaves who have no voice hardly seems like a democracy at all. Yet, as Agard points out, for the majority it was not slavery as we usually think of it. He estimates that while one-fifth of the slave population was confined to the mines where life was hard and short, the remaining slaves had many economic advantages. They were also protected from bodily harm by legislation.

Moments in Time

While the Athenians paid homage to their goddess, Athena, they repressed their wives and daughters. One of the few women of Athens to participate in Greek culture was Aspasia (470–410 B.C.). A companion to Pericles, Aspasia was a scholar who took part in the intellectual dialogues of the day. She discussed the role of women in society and openly asserted woman's right to live as man's equal. Eventually, she was charged and tried for her outspoken behaviour. This treatment was in keeping with Thucydides' famous remark: "That woman is best who is least spoken of among men, whether for good or evil."

Domestic slaves were often regarded with respect and affection. Others, who worked as artisans or for the state, were actually paid for their labours. If they saved enough money they could eventually buy their freedom. Slaves often worked alongside citizens and metics in both unskilled and highly skilled jobs.

From an economic perspective Agard feels there were probably many Greek slaves who were secure and happy. As support, he notes that there were no serious slave revolts in Athens until 103 B.C.

Athenian democracy also excluded women, even those who were the wives of citizens. Although they had the responsibilities of managing the households and educating the children, Athenian women had very little freedom. From birth to death their lives were controlled by men. Their fathers arranged their marriages, and if these ended in divorce, male guardians took control of their purse strings. The husbands were always given custody of the children in such situations.

Xenophon, the Greek historian, described a good wife as having habits of temperance, modesty, and teachableness. Athenian women did not participate in public affairs, and they socialized mainly with other women. Oddly enough, metic women enjoyed more social freedom than Athenian women.

These gold dove pendant earrings were worn by women during the Hellenistic period.

Questions

1. a) What were the qualifications needed to participate in Athenian democracy?
   b) How many citizens were there in Athens?
   c) What proportion of the total population did they represent?
   d) Is this the impression Pericles left in his "Funeral Oration"? Give evidence to support your answer.
   e) What proportion of the total population can vote in Canada?
   f) Is Canadian democracy more democratic than the system used in ancient Athens? Explain your answer.
2. a) How were members chosen for the Council of Five Hundred, the chairmanship of the council, and the jury?
   b) To what extent was this procedure democratic?
   c) What advantages did this system offer?
   d) What problems did the system create?
   e) How does this system compare with the procedures used in Sparta?
3. a) What is meant by the term "ostracism"?
   b) How could the use of ostracism be abused?
4. a) Describe the rights and living conditions of slaves in Athens?
   b) The existence of slavery seems impossible in a democracy. How, then, can the existence of slaves be explained in terms of Athenian life?
5. a) Describe the living conditions of women in Athens.
   b) Suggest why women in Athens were treated so differently from women in Sparta.

ANSWERING THE PROBLEM QUESTION

Comparing systems of government and their impact on people is a different type of problem from those previously studied. Physical evidence in the form of fossils, artifacts, monuments, and geology has until now played a major, if not the only, role in helping us select and develop the most persuasive argument. In examining the relationship between government and people, however, the issue is primarily abstract. It involves competing ideas and ideals. In comparing Athenian and Spartan ideals, several key areas must be explored before judging those city-states in their historical context.

In both Sparta and Athens citizenship was not automatic and did not include the entire population, but the qualifications for each were different. Although an assembly existed in each state, the intended purpose and actual operation of each were, again, much different. Why did such a contrast exist? What was each state trying to achieve with its particular system? People of all classes were treated one way in Sparta and another way in Athens. Why was there such a contrast in the way Spartans and Athenians treated women, slaves, and those involved in trade? Was the demise of Athens and Sparta a direct result of the goals they set for themselves and the systems they developed to reach their ideals? Or was it perhaps related to external forces over which they had little control? How, then, can these criteria be ranked and applied to the question about the extent to which the oligarchy of Sparta and the democracy of Athens best served the people in their city-states and throughout all of Greece?

THE STORY CONTINUES . . .

The Decline of the Greek City-States

The military victory finalized in 404 B.C., after the long, drawn-out Peloponnesian War, appeared to open the way for Sparta to assume Athens' former position of leadership in the Aegean and Asia Minor. Attempts by Sparta to dominate, however, resulted in thirty years of intermittent land and naval skirmishes with several city-state rivals. The Second Athenian League, which, in contrast with the Delian League, was closer to a true democracy, crippled the Spartan fleet at Naxos in 376 B.C. Five years later, Thebes ended the legend of Sparta's invincibility on land by inflicting a crushing defeat at Leuctra. The following year, the Messenians revolted against Sparta as they had in 620 B.C., but this time they were successful.

A lack of soldiers certainly contributed to deterioration as the scale of Sparta's ambition grew. The problem was increased when city-state policies began to concentrate wealth into the hands of Spartan citizens at the expense of other city dwellers. This weakened the high morale of city life which had been one of Sparta's greatest assets. New inheritance laws resulted in the gradual absorption of small lots into large estates. Many Spartans, left landless, lost their citizenship and emigrated, leaving fewer dedicated soldiers for the Spartan army.

CONFLICT WITHIN GREECE

Allied briefly with Athens in 362 B.C., Sparta was again defeated by Thebes, but no city-state could gain control or even continuous leadership of the Greek world. By 340 B.C., Sparta's once-proud army numbered only about one thousand men.

The inability of individual Greek city-states to understand the advantages of political units larger than their own kept Greece divided and led to its demise. Brief loyalties for immediate gain led to alliances in one battle which would be quickly abandoned in the next. This failure to overcome mutual suspicion made Greek city-states vulnerable to external forces that could impose unity through military force.

THE FAILURE OF SPARTAN LEADERSHIP

The Macedonian Era

Although Macedonia had already been exposed to the impressive accomplishments of Greek culture when Philip II came to the throne in 359 B.C., it was still an agricultural society dominated by an aristocracy of horse breeders who were seen as barbarians by the Greek city-states. In Philip, however, Macedonia had a shrewd soldier and calculating diplomat able to bring order to the entire Greek world. To accomplish this goal, Philip waited patiently for the right moment and then acted decisively with the most efficient military organization the world had yet seen.

PHILIP II

In previous centuries, the bravery of the individual hoplite soldier had been overcome by the Spartan phalanx of soldiers armed with spears in close, disciplined formation. At Leuctra in 371 B.C., however, the Theban column, of uneven depth and distribution and organized to strike on command, thoroughly defeated the Spartans and their military system. In turn, the value of the Theban column was surpassed when Philip integrated a Macedonian phalanx and a heavy cavalry into a single fighting machine.

IMPROVEMENT OF THE PHALANX

A cautious planner, Philip took pains to secure his northern and eastern borders from attacks by hill tribesmen. While the Greek city-states squabbled among themselves, Philip slowly advanced into Thrace, where, by 356 B.C., he had taken control of the rich gold mines of the Pangaea Mountains. During the Third Sacred War among the Greek city-states, Philip also secured Thessaly, with its important reserves of grain and horses. A brief attempt to penetrate central Greece was unsuccessful.

The Athenians, inspired by their masterful orator, Demosthenes, realized that the growth of Macedonian power under Philip's leadership was a threat to their existence. Few of the other city-states were willing to commit themselves to Demosthenes' warning, and fighting continued in minor skirmishes until a tenuous peace between Athens and Macedonia was arranged in 346 B.C.

DEMOSTHENES

Philip's promises of peace, however, were soon forgotten. He repeatedly pressed his advantage over small, isolated communities and, though unsuccessful in permanently cutting off Athens from its supply of wheat in the Black Sea or in holding Thermopylae, Philip gained access to northern Greece through a stroke of diplomacy. The Phocians, earlier defeated and harshly treated by Philip,

CHAERONEA

THE LEAGUE OF CORINTH

gave up their capital city, Elatae, to Macedonia in return for reduced tribute. This stunned the Athenians as Elatae gave Philip a strategic route to enter Greece. The danger enabled Demosthenes to seal a shaky alliance with Athens' former enemy, Thebes.

On the battlefield of Chaeronea in 338 B.C., the efficiency of Philip's Macedonian army annihilated the combined forces of Athens and Thebes. Philip, now master of all Greece, summoned the defeated city-states and their neighbours to Corinth. Here, a league of Hellenistic states, with the exception of Sparta, was formed and bound by decisions of an assembly which met at Corinth. The league was then allied with Macedonia who could command Greek forces upon request in time of war.

Philip was now ready for the greatest military adventure of his career–the conquest of Persia. In spite of personal suffering, such as having his right eye gouged out by an arrow, Philip remained ambitious, though careful, in implementing his vision for Macedonia. Such dreams, however, were rudely cut short when he was assassinated at his daughter's wedding feast in 336 B.C. It would be left to his son, Alexander, to bring the dream to reality.

COMMENT

The city-state bickering that dominated the first half of the fourth century B.C. should not cloud the remarkable and varied achievements of Hellenic civilization. Despite the contrast in their political organizations, both Sparta and Athens made major contributions that would endure beyond their time. Yet each state also displayed the suspicion and narrow-minded aggressiveness that led to a general decline in power and growth.

To today's democratic eye, Sparta often appears as a merciless, armed, and rigid city-state. Greeks of the fifth century, however, regarded Spartan self-sacrifice for the good of the state as admirable because it was a choice made willingly by a free people. The bravery shown by King Leonidas and his personal bodyguard when they fought to certain death at Thermopylae in the face of overwhelming Persian strength, became a standard praised by all of Greece. Spartan leadership and prestige were reaffirmed when the Persians, again with superior numbers, were defeated at Plataea. Rather than view the lack of monumental buildings as a cultural limitation, Sparta should be seen as a society that emphasized strength of character through a life of simplicity, loyalty, and service. To their lasting credit, the victorious Spartans did not destroy the Athenian Acropolis at the end of the Peloponnesian War, because they appreciated the exceptional artistic and architectural achievement of their long-time enemy.

Athenians were equally proud of their own military tradition. The ''miracle of Marathon'' not only prevented Persian domination of the Western world, but inspired all Greeks to protect their homeland. Later victories against Persia increased Athens' status and seemed to justify Athenian domination of the

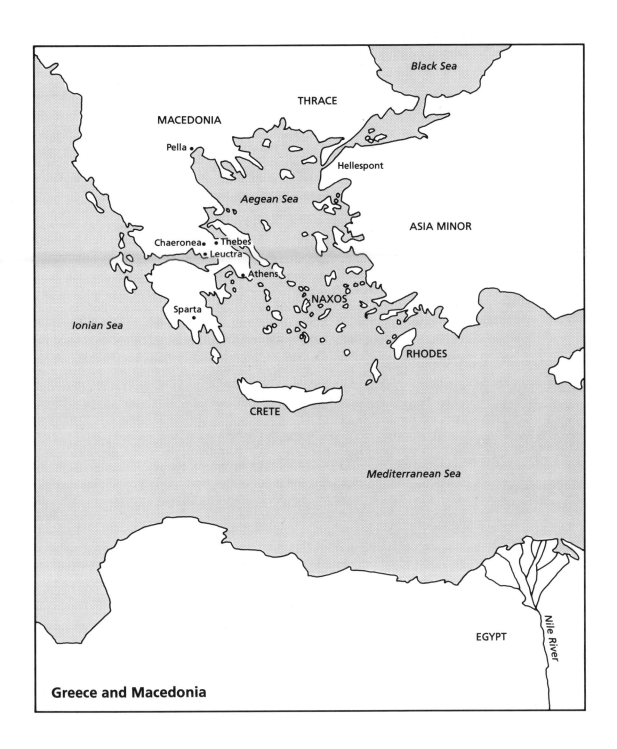

Black Sea

THRACE

MACEDONIA

Pella

Hellespont

Aegean Sea

ASIA MINOR

Chaeronea
Thebes
Leuctra

Athens

NAXOS

Ionian Sea

Sparta

RHODES

CRETE

Mediterranean Sea

EGYPT

Nile River

Greece and Macedonia

Delian League. By extending control over city-states along the Aegean coasts in imperialistic fashion, Athens was able to use the league's wealth to maintain a large navy and to support an ambitious program of public building. Ironically, the treasury was moved from Delos to the second of two large rooms within the recently completed Parthenon, the construction of which had been financed largely from league funds! When war broke out in 431 B.C., Pericles' rousing tribute to the noble cause of Athens illustrated the pride with which Athenian leaders sent their young men to fight. Living in the shadow of the Acropolis, Athenians had visible proof of the greatness they eagerly sought to defend.

As children, most Greeks had learned of the exciting adventures of the Trojan War as described in Homer's *Iliad* and *Odyssey*. Yet it was a real war, the Peloponnesian War, justified as it was with such high-minded purpose at the outset, that ultimately bled the soul of the Greek city-states. As people flooded into Athens for protection, conditions became unsanitary, which resulted in an outbreak of typhus. The death of Pericles in the plague that followed opened the way to power for the war-hungry and talented Alcibiades, who was given to extremes. As the war laboured on, Athens became less and less tolerant of city-state freedom. When the residents of the tiny island of Melos refused to pay tribute in 416 B.C., Athens, at Alcibiades' urging, massacred every man and enslaved the women and children. Spartan pride would later lower itself in a desperate and successful bid for victory when assistance was sought from the once-dreaded Persians. The glory of Marathon was now only a faint echo in the Greek past.

The social practices of Sparta and Athens must be examined carefully. The Spartan policy of leaving infants with identifiable defects to die on Mount Taygetus was regarded as humane and necessary. From the stronger youths, state-controlled education could produce the brave, dedicated soldiers needed to protect Sparta from rebellious city-states or foreign enemies. In Athens, population pressure produced similar results for different reasons. Just behind the spectacular public buildings of the Acropolis and agora, twisting crowded alleyways enclosed some of the worst slums and unsanitary conditions of the age. Unwanted or deformed children were often placed in earthenware jars or left at isolated street corners to be picked up by slave traders, eaten by dogs, or simply to die. Such actions are difficult for us to understand, but they were at least tolerated, if not approved, in many Greek city-states.

Athens' approach to education evolved as the city grew. At first suspicious of practical training, Athens attempted to develop a cultured citizen who would realize his physical, mental, and moral potential. Although every male citizen learned to read and write, it was usually the upper-class Athenian who received a complete education in the art of politics, public speaking, and the music of ballads sung to tunes played on the strings of a lyre. Indeed, lyric poetry recited to music filled almost every corner of Athens. Between 450 and

"*You may be right,
Pythagoras, but everybody's
going to laugh
if you call it a 'hypotenuse.'*"
BOB THAVES © 1984 NEWSPAPER ENTERPRISE ASSN.

400 B.C., wandering scholars known as **Sophists** began to stress the need for practical training in politics, a need that was created by a steadily expanding empire. By teaching any young man who could afford to pay how to win any side of an argument, education became available even to the lower classes.

The importance of free thought became the foundation of Athens and much of the Greek world. As the male citizens of the Athenian Assembly gathered on Pynx Hill facing the Acropolis to practise democratic self-government, a rope dipped in red paint coralled the stragglers for the meeting. Those left with the tell-tale smudge were fined for their apparent lack of enthusiasm! Playwrights such as Aristophanes wrote biting satires and comedies that ridiculed public figures in a manner that would probably lead to a libel suit if repeated today. Socrates, a greatly respected teacher and philosopher, used free speech to search for the "truth." In contrast to the Sophists, Socrates felt that "truth" did exist, and by asking a series of precise questions, he intended to help each man identify errors in logic until his own "truth" was discovered.

Individual freedom in thought even tempered Greek attitudes towards religion. Although festivals were created and cities dedicated to Zeus and his family of gods on Mount Olympus, even the earliest philosophers rejected the gods as described in Homeric myths. The gods were regarded as larger-than-life human forms showing not only great strength and bravery, but also the common human failings of dishonesty and jealousy. Rather than fear the gods' wrath, Athenians thought they could be appeased through proper ceremonies such as sacrifice and the celebration of special rites and occasions. The Olympic Games, first held in 776 B.C., combined widely accepted religious beliefs with the Greek love of physical fitness and fair play.

The oracle of priests established at Delphi, on the awe-inspiring site of Mount Parnasus, illustrates many of the major Greek attitudes towards religion. Believed by the Greeks to be the centre of the world, Delphi was showered with gifts by city-states before every major battle and became the final word in all religious matters. Within the sacred temple of Apollo, a Pythian priestess would drink from a special spring, chew a laurel leaf, become possessed by a god, and utter cries that priests would interpret as the oracle. Usually, such predictions were vague and could be viewed in many ways. In fact, predictions rarely changed or discouraged plans that had already been made. It was, however, the participation in festivals like the Olympics and rites such as the oracle at Delphi that helped to generate a common set of values throughout the Greek world.

The turning point in Greek history was the Peloponnesian War. As corruption spread throughout Athens under the pressure of constant war, freethinkers became suspect. Following the peace and continued public outcry, Socrates—the most praised freethinker, who felt that individuals should act according to their consciences—was arrested in 399 B.C. because, it was claimed, his ideas misled Athenian youth. Although an admission of error would have saved

Geometric krater, 450–350 B.C., is typical of the pottery for which Greece is famous.

On Mount Parnasus, this ruin, built
by Theodorus of Phocaea, was
known as a tholos or round building.
It was near the site where the oracle
at Delphi made predictions about
the Greek city-states.

his life, Socrates chose to uphold the ideas for which he lived. In one of the most famous death scenes in history, Socrates drank a cup of poisonous hemlock, as instructed by the court, then talked to his friends until he died. Plato, a student and friend of Socrates, rejected the once-revered democracy and the chaos of its political life. In his greatest work, *The Republic*, Plato argued that an elite of "philosopher kings" prepared by training from youth was the best blueprint for society. Greece was now doomed to permanent division when the only force of cultural unity, the oracle at Delphi, was discredited by making too many one-sided predictions in favour of Sparta.

Like the ancient Greeks, the Western world has more to praise than to criticize in the Spartan oligarchy and Athenian democracy. The Golden Age perfected the architecture often seen today in many public buildings and monuments. The roles of the individual, society, and the state were first discussed, if not resolved, among Greek philosophers. Greek plays, poems, sculptures, and pottery remain admired today for the original achievements they represent.

Ancient Greeks saw themselves as freemen with free choices, and hence developed a fierce loyalty to the system of government, whether oligarchy or democracy, they wished to follow. It is ironic that these many accomplishments depended on the social division and economic importance of slavery, an evil in any age. Despite the imperfections of the Greek world, it is the concept of individual freedom, amongst all Greek legacies, that has influenced the widest number of people, male and female, of mixed cultural and economic heritage.

Date B.C.	Event
1200–1100	Canaanite traders (Phoenicians) settle on coast of modern Lebanon and establish independent cities Sea peoples destroy and sack all Mycenaean palace states
1000	First city built by Latins on site of Rome
c.814	Tyre founds the city of Carthage in North Africa
800	Greek city-states emerge
753	Legendary founding of Rome by Romulus
616	Etruscan rule of Rome and central Italy
c.550	Carthaginians battle Greeks in Sicily Magonid Dynasty is established and lasts 150 years
509	Romans overthrow Etruscans and Rome becomes a Republic
494–480	Phoenicians supply Persians with ships in war against Greek city-states
431	Peloponnesian War begins
338	Philip II of Macedonia defeats Athens and Thebes at Chaeronea
336–323	**Leadership of Alexander the Great**
264–241	First Punic War–Rome versus Carthage
218–202	Second Punic War–leadership of Hannibal
150–146	Third Punic War–Carthage is destroyed by Rome
73–71	Spartacus revolts
61–44	**Leadership of Julius Caesar**
41	Antony and Cleopatra at Tarsus
31	Octavian defeats the combined forces of Antony and Cleopatra at Actium
27	Octavian becomes Caesar Augustus, the first Roman emperor

6

Alexander, Hannibal, and Julius Caesar

BACKGROUND

Alexander

Do great leaders control the course of historical events? If ever that question could be answered with a "yes" it was during the life of Philip of Macedonia's son Alexander who, as a young man of twenty, became king when his father was assassinated in 336 B.C. Where Philip had been a cautious military planner and shrewd bargainer, Alexander was an impulsive and decisive man of immediate action. Relying on the extraordinary force of his own personality, indeed an almost-instinctive ability to make the right move at the right time, Alexander usually overcame the extreme risks he eagerly undertook. Alexander fashioned himself as a second Achilles, a hero described in his favourite book, the *Iliad*. Heroic strength, courage, and strong will made it easy for Alexander to believe he possessed special gifts, and that he was destined to achieve the glory that was denied ordinary mortals. At the same time, he could celebrate with unrestrained spirit, lapse into fits of rage, or be extremely generous to his enemies.

Alexander was also inspired by a grand vision of the future. He had been instilled with a continuing interest in art, poetry, and science by his childhood tutor, Aristotle, one of the most respected Greek thinkers. Yet, where Aristotle felt that the tiny city-state was the ultimate political unit, Alexander saw the creation of an imperial partnership of Macedonian pride, Greek culture, and Persian wealth as his personal ambition.

After a brief but spectacular career in which he never lost a battle, tales of Alexander's exploits became legendary as they spread throughout the civilized world. From Britain to Malaya, over eighty versions in twenty-four languages told and retold his story of conquest. Although Greece never regained its former political power, the influence of Greek culture after Alexander was wider than it had ever been before.

PERSONAL CHARACTERISTICS

AMBITION

REPUTATION

In coin and in art, Alexander was usually pictured as a beautiful youth with long, flowing locks. His clean-shaven face set a fashion in Greece and Italy that lasted centuries.

Rise of the Phoenicians

Over a thousand years before Alexander, the Minoan civilization centred on Crete had ruled the Aegean and eastern Mediterranean as the world's first true maritime power. The rapid decline of Minoan influence following the eruption on Thera in the fifteenth century B.C., left a vacuum of power. Weakened city-states, the Egyptians, the Hittites, and the marauding "peoples of the sea" struggled for control of trade routes and colonies. No single power was able to gain the upper hand.

In this world of turmoil and change, Canaanite traders, located in centres along the coast of modern Lebanon, extended their influence. Known as the Phoenicians, these people became the greatest seafarers and traders in the Mediterranean. The "Phoenician" label given to them by the Greeks was a word that was probably unknown to these people. They saw themselves as citizens of their individual cities–Sidon, Tyre, or Byblos–and they were very jealous of each other. Although they spoke the same language and worshipped the same gods, they never formed a country known as Phoenicia. As the volume and profit of their trading ventures increased, however, Phoenician cities were established in the western Mediterranean, including the city of Carthage founded by Tyre in the eighth century B.C.

With the spread of Greek colonization and the Golden Age during the next three hundred years, several clashes between the two sea powers occurred. Carthage launched a successful campaign against the Greeks in Sicily and created the Magonid Dynasty. It was also the Phoenicians who supplied the Persian kings, Darius and Xerxes, with ships in their costly effort to conquer Greece.

Carthage became the dominant trading city and best-fortified port in the western Mediterranean. Situated on an arrowhead peninsula on the north shore of Africa, Carthage was protected by triple walls 15 m high and 10 m wide with four-storey towers every 60 m. The sheltered harbour had anchorage for about two hundred ships. Increased military strength on land and sea was supported by growing wealth through trade in grain, metals, resin, wax, honey, slaves, and wine from far-flung contacts throughout the Mediterranean.

HUMAN SACRIFICE

Resentment of the Carthaginian domination of trade was matched only by revulsion for the Phoenician practice of human sacrifice to please their gods. One burial ground in Carthage had thousands of clay pots with the remains of babies and young children while others contained the remains of young animals. Carthage continued this religious rite for over four hundred years after it was abandoned in the eastern Phoenician cities.

THE FIRST PUNIC WAR

As a strong commercial power with an imposing fleet, Carthage became involved in a local dispute with the city of Syracuse, on the island of Sicily. Syracuse appealed to Rome, a new power that had just completed the conquest of the Italian peninsula, for assistance. When Rome answered the call in 264 B.C., the First Punic War broke out and continued with heavy losses on both sides until Rome emerged victorious in 241 B.C.

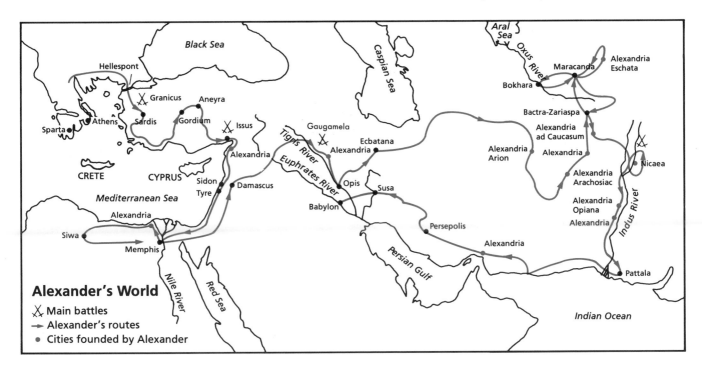

Alexander's World
X̱ Main battles
→ Alexander's routes
• Cities founded by Alexander

Hannibal

During the next two decades, Carthage turned its attention to the western Mediterranean and gained territory in Spain. Fearing additional expansion, Rome reached an agreement with Carthage to divide Spain at the Ebro River. Yet, in 219 B.C., a young general named Hannibal attacked the hill fort of Saguntum, which had been placed under the protection of Rome. Hannibal knew this would lead to war and he was ready for the challenge.

Military leadership in Carthage was not easy. The city government retained tight control over generals in the field. One unsuccessful general was crucified on the battlefield, while another suffered the same fate at home after a defeat at sea. Hannibal, who had taken an oath as a boy of nine to dedicate his life to the destruction of Rome, had absolute confidence in his ability to command and in the quality of his troops. Although the Carthaginian army was made up largely of mercenaries, including Spanish infantry, Numidian cavalry, and Celtic warriors, each group was fiercely loyal to Hannibal. He ate the same food, wore the same clothes, slept on the same ground, and suffered the same hardships as his men. Hannibal's personal bravery as the first man in and the last man out of any battle was equalled only by the brilliance of his successful military strategy that made him the greatest general of his time. If he could battle the Romans in Italy, away from the interference of the Carthaginian government, he felt sure he could win.

SAGUNTUM

COMMAND IN CARTHAGE

HANNIBAL AS LEADER

Carthage

B.C.

c.1500	Volcanic eruption on Thera ends Minoan civilization
1450–1200	War dominates the Aegean and eastern Mediterranean Mycenaens, Egyptians, the Hittites, and the peoples of the sea struggle for control of trade and land
1200–1100	Canaanite traders (Phoenicians) settle on coast of modern Lebanon and establish independent cities such as Sidon and Tyre
c.814	Tyre founds the city of Carthage in North Africa
c.550	Carthaginians battle Greeks in Sicily Magonid Dynasty is established and lasts 150 years
494–480	Phoenicians supply Persians with ships in war against Greek city-states
333	Byblos and Sidon fall to Alexander the Great
332	Tyre falls to Alexander the Great
264–241	First Punic War between Carthage and Rome for control of the Mediterranean Rome wins after a long difficult struggle
237	Hamlicar Barca of Carthage develops a base in Spain
239	Hasdrubal of Carthage founds New Carthage in Spain

The Birth and Development of the Roman Republic

ROMULUS AND REMUS

Shortly after the emergence of the Phoenician cities as a distinct cultural, if not a political group, the first settlement on the site of Rome was established. According to legend, as babies, the twin brothers Romulus and Remus were set adrift on the Tiber River, but were grounded and managed to survive. They were suckled by a she-wolf, then raised by a shepherd's wife. Romulus established the city of Rome, in 753 B.C., on the site where they had been nurtured. Later, the two quarrelled and Romulus killed Remus. The image of the she-wolf caring for the two boys was immortalized in sculpture in the ancient world and remains a highly visible symbol in public buildings and on tourist souvenirs in Rome today. In fact, however, Rome had already been occupied for several centuries and it seems likely that the Latins had first built on the location by about 1000 B.C.

FOUNDING OF ROME

THE ETRUSCANS

As a small town, Rome was only one of several population centres in the Italian peninsula, many of which were either developed or taken over by the Etruscans. A rather mysterious people from the north whose writing has not

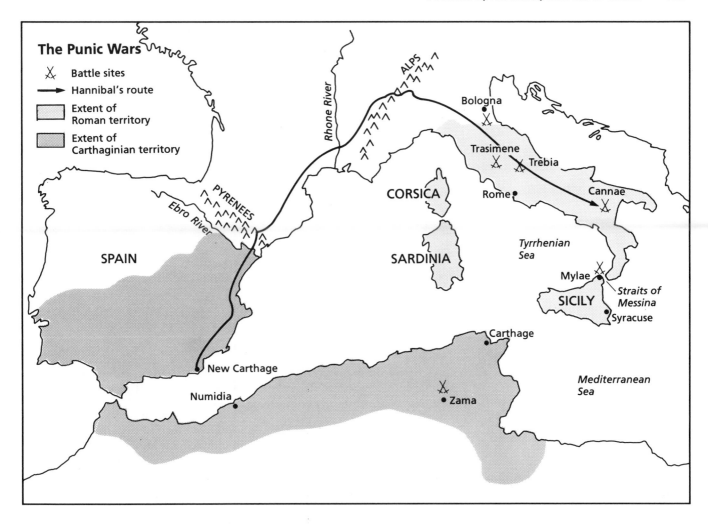

The Punic Wars

- ✗ Battle sites
- → Hannibal's route
- Extent of Roman territory
- Extent of Carthaginian territory

yet been deciphered, the Etruscans placed their first king on the Roman throne in 616 B.C. and eventually controlled a domain that focussed on the area between the Arno and Tiber rivers. The invaders brought with them improved methods of farming, manufacturing, trading, and building skills that enabled Rome to flourish as a city-state. In 509 B.C., the Romans rebelled and established a Republic that would last until 27 B.C., but many later Roman achievements owe a debt to the impetus given by Etruscan influence.

Initially, Rome simply hoped to survive, isolated as it was in a sea of city-states. The collapse of Etruscan power throughout the Italian peninsula, however, resulted in several subject peoples warring against each other and opened the region to invasion. In 390 B.C., warlike tribes from Gaul conquered and sacked Rome, but the city was quickly rebuilt and a new outlook prevailed.

THE ROMAN REPUBLIC

Rise of the Roman Republic

B.C.

1000	First city built by Latins on site of Rome
753	Legendary founding of Rome by Romulus
616	Etruscan rule of Rome and central Italy
509	Romans overthrow Etruscans and Rome becomes a Republic with a city-state government
390	Rome sacked and destroyed by Gauls but it is quickly rebuilt
326	Enslavement of citizens abolished
270	Roman conquest of Italy complete
264–146	Three Punic wars against Carthage A victorious Rome now dominates the Mediterranean
135–132	Slaves revolt in Sicily
85	Intermittent civil war begins
73–71	Spartacus revolts
50	Roman control around the Mediterranean complete Extent of Republic makes it difficult for city-state to administer to outlying provinces
44	Julius Caesar uses slaves and freed men in his administration Caesar attempts to secure a hereditary monarchy Caesar is assassinated
27	End of Roman Republic City of Rome has two hundred and fifty thousand slaves

DIVIDE AND RULE

Territorial expansion was considered the best defence against unfriendly neighbours. Rather than attempt to conquer large areas, they would take over the land between two potential enemies to avoid a conflict. At other times, Rome would temporarily ally with one enemy to defeat another. This policy of "divide and rule" greatly increased the area under Rome's control and far exceeded the city's original goals. Once a city was conquered, it was offered friendship, control over local matters, and an alliance with Rome in return for Roman citizenship. This flexible policy allowed Rome to maintain control after it was first established and resulted in the unification of the entire Italian peninsula under Roman rule by 270 B.C.

EXPANSION IN THE MEDITERRANEAN

The first of three Punic wars against Carthage marked the beginning of a period of expansion throughout the Mediterranean region. Again, Rome did not have a master plan, but was determined to defend the position already established. At the outset, Rome was at a disadvantage since it had no navy. Always willing to learn from others, the Romans used a captured Carthaginian ship as a model and quickly built a fleet of their own. They then developed a boarding plank so that enemy ships could be boarded easily when locked in combat at close range. This turned a naval encounter into an infantry battle and soon gave Rome control of the sea.

Carthage was the most serious military threat that Rome ever faced. When Rome was successful at the conclusion of the Third Punic War, the city of Carthage was so thoroughly dismantled that Carthaginian culture virtually ceased to exist. By the first century B.C., Rome had grown from a small city-state to become the major power in the Western world with control over the north coast of Africa, Sicily, Sardinia, Corsica, southern Gaul, Macedonia, and Asia Minor.

The Roman Legions

Rome's military success was due to the development of the most disciplined and efficient infantry in ancient history–the Roman **legion**. The basic unit was a century of eighty men, six of which were united to form a cohort; ten cohorts made up a full legion of forty-eight hundred men. In battle, the legion standard, a silver eagle which was considered sacred, was always kept near the commanding general. The lead century formed a tightly closed row behind protective shields as the men remained still until ordered to throw their spears the instant before the enemy was upon them. With the enemy at close quarters, the century line moved forward for hand-to-hand combat. After twelve minutes, the period of peak efficiency, the first century fell back to be replaced by a second and then a third.

In addition to the co-ordination of tens of thousands of men, the Romans developed huge war machines that included the catapult–that could hurl a 27-kg boulder 500 m–and the battering ram–that was so large one thousand men were required to mobilize it for action. The ceaseless bombardment was so intense that enemy commanders orderd their men to cover their ears against the noise from the whine and crash of the Roman projectiles.

At night, after a battle or a hard-day's march with a 25-kg pack on his back, every Roman soldier in the legion helped to build an overnight marching camp. Discipline was maintained by long hours of drill in summer and winter through which every battle tactic was practised with weapons of double weight. The drills were so intense that they have been described as ''bloodless battles,'' while their battles were regarded as ''bloody drills.''

Failure to perform the required duties was corrected by brutal measures such as stoning and if an entire unit was negligent or cowardly in battle it was greeted with decimation, which meant that every tenth man was executed. The soldier who first mounted the wall during the siege on a city, however,

LEGION ORGANIZATION

TACTICS

OVERNIGHT CAMPS

PUNISHMENT AND REWARD

Roman Siege Equipment. The Romans developed their weapons from Macedonian, Carthaginian, and Spanish originals.

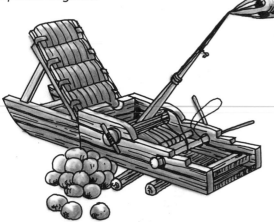

The Battering Ram. The ram, protected against enemy fireballs and molten lead by a roof of wet animal skins, was swung back and forth against the defending town's gate until the gate finally gave way.

Catapult. Built with a series of levers and ropes, this machine hurled rocks and other projectiles into the enemy town.

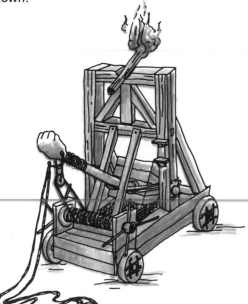

Ballista. A type of catapult, the ballista shown here shot balls of fire across the town walls.

Assault Tower. This several-storey structure was wheeled to the town walls. The drawbridge then swung down into the town, enabling soldiers to storm in.

received a crown of gold. Through this combination of harsh punishment and generous reward, Rome produced loyalty, self-sacrifice, dedication, and a high morale that resulted in a continuing story of military success.

Above the military efficiency generated by legion organization, construction works on aqueducts, bridges, and roads followed the path of victory. Here Roman engineering was superb. Using either concrete or stone, eleven major aqueducts fed the city of Rome from distances of 58 km and provided 1100 *l* of water daily for each person (almost twice as much as in New York City today). Eventually, over 310 000 km of Roman roads were built on foundations over 1.5 m deep. Some of these are still in use today. Caesar used this vast network to pursue Pompey's armies with lightning speed to Spain and back to Greece.

CONSTRUCTION PROJECTS

The Emergence of Slavery

The outstanding success of the Roman army, complemented by an improved navy, created many problems. Grain from conquered provinces poured into Rome as the Republic grew in strength, and sold at much cheaper prices than Italian grain. This forced many small farmers out of business and much of their land was purchased by a few wealthy men. These new holdings were organized into large farms called **latifundia** that required large amounts of skilled labour for cultivation and shepherding. The labour was provided by the conquered peoples. The success of Roman legions was so great that Rome became a slave-based state in a very short time. The number of slaves in Rome grew from forty thousand in 325 B.C. to two hundred fifty thousand by 27 B.C., out of a total population of 1.25 million. The wealthy Romans became so accustomed to the luxury and the status of owning a large number of slaves, that even military conquest could not satisfy the demand. Pirates turned slave trading into a very lucrative business. The small, independent farmer who had been the mainstay of the early Republic became part of an unemployed mob, depending on the government for food and entertainment as a necessary bribe to prevent the outbreak of revolution.

LATIFUNDIA

THE GROWTH OF SLAVERY

Even though the idea of slavery is morally offensive today, it was a natural part of the Roman world. Slaves were often employed in the households of wealthy Romans in capacities ranging from cooks to tailors to chambermaids. Greek slaves were often sought to educate the Roman children. Room and board and training in a profession were sometimes provided and, for years of good service, a slave might even be allowed to buy his or her freedom. Those who toiled in the mines and quarries or rowed the ships of the Roman fleet, however, clearly suffered the harshest and most hopeless existence. In general, the life of a slave depended on the time in which s/he lived and the occupation thrust upon her or him. When conditions became extreme, as they did in 135 B.C. on a latifundia run by wealthy Romans on Sicily, the slaves rebelled against their masters. Despite the limited chance of success and certain death by crucifixion if captured, slave revolts against cruel treatment continued until the end of the Republic.

WORKING CONDITIONS FOR SLAVES

Spartacus

Often those slaves who were in the best physical condition were trained as gladiators to fight to the death in public arenas for the entertainment of the Roman mob and upper classes. For most gladiators, life was measured in months rather than years. In 73 B.C., a slave from Thrace named Spartacus was taken from his toil in the quarries of Libya to be trained in the gladiatorial school at Capua. His resentment to fighting for the amusement of others sparked a revolt of seventy gladiators who broke from the compound with him and began a war that ravaged the Italian countryside for three years.

As described by the Greek historian Appian, Spartacus unintentionally also hurled himself into the complicated world of Roman politics. According to Appian, the escaping gladiators armed themselves with clubs and daggers taken from people on the roads and eventually took refuge on the slopes of Mount Vesuvius after plundering the countryside. At first, the Romans regarded such activity as little more than a raid. When the slave army was attacked, however, the Roman general Varinius not only lost the battle but had his horse captured by a mere gladiator!

As refugee slaves and freemen flooded into his camp, Spartacus's army increased until it numbered about seventy thousand. Spartacus attempted to leave Italy by heading north to the Alps and Gaulic country, but was hindered by advancing Roman armies. Somewhat frustrated, Spartacus turned on the pursuing soldiers and beat several Roman armies in succession, killing every prisoner in the process.

Rome was now fully aware of the severe military threat and dangerous symbol of a slave defying his master that Spartacus represented. At first, no one was willing to accept the challenge of facing a now well-equipped and well-trained army of gladiators. Finally, Licinius Crassus, a wealthy and distinguished Roman, offered to take command of the army assigned to crush the slave revolt. Crassus hoped to use his victory over Spartacus to gain personal glory and enhance his political power within the Roman government.

With the help of ten legions, Crassus advanced on isolated groups of the slave army and weakened the overall strength of Spartacus's fighting force. Rome, still concerned that the war might drag on, now engaged the army of Pompey to assist Crassus, even though it had just recently arrived from Spain. Crassus, however, wanted no such assistance and did everything he could to manoeuvre Spartacus into battle before Pompey arrived. When Spartacus invited Crassus to negotiate a settlement, his terms were rejected. A third Roman army, led by Lucullus, had landed at Brundesium, blocking any possible escape for Spartacus who was now boxed in on three sides.

Spartacus chose to engage Crassus directly, as Crassus had originally planned, but after a long, bloody battle, the Romans were victorious. Spartacus, speared in the thigh, continued to fight on one knee with shield in hand until he was slain. His body was never found. Those few slaves who escaped to the north were killed by the late advance of Pompey's army and Pompey claimed part of

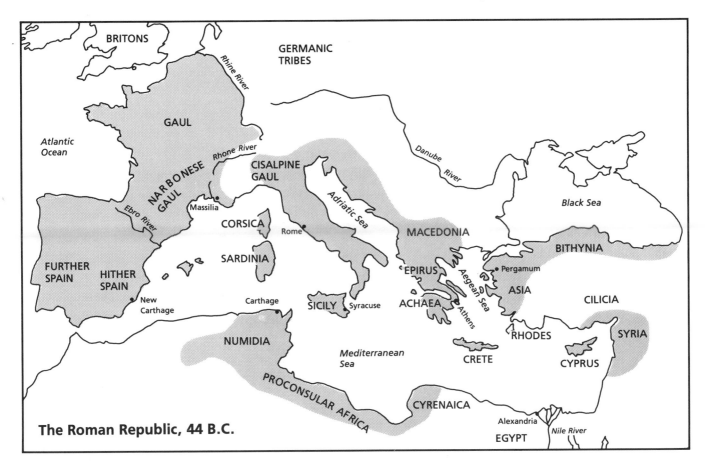

The Roman Republic, 44 B.C.

the credit for suppressing the slave revolt. This greatly annoyed Crassus. It also marked another step in the political struggles that plagued Rome throughout the first century B.C. as the two successful generals continued to compete with each other for prestige and power. As a final reminder of the fate that a rebellious slave could expect, six thousand slaves captured from Spartacus's army were crucified along the road from Capua to Rome.

The Struggle for Power

As Rome expanded from a mere city-state to dominate Italy and the Mediterranean, it enjoyed a period of relative political stability. In theory, it had become a democracy, although somewhat limited, like the Athenian system had been in the Golden Age. The **plebians**, or lower classes, had achieved all of their political objectives. The fact that they were needed as soldiers to defend the state gave them a strong bargaining position. Nevertheless, the **patrician** or aristocratic upper classes enjoyed representation and power beyond their numbers in the structure and operation of the government.

PLEBIAN AND PATRICIAN

Julius Caesar

THE SENATE

SULLA

The most prestigious political body was the Senate, even though it only had the power to advise. The Senate had considerable moral authority and it usually spoke and acted on behalf of the patrician class as a whole. Unfortunately, Rome did not adjust the operation of its city-state government to deal with the representation and administration of the many regions now under its control. Local government in outlying provinces remained in local hands and bad governors were rarely disciplined even by Senate committees set up for the purpose. If serious problems resulted, as they often did, an army would be dispatched to settle the issue.

Within the Senate, competition for power between the aristocratic families and those of the popular party, from less distinguished backgrounds, created other problems. When Sulla, defender of the aristocratic families, became dictator in 82 B.C., he methodically slaughtered all of his political opponents in the popular party. A young man named Julius Caesar, who had been born an aristocrat but who sided with the popular party, was forced to flee from Rome. Although the Senate's position was restored after this political blood bath, it was becoming increasingly clear that the army was the key to power in Rome. In turn, to maintain support from the army, considerable wealth was needed. Sulla had executed many of his opponents only because he needed their money to pay his veteran soldiers a bonus.

Julius Caesar

It was in this complex world of political upheaval and intrigue that young Julius Caesar began his career. Initially, Caesar lacked the popular support required to win even minor offices and the money to engage in the common practice of bribing the electorate. Caesar was, however, extremely talented in many ways. He was a charming and convincing talker who became one of the best orators of his day. An excellent horseman, he could ride and fight with exceptional endurance. In his later years, he had enough concentration to dictate literary works and reports to two or three secretaries at a time. Like Alexander, he was subject to fits of epilepsy, but otherwise enjoyed good health. His unusual habit of keeping his belt loosely tied became a style that was eventually copied by everyone.

Caesar was very sensitive about his public image and pride. It is possible that he divorced his first wife because she was merely suspected of unfaithfulness. When his hair began to thin at an early age, he combed it forward, and in later years frequently wore a laurel wreath to improve his appearance.

Caesar was overshadowed by public competition from the wealthy Crassus and the military exploits of Pompey following the suppression of the slave revolt in 71 B.C. Shrewdly, Caesar cultivated the support of both men. In 65 B.C., rumours circulated that Caesar had been part of an abandoned plot to make Crassus dictator. Nothing came of the attempt, but Caesar was soon spending part of Crassus's considerable riches to get himself elected to office. As Caesar improved his status, he eventually served as governor to Further Spain. His success in the wars against looting bandits not only made him rich, but earned him a public "triumph" recommended by the Senate. This meant that Caesar, as the victorious commander, entered the city in ceremonial procession, displaying the spoils of his campaign to the cheering crowds. Caesar then sought to add a political alliance to his own prestige by giving his daughter Julia permission to marry Pompey, while he himself married Calpurnia, whose family connections were also a political advantage. By virtue of his ties and the support of both men, Caesar was now in a position to manipulate the ambitions of Crassus and Pompey in a careful and calculated climb to the top of the Roman political world.

PERSONAL CHARACTERISTICS

THE CLIMB TO POWER

Great Leaders in History

When civilizations rise and fall, the role of an individual often shrinks in scale. Yet Alexander, Hannibal, and Julius Caesar achieved greatness that was recognized in many ways by their contemporaries and by later generations. Each man faced a unique historical situation with problems and goals that demanded unique solutions. For Alexander, the dream of glory and empire seemed to inspire his every move; for Hannibal, the conquest of an expanding Mediterranean power that threatened his homeland was a childhood promise that became the toil of his life; while Caesar clawed his way to power in a Roman state that could not peacefully manage the citizens it served or the provinces it controlled. The leadership required to meet any of these considerable challenges revealed in each man a set of characteristics that were at times shared and at times geared to the immediate circumstances. What were these characteristics? Why do they seem to be lacking in the political leaders of today? Perhaps the answers to these questions can be approached by examining the careers of Alexander, Hannibal, and Julius Caesar.

PROBLEM QUESTION

To what extent was the leadership of Alexander more or less consistent with standards of greatness than the leadership provided by Hannibal or Julius Caesar?

ALTERNATIVE ONE

Alexander the Great—Based on *Classical Greece* by C.M. Bowra, 1965

Within a year of his accession Alexander extended his dominion northward to the Danube River and westward to the Adriatic Sea. He then turned his attention to Greece, where Thebes and Athens were threatening to bolt the League. Alexander put down the insurrection in Thebes in 335 B.C. Then, to punish the city for what he regarded as treachery, he had its inhabitants slaughtered or sold into slavery and razed all of its buildings except for temples—and the house of Pindar the poet. Pindar himself was dead long since, but Alexander revered him and was eager to prove that even a Macedonian conquerer could be a Hellene. The savage lesson of Thebes brought results. The Athenian Assembly quickly congratulated Alexander, and the Greek states, with the continuing solitary exception of Sparta, remained Macedonian allies.

Alexander now took on a project that Philip had planned but never carried out: an invasion of Persia. Solid political reasons led him to this decision. For a century Persia had interfered increasingly in Greek affairs and had constantly oppressed the Greek cities in Asia Minor. There was always the dangerous possibility that, under a strong king, it might step up its troublemaking and once again actively take the offensive against Greece. Alexander had personal reasons for the invasion, too. Avid for glory and for identification with Greece, the young King knew no better way to win both than by attacking Greece's ancient foe. . . . Alexander, with his far stronger army, had good reason to believe that he could win. In 334 B.C. he crossed the Hellespont, which Xerxes had crossed in the opposite direction nearly a century and a half before. Soon afterward he defeated the Persian forces gathered to meet him on the Asian side of the River Granicus. From the spoils of this victory he sent 300 suits of Persian armour back to Athens. With them went the message, "Alexander, the son of Philip, and the Greeks, except the Spartans, have won this spoil from the barbarians of Asia," thus expressing in one brief and self-assured sentence his contempt for the Persians, his even greater contempt for the Spartans, and his conviction that he was furthering a Greek cause.

As the campaign progressed, Alexander's plan expanded. Originally his purpose had been simply to destroy the Persian army. Before long he had decided to take over the whole Persian Empire. And he went on to achieve this aim without losing a single battle. Of all the great generals of the ancient world, Alexander was surely the greatest. He possessed an almost clairvoyant insight into strategy and was a consummately resourceful tactician. Like Napoleon, he believed in swiftness of movement, but he could be patient too, as he showed in his long siege of the formidable fortress of Tyre.

He was enormously skillful at dealing with unfamiliar tactics of warfare, such as the use of chariots armed with scythes, elephants deployed in battle, and evasive, encircling movements by nomad horsemen. Sometimes he got unexpected help from the enemy. Darius, who was cruel as well as cowardly, treated prisoners with a harshness that embittered the Macedonian soldiers. In two major battles, at Issus in 333 B.C. and Gaugamela in 331 B.C., Darius fled from the field. With these two victories Alexander broke the main Persian resistance and in the autumn of 331 B.C. he entered Babylon, the winter capital of the Persian kings. In December of the same year he entered the summer capital at Susa. From Susa he went on to the ceremonial capital at Persepolis. Here he collected a treasure so vast, says Plutarch, that it took 20,000 mules and 5,000 camels to remove it. Before leaving Persepolis, Alexander burned the huge palace of the Great King for reasons that have never been clear. Possibly it was a whim, possibly he did it in a fit of drunken excitement, or possibly he did it to signify that the Persian invasion of Greece had at last been avenged.

Alexander already considered himself King of Persia, but his right to the throne was in question as long as Darius was still at large. In the summer of 330 B.C., Alexander marched north in pursuit of him. He had almost caught up with his quarry when the Persian leader was suddenly slain by his own men, finally brought to rebellion by their long resentment of his mismanagement of the Persian defense. Alexander came upon Darius' body near Hecatompylo, and ordered it sent back to Persepolis for burial in the royal cemetery of the Archaemenid kings. Now, at last, Alexander was officially the Great King of Persia. In his new role he headed east to take possession of the remaining Persian provinces. After two years he reached and subdued Bactria and Sogdiana; he now controlled all the lands that belonged to Darius.

Since his main concern was to keep the Empire functioning, Alexander tolerated many local religious and social customs. He even, to some extent, permitted each country to keep its national institutions. At the same time he introduced a number of Hellenic ideas. The most important one was that of the Greek city-state. He was liberal with his name and among cities he founded were no fewer than 16 Alexandrias. Most of them were built from the foundation up. The first and most famous one was the Egyptian city which became, a century later, the center of the Hellenistic world.

As his empire grew Alexander saw that Asia could not be administered simply as a colony of Greece. Somehow he had to bring Persians and Greeks together into a single unit. In 327 B.C., partly for political reasons, but perhaps for love, he married a Sogdian Princess, Roxane. Alexander does not seem to have cared much for women. Plutarch writes that "he was wont to say that sleep and the act of generation chiefly made him sensible that he was mortal; as much to say, that weariness and pleasure proceed from the same frailty and imbecility of human nature." Three years after his marriage to Roxane, he married the elder daughter of Darius in a purely political union. This wedding was a communal affair: at the same time, on Alexander's order, 80 of his top-ranking officers married 80 Persian girls of noble birth.

Further to consolidate his Empire Alexander drafted Persian calvary into his own army and ordered 30,000 Persian boys to be trained in Macedonian combat techniques. He adopted Persian dress for himself and for a time even tried to get his soldiers to follow the Persian custom of prostration before the King. But his Macedonian captains were affronted by this. They felt that it implied worship, and they did not think that Alexander was a god.

Most of Alexander's ideas for consolidating the Greek and Persian peoples made little impression on his Macedonian companions. They were soldiers, not political scientists. His concept of empire did not fit their own crude ambitions and they had no sympathy for his desire to govern responsibly. They felt that he was setting himself above them, spoiling the old sense of comradeship-in-arms which had once characterized the Macedonian army. They resented his treatment of the Persians as their equals, which obliterated the age-old distinctions between Greeks and barbarians. They were dismayed when he put Greeks under the command of Persians, and made Persians governors. More than once, Alexander was faced with conspiracy. He could never be sure that forces left behind to govern occupied cities would not revolt. He could never rule out the danger of assassination. And yet he held his enormous Empire together.

After he had taken over the provinces of Bactria and Sogdiana, completing his conquest of the Persian Empire, Alexander turned south and headed into India. Nearly two centuries before, in the reign of Darius I, the Persian Empire had included part of that subcontinent. Determined to recapture it, Alexander crossed the Hindu Kush mountains, followed the Kabul River down to the Indus River and crossed overland to the Hydaspes River. At the Hydaspes, near a place now called Jhelum, he fought one of the most difficult battles of his entire career. His opponent was the Indian King, Porus, whose army was several times larger than Alexander's and superbly trained. It included war elephants, and the huge beasts reduced Alexander's striking power because his horses would not go near them. By feinting a series of attacks and finally attacking from an unexpected quarter, Alexander defeated Porus. One of the casualties of battle, however, was his own horse, Bucephalus.

Alexander had earned him as a boy of 12 by riding him when no one else could. He founded a city in his memory on the site of the battle, naming it Bucephala.

From the Hydaspes Alexander advanced deeper into India. Like most men of his time he believed that the Indian continent was a small peninsula jutting eastward, and that its uttermost extremity was washed by the body of water, called simply Ocean, that encircled the world. He expected to reach Ocean and explore it as the climax of his long campaign. With this in mind he had brought with him rowers and shipwrights from Phoenicia, Cyprus, Caria and Egypt, and had even chosen his admiral, a boyhood friend named Nearchus. But his troops had other ideas. They could see the point of the Persian campaigns, but not of an invasion of India. They had heard rumours of vast deserts and fierce warriors and great armies of elephants lying ahead. Besides, they were tired and yearned for home. They refused to march.

Alexander waited three days for them to change their minds. When he was convinced that they would not, he agreed to start home. . . .

In the spring of 323 B.C. he reached Babylon, and began almost at once to regroup his army and plan an invasion of Arabia. But in June a fever struck him. The efforts and privations of the journey had undermined his hitherto magnificent health. He grew rapidly worse and soon could no longer speak. One by one his captains filed past his bed; he was unable to do more than lift his hand and make a sign with his eyes. On the 13th of June, 323 B.C., not yet 33 years old, he died.

Great Ages of Man/CLASSICAL GREECE by C.M. Bowra and The Editors of Time-Life Books © 1965 Time-Life Books Inc.

Questions

1. In what way did Alexander's treatment of Thebes affect Athens?
2. Why did Alexander decide to invade Persia?
3. Compare the personal qualities of Alexander and the Persian king, Darius.
4. a) How did Alexander administer his empire?
   b) What were the Hellenic ideas that he introduced?
5. a) Why did Alexander try to bring Persians and Greeks together in running the empire?
   b) How did Alexander's Macedonian followers react to this?
6. a) Give examples to show that Alexander often acted for purely political reasons.
   b) Did Alexander regard himself as an equal to his followers? Explain your answers.
7. What tactical problems did Alexander overcome in his battle against the Indian king, Porus?
8. a) Why did Alexander's men refuse to complete the Indian campaign as he originally intended?
   b) What does this tell you about Alexander's leadership qualities?

Alexander

B.C.

338 At age eighteen, Alexander commands Philip's cavalry at Chaeronea

336 Philip is assassinated
At age twenty, Alexander becomes king of Macedonia

335 Alexander crushes revolt in Thebes
Survivors are sold into slavery

334 Alexander defeats Persia at Granicus

333 Alexander defeats Persia at Issus
Darius III of Persia flees battle site

332 Alexander occupies Egypt and plans the city of Alexandria
Alexander travels to Ammon to seek confirmation of his divine origin

330 At Arbela Alexander defeats Darius again
Darius retreats and is eventually killed by his men
Alexander marches into the Persian cities of Babylon, Susa, and Persepolis
Alexander kills Philotus and his father for daring to share credit for Alexander's victories

328 Clitus criticizes Alexander and praises Philip
In a drunken rage, Alexander spears Clitus

326 Alexander expands his empire to India where he defeats King Porus in a difficult battle at the Hydespas River

324 Alexander is forced to return to Susa when his generals will go no farther

323 Alexander dies of a fever in Babylon

311 Roxane and the son she bore Alexander are murdered
Alexander's empire is divided among his generals
India and Greece regain their independence

ALTERNATIVE TWO

Hannibal–Based on *The Enduring Past* by John H. Trueman and Dawn Cline Trueman, 1982

In April 218 B.C., a twenty-nine-year-old Carthaginian known as Hannibal set out from New Carthage in the south of Spain. His destination was Italy; his goal was to crush the Romans once and for all. Hannibal believed the Romans could only be defeated in Italy, where the people, once liberated, would ally with him against their oppressors.

Leading forty thousand infantry, eight thousand cavalry, and sixty elephants, Hannibal managed to cross the Rhone by mid-August, just three days before a Roman army arrived to intercept him. By autumn, he had reached the Alps, which were already deep in snow. This made the trek through the treacherous passes even more dangerous. It also gave the hostile mountain tribes who were accustomed to these conditions a fighting advantage. Still, Hannibal pushed on. Indeed, it is this seemingly insurmountable feat that most people associate with the name Hannibal.

The struggle across the Alps took its toll. By the end of the fifteen-day trek Hannibal had lost forty elephants and twenty-two thousand men. Considering the loss, it was a strange victory.

The Romans had missed capturing Hannibal on both sides of the Alps. Now, they hoped to catch him in northern Italy crossing the river Trebia. Hannibal, however, had his own plan. Early one bitterly cold December morning, he dispatched a small cavalry detachment across the river. It fought the Romans just long enough to be convincing, then retreated in defeat. The Romans charged after them through the icy waters. The retreating Carthaginians led them straight into an ambush. Of the forty thousand Romans, twenty thousand men were lost. The Romans retreated to the south, leaving northern Italy to Hannibal.

The Carthaginian army spent that winter in Bologna, while the Romans fervently recruited more men. In the spring, Hannibal headed southward. He crossed the Apennines and made his way through the marshland of the river Arno where he contracted an infection and lost the sight of one eye. Nonetheless, he pressed on towards Rome, ravaging the land in his path.

A Roman army of twenty-five thousand followed Hannibal's forces at a distance but they were not prepared to fight the Carthaginian force that outnumbered them. Hannibal had other ideas. He sent his men to hide in the hills surrounding Lake Trasimene. The next morning, as the Romans marched through a particularly narrow valley, the Carthaginians attacked, killing fifteen thousand in just two hours, and capturing most of the survivors.

Hannibal had now outwitted the Romans twice and their casualties had been high. He must be stopped before he reached Rome. The Roman people decided the man to defeat the Carthaginian was Quintus Fabius Maximus.

Since Hannibal's cavalry had played a decisive role in his previous victories, Fabius decided to wait until Hannibal was in a position in which he could not use his cavalry. As Hannibal continued to lay waste the countryside, Fabius was resolute in his decision not to fight until the time was right. The Romans were soon referring to Fabius as "the delayer." Eventually, Fabius's patience was rewarded. Hannibal was trapped by a mountain pass commanded by Fabius.

Yet again, Hannibal outwitted the Romans. Hannibal had his men roundup two thousand head of cattle and tie bundles of twigs to their horns. Then, under the cover of darkness, they drove the cattle towards the pass, lighting the twigs on command. To the Roman guards, it looked like an advancing army bearing torches. Suddenly the paradelike ranks dissolved into a scattered arrangement. What the Romans thought was a sudden attack was in reality the cattle wildly shaking their heads as the burning twigs singed their flesh. As the fire spread through the valley, the Romans abandoned their vantage point to Hannibal and his cavalry. With this protection, the Carthaginian infantry passed through unchallenged.

Fabius's strategy had failed. Hannibal continued to ravage Italy, and the Romans were growing increasingly more impatient. When Fabius's term of office expired in 216 B.C., the consuls were ready for action. They chose a battle site near Cannae in the plains by the Adriatic, an ideal location for a cavalry engagement. Although the Romans outnumbered the Carthaginians fifty-four thousand to forty-five thousand, the Carthaginian cavalry was stronger by four thousand. Hannibal planned his strategy around this advantage. His battle formation was crescent shaped with the cavalry on each end and the infantry at the centre bulging towards the Romans. As the Roman legions pushed forward, the bulge gave way to a hollow. Still the Romans drove forward. Meanwhile, the Carthaginian cavalry had routed the Roman wing and had regrouped to strike a second time. Advancing in a wide sweep around the rear of the legions, they completely surrounded the Romans. As they tightened their formation, the Romans found themselves in a slaughterpen. Once again, Hannibal was victorious.

At Cannae, the Romans lost twenty-five thousand men in battle and ten thousand as captives compared with the loss of only fifty-seven hundred Carthaginians. They also lost support from many of the towns in southern Italy which now allied themselves with Hannibal. Nonetheless, they still had the loyalty of central and northern Italy, and Rome itself was safe for the moment. Hannibal did not have the siege weapons necessary to storm the city's high walls.

Their defeat at Cannae had taught the Romans one thing: Direct combat was not the way to conquer Hannibal. Instead, they adopted a strategy of delay tactics to wear down their enemy. Hannibal's plan, to surround Italy with enemies, meant that he must stay in Italy without reinforcements. As long as he remained in the south of Italy, Hannibal had the freedom of the countryside. It was only when he ventured northward that he encountered difficulty. There, the Romans and their allies either protected their crop harvests within the city walls or burned them to the ground rather than leave them for the Carthaginians. Once their food supply ran out, Hannibal and his men were forced to return to the south.

Neither side seemed able to defeat the other. However, the Romans had one trump card left, **Publius Cornelius Scipio,** a general as capable as Hannibal. Scipio had experience fighting Carthaginians. He had ended the Carthaginian Empire in Spain in 207 B.C. using a troop formation similar to the one Hannibal had used in Cannae.

In spite of Scipio's success, however, Hasdrubal, Hannibal's brother, had managed to lead thirty thousand men out of Spain and was determined to join Hannibal. The Romans, just as determined to keep them apart, dispatched one army to intercept Hasdrubal while another watched Hannibal's movements.

Hasdrubal made one critical error. He dispatched a messenger to Hannibal disclosing the rendezvous point. The Romans intercepted it, and, acting quickly, the two armies marched to the meeting place to await Hasdrubal's arrival. The battle at the Metaurus River was the first major Roman victory in eleven years. A week later, the Romans took pleasure in announcing the defeat to Hannibal by throwing his brother's head into his camp.

Scipio's next move was to convince the Senate that the only way to ensure Rome's safety was to crush Carthage itself. Towards this end, he set sail for North Africa in 204 B.C. with a force of thirty thousand Romans. It was a hard campaign, but a year later the Carthaginians were ready to discuss peace terms.

In the meantime Hannibal, who had spent sixteen years in Italy, returned to North Africa having neither won nor lost the war. His return gave the Carthaginians the courage to challenge Scipio one more time.

The two generals met at Zama. Although Hannibal's force outnumbered the Roman legions, his cavalry was slightly weaker. Once again Hannibal displayed his genius for strategy. His plan was to draw the Roman cavalry in by staging a retreat of his own cavalry and then to attack with his infantry, holding back a reserve force for the final onslaught. It appeared as though the plan was working; however, the Roman cavalry regrouped before the reserves could deliver the decisive blow. Although Hannibal escaped, his army was cut to pieces. At last the war was over.

Rome imposed harsh penalties in the peace agreement. The Romans were not about to forget what the war had cost them, and they demanded that Carthage make reparations.

The Romans were not about to forget Hannibal's role in the war, either, and he was forced to flee to Syria. But even there, his safety was threatened by the long arm of Rome. Seeing his house surrounded by soldiers, Hannibal took the poison he always had with him. In 183 B.C., the noblest failure in antiquity died.

Questions

1. a) Once embroiled in a war with Rome, what was Hannibal's plan of attack?
   b) What hardships were encountered in the march across the Alps?
   c) Why did this trek capture the imagination of later generations?
2. a) Describe Hannibal's military tactics at Trebia, Lake Trasimene, and

Hannibal

B.C.

218	Second Punic War begins when Hannibal invades Italy by crossing the Alps
	Hannibal defeats Rome at Trebia
	War elephants are used for the first and only time in the Italian campaign
217	Hannibal defeats Rome at Lake Trasimene
	Rome elects dictator Quintus Fabius Maximus
216	Fabius's strategy is ineffective and he is removed from office as Rome grows impatient
	Hannibal defeats Rome through the brilliant use of infantry and cavalry
	Ill equipped to attack Rome itself, Hannibal's forces wander the Italian countryside winning every battle but not the war
207	Roman general Scipio ends Carthaginian Empire in Spain
	Rome is now virtually assured of victory
202	Hannibal returns to Carthage for a last stand
	The Numidian cavalry switch their allegiance to Rome
	Hannibal is defeated by Scipio at Zama
183	Hannibal commits suicide
150–146	Third Punic War–Rome destroys Carthage and creates the province of Africa
	Rome now dominates the Mediterranean

Cannae.

b) What feeling swept Rome as a result of Hannibal's success?

c) Why was Rome itself safe from Hannibal's attack?

3. Describe the situation in Italy by 207 B.C. after Hannibal's many successes.

4. How did the Roman general Scipio undermine Hannibal's victories in Italy?

5. Why was Hannibal finally defeated at Zama?

6. Were Hannibal's military victories as impressive as those of Alexander? Explain your answer.

ALTERNATIVE THREE

Julius Caesar–Based on "The Enigma of Caesar" by Luigi Barzini, 1966

At the news of Sulla's death in 78 B.C., Caesar returned to Rome to try his hand at politics and law. Exercising his right as a citizen to sue a public official, he chose a powerful opponent . . . and lost the case. The young lawyer's eloquence won many admirers; people talked about him and he began to have a following. He decided to broaden his education and set out for Rhodes.

On the way there, he was captured by pirates, whom he promptly treated as servants. When he wanted to sleep he sent orders to his noisy captors to be quiet; he joined in their games, practiced his rhetoric on them, called them illiterate barbarians to their faces and, in raillery, promised to have them crucified. They admired and obeyed him meekly, sensing the leader in him. Six weeks later, after his ransom arrived and he was freed, he hired several galleys, returned to surprise the pirates in their lair and crucified the lot as he had promised.

He returned to Rome and, to make friends, went into debt. He kept an open house; according to Plutarch, "the splendor of his life increased his political influence." His opponents did not suspect his aims. They thought he was one more frivolous young man who frittered away money on entertainment and that his growing influence would vanish when his credit gave out.

The borrowed money soon did give out and Caesar plunged further into debt which reached such an unheard-of magnitude that his political backers, men of considerable power, began to worry. Caesar must have figured out that some of these creditors would help him get an army command in hopes of being paid back. This, of course, was his great gamble . . .

He ran for election to a succession of minor posts, climbing steadily. In 61 B.C., . . . when his debts were on the point of overwhelming him, he reached his first substantial and profitable position: he was appointed propraetor in charge of quelling some rebellious Spanish tribes. At the last minute an apparently insurmountable obstacle threatened to prevent his voyage and defeat his plans to find power and wealth in Spain. Some of his creditors insisted he pay a large part of the money owed them before he left and they had his baggage, carriages, and horses seized.

Caesar turned to the only man who could save him—Crassus. Crassus was the richest man in Rome . . . and, like many very rich men in those times of anarchy and chaos, so nervous he had been playing every side. Crassus needed as many strong friends as he could find: ruthless, ambitious, clever, bold men, possibly in need of money but with a strong popular backing.

So Crassus paid off most of Caesar's debts and pledged himself to finance the young propraetor's expedition. On Caesar's arrival in Spain, "he not only begged for money to settle his debts, but wantonly sacked several Spanish towns," Suetonius reports, and proceeded to subdue the local tribes in a blitz campaign. "Advancing as far as the ocean, he conquered new tribes which had never been subject to the Romans," says Plutarch and which had never therefore been thoroughly plundered before. Caesar sent some of the booty to the Roman treasury, distributed more than a fair share among his soldiers and began to get rich himself. He was ready to try for bigger stakes.

The situation in Rome in 60 B.C. was extremely precarious. Once again the time was ripe for a great leader, with the means and the will, to reach for supreme power. But who? There were three candidates in sight–Crassus, Pompey, and Caesar. Crassus had his immense wealth, the backing of a large section of the population and of a fair share of the Senate and could easily find military commanders who would lend him their legions for a price. Pompey was the great military conqueror, who had destroyed the pirates infesting the Mediterranean, had defeated the Eastern rebel king Mithridates and had amassed money and men. Caesar was clearly the weakest of the three: he had neither the money of one nor the armies of the other. What should he do? The obvious course was to encourage the enmity between Crassus and Pompey and hope to come out as sole survivor of the struggle. When one of them seemed to be winning, he could rush to his aid. But it was a risky plan. Would the winner tolerate a minor rival for long? Would he not destroy Caesar, too, in the end?

Caesar's course shows the magnitude of his political genius. It took immense diplomatic ability and exceptional persuasive power. It probably would have been impossible for any other man. Afterwards, the main developments of Caesar's life fell into place, one after another, as predictably as the moves of a chess game played by a champion after the opening gambit. He simply convinced Pompey and Crassus to make peace and secretly join with him in a partnership to dominate Rome. What none of them could hope to achieve without an exhausting war, the three of them could do overnight by sealing a pact.

It was obvious that the alliance could dispose of the people's assemblies, all public officials, the banks; they were . . . the bosses of an all-powerful political machine. With the help of his partners Caesar in 59 B.C. easily became consul and, within a year, governor of the two Gauls (Northern Italy and France). From the age of 44 to 53 he was away in Gaul (frequently coming back to North Italy, but not to Rome, to mend political fences and direct the work of his agents in the city). He consolidated his conquest and pacified the inhabitants, Plutarch says, simply by killing one million of a total of three million. Meantime, he amassed a fortune possibly larger than Crassus', and became one of the most successful generals of all ages, with a brilliant and tested staff of officers and a number of practically invincible legions, all loyal to the death.

His nature irresistibly drove him to face the greatest dangers. In his military campaigns he played for safety only when he faced an inferior and weaker enemy: he did not want to waste his own men's lives to achieve a practically certain victory. But when he found himself on unfavorable ground–with a small army worn out by marches, without supplies and far from his base, facing a superior, confident, well-entrenched enemy–he always attacked. He attacked because, at such times, the enemy least expected him to.

Many times, in those desperately uneven battles on which Caesar liked to stake his luck, he saved the day by rushing in where his men were being beaten back. During one of his early campaigns in Gaul, his troops were surprised by an overwhelming onslaught of Nervii. Caesar says in his *Commentaries* that he himself "had everything to do at one moment": raise the flag, sound the alarm, bring in the men who were digging trenches, and give orders. He then rushed over to the Twelfth Legion, which was falling back in disorder. He seized a shield from a soldier in the rear ranks, pushed his way to the front, called upon the centurions by name, then sounded the charge. The mere gesture revived his men and made them surge forward. At the end of the day, the Nervii were hacked to pieces. In the last battle he ever fought near Munda, Spain in 45 B.C., Caesar again turned panic among his troops into victory. Feeling that this was his moment to die, Caesar charged to within 3 m of the enemy line. According to Appian, a "hailstorm of 200 arrows descended upon him; some passed without touching him, his shield protected him from the others." First the tribunes, then the entire army turned with vehemence and defeated the enemy.

In all this time the day was approaching when the ruling partnership–Caesar, Crassus and Pompey–would be reduced to two and make civil war inevitable. That moment came in 53 B.C. when Crassus, leading his privately financed army, was killed fighting the Parthians in the East. Pompey made himself the buttress of the patrician Old Guard and agitated against his former partner, Caesar, who was still in Gaul. The Senate ordered Caesar to leave his legions in Gaul (north of the River Rubicon) and return home as an unarmed private citizen. Instead, Caesar waited, weighed the risk, and finally crossed the Rubicon with a legion. It was Jan. 11, 49 B.C., four years after the death of Crassus. . . .

So swift and unexpected was his advance that Pompey fled first to southern Italy, then to Greece. Everybody recognized that this was not a war between the Republic and a seditious general; it was a conflict between two candidates for supreme power. Whoever was going to win, the Republic would lose. "I cannot endure the sight of what is happening," Cicero wrote, "or what is going to happen."

Caesar entered Rome (where he emptied the treasury), then went on to Spain, came back and crossed the Adriatic in pursuit of Pompey. He finally destroyed Pompey's army at Pharsalus, in Thessaly, on Aug. 9, [48 B.C.]. Pompey, together with his wife, his son, and a small band of soldiers, escaped to Egypt, only to be murdered there by the Egyptians, who offered his embalmed head in tribute to Caesar when he landed there. Victorious Caesar refused it and wept. But he went on to wage wars against Pompey's sons and successors in command. Among them were patrician lovers of the ancient liberties, the men who, in the end, murdered him. Caesar triumphed over them all and, at 57, returned to Rome absolute master of the state.

The real problem of Caesar's generation was to find a simple method to pick supreme leaders, to govern far-flung domains with stability and establish a reasonably durable peace. The Senate was no longer able to start or stop the wars, curb the generals' ambitions, discipline the rich, keep order in the city, or defend the Roman world from invasions. The constitution, which had been good enough for a small city, for short and necessary wars, and for a few subjected peoples, was obsolete.

There was not much time to devise a new government capable of coping with the new problems, yet preserving at least the forms of the old institutions and providing a smoother way to transfer power from one leader to the next. It was with this dilemma that Caesar grappled and which he almost solved. He sometimes believed that he had been forced by circumstances to restore the legendary Roman monarchy. In the end he suspected he had introduced something new: despotic and absolute one-man rule over slavelike subjects, based on the divine worship of the ruler as god, after the example of Eastern autocracies.

Shortly before his death Caesar had assumed some of the outward forms of sovereignty: he not only installed a gilded throne in the Senate but stayed seated in the presence of standing senators, his supposed peers. He had his image stamped on coins; his birthday was celebrated by public sacrifices; the month of Quintilis was renamed July after him. Senators addressed him as Jupiter Julius and ordered a temple consecrated to him and to his clemency. Caesar was delighted. Yet he had ostentatiously and publicly refused a royal diadem, saying loudly: "Jupiter alone is king of the Romans"; and after a feast, when his supporters started hailing him as their king, he cried, "My name is Caesar not Rex."

At the same time Caesar realized that he could not surrender absolute power without becoming a party to his own destruction. Forced by logic to follow one move with another in his game, he had never clearly known what he would do in the end, after final victory. He tackled legislative problems, packed the Senate with his friends (some of whom were trousered Gauls who did not know their way about the city), and carried out some reforms, but more to consolidate his power and repress possible revolutions than to reorganize the government. His most famous contribution to civilization, the reform of the calendar, seems insignificant compared to [sic] the number of battles fought, the men killed, the countries ravaged in order to bring it about.

On the day of the assassination he walked into the Senate meeting . . . alone, unarmed, unescorted and apparently unperturbed. The conspirators had sworn each would plunge his blade into Caesar's body, so that all would be held equally responsible for his death. They were so awed by what they were doing that their hands trembled and, in the confusion, wounded each other at the same time.

After the first blow, Caesar did not utter another sound. But finally, when he saw Brutus—the son of his old mistress, the woman he cherished all his life—about to deliver his blow, Caesar said in Greek (as a Russian aristocrat would speak in French): "You, too, my son?" The dictator then drew himself

Julius Caesar

B.C.

82 Sulla become dictator
Marius's supporters are massacred
Caesar flees Rome

75 Caesar is captured by pirates and released for ransom
Caesar returns with fleet and executes former captors

69 Caesar is elected pontifex maximus with financial aid of
Crassus

62 Pompey returns from the east after successful military
campaigns
Pompey and Crassus manoeuvre for political power

61 Caesar wins renown as governor of Further Spain

60 Pompey, Crassus, and Caesar form First Triumvirate
Caesar has the least power

58 Caesar becomes governor of Gaul (France)
Caesar gains personal wealth from plunder and fame from
military victories

53 Crassus is killed in battle
Pompey conspires against Caesar to get supreme control
Pompey becomes virtual dictator of Rome

49 Caesar and his army cross the Rubicon River in defiance of
the Senate and Pompey
Civil war against Pompey begins

48 Pompey is defeated at Pharsalus and murdered in Egypt
Caesar arrives in Egypt and makes political and personal
alliance with Cleopatra

46 Civil war ends and Caesar is appointed dictator for ten years

44 Caesar is appointed dictator for life
Caesar's attempt to secure a hereditary monarchy leads to
his assassination

up against the statue of Pompey, his old ally and defeated enemy–the statue
he himself had generously ordered–pulled his gown over his face and allowed
himself to be butchered in silence.

Questions

1. a) On his journey to Rhodes, Caesar was captured by pirates. Describe how
   Caesar treated his captors.

b) Was Caesar a man of his word? Explain your answer.
2. Caesar was often in debt early in his career. How did he use this to his political advantage?
3. How did Caesar acquire personal wealth during his years in Spain?
4. a) Who were the three most powerful men in the Roman world in 60 B.C.?
    b) Who was the most powerful of these three leaders?
    c) How did Caesar make this situation work to his advantage?
5. a) What event changed the balance of power in 53 B.C.?
    b) Why was crossing the Rubicon River in 49 B.C. a key event in Caesar's career?
    c) Did Caesar's gamble pay off? Explain your answer.
6. a) What was the key problem facing Rome at this time?
    b) What seemed to be Caesar's answer to this problem?
7. a) How well did Caesar handle the military and political problems he faced during his career? Explain your answer.
    b) Would Alexander or Hannibal have dealt with these problems differently? Again, explain your answer.

ANSWERING THE PROBLEM QUESTION

It is difficult to determine the standards for greatness as they apply to exceptional leaders. To some extent, greatness is measured by the ideals that dominate a society in any given era. When a person reflects the ideals of his or her society, due recognition is sometimes given during that person's lifetime. Often, however, a person's accomplishments are not fully appreciated until after his or her death, in which case greatness is identified through the eyes of later generations. The special abilities of Alexander, Hannibal, and Julius Caesar were clearly seen while they lived, and have since been appreciated by writers throughout the centuries.

To compare the degree of greatness among people, you must consider the merits of several factors that vary in importance from case to case. Confidence in the chosen course as the best possible course of action is a key characteristic for any leader. This self-assurance is available only if it offers a sense of direction to those who follow. In battle, this can depend on the leader's decisiveness and bravery under pressure. A leader who clearly demonstrates these traits can generate a personal magnetism or charisma that inspires others to achieve more than they normally would. Charisma also springs from sheer force of personality. Alexander, Hannibal, and Julius Caesar had confidence and charisma. But to what extent did each of them have the ability to inspire their men to achieve either short- or long-term objectives? And was each man successful in reaching the goals he set for himself?

Keep in mind that Alexander, Hannibal, and Julius Caesar lived in different societies and in different times. Alexander was very much a product of the Greek world even though his vision far exceeded the tiny city-state; Hannibal fought bravely for the extension of Carthaginian power; while Julius Caesar grappled with the complexities of Roman civil war. In what way did these men reflect the values held dear by their own societies? Perhaps it is equally important to know how these men were regarded by their enemies, who had to contend with the exceptional talent each man brought to his era. How, then, can the many criteria involved in leadership be ranked and applied to determine the greatest of the great?

THE STORY CONTINUES . . .

The Impact of Caesar's Assassination

In pursuit of Pompey in 48 B.C., Caesar arrived in Egypt only to find a struggle for rule between a ten year old, Ptolemy XII, and his sister Cleopatra. Heeding bad advice, Ptolemy had Pompey murdered and presented his head to Caesar in a vain gesture to win approval. Caesar was not impressed and after initial caution, the arrival of additional legion support enabled Caesar to take control of the situation and assert the authority of Rome.

CAESAR IN EGYPT

During this time, however, Caesar had met and fallen in love with Cleopatra despite the difference in their ages–he was fifty-two, she was twenty-one. Although not a striking beauty, Cleopatra's intelligence, charm, and wit fascinated Caesar. The famous incident of Cleopatra's gaining access to Caesar by having herself wrapped in a carpet, delivered by a friend, and unrolled at Caesar's feet was the kind of dramatics that only increased her appeal. With Caesar's support, Cleopatra's position as queen of Egypt was secured.

CLEOPATRA

It is possible that Cleopatra's influence, and the year of leisure in Egypt experiencing the impact of absolute power might have encouraged Caesar to see monarchy as a solution to the political troubles facing Rome. Rumours circulated that Caesar intended to shift the capital of the Roman world to Alexandria and establish a joint monarchy with Cleopatra.

The foundation for these rumours seemed confirmed when, in 47 B.C., Cleopatra bore Caesar a son, much to the humiliation of Caesar's Roman wife, Calpurnia. Cleopatra's spectacular entrance into Rome with her son, Caesarion, in 46 B.C., won the admiration of the adoring crowd. This heightened the politicians' fear that an alien queen in concert with Caesar would assume complete political authority.

CAESARION

Privately, Caesar left his estate and authority to his adopted grandnephew, Octavian. Perhaps Caesar realized that his son by Cleopatra would have little chance for survival after his father's death.

On the day he was assassinated, 15 March 44 B.C., Caesar had convened a meeting of the Senate to grant him authority as king outside of Rome. For his assassins, including his personal friends Brutus and Cassius, granting such a request would only help establish Caesar as tyrant. They wanted political authority restored to the Senate, but Caesar knew Rome needed him alive if peace was to continue. He once said:

> It is more important for Rome than for myself that I should survive. I have long been sated with power and glory; but should anything happen to me, Rome will enjoy no peace. A new Civil War will break out under far worse conditions than the last.[1]

CAESAR'S REACH FOR ABSOLUTE POWER

Although Caesar was convinced that only he could give Rome the stability it desperately needed, his assassins felt he was ambitious for too much power. Caesar had accepted a golden chair in the Senate chamber and the right to wear the purple dress of the triumphal toga, honours that were usually reserved for kings. After his last battle at Munda in 45 B.C., he had allowed statues of himself to be placed in temples to help confirm his semidivine character. The previous year, Caesar had been appointed dictator for ten years, while in 44 B.C. the term was extended to life. During the festival of Lupercalia, one month before his assassination, Caesar's trusted general, Mark Antony, had placed a crown on Caesar's head. At first, the crowd remained silent, but after the initial pause, Caesar removed the crown and was applauded. Caesar seemed to be consolidating his position and power to establish a hereditary monarchy.

MARK ANTONY

Following the assassination, Mark Antony, Caesar's cavalry commander, seized the initiative by directing the Roman mob to read Caesar's will, honour him, and condemn the assassins. Yet Antony–and everyone else, including the Senate–did not reckon with the legal heir, Octavian, who, though only eighteen, was mature beyond his years, confident, and aggressive. While Antony doggedly pursued Caesar's assassins, Octavian returned to Rome, claimed his inheritance, raised an army, and, when the Senate refused to make him consul, marched on the city and secured the position anyway.

OCTAVIAN

In 43 B.C., Antony, Octavian, and Lepidus, a lesser provincial governor, formed a Second Triumvirate to stabilize political power just as Crassus, Pompey, and Caesar had done in 60 B.C. The combined forces of the Second Triumvirate, led by Antony's skill and daring on the battlefield at Philippi, defeated the armies of Brutus and Cassius, who both committed suicide. Caesar's inability to gain acceptance for a hereditary monarchy and a smooth transition of political power had thus resulted in continued strife and conflict. The thinly veiled ambition of each member in the Second Triumvirate to achieve undivided power promised more of the same.

THE SECOND TRIUMVIRATE

Antony and Cleopatra

Octavian was the first to consolidate his position. Pompey's son, Sextus, had occupied the western provinces of Corsica and Sardinia and, in so doing, threatened the food supply of Rome. At first, Octavian negotiated while Agrippa, Caesar's former admiral, built a strong fleet. In 36 B.C., however, with the fleet prepared, Octavian took the initiative and defeated Sextus. That same

1. Gaius Suetonius Tranquillus, *The Twelve Caesars*, trans. Robert Graves (London: Cassell, 1962), p. 20. Cited in Hugh Parry, *Julius Caesar: The Legend and the Man* (Toronto: Macmillan of Canada, 1972), p. 36.

year, Lepidus occupied Sicily, and Octavian, fresh from victory, turned on the weakest member of the triumvirate and won a second triumph. Octavian was now supreme in the western Roman world.

Mark Antony, Octavian's only rival, was intent on expanding his control in the east in the name of Rome.

After the battle at Philippi, Antony needed money and supplies for his legions and Egyptian wealth seemed to be the solution to his problem. He summoned Cleopatra, who sailed her spectacular barge to Tarsus. Virtually all of the townspeople flocked to the riverbanks as the smell of incense offerings to the god Bacchus spread from the ship, filling the fresh country air. Cleopatra, who reclined beneath a spangled gold canopy, was the focal point of attention. Antony, like Caesar before him, fell under Cleopatra's spell.

After his meeting with Cleopatra at Tarsus in 41 B.C., Antony's objective changed drastically. Antony, who had always admired Greek culture, now saw himself as a Hellenistic sovereign who wanted to strengthen Cleopatra's influence rather than subdue threats to Roman peace and security. He slavishly followed Cleopatra back to Alexandria while his legions suffered reverses in poorly organized military campaigns. He used his authority as consul of the eastern Roman world to restore to Egypt much of the territory lost since early Ptolemaic times. The children that Cleopatra bore him were given Roman provinces and pronounced kings.

While Antony enjoyed a lavish life with his Egyptian queen, Octavian restored stability and order to Rome. Backed by a well-disciplined army, Octavian had himself appointed consul. He secured Antony's will, held by the priestesses of Vesta, and made it known that Antony left his possessions to Cleopatra and her children. As they had with Caesar, rumours spread that Antony wished to move the capital to Alexandria, a bustling commercial centre of commerce second only to Rome. Again, however, the people and the Senate rejected the influence of a foreign queen on a Roman leader, and in 32 B.C., the Senate deposed Antony from his command in the east.

The Triumph of Octavian

Octavian's fleet confronted the combined naval forces of Cleopatra and Antony at Actium in 31 B.C. With the outcome still uncertain, Cleopatra unexpectedly withdrew sixty ships, throwing Antony's fleet into total confusion. It is possible that Cleopatra may have had an understanding with Octavian, but this has never been determined. Antony fled the battle in mournful pursuit of Cleopatra, leaving his navy to face destruction and death. After joining Cleopatra in Alexandria, Antony wallowed in shame and self-pity. When Octavian and his legions marched on the Egyptian city in 30 B.C., Antony, who had few loyal followers left, challenged Octavian to settle the issue by personal combat. Before the fight, however, Antony, who was told Cleopatra had committed suicide, promptly stabbed himself. Antony's wound was not instantly fatal, and when

This relief shows a Roman warship in the process of landing.

OCTAVIAN AND CLEOPATRA

he learned that he had been tricked, he asked to be taken to Cleopatra where he died.

After Antony's death, Cleopatra met with Octavian, perhaps hoping to win over yet another Roman commander. Octavian had other ideas. His main interest in Cleopatra was to make her second entrance into Rome even grander than the first. A victory procession with the queen at his side would certainly enhance his own prestige. During the interview, Octavian consciously kept his eyes lowered so that he would not be seduced by the lightly clad Cleopatra, who always seemed to get her way. Recognizing her failure, Cleopatra arranged

THE ASP

to have an asp smuggled past the Roman guard in a basket of figs. She then committed suicide by letting it bite her.

The power of Rome was now and would remain in Octavian's capable hands. He maintained his position not because of military force but because of his realistic approach to the problems facing the city and its provinces. The first century B.C. had seen a continual struggle between the people's party and the senatorial party that had fanned the flames of civil conflict with no apparent solution. Rather than seize what he had won, Octavian shrewdly gave up his authority in 27 B.C. only to have it restored by the Senate through his appointments to several key public offices. Although he appeared to be reestablishing the Republic through his unselfish gesture, Octavian had, in fact, managed to

OCTAVIAN, THE FIRST ROMAN EMPEROR

become the first Roman emperor. The Senate had realized that a lone ruler in the person of Octavian was the best hope for peace and stability.

Octavian

B.C.

43 Antony, Octavian, and Lepidus form a Second Triumvirate
The armies of Brutus and Cassius are defeated at Philippi
Caesar's assassination is avenged

41 Cleopatra's barge arrives at Tarsus where she and Antony
join personal and political forces
Antony lives a life of luxury with Cleopatra as the dominant
figure of the eastern Roman world

36 Octavian defeats Lepidus in Sicily and dominates the
western Roman world
The Triumvirate is reduced to two

34 At the assembly of Alexandria, Antony's children by
Cleopatra are pronounced kings and given Roman lands

32 Octavian has himself appointed consul by the Senate
Octavian discredits Antony by publicizing Antony's intention to leave all his possessions to Cleopatra and her children, and his wish to be buried in Alexandria

31 Octavian defeats Antony in naval battle at Actium
Cleopatra flees with her ships in the midst of the battle
Antony follows Cleopatra abandoning his men to defeat

30 Cleopatra commits suicide after Antony when it becomes
clear that Octavian cannot be managed

27 Octavian becomes Caesar Augustus, the first Roman
emperor

COMMENT

It is always difficult to weigh the impact of a leader on the people he led, the ambitions he realized, the legacy in fact, and the impression that he left for future generations. Today, the names of Alexander, Hannibal, and Julius Caesar leap out of the pages of history with a grandeur that seems to be denied to leaders of our time. Perhaps the complex problems of the modern world stand too tall for any leader in any position of power to control or even dominate. Certainly the impact of television, radio, and newspaper coverage of daily events more often than not exposes flaws in policy and personality that keep the reputations of public figures at a less than superhuman level. The pressure to say something about each fast-breaking news event results in an endless line of generalities, clichés, and empty rhetoric that is only occasionally punctuated with significant comment.

Leaders of the ancient world were able to save their public comments and proclamations to mark religious ceremonies, military victories, and personal accomplishments. Often days, weeks, and even months were required for such news to spread throughout their lands and provinces. Possibly this and the distance of time has led us to see these men as larger than life, to focus on the more glamorous side of their careers, and to romantisize their images. The worries, uncertainties, and weaknesses that they undoubtedly possessed somehow became hard to believe and are, at times, simply ignored.

Of all the exceptional leaders in antiquity, none was more carefully groomed for his role than Alexander. Philip saw to it that Alexander received the best education that Greece could offer and, under his own watchful eye, gave Alexander command of his cavalry at Chaeronea though Alexander was only eighteen. At age twenty, Alexander was king of Macedonia.

Hannibal also had direct access to military power, although the Carthaginian political system limited his authority. As the son of the administrator and general, Hamilcar, Hannibal had been warned of the Roman threat since childhood. Following the death of his brother-in-law, Hannibal became the leading Carthaginian commander of his day and the dominant public figure of the Second Punic War.

Of the three, only Caesar had to spend most of his early years manoeuvring for public office. Brilliantly playing the shifting tides of Roman politics, it was not until Pompey's defeat at Pharsalus, when Caesar was fifty-two years old, that he secured undivided authority in Rome.

In the modern world, political leadership, particularly in unstable Third World countries, can be secured through a military takeover or a revolution. Among the major powers, military service may enhance an individual's reputation and personal success, but systems of election or party policy have established an orderly transfer of power. No one expects a Canadian prime minister, an American president, or a Soviet premier personally to lead a military campaign to protect their country's interests! In the ancient world, however, personal bravery and the respect it created could be critical to achieving and even maintaining high public office.

Alexander, Hannibal, and Julius Caesar stood out among their peers as brave leaders who inspired their men in battle and could devise a strategy, in advance or on the spot, to win the day. Alexander's military campaigns conquered the widest expanse of territory on a scale that was unimaginable at the time and is still impressive today. Yet, Hannibal never lost a battle in sixteen years of fighting in Italy against a Roman foe that was far better organized than the decaying Persian Empire Alexander faced. Caesar's conquests in the western provinces took him from severe debt to immense wealth and gave him the disciplined legions that sent the forces of Pompey, then the most acclaimed general in Rome, into flight and eventual defeat.

Once the image of a leader becomes clearly engrained, it is easy to forget that men change as their careers progress. Initially, Alexander fought with ambition, pride, and friendship amidst his fellow Macedonians in winning victory after victory against Persia. Alexander, however, gradually became convinced that he was a god, ranking in importance above his fellow soldiers. He became suspicious of any comment that did not focus attention and glory upon himself.

In 330 B.C., his faithful general Philotus boasted to a ladyfriend that Alexander needed himself and his father to subdue Persia. When Alexander heard about the remark, he had both the father and son executed. Two years later, at a party where everyone had drunk too much, Alexander's closest friend, Clitus, praised Philip and voiced his resentment of Alexander's Persian dress and his personal claim to victories that had been won by thousands. When Clitus persisted, Alexander grabbed a spear from a guard and slew his friend–a man who had once saved his life in battle at Granicus.

In 324 B.C., after eleven years of fighting, Alexander's Macedonian generals would go no further and forced a long, difficult return to Susa. Here Alexander escaped the assassination he feared, but fell victim to a fever and died. Alexander's men respected his many talents, but did not, perhaps could not, love a man whose vision of himself and of a cultural blending of Greek and Persian custom they were unable to share.

Hannibal's ability to lead and inspire never faltered. The Carthaginian infantry was made up largely of foreign mercenaries that included Celts, Spaniards, Balaeric Islanders known for their slingers, and Ligurians who were mostly deserters and runaway slaves. Hannibal wisely let each group fight together using familiar tactics and made no attempt to impose uniformity. Hannibal was able to keep their support throughout the entire Italian campaign with no hint of mutiny or revolt. Similarly, the famed bareback-riding cavalry from Numidia, now Algeria, remained loyal and proved crucial to the success of Hannibal in several battles against Rome. After sixteen frustrating years of endless victory in battle, however, Hannibal knew that Carthage would not win the war. The Roman general, Scipio, had won back the lost territory in Spain and moved the site of battle to North Africa. Even more important, however, was Scipio's agreement with the Numidians, who now offered to support Rome against Carthage in return for territory and the prospect of additional weath.

Hannibal returned to defend his homeland. Although the opposing forces were close in number, Hannibal had to contend with the loss of his Numidian cavalry and the fact that the mixed bag of hastily assembled Carthaginian forces had never worked together. In the battle at Zama, Hannibal's tactics kept the fighting close until his largely untrained troops faltered under the pressure of Scipio's superior infantry. Although war weary and tired, Hannibal had remained a talented leader, respected by his men and his city until the end.

Caesar's strength as he climbed the top rungs of the ladder in Roman politics had always been the loyalty of his legions. While he encouraged public acceptance of his own divinity, there is no evidence that he believed it himself. Certainly his legions were not offended as their support never wavered. Nevertheless, as his public image of at least a semidivine leader took shape, Caesar

The silver laurel wreath was symbolic of the power of the Caesars.

began to alienate many of his friends, as Alexander had done in an earlier era. Caesar was not given to fits of rage like Alexander, but his steady move towards being a lone ruler in a hereditary monarchy led his previous admirers, Cassius and Brutus, to hatch a successful plot against his life. Caesar's apparent divinity emerged only after he began his affair with Cleopatra. An indiscretion between a middle-aged, married man and a young woman might have been left at the level of spicy gossip, but when such a relationship threatened to alter the form of government in the Republic, even friends could not stand idly by. The ease with which Antony roused public outrage against the assassins, however, might well reflect the degree of loss felt by most Romans rather than the fickleness of the mob or Antony's self-serving sense of revenge.

Alexander's emotional condition was more extreme than either Hannibal's or Julius Caesar's. A partial explanation may be the influence of Olympias, his mother. Olympias, who was estranged from Philip shortly after Alexander's birth, transferred her resentment of Philip to Alexander. It was she who planted the notion in Alexander's mind that he might be a god and destined to achieve greatness as leader of Macedonia. When Philip took a second wife, as was the custom among kings, Olympias used the occasion to impress upon Alexander that a son from this new marriage would give Macedonia a new heir to the throne. When Philip was assassinated, Olympias made sure that Philip's second wife was murdered along with her newborn child. This action might have shocked Alexander, but he left his mother with considerable power when he began the Persian campaign and always sent her a large share of the booty. Alexander's own behaviour became much more brutal on a grander scale. Victories over Thebes, Tyre, and Gaza followed a familiar pattern of massacring, plundering, and selling survivors into slavery. Although Hannibal and Caesar were ruthless in battle as any capable leader had to be, neither man seems to have indulged as often and with so little to be gained as Alexander in the harsh treatment of an already-defeated foe.

Each of the three leaders fell short of the goals he had set for himself. Alexander's dream of a unified political and cultural empire was an illusion. Many of the conquered cities and towns kept their traditional way of life with newly appointed provincial governors who paid only lip service to Alexander's authority. Upon his death, Alexander's empire fell into chaos. Roxane, his first wife, soon murdered the daughter of Darius, his second wife and Roxane's main rival for Alexander's inheritance. Roxane bore Alexander a son posthumously, but mother and son were both killed in 311 B.C. Alexander's generals divided his empire among themselves. Selecus established the Seleuced Kingdom in Persia; Ptolemy established his own dynasty in Egypt; while Antigonus became king of Macedonia. The cities and land captured by Alexander in Greece and India regained their independence.

Hannibal's military success was tempered by the fact that he lacked the siege equipment necessary to scale the ramparts of Rome itself. With little support in men or material from Carthage, Hannibal was forced to rely on what he could scour from the Italian countryside. Hannibal's loss at Zama illustrated more about the weakness of Carthage than it did about the shortcomings of Hannibal as a general.

Caesar faced the challenge of sorting out the problems of a Roman world more complex than the eastern empire that Alexander had tried to create. Rome was supreme in the Mediterranean but had been torn by half a century of civil war. Caesar felt that peace and stability could only be achieved by a lone ruler in a hereditary monarchy. Although he took steps in that direction, Rome was not yet ready to give up the trappings of republican government. It would take another fifteen years of Romans fighting Romans before an absolute ruler would govern.

Great leaders are remembered by the impact they made on the events of their time, the extent to which their careers helped to shape the future, and the image they call to mind. From a community of tiny city-states, Alexander grasped the boldest objective of an empire that was continental in scope and Greek in spirit. That he conquered a territory almost as expansive as his dream reinforced the picture of a youthful, clean-shaven warrior with flowing locks as depicted on the coins that preserved his likeness. Alexander became the symbol of world order, law, and organization even though he did not live long enough to deal with the problems of administering the lands he had won. A century later, Hannibal challenged the growing power of Rome for the right to dominate and control the Mediterranean. Hannibal's dramatic crossing of the Alps with his army and a herd of war elephants in a mere fifteen days captured the imagination of history. His mastery of tactics in battle made him the most serious threat that Rome ever faced. With the defeat of Hannibal and the total destruction of Carthage in the Third Punic War (146 B.C.), Rome soon controlled much of the land from the edge of Asia to the Atlantic. It was the problem of adapting Rome's city-state government to a collection of provinces so vastly distributed that confronted Julius Caesar. The final solution of a hereditary monarchy was achieved by Octavian. That Caesar had made such a solution possible, however, was clearly recognized when Octavian, as Emperor Augustus, took the title of "Caesar" for himself and all of the emperors that followed.

Modern political leaders, like their ancient counterparts, rarely satisfy the objectives they establish for themselves at the outset of their careers. They too, however, can leave a striking impression of the uncontrollable tide of the world events through which they live. Only with hindsight can their achievements and lasting impact be adequately measured against the issues they faced and the people who served before them.

Date	Event
B.C.	
27	End of the Roman Republic Octavian becomes Caesar Augustus, first Roman Emperor
c.3	Birth of Jesus
A.D.	
14	Tiberius becomes emperor
30	Jesus is crucified
37	Caligula becomes emperor
41	Claudius becomes emperor
54	Nero becomes emperor
64	Nero blames the Christians for the burning of Rome Persecution of Christians begins
70	Revolt of Jews is crushed and they are banished from Palestine
79	Mount Vesuvius erupts burying Pompeii, Herculaneum, and other towns Dedication of the Colosseum
82	Arch of Titus, marking Titus's victory over the Jews, is built
100	Punishment for being a Christian is death
118	Hadrian begins rebuilding the Pantheon in Rome
135	Hadrian suppresses the revolt of the Jews and denies them access to Jerusalem
212	Caracalla grants Roman citizenship to all free residents of Roman provinces Decline of the Western Roman Empire
476	The German barbarian, Odoacer, deposes line of Roman emperors in the West
480–543	Saint Benedict revives the early Christian institution of the monastery
527–565	Reign of Justinian Golden age of the Byzantine Empire in the East
622	Hegira of Muhammad from Mecca to Medina
732	Charles Martel stops the Muslim advance into Europe at Tours
800	Charlemagne crowned by Pope Leo III
843	Treaty of Verdun divides kingdom of Charlemagne
800–1000	Muslims and Magyars threaten Vikings raid coasts of Europe from Ireland to Spain, and France, Russia, and Constantinople Old Western Roman Empire blossoms into a new civilization, Europe

7

The Triumph and Decline of Rome

BACKGROUND

Pax Romana

Beginning with the rule of Augustus, Roman civilization thrived in the general peace and stability known as the **Pax Romana**. The Empire comprised forty-three provinces that stretched from the Caspian Sea to the Atlantic and from Britain to Africa. For two centuries, 90 million people lived through an age of material well-being, order, and security that had never been known before. One government, one system of coinage, and one set of laws unified the civilized world.

The administrative structure for the Roman Empire was developed by Augustus. His authority as **princeps**, or first citizen, was backed by the Roman army of almost three hundred fifty thousand men, each of whom took an oath to protect the frontiers of the Empire. Within Italy, an imperial force of nine thousand men known as the Praetorian Guard was created by Augustus to protect the heart of the Empire. Although he presided at meetings of the Senate and occasionally asked its advice, Augustus himself made the decisions on appointments to major public offices. The traditional posts of republican government were kept, but Augustus used an imperial household responsible only to him to run the everyday business of government. This marked the beginning of a civil service that became divided into departments controlled from a central office in Rome and responsible only to him. Governors of provinces were chosen on the basis of ability and, while considerable freedom was given to local communities, a careful watch was maintained on officials and tax collectors.

Augustus was a great statesman and his system of government survived with limited changes for two hundred years. His administrative reforms, so smoothly created and enforced, endured the rule of less-able emperors such as Nero and tyrants in the worst sense of the word like Dominitian. More talented leaders like Trajan, Hadrian, and Marcus Aurelius used the bureaucracy to keep the Empire in fairly stable operation.

THE ROMAN PEACE

GOVERNMENT OF THE ROMAN EMPIRE

GOVERNMENT OF THE
ROMAN REPUBLIC

S.P.Q.R.

The Senate . . .

Purpose:

Advisory council to public officials

Gained the right to approve or disapprove proposals of other assemblies

Supervised foreign affairs including planning and leadership in war

Could declare martial law in wartime

Membership:

Three hundred members appointed for life by consuls

Usually from a list of ex-magistrates who had served in at least ten military campaigns

Usually members of the patrician upper class

And People of Rome

Centuriate Assembly

Purpose:

Elect senior officials including the consuls

Membership:

Favoured wealthy patrician classes over plebians in membership and operation

Pro-Consul

Dictator endorsed by the Senate for six months during war

Consul

Purpose:

Convene and preside over the Senate

Raise and lead armies in time of war

Administer public affairs and justice

Initiate laws

Conduct public religious ceremonies

Membership:

Two consuls

In peacetime each consul led in alternate months

In wartime leadership changed daily

Tribal Assembly

Purpose:

Elect the remaining officials including tribunes, who protected the rights of plebians

Membership:

Thirty-five tribes or electoral districts

Four tribes near Rome dominated which limited democracy in practice

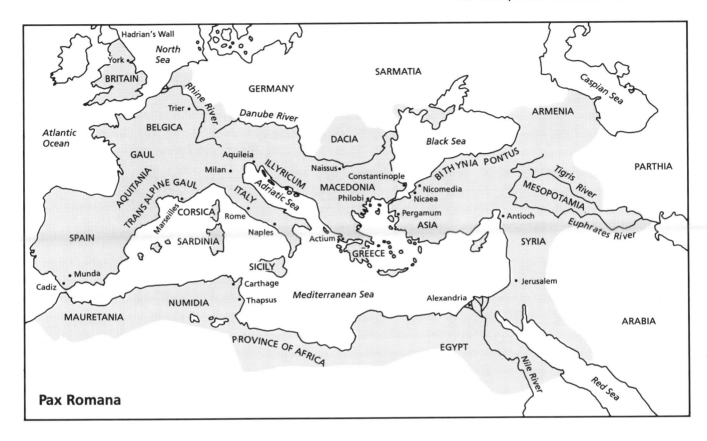

Pax Romana

Rome the Splendid City

The expansion of Rome throughout the Mediterranean produced new markets and opportunities for trade that improved the standard of living throughout the Empire. The Egyptian city of Alexandria became a centre of Hellenistic grandeur with its emphasis on large structures such as the 120-m-high Pharos lighthouse and the great library. Antioch, on the Phoenician coast, was almost as striking. The focal point and most-valued jewel of the Empire, however, was the city of Rome itself. Nowhere were the material achievements so lavishly displayed on such a magnificent scale.

Concrete construction was the major technological breakthrough that produced interlocking domes and vaults that were unsurpassed until the use of the steel beam in the nineteenth century. A wooden shell, framed by scaffolding, was used to give shape to the domes and arches of public baths and temples. Such splendour created a permanent atmosphere of awe and celebration for those who lived in the city as well as for visitors from the far reaches of the Empire. The sheer magnitude of the setting was a wonder in itself. It included

THE GRANDEUR OF ROME

This Roman bath in Bath, England is evidence of the far-reaching influence of Roman activity throughout the Empire.

2 circuses, 2 amphitheatres, 5 lakes, 4 gladitorial schools, 11 imperial baths, 926 private baths, 2000 fountains, 18 squares and forums, 38 parks and public gardens, 290 warehouses, 700 public pools and basins, 36 marble arches, and 37 monumental gates! The almost universal presence of statues decorated every conceivable meeting location, if a fourth-century inventory list of ten thousand figures in stone and bronze is to be believed. Although major building had started before and continued after Augustus's reign, the usually humble Augustus claimed to have converted Rome from a city of brick to a city of marble.

THE ROMAN BATHS

As physical and social institutions, the Roman public baths were unique. Constructed during the reign of third-century Emperor Caracalla, the baths were fed from a 100 000 000-l cistern of water and would accommodate sixteen hundred bathers on a 12-ha site. Those of fourth-century Emperor Diocletian were even larger, holding two thousand bathers comfortably. Beneath spacious domes over 30 m in diameter, brilliant glass mosaics hung on multi-coloured marble walls. Bathers could admire this extravagant interior as hot water poured through the silvered mouths of statues and troughs into the sunken baths of the *calidarium*. The baths also provided lukewarm showers in the *tepidarium*, and cold water in the *frigidarium*. Women and men bathed in separate baths.

Although the baths were the only places where many Romans could get clean, they also provided reading facilities, lounges, and art galleries that bordered parks with manicured groves, gardens, and statues. Recreation was encouraged in areas reserved for the athletic events adopted from the Greeks, such as wrestling, discus and javelin throwing, and boxing. Heat circulated under the floors of the entire complex to the bathing areas from underground chambers

The Palatine Hill, seen here across the Roman forum, was the home of the wealthiest Roman citizens.

called **hypocausts** where hot air was trapped from furnaces that were continually stoked. For about a quarter of a cent, even the lowliest slave could gain admittance.

Bathing took place between the sixth and ninth hour after sunrise, during which time all other activity ceased. The closing hour was shouted aloud by a slave who used a water clock as a guide. By this time, most Romans were ready for their evening meal.

Dinner was the most elaborate meal for all Romans, often lasting for hours, but the food for the average citizen was not much different from what it is today. Only a few of the wealthy patricians gave the Romans their reputation for gluttony. Here, the more exotic and rare the dish was, the more desirable it became and a multicourse dinner might include tongues of parrots that had been taught to speak, mackerel livers, pheasant and peacock brains, and lamprey milk. Lucullus, a contemporary of Caesar, seldom paid less than the modern equivalent of $5000 for a dinner party and would send a fleet out to search the Mediterranean for the precious ingredients in such a meal. Special delights for the common people, who ate pork but little beef, were guinea pigs and dormice. Although the quality of the wine varied, it was usually diluted with water and almost never taken straight.

During dinner, those with status reclined on couches, believing that to dine sitting up was not good for one's constitution. Knives and spoons were used but not forks, and much of the food was picked up with the fingers. Washing as the meal progressed was common practice. It was a Roman custom to express appreciation by belching.

Moments in Time

Six vestal virgins were selected by the Pontifex Maximus, the high priest in the Roman religion, to maintain a continuous watch over the round temple of Vesta in the Roman forum. Vesta was the goddess of the hearth and her shrine was symbolic of the safety of the city. The vestals were vowed to thirty years of chastity and service including the annual renewal of the sacred flame and the preparation of the sacrifices. Any vestal who broke her vow was buried alive.

Samnite

Gaul

Thracian

The Spectacle of Entertainment

Nearly every day of the year had a public or private significance for Roman citizens. Many ancient festivals were carefully observed, and new festivals were added to celebrate military victories, birthdays, and historical events throughout the history of the Empire. In the late Republic, politicians who wanted to increase their popularity often sponsored ruthless spectacles. Bizarre combinations of animals, such as a rhinoceros and a bull, were often pitted against each other.

Occasionally, humans were tied to stakes or set free in artificial landscapes of groves and brooks populated by lions and other wild beasts. Onlookers made bets as to how long the people would last, while tokens for door prizes and lunch were dispersed throughout the crowd. To celebrate the one thousandth anniversary of Rome's legendary founding by Romulus, thirty-two elephants, ten tigers, sixty lions, thirty leopards, ten hyenas, and six hippos were killed. Following Emperor Trajan's triumph over the Dacians, a festival lasting 123 days had combats staged involving eleven thousand animals and ten thousand gladiators. Emperor Hadrian so loved this kind of activity that he stepped into the arena himself and killed a lion with his bare hands. Another emperor, Commodus, often boasted that he had personally defeated one thousand gladiators!

Gladiators

The Roman practice of human combat was adopted from the Etruscans, who had often forced Roman prisoners of war to fight to the death to please the spirits of the underworld. Rome, however, used the gladitorial games to entertain the underemployed city masses. The earliest official gladitorial games staged by Rome were held in 105 B.C., and they quickly became an essential element in public celebration.

Gladiators were recruited from slaves and prisoners of war, sources that seemed inexhaustible as Rome expanded its Empire through military conquest. The men were taken to training grounds known as "schools" where they were treated harshly in preparation for their battles in the arenas of the Empire.

Originally, gladiators, which means swordsmen, were named according to their equipment which, in turn, was associated with their home countries. The lightly armed **Thracian** had a sword, helmet, round shield, and curved dagger; the **Gaul** had a sword and shield but was easily recognized by the image of a sea creature on the helmet; while the heavily armoured **Samnite** fought with a large, rectangular shield and axe. These three types were pursuers who were always on the attack and were often matched against the net-fighter who used a trident, shoulder guard, and net to capture his foe and ready him for the kill. Other gladiators were specialists such as boxers, archers, horsemen, and the well-trained *bestiarii*, who fought only in the wild beast hunts.

Although gladiators usually fought to the death, a man could be spared if he distinguished himself in battle. A fallen gladiator asked for mercy by throwing away his shield and raising a finger on his left hand. If the emperor approved, or, in his absence, the crowd or the opponent, the beaten gladiator might walk away. A down-turned thumb meant immediate execution. Gladiators who won many victories often became heroes worshipped by the adoring crowds much as modern athletes are praised today. A gladiator of such recognition could be presented with a wooden sword, an honour that gave him freedom if he was a slave and, if already free, retirement from the arena.

The Colosseum

The most famous setting for the Roman spectacles was the Flavian Amphitheatre, more popularly known as the Colosseum. It is not known how the more popular name originated. It may have been in reference to the structure's gigantic size or the 30-m statue or **Colossus** of Nero as the sungod, which stood nearby until the fourth century A.D. The elliptical-shaped stadium was clearly built to impress all onlookers. It consisted of three floors built with arches adorned by half columns of Doric, Ionic, and Corinthian orders and a fourth floor with rectangular windows framed with pilasters and topped with Corinthian capitals. On the first three levels there were eighty arched passageways; those on the first floor were numbered so that spectators could quickly reach the seating area accorded their social rank. The arches on the second and third levels were originally decorated with statues. The first four passageways were reserved for processions and the entrance of the emperor who, along with the senators, vestal virgins, and top civil servants, sat in special seats on the imperial podium in the front rows. This gave them the best view of the almost-daily blood bath of public entertainment. Each of the lower classes sat in progressively higher tiers as the importance of their rank decreased.

ORIGIN OF THE NAME

The arena itself consisted of a surface area of wooden boards covered with sand that measured about 80 m long and 50 m wide. At the long ends of the arena there were two passageways, the first of which was used by the gladiators as they were paraded in front of the emperor to give the address, *Caesar, Morituri te salutant*! (Caesar, those about to die salute you!) Dead gladiators and wild beasts were removed through the other passage. Below the floor of the arena was a maze of cages that held the animals about to be used in the show. They were raised to the floor level by mechanical elevators powered by beasts of burden. It was even possible to flood the entire surface to reenact naval battles with gladiators in marine costume fighting to the death on swaying decks.

THE ARENA

To protect the crowd from the burning sun, a canopy called a *velarium* was raised manually by sailors of the Imperial Fleet of Miseum. A complicated series of cables, pulleys, and winches anchored on stones that surrounded the Colosseum required about one thousand men to work in unison to complete the task. With the action of the wind passing under the canopy, and the roar of nearly fifty thousand spectators and wild animals, the noise must have been deafening.

THE VELARIUM

The model (above) is how the Colosseum probably looked at the height of the empire, and (right) as it appears today. Notice the three layers of stone rings supported by the arches and vaults. Passage through these went in two directions: one was around each of the three eliptical rings; the other crossed the rings towards the centre of the arena.

CHARIOT RACES

Much of the Colosseum was built with travertine stone (limestone) shaped into blocks that were held together with iron pins rather than mortar. Later generations in history dismantled and removed large portions of the amphitheatre, and earthquake damage was considerable, but it remains an impressive structure even today.

The Circus Maximus

Rivalling the Colosseum in popularity was the Circus Maximus, one of four major stadiums used for chariot races about two hundred forty days a year. Under Augustus, about twelve races a day were held; under Caligula, as many as thirty-four. Emperor Domitian changed the standard seven-lap (8-km) race to five laps so that a hundred races could be run each day. Charioteers were not just able racers, they had to balance and jump from one horse to the other, stand on a horse's back and pick up a cloth from the ground at full gallop. The risk of an accident was so great that most died at an early age: Fuscus was killed after fifty-seven victories at age twenty-four; Crescens was fatally injured at twenty-two after winning 1.5 million sesterces (about $300 000). The successful drivers, like the gladiators of the arena, became the idols of the mob. A second-century charioteer named Diocles retired after winning 3000 races with two-horse chariots and 1450 races with four-horse chariots, earning 35 million sesterces in the process. The most famous stables were the Reds, the Whites, the Greens, and the Blues, each of which had its own trainers and financial supporters who made great profits on the races. Emperor Caligula became such an avid supporter of the Greens that he once had the horses and charioteers of the Blues poisoned. Vitellius was such a fan of the Blues that he had men executed for shouting "Down with the Blues!" Nero even wore green to the circus and

This is the floor of the Colosseum as it appears today. These cages, which housed the animals destined for the arena, were hidden by the floorboards in Roman times.

on at least one occasion had the entire floor covered with green copper-oxide dust.

The Circus Maximus was of ancient origin, dating back to the early days of the Republic, and reached truly overwhelming size by the third century B.C. Measuring 600 m long and 200 m wide, each side had three tiers of seats, the first of which was made of stone, the others of wood. About two hundred fifty thousand people could cheer their favourite stable to victory as chariots wheeled around the *spina* that divided the race-track with a central line of statues, obelisks, and lap counters. On special occasions, such as the triumph of the third-century emperor Probas over the Germans, the Circus Maximus was transformed into a forest filled with game—one thousand ostriches, one thousand wild boars, one thousand stags, and one thousand sheep. The spectators were then allowed to rush in to capture or kill whatever they could grab. It took an army of game hunters working full-time to keep all the arenas of the Empire supplied with animals. They were so efficient that elephants vanished from Libya, lions from Thessaly, and hippos from the lower Nile.

Roman Theatre

The most popular, nonviolent form of public entertainment enjoyed by the Romans were the plays performed in the theatre. Borrowed and modified from the Greek original, the Roman theatre consisted of a D-shaped orchestra at floor level surrounded by an auditorium of seats that faced a stage and stage wall at the end. The Romans reduced the size of the orchestra but enlarged the size of the

Little remains of this roman theatre discovered during the excavations of the lost city of Pompeii.

stage buildings, reaching a peak in the Roman theatre at Orange, France, which has a stage wall 103 m long and 38 m high. In Rome, the only remaining theatre is the twelve-thousand-seat Theatre of Marcellus, although the Theatre of Pompey, which has not survived, had a capacity of forty thousand.

The open-air setting in which either tragedies or comedies were performed had characters that were easily identified by special masks and costumes. The actors and the play were aided by revolving screens of painted scenery, cranes that could raise the blessed from earth to heaven, and trap doors for a quick exit. If the performance was dull, however, the audience whistled and hissed just as they might today and, if the play was really bad, they threw apples!

Behind the Grandeur

ROMAN SLUMS

The facade of continuous entertainment, opulent wealth, and architectural beauty could not hide the existence of some of the worst slums known to history. Almost forty-seven thousand tenements divided into small, poorly vented cubicles provided the cramped living space for the bulk of Rome's population. Although water abounded in public baths, pressure from the aqueducts provided water for only the first floor of an apartment building, which meant that water had to be carried up flight after flight as high as seven stories. Construction was so shoddy that walls were too flimsy for the weight that they had to support. Most rooms were foul smelling, rodent infested, and filthy. Fires broke out continually since all cooking was done with small charcoal braziers that were constant dangers in wood-framed structures.

On 24 August, A.D. 79, Mount Vesuvius (shown in the background) exploded sending up a black cloud of pumice and lava fragments. The city of Pompeii, seen here, was soon buried under 3 to 5 m of volcanic ash. Pompeii was rediscovered by chance at the end of the sixteenth century.

The forums of Rome were all drained by an impressive network of sewers that equalled other engineering achievements in scale, but nothing was done for the slums. Without toilets, people either walked to public latrines or used small sewage tanks that were picked up by night-soil merchants for sale to truck farmers. If laziness prevailed, slop was dumped into the narrow, crowded streets, which often had small sewage trenches running down the middle. The smell was rivalled only by that of the garbage pits that ringed the city, which were used not only for refuse but also for the disposal of animal and human carcasses from the arena.

For many needy Romans, the streets were the only place to sleep when rent money was not available. Most streets in Rome were no more than alleyways and few were wide enough for carts to pass each other. To reduce the never-ending traffic jams of carts and people, Julius Caesar banned vehicles from the city centre until dark unless they were needed to shore up sagging buildings. After dark, the noise of wagon wheels exceeded that of the great baths during the afternoon. Without street lighting and with few night watchmen, murderers and thieves threatened any who ventured alone.

Changes in the Empire: Slavery and the Stoics

Although the Empire reached its maximum extent in the second century, Rome under the emperors fought fewer wars of aggression and became more concerned about preserving the gains that had already been made. This reduced the slave supply for the slave-based economy, however, and as the labour supply became scarce, it also became more valuable. The result was a more humane

Over the centuries, the bodies of those buried beneath volcanic ash in Pompeii decayed, leaving a space that outlined their exact shape at the moment of death. By pouring plaster into the space, excavators were able to create casts of the former occupants. This twisted body suggests the agony this dog must have experienced trying to escape.

The Roman Calendar
Month

Martius–Mars, god of agriculture

Aprilis–the goddess of sprouting

Maiius–Maia ("increase")

Junius–Juno ("thriving")

Quinctilis–fifth month

Sextilis–sixth month

Septembrus–seventh month

Octobrus–eighth month

Novembrus–ninth month

Decembrus–tenth month

Januarius–Janus

Februarius–Februa ("fever")

The early purpose of the calendar was to list the many festivals. There were twelve lunar months in a year of 355 days. The month was divided into three parts by the **Nones** (the fifth or seventh day of the month) and the **Ides** (the thirteenth or fifteenth day).

JESUS

treatment of slaves, who were now kept working only by promises of freedom after a certain number of years of service. Many slaves thus were freed, much to the resentment of the Roman population.

More humane attitudes towards slavery may also have been shaped by two new forces within the Empire, the first of which was the impact of the Greek philosophy of **Stoicism**, imported to Rome as early as the second century B.C. Stoics stressed that happiness was in accepting one's fate since this was the result of the laws of nature that operated under God's direction. What was important was the way the individual responded to his or her situation. All people possessed the spark of God within them and as members with a universal bond, equal respect was implied in human relations. The second force that may have influenced attitudes towards slavery was a new religion–Christianity.

Changes in the Empire: Cults, Christ, and Christianity

After some hostility during the Republic, Rome became very tolerant of foreign religions and, for largely practical reasons, willingly accepted foreign deities. Indeed, the first two centuries A.D. were dominated by the spread of oriental cults, such as those of Cybele and Bacchus, and the Egyptian cult of Isis. Perhaps the most influential was the cult of Mithras, which came to Rome from Persia and was spread by the contact of oriental slaves in seaports and by Roman soldiers to the outposts of the Empire. Even as late as the reign of Emperor Diocletian (third century A.D.) armies fought under the banner of the Invincible Sungod associated with Mithras because the god was so popular among the soldiers. This religious toleration helped in the successful administration of the outlying provinces of the Empire. In return for religious freedom, the locals were expected to respect Roman gods in a Roman setting.

Rome had been less tolerant, however, of Jews and their religion of Judaism. As detailed in the Old Testament of the Bible, the Jews had a long history of struggle that dated to the era of Abraham and Moses. Their unwavering faith in one God whose word would be revealed by enlightened prophets, had enabled the Jewish people to maintain a solidarity that brought them through the darkest hours of oppression. Spread throughout the commercial and trading cities of the Roman Empire and eastern Asia, the Jews looked forward to the arrival of a Messiah, or king, who would deliver them from hardship and establish God's rule on earth.

During the reign of Tiberius, a Jew named Jesus of Nazareth emerged as a popular leader because of his dramatic sermons in the countryside of Judea. His teaching is now so familiar that it is easy to overlook the fact that it was one of the most revolutionary doctrines ever to stir the human mind. Jesus focussed on the existence of one God as Father of all people and of the kingdom of Heaven into which all may enter. Many of his earliest converts were Jews who felt that Jesus was the Messiah whose arrival had been prophesied in the Old Testament. Nevertheless, Jews had been bonded together by close family ties and the special promise God made to their patriarch, Abraham, which recog-

Greek and Roman Gods

Greek	Function	Roman
Zeus	king of the gods–father of the sky	Jupiter
Hera	queen of heaven–marriage	Juno
Ares	god of war and agriculture	Mars
Athena	goddess of wisdom, memory, actors–handicrafts	Minerva
Aphrodite	goddess of love	Venus
Artemis	moon goddess–hunting	Diana
Hermes	god of merchants, orators, thieves	Mercury
Heracles	god of joy	Hercules
Demeter	earth goddess	Ceres
Dionysus	god of wine and the grape	Liber
Apollo	health–prophecy	Apollo
Poseidon	god of the sea	Neptune
Hephaestus	god of the forge (vulcanize)	Vulcan
Hades	god of the underworld	Pluto
Hestia	goddess of hearth and household	Vesta

nized them as the chosen people. Jesus' stress on universal entry into the kingdom of Heaven threatened the Jews' unique status in the eyes of God, one which had meant so much for so long. For the Jewish community as a whole, Jesus was not the Messiah. Today, they still patiently wait with steadfast faith for the Messiah's arrival.

The Romans accepted, if not approved, the idea that Judaism was concerned with only one God, and they even allowed Jews to become Roman citizens with special exemption from participating in Roman religious practices. Only after the Jews revolted against their Roman masters between A.D. 66–70 and A.D. 132–135 were many of their privileges either revoked or limited.

As Jesus travelled and preached over a three-year period, however, he stressed in uncompromising terms the moral obligation people had to God. He denounced personal wealth and asserted that service to God's will was the path for anyone–merchant or beggar, man or woman, black or white–who wished to enter the kingdom of Heaven. For Jesus, there were no temples, no altars, no ceremonies; only the word of the preacher and the sermon spreading the word of God.

THE CRUCIFIXION

Jesus' entry into Jerusalem was regarded by the Jews as a potential source of protest against Roman authority. This prompted Jewish priests, with the assistance of Judas (one of Christ's disillusioned disciples), to help the Romans secure the arrest of Jesus. He was charged with attempting to set up a new kingdom in Judea, tried, convicted, and reluctantly sentenced by the Roman procurator, Pontius Pilate, in A.D. 30. The crucifixion ended the story of Jesus. Reports of his resurrection inspired the emergence of the Christians.

PAUL

One of the greatest of the early Christian teachers was Saul of Tarsus, a man who was not a disciple and had never met Jesus. Saul was a Jew who was educated in Greek and who was a Roman citizen. On the road to Damascus in A.D. 35, Saul experienced a dramatic conversion to Christianity. Thereafter he changed his name to Paul and travelled to the major cities of Asia, Syria, Greece, Macedonia, as well as to the capitals of Alexandria and Rome and established Christian cells in all places. His dedicated journey would be difficult to duplicate even today. Of equal importance was the disciple Peter who also travelled the eastern Mediterranean as an Apostle spreading the word of God. Christianity, in the thirty years that followed the crucifixion received little opposition in Rome, and even in the harshest times Christians were protected by Roman law. When Paul (who along with Peter founded the Christian diocese of Rome) faced charges of misdeeds by Jewish leaders in Palestine, he appealed to the emperor to assure himself of a fair trial.

PETER

As conditions grew worse in Rome during the first century A.D., however, people became more sensitive about Christian criticism and faith. In contrast to the Jewish community, the Christians possessed intense missionary zeal and repeatedly condemned worldly success. Christians not only refused to recognize and sacrifice to Roman gods and deified emperors, but insisted their God was the only God. A misunderstanding of the Communion service held in secret meetings at night even brought charges of cannibalism against them. Under Emperor Nero, Christians were used as scapegoats for the great fire that ravaged Rome, and both Paul and Peter were executed in the immediate aftermath of persecution that followed in A.D. 64. By A.D. 100, a confessed Christian could legally be put to death. Despite the harsh treatment and later mass executions under the emperor Decius in A.D. 250, and then Diocletian in A.D. 303, Christianity spread throughout the Empire. In A.D. 313, Emperor Constantine expanded an earlier edict of toleration to grant Christianity an equal status with other religions. On his deathbed, Constantine was baptized a Christian. Later in the fourth century A.D., the emperor Theodosius made Christianity the official religion of the state and declared pagan worship illegal.

THE SPREAD OF CHRISTIANITY

REASONS FOR SUCCESS

Why was Christianity so successful? Ironically, the widespread distribution of Christianity accomplished by the early Apostles was made possible by the general political and military stability of the Roman Empire, with the roads it maintained and the sea lanes it protected. The use of Greek as a universal language of culture and business, particularly in the east, had survived since the days of Alexander and was the language that preserved most of the Gospels of the New Testament.

Above and beyond the unflinching faith of the early Christians, part of the answer lies in the living conditions of the Roman Empire. It should be stressed that Christianity was in competition for converts with several pagan cults, and that Christianity became a sizeable minority only in the third century A.D. The average Roman did not share in the wealth suggested by magnificent architecture, and the daily hardship of economic survival led many to seek answers in any religion that promised a better life. Christianity won out over pagan cults because it offered a simple and clear message that would benefit the lot of any slave or plebian no matter how lowly his or her plight. Where the powerful in Rome saw unbending faith to the Christian God as a threat to their social status and control, the people saw possible rewards of life after death and an equality for all that was denied on earth. Jesus had been a real person rather than a mythical figure of pagan legend, and as more and more martyrs sacrificed their lives with faith unshaken in times of persecution, the Christian cause grew in appeal.

Roman emperors were always willing to embrace a religion that promised to increase their popularity with and power over the common people. Believing that the sungod had helped him secure military victory, Aurelian established a state for Sol Invictus in A.D. 274 and a festival to mark the birth of the sun on 25 December. The Christians later used the date to celebrate the birth of Jesus. Similarly, while Christians separated themselves from the Jewish Sabbath of Saturday, the Christian Sabbath honoured the Sun-day familiar to the many followers of the cult of Mithras. Indeed, the worship of Mithras involved the burning of candles in front of an altar, a practice that resembled ceremonies that gradually appeared in the Christian Church. The Isis religion dramatized the Finding of Osiris in a November celebration. This event told a story of death and resurrection that, to the uneducated pagan, was much like the central event in the life of Jesus. Diocletian continued to march with the banner of the sungod on his soldiers' shields. Constantine, however, apparently saw a cross in the sky while he was praying to the sun and a later dream confirmed to him that this was a sign from the Christian God. Constantine's approval of Christianity was supported by the knowledge that earlier persecution had not prevented the rapid spread of the religion and that such an organized force might help to preserve unity throughout the Empire.

The progress of Church organization at a time when the political and military state of Rome began to decay also contributed to Christian success. During the second and third centuries, the clerical orders of deacon, priest, and bishop were created, and in A.D. 325, Constantine called the First General Council of the Christian world at Nicaea. The council attempted to standardize Christian beliefs and practices and gave to history the form of the Church that is known today. For the Christian, the teachings of Jesus became embod-

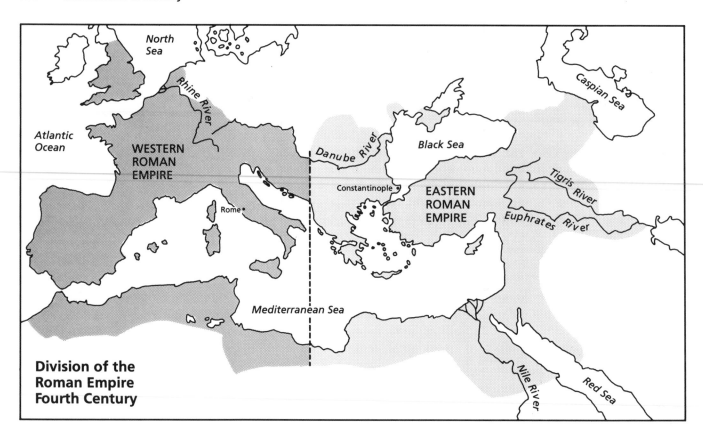

Division of the Roman Empire Fourth Century

ied in the purpose and ritual of services far more elaborate than anything practised by Jesus himself. For the pagan, a tradition of religious trappings in many
cult practices made the observable rituals of Christianity more familiar and thus
more readily acceptable.

Decline of the Western Empire

While Rome basked in the glory and stability of the *Pax Romana*, it seemed as if
the Empire would last indefinitely. The changes that occurred in the three centuries that followed have been referred to as the decline of Rome, although
there is no specific event that signalled this demise for a Roman of the time.
This decline, however, was not universal. Ruling the vast Empire had become
so awkward that Diocletian (A.D. 285–305) divided the Empire into two sections ruled by coemperors, an administrative change that was completed under
Constantine (A.D. 312–337). The Western Empire, with Latin as a language
and Roman Catholicism as the major religious force, was administered from
Rome; the Eastern Empire, with Greek as the language and the Greek Orthodox Church as the major religious force, was administered from Constantino-

ADMINISTRATIVE CHANGE IN THE
EMPIRE

Decline of Rome

A.D.

270   Emperor Aurelian builds a new wall around the city of Rome as protection against barbarian attack

303   Diocletian intensifies persecution of Christians
Diocletian divides Empire into Eastern and Western sections as his governmental reforms seek to control almost every aspect of Roman life

313   Constantine grants toleration to Christianity

325   Universal Church Council of Nicaea

330   Constantine makes Constantinople the new capital in the Eastern Empire

378   Barbarians defeat Romans at Adrianople

380   Christianity becomes the official religion of the Empire

395   Roman Empire permanently divided into East and West

410   Rome sacked by Visigoths
Saint Augustine writes *City of God* in defence of charges that Christianity was responsible for the decline of the Empire

451   Attila the Hun is defeated by a combined force of Romans and barbarians at Troyes

455   Rome sacked by Vandals

476   End of the Western Empire
The German barbarian, Odoacer, deposes line of Roman emperors in the West

ple. When historians speak of the decline or fall of Rome, it is the Western Empire to which they refer; the Eastern Empire survived as a civilizing force until the fall of Constantinople to the Turks in 1453.

What is clear about the fate of the Western Empire is that it gradually lost control of more and more territory to tribes of Germanic people identified by Romans and known to history as barbarians. In the third century, the Franks pushed westwards across the Lower Rhine into Gaul while the Alamanni moved into Alsace. The Eastern Empire was threatened by the Goths who moved out of southern Russia and crossed the Danube in search of plunder. Initially, these raids were checked or pushed back by Roman legions, but the insecurity they created was reflected in the massive walls built under the direction of Aurelian (A.D. 270–275) to fortify the open city of Rome. During the fourth century,

GERMANIC TRIBES

ADRIANOPLE

THE HUNS

ODOACER

the barbarians themselves were threatened by an even more warlike people, the Huns, who broke out of central Asia and subjected several German tribes to their harsh rule.

Germanic people fled to and settled on Roman land in Gaul and in what is now Bulgaria to escape the threat posed by the Huns. The barbarians living within the frontiers of the Empire quickly tired of Roman rule and they rebelled. A major victory over Rome at Adrianople in A.D. 378 opened the way for barbarian infiltration and eventual domination of large parts of the Empire. The West Goths, known as Visigoths, swarmed into Greece and, led by their king, Alaric, sacked Rome in A.D. 410. They continued their march into southern Gaul and Spain. Similarly, the Vandals pushed outward from Hungary into central Gaul, Spain, and the north shore of Africa. Under the leadership of Clovis, the Franks established a kingdom in northern Gaul while the Angles, Saxons, and Jutes invaded Britain.

Perhaps the greatest military threat to Roman security came from the Huns. These powerful barbarians had originally turned westward because their expansion in Asia was halted by the Chinese. As they swept into Europe, terrorizing and brutalizing the Germanic barbarians with unrivalled fury, the latter were forced into increasing their contact and then conflict with the Roman Empire. By the middle of the fifth century, the Huns, led by the stocky, swarthy-skinned Attila, had established control over several Germanic peoples, and in A.D. 451 declared war on the Western Roman Empire. The Hun threat was so severe that the Franks and Visigoths joined the Roman forces and defeated Attila's army at Troyes where over one hundred fifty thousand men were killed in one of history's bloodiest battles. The Huns continued to plunder southern Europe until Attila's mysterious death in A.D. 453, after which they disappeared as a distinct group.

The German barbarian Odoacer deposed the historic line of emperors in Rome in A.D. 476, a date that later became the traditional reference for the end of the Western Empire. What caused the Western Empire to topple from its former position of dominance? The lapse of the once-formidable military defences that could not prevent the penetration of foreign barbarians suggests that the quality of the Roman army should be examined. Historians agree that several factors relating to almost every aspect of Roman life played a part in the general decline. Any such explanation, however, must account for the fact that the Eastern Empire survived its Western counterpart for almost a thousand years. Was the decline of the Western Empire inevitable or did it fall victim to an unusual series of events which could have been changed in a way that preserved, rather than ended, an age of accomplishment?

PROBLEM QUESTION

Why did the Western Roman Empire falter after providing centuries of strong political and military leadership and a relatively stable economic and social organization?

ALTERNATIVE ONE

The Roman Army—Based on "The Roman Army and the Disintegration of the Empire" by E. Togo Salmon, 1963

In its heyday throughout the 1st and 2nd centuries A.D., the Roman army was a magnificent instrument of power. It met all the basic requirements for a first class fighting force: the soldiers were well trained and the system of command was well organized. Yet gradually the personnel composing this incomparable force ceased to be respectable elements of the Empire's population. As time went on, the army became so barbarized that, by the 5th century A.D., the defense of the Empire was quite literally in the hands of the Germans. Why and how this happened to the Roman state is an important question relating to the decline and fall of Rome.

The Roman state, under the Republic and the Empire, had the right to draft or conscript its subjects, citizens or others, for military service, and in time of war this approach was occasionally used. But short-service conscripts were not the answer for the defence of the Empire. Without the assistance of railways, the conscripts would have spent most of their time travelling to outlying trouble-spots rather than in training. Their combat efficiency would not have been very high. The Roman army became, for the most part, an army of volunteers even though the normal length of service until the 3rd century A.D. was twenty-five years! Although small by modern standards, the Roman army was enormous in size for the time: in the 1st and 2nd centuries it consisted of about 300,000 including legionaries and auxiliaries. Such an army needed an annual intake of about 30,000 new soldiers to maintain it.

The hard life of a soldier and low pay offered little reason to volunteer, moreover, those born into Roman citizenship felt it was their right to escape military service. The average Roman citizen was deliberately discouraged from taking any interest or participating in public affairs. It was the emperor who decided everything. With no universal state education and no popular press, information about imperial policies was never dispersed in a systematic fashion. A Roman citizen felt that he belonged to an invincible empire and that he was expected to leave its administration to others. If he was not needed to run the Empire, then it also seemed that he was not needed to defend it. Thus, the Roman army was not likely to be kept up to strength by volunteers amongst the Roman citizens. Citizens of the better classes enlisted only if their background encouraged confidence of promotion to a high rank.

The standing Roman army from the days of its founder, Augustus, included many non-Italians from the provinces of the Empire. By the 2nd century A.D. their numbers were overwhelming. The big inducement was Roman citizenship and the advantages it offered. Roman citizenship improved social standing and opened more doors for the soldier and his family. All provincials–those who lived outside of Italy but within a province of the Empire–were eager to acquire it and there was virtually only one way to get it: service in the Roman army. If provincials served in the legions, they obtained citizenship the moment they enlisted. But usually recruits for the legions were taken only from those living in an organized town, a setting that officials felt provided the best environment for the Roman spirit and civilization. If the volunteer served in the auxiliaries, he obtained citizenship twenty-five years later, upon his release from service. Usually, he had been a country-dweller who, in Roman eyes, was far from civilized and needed more exposure to Roman ways and outlook. Thus a highly urbanized region like Greece provided legionaries and no auxiliaries, while in the rural Gallic provinces the pattern was reversed.

Certainly the army would not have remained at full strength if it had depended on those who already possessed Roman citizenship. By A.D. 100, serious attempts to find legionaries in Italy were abandoned. Unfortunately, the more widespread Roman citizenship became, the more restricted was the area from which recruits were likely to be obtained since Roman citizens, as we have seen, were reluctant to serve. Thus, the quality of the soldier enlisting was reduced to the lowest elements in society since many in the better classes already had citizenship by the 2nd century.

A critical decision was made by Emperor Caracalla in A.D. 212 that proved disastrous for the army. In that year, Caracalla enfranchised all of the free-born inhabitants of the Empire regardless of their race, origin, creed, or mother tongue. Whatever Caracalla's motives, one effect was to eliminate what had been a prime reason for men to enlist. Thus, it eventually became necessary to go outside the Empire to search for soldiers as the number of volunteers quickly dropped off; and so did their quality.

After A.D. 212 the army was often at odds with civilians. The Roman army, like any other, had always contained a few adventurous roughnecks and even criminals in its ranks. But so long as the prospect of acquiring Roman citizenship had spurred men of a different stamp to enlist, it had not got out of hand. In the 3rd century, however, it became quite uncontrollable. It kindled an unending series of civil wars, it spawned a well-nigh inexhaustible list of pretenders, it made and unmade emperors with almost reckless abandon and greedily extorted from the civilian population whatever it could.

It would not have been easy in any case to maintain the army at full strength in the Western Empire because the population was beginning to decline. Changed conditions of warfare also made recruiting more difficult. As cavalry came to play an ever more important role, the wild cowboys of the frontier would be more in demand. But probably it was not so much the decline in population or the need for skilled riders as the universal grant of citizenship that was responsible for the deterioration in army personnel. Men of the better type no longer had any reason to volunteer.

With citizenship no longer available as a bribe, various devices were used to attract recruits: increased pay, free rations, a more frequent share of the booty from battle, and the right to legal wedlock. But it was all to no avail: none of these makeshifts improved the calibre of the troops. During the 3rd century, the men who fought for Rome knew little and cared less about Rome's mission and, when not preying upon the civilians, had not the slightest hesitation about preying upon one another.

It was the chaos caused by these unruly soldiers which provided the barbarians beyond the frontiers with their chance and they quickly seized it. The assaults of these barbarian hordes led directly to the most obvious, if not the most important, of all the causes for the decline and fall: military collapse. An Empire whose defenders were few in quantity and poor in quality must have been tempting bait to the outer barbarians. Small wonder is it that they fell upon the Empire and thereby set in motion that fateful sequence of events which resulted finally in its disintegration.

Questions

1. Describe the quality of the Roman army during the first two centuries A.D.
2. Why did the Romans usually rely on volunteers to keep a full complement of three hundred thousand men?
3. Why did the average Roman citizen *not* volunteer for military service?
4. How were people living in the provinces of the Empire encouraged to join the Roman army?
5. a) What was the critical decision that reduced the overall calibre of the Roman army?
   b) What were the effects of this decision during the third century?
6. What other factors also reduced the effectiveness of the Roman army after the second century?
7. How did the barbarians react to Roman weakness?

ALTERNATIVE TWO

Decline and Fall–Based on *The Civilization of Rome* by Donald R. Dudley, 1962

Our own times understand technology, if nothing else, and there were certainly grave weaknesses in the technology of the Roman Empire. Judged by modern standards, there was little general advance in the five centuries after

Rome had taken over the technology of the Hellenistic world. Large-scale exploitation, not advances in technique, were the strong point of the Romans. No doubt this stagnation can be partly explained by the influence of slavery. By providing a cheap and expendable supply of human labor, slavery discourages invention, which tends to replace human labor by the machine. In all periods of history slavery has affected enterprise and efficiency as deeply as it has morals and humanity. And yet slavery cannot be the whole answer. The number of slaves in the Roman world declined after the great wars of conquest under the Republic. There were no more slave markets on the scale of Delos in the Aegean. The early Empire is marked by the increased use of free rather than slave labor. This, and the economic boom of the period, should have provided conditions to suit the inventor. But there was no large-scale advance—certainly nothing to equal even the earliest phases of the Industrial Revolution. It is not enough to ascribe this to the Roman bent for the practical and dislike of theory. Some of the inventions that would have been of most benefit to the Roman world were precisely those which might have been expected from men of practical skill. Why did none of the thousands of Roman teamsters invent a harness that would not half-strangle a draft animal by pulling on its windpipe? Why was there no improvement in the clumsy rigging of Roman ships? Above all, why did no employee of a Roman mint ever take the easy step from stamping to printing—a discovery which would have been of incalculable importance to the spread of knowledge? There is something here as hard to explain as the failure of Peruvian civilization to invent the wheel.

Partly, no doubt, this failure in technology is bound up with the failure in education. Despite the patronage of the emperors and the eagerness of the municipalities to found and maintain schools, education under the Empire was neither sufficiently wide nor sufficiently deep. It was certainly a grave weakness that natural science and practical subjects were neglected, but it is not enough to say that the Romans were satisfied with a mere literary education. The real weakness was the undue attention paid to rhetoric and this was due to a short-sighted preference for the form of vocational training which seemed to offer the quickest way to success. Roman education produced lawyers, administrators, and teachers of rhetoric. In doing so it gave them considerable powers of expression, some feeling for literature, and the rudiments of an education in morals. But it failed to stimulate intellectual curiosity, and it added nothing to knowledge.

More obvious are certain political and military weaknesses. The failure to establish a lasting and generally accepted basis for the succession of emperors stands out. Had the hereditary principle been accepted, it would no doubt have produced many weak or vicious emperors. But it would have been a principle that all could understand, and usurpers would have been seen for what they were. Had the principle of adoption been accepted for the succession of emperors, palace intrigues rather than arms of the battlefield would more likely have settled the issue. But the Romans did not consistently follow either system, and so often got the worst of both worlds. Hereditary succession produced some bad emperors in the first century. A disputed succession, especially after the time of Commodus, led to many struggles which gravely weakened the state, and not only in loss of manpower and material resources. The army became corrupted by the discovery that it was more profitable to plunder the civilized world than to defend it against the barbarians. Little more than a century separates the unruly army of Maximinus Thrace from that of Trajan, but they were poles apart in discipline, morale and fighting spirit.

In any case the system of defense against the barbarian world established by Augustus would only work so long as Rome retained a clear military advantage over her enemies. Things do not stand still on a frontier. The barbarians would become Romanized, at least in the sense that they understood Roman methods of warfare; the barbarians Arminius and Alaric both served in the Roman army. And the Roman army itself became increasingly barbarian in its personnel—even, in the fourth century, in the higher command. Under such circumstances Roman superiority could only have been maintained by greatly superior technical resources such as the use of firearms. It is true that various ballistic devices in the third and fourth centuries gave it a superiority of a kind, but not sufficiently effective to give a decisive margin over the enemy. By the middle of the fourth century an army of Goths, Vandals, or Huns could take the field against the Roman army on at least equal terms. Even at that stage the Empire must have had far superior resources of manpower, but these could not be mobilized and brought into action without increasing the already-staggering burden of taxation.

Crippling taxation was only one of the burdens which the late Empire imposed on its citizens. From the time of Diocletian on it had degenerated into a totalitarian state, controlling and directing all activities in its own interests. The agents of the state were everywhere; its regulations covered every side of life. Frozen into their hereditary occupations, struggling under the twin burdens of taxes and inflation, further harassed by incessant demands for loans, gifts, and labor, exposed to the greed of an army of corrupt officials, the citizens of the late Empire had neither the means nor the motive to better their lot. The emperors of the third and fourth century had no choice but to act as they did if the state was to survive. Their reforms did indeed make survival possible, for a time, but at the terrible price of the destruction of all enterprise and public spirit. The citizen was reduced to a helpless individual to whom the state and its agents were not responsible. The barbarians must often have seemed preferable to the officials of Rome. The excessive demands of the state were, without doubt, the chief cause of the final downfall of the West.

Since these conditions also existed in the East, the question arises as to why there was no such collapse there. It is clear that the main force of the barbarian invasions fell on the West, which had to face the worst assaults of the Goths and the Huns. There are no parallels in the East to the Frankish kingdom in Gaul, and those of the Vandals in Spain and Africa. Above all, the comparative immunity of Asia Minor meant that the East had a reserve of manpower and material resources such as Italy could not afford to the West. From this springboard in the East, Justinian, in the early sixth century, launched the great offensives which offered a brief hope of the restoration of the Empire.

Questions

1. a) Why did the Romans fail to make any major advances in technology?
   b) What inventions might have been of great benefit to the Romans if they had been made?
2. Why did the failure to find an acceptable basis for the succession of emperors cause such a problem for the Roman Empire?
3. Why did the Roman army gradually lose its military superiority over the barbarians?
4. Describe the impact on the Roman Empire of the heavy taxation begun by Diocletian.
5. Why did the Western Empire collapse in the fifth century while the Eastern Empire continued to prosper?

ALTERNATIVE THREE

The Later Roman Empire—Based on *History of the Later Roman Empire* by J.B. Bury, 1923

No general causes can be assigned that made the fall of the Western Empire inevitable. Consider depopulation. The depopulation of Italy was an important factor and it had far-reaching consequences. But it was a process which had probably reached its limit in the time of Augustus. There is no evidence that the Empire was less populous in the fourth and fifth centuries than in the first. The "sterility of the human harvest" in Italy and Greece affected the history of the Empire from its very beginning, but does not explain the collapse in the fifth century.

There are really two distinct questions here which are often confused. It is one thing to seek the causes that *changed* the Roman state from what it was in the Republic to what it had become in the later Empire—a change which may be called a "decline". But it is another thing to ask why the Roman state could resist its enemies on many frontiers in the fourth century under Diocletian and Constantine and then give way a century later in the days of Honorius. "Depopulation" may partly answer the first question, but it is not an answer to the second.

Nor can the events which transferred the greater part of western Europe to German masters be accounted for by the number of peoples who invaded it. The notion of vast hordes of warriors, numbered by hundreds of thousands, pouring over frontiers, is perfectly untrue. The total number of one of the large East German nations probably seldom exceeded 100,000, and its army of fighting men can rarely have been more than from 20,000 to 30,000. They were not a deluge, overwhelming and irresistible, and the Empire had a well-organized military establishment, fully sufficient in capable hands to beat them back. As a matter of fact, since the defeat at Adrianople in A.D. 378 which was due to the blunders of Valens, no very important battle was won by German over Imperial Roman forces during the whole course of the invasions.

It has often been alleged that Christianity in its political effects was a disintegrating force and tended to weaken the power of Rome to resist her enemies. It is difficult to see that it had any such tendency, so long as the Church itself was united. In the political calculations of Constantine, it was probably this ideal of unity that was so appealing. As a result, he raised the Christian religion to power to offset other forces that threatened to break up the Empire. Early in the fifth century, a pagan senator posed the question whether the teaching of Christianity is not fatal to the welfare of the state because a Christian smitten on one cheek would have to turn the other cheek as indicated in the Gospel. In a skilfully written reply, Augustine, a leading Father of the Church, suggested that those who wage a just war are really acting in a spirit of mercy and kindness to their enemies, as it is to the true interests of their enemies that their vices should be corrected. Unintentionally, by stating that the Christian discipline does not condemn all wars, Augustine had argued that Christians were bound as much as pagans to defend Rome against the barbarians. All the leading Churchmen of the fifth century were devoted to the Imperial idea and when they worked for peace or compromise, as they often did, it was always when the cause of the barbarians was in the ascendant and resistance seemed hopeless.

The truth is that the gradual collapse of the Roman Empire in the West was the result of a series of unpredictable or contingent events.

The first such event was the irruption of the Huns into Europe, an event resulting from causes which were quite independent of the weakness or strength of the Roman Empire. It drove the Visigoths into the Illyrian provinces of the Empire and the difficult situation was mismanaged. Emperor Valens lost his life as a result of his own errors when Rome suffered defeat at Adrianople. That disaster, which need not have occurred, was a second unpredictable event. Valens's successor, Theodosius I, allowed the Goths to settle south of the Danube on Roman soil, which set an unfortunate precedent. Barbarians, with Roman consent, were now living within the Empire as well as pressuring Roman resistance from the outside. The premature death of Theodosius could not have been foreseen and would not have mattered if a strong emperor had succeeded to power. The government of the West,

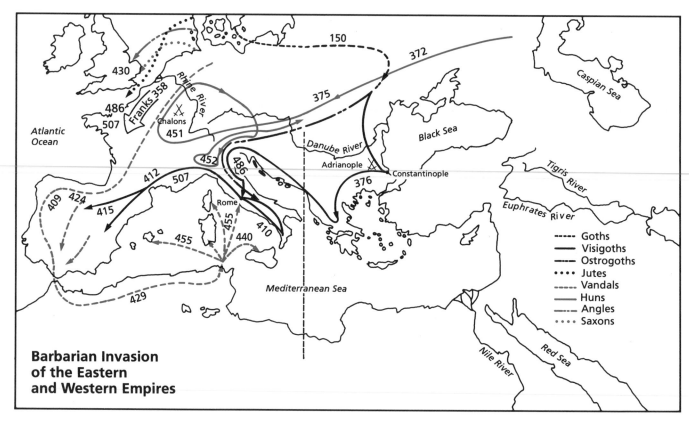

**Barbarian Invasion
of the Eastern
and Western Empires**

Legend:
- – – – Goths
- —— Visigoths
- –··– Ostrogoths
- •••• Jutes
- – – – Vandals
- —— Huns
- –·–·– Angles
- •••• Saxons

however, was inherited by a feeble-minded boy named Honorius. That was a fourth event, dependent on causes which had nothing to do with the conditions within the Empire.

In themselves, even these events need not have led to disaster. If the guardian of Honorius and director of his government had been a man of Roman birth and tradition who commanded the public confidence, all might have been tolerably well. But there was a point of weakness in the Imperial system, the practice of elevating Germans to the highest posts of command in the army. The German in whom Theodosius reposed his confidence and who assumed the control of affairs on his death was a Romanized German named Stilicho. Although Stilicho probably believed that he was serving Rome faithfully, it was a singular misfortune that at a critical moment when the Empire had to be defended not only against Germans from without but against a German nation which had penetrated inside, the responsibility should have devolved upon a German. Stilicho continued the policy of barbarian settlement on Roman land and even allowed Huns to serve as auxiliary troops in the army. Invading tribes freely roamed the countryside and when Stilicho died the Goths had Italy at their mercy while Gaul and Spain were overrun by other peoples. His Roman successors could not undo the results of events which need never have happened.

The supremacy of Stilicho was due to the fact that the defence of the Empire had come to depend on the enrolment of barbarians, in large numbers, in the army and that it was necessary to render the service attractive to them by the prospect of wealth and power. This was, of course, a consequence of the decline in military spirit, and of depopulation, in the old civilised Mediterranean countries. The Germans in high command had been useful, but the dangers of such a policy were becoming apparent. Yet this policy need not have led to the dismemberment of the Empire, and but for that series of chances its western provinces would not have been converted, as and when they were, into German kingdoms. It may be said that a German penetration of western Europe must ultimately have come about. But even if that were certain, it might have happened in another way, at a later time, more gradually, and with less violence. Rome's loss of her provinces in the fifth century was not inevitable and might not have occurred but for the sequence of unpredictable events pointed out above.

From J.B. Bury, *History of the Later Roman Empire* (London, rev. ed., 1923), vol. 1. Reprinted by permission of Macmillan & Co. Ltd.

Questions

1. a) How important were the effects of depopulation and Christianity with regard to the survival of the Western Roman Empire? Explain your answer.
   b) What two distinct questions must be considered when examining the fate of the Western Empire?
2. a) What is meant by Bury's reference to "contingent events"?
   b) What were the six contingent events that Bury identifies in the sequence leading to the collapse of the Western Empire?
3. To what extent does Bury's view of the decline of Rome agree with the explanations given in Alternatives One and Two? Explain your answer.

ANSWERING THE PROBLEM QUESTION

There is rarely a single, isolated answer to a complex question that involves the fate of an entire civilization. Usually there are several factors, operating in combination, that can best explain why things turned out the way they did. This type of analysis, in which causes are identified, related to each other, and ranked on the basis of the evidence presented, is known as **multiple causation**. The causal question through which a reasoned explanation of an issue is developed is the focal point of historical study.

Unfortunately, there is no magic formula which, if carefully applied, will guarantee the right answer to a causal question. For such a formula to work, people would have to be entirely predictable. But human behaviour is not governed by a rigid set of laws. People do not always react in the same way in the same situation. However, there are recognizable patterns that emerge from an evaluation of any historical situation. These can provide a meaningful explanation and understanding of the relevant series of events. This means that conclusions about people and the times that shape their lives are usually phrased in a tentative way because they are based on certain assumptions, rather than in absolute terms that leave no room for additional consideration.

The following guide represents one way to develop an answer to a causal question. While adjustments must always be made in the way any specific issue is studied, a systematic approach will help to organize the major elements of an argument.

Developing an Answer to a Causal Question

1. List all the major events or facts that could be used to evaluate the question.
   In the given question about the fall of the Roman Empire, the events would be identified from the background information and the three alternatives.
2. Classify the events or facts under major headings or criteria such as economic, religious, national, or political.
   In the given question about the fall of the Roman Empire, the criteria are political, military, economic, and social.

Political	Military	Economic	Social
event a	event c	event b	event e
event d	event g	event f	event h
event i	event k	event j	event l
event p	event m	event n	event o
etc.	etc.	etc.	etc.

3. Now, classify the events or facts listed under each criterion by the subheads *long term* and *short term*. Deciding whether an event or a fact is of long-term or short-term importance is a matter of judgement. Usually, long-term considerations are those conditions that existed for most of the time frame under discussion. Short-term considerations are usually those conditions that represent a specific peak or climax in a long-term trend or events that bring an immediate, often unforeseen change in the situation.
   In the given question about the fall of the Roman Empire, the long-term causes would be measured in centuries while the short-term causes would be discussed in decades.
   Your classification chart should look something like this:

	Political	Military	Economic	Social
Long Term	event a	event c	event b	event e
	event i	event m	event f	event l
	etc.	etc.	etc.	etc.

	event d	event k	event j	event h
Short Term	event p	event g	event n	event o
	etc.	etc.	etc.	etc.

4. The next step is to rank each of the events or facts in the order of its importance. Assign a "one" to the most important, a "two" to the second most important, and so on. Rank the long-term group and the short-term group separately under each criterion. Your chart should now look something like this:

		Political	**Military**	**Economic**	**Social**
	1	event a	etc.	event b	event l
Long Term	2	etc.	event m	event f	event e
	3	event i	event c	etc.	etc.
	1	etc.	etc.	event j	event h
Short Term	2	event p	event g	etc.	event o
	3	event d	etc.	etc.	etc.

5. Now, you must decide which of the major headings or criteria is most important, which is second most important, and so on. You must be able to explain your reasons for the order you have selected.

		1 Military	**2 Political**	**3 Economic**	**4 Social**
	1	etc.	event a	event b	event l
Long Term	2	event m	etc.	event f	event e
	3	event c	event i	etc.	etc.
	1	etc.	etc.	event j	event h
Short Term	2	event g	event p	etc.	event o
	3	etc.	event d	etc.	etc.

6. Events and facts do not occur in isolation. They are interrelated. Before you can begin to explain the interrelationships of the events and facts in your chart, arrange the criteria in sequence of importance. Your task now is to determine why a long-term military cause, for example, is more or less important than a short-term economic cause; or why a short-term social cause is more or less important than a long-term political cause, etc. At the same time, you must also consider the relationship between long-term and short-term causes under each criterion.

7. In most cases, a thorough study of the interrelationships will give you a framework on which you can base a reasoned conclusion. It is possible, however, that certain major questions can be missed in the overall process. If such questions come to mind, they should be dealt with at this point.

   In the given question about the fall of the Roman Empire, it could be asked if the economic problems of food supply were related to the fewer numbers of slaves available to work on the farms to produce the food; or whether the

Barbarian Gods

Germanic God	Symbol	Function	Day of the Week
Tieu	spear	god of the sky	Tieu's day
Wodan	black horse and wolf	god of the under-world (death)	Wodan's day
Thor	axe	god of thunder	Thor's day
Freyja	seated goddesses with fruit, bread, or horns of plenty	goddess of fertility and bounty	Freyja's day

The role of each god varied from tribe to tribe and with the passage of time.

reduced supply of slaves was linked to the military fact that the Empire conquered fewer provinces and hence gradually lost the source of human labour.

Once you have thoroughly researched and analyzed questions such as these, you should be able to state your conclusion in terms that answer the causal question.

THE STORY CONTINUES . . .

The Dark Ages (A.D. 476–1000)

In the five centuries that followed the German Odoacer's ascent to power over the Western Empire, Europe entered the so-called Dark Ages. This name is usually applied because of the contrast between Roman and barbarian life and because relatively little is known about the period. More accurately, the era should be seen as the result of mixing Roman, Christian, and barbarian cultures–a mixture that provided the basis for the emergence of European civilization. Indeed, the Dark Ages really represent the first half of the medieval period (Middle Ages) between Rome and the modern world.

DECAY OF THE ETERNAL CITY

To the average Roman of the time, the date A.D. 476 had little significance after a century of chaos, conflict, and change. Of greater impact was the physical and symbolic demise of the Eternal City itself as the invasion of different groups of marauders continued in the sixth and seventh centuries. Death from the sword, the plague, and the destruction of the aqueducts that fed water to the city reduced the population drastically. When Totilla, a barbarian invader, entered Rome in A.D. 546, he found only five hundred people. The half-deserted city, once the centre of the civilized world, was looted of its bronze statues, artwork, and pride as its now-roofless buildings began to crumble. Although still a show-piece of architecture, grass began to grow over the seats of the Colosseum that had once provided a setting for savage entertainment for the Roman mob from dawn until dusk.

The barbarians, whose warlike migrations infiltrated the weakened Western Empire, were mainly an illiterate, artistically limited, agrarian people. Their impact was both immediate and long lasting. They settled everywhere in what is now northern Europe, squeezing out the inhabitants they encountered through population pressure as well as conquest. To the south, the barbarians, though dominant in war, were less numerous and they shared the land with the original people whose lives they so drastically changed. This difference between north and south is reflected in Europe's population today.

Neglect and sometimes deliberate destruction of roads for building material destroyed the commercial patterns and life of the Roman world. Town after town decayed and was often reclaimed by the forest. This was a time of confusion, without law or administration, in which the local village became the focal point of social and economic life. Instead of having a surplus of food for trade, farmers tried desperately to produce enough food to survive.

The German barbarians were organized into war bands or tribes each headed by a chieftain of their own choosing. In return for his leadership and promise to share the spoils of battle, individual warriors swore their personal allegiance. Major decisions were made by proposals presented to a general assembly or council of men of military age. Acceptance was signified by the clashing of spears on shields.

Justice, where it could be enforced, was administered by oath if the crime was minor, and by ordeal if the crime was major. For a lesser offence, a person could be cleared by having friends and neighbours swear that he was honourable and innocent. This practice of listening to testimony before passing sentence provided the basis of the jury system of later centuries. A person accused of a more serious crime, however, had the case referred to the "Judgement of God," which was determined by the success of certain experiments using fire, water, or combat. The ordeal by fire, for example, required that the accused carry a red-hot iron for a specified distance or walk barefoot and blindfolded across a 3-m space of red-hot ploughshares. The hand or foot was bound up for three days, then unbandaged and inspected. If the wounds were healing, the accused was pronounced innocent; if the wounds were festering, the accused was judged to be guilty. The use of ordeal was continuous in England until the middle of the thirteenth century, although it seems to have been abolished earlier throughout most of the continent.

The Emergence of Feudalism in the Dark Ages

In the lawless countryside of Europe, no individual was safe from common thieves, barbaric chieftains, and looting invaders. Without a civilized government to offer protection, individuals were forced to associate themselves with the most powerful man in the local district, in short to become *his* man. The process was not altogether new. During the Roman Empire, men without rank often offered their toil in work or battle to a patron of standing in return for

GERMANIC "BARBARIAN" CULTURE

POLITICAL ORGANIZATION

JUSTICE

THE LAWLESS COUNTRYSIDE

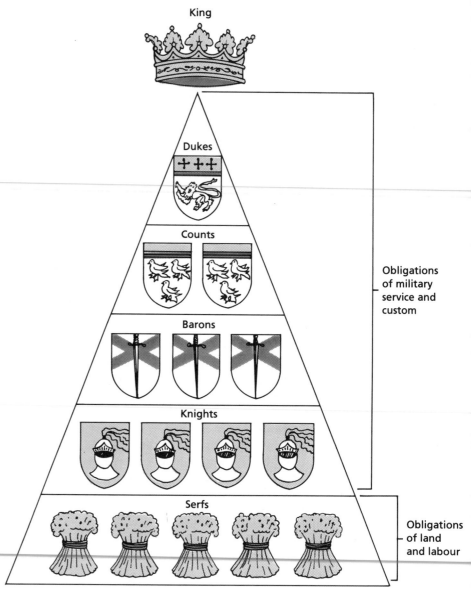

The Feudal Pyramid. The feudal order was a political and social pyramid. Feudal territories ranged in size from local estates of a few km² to large kingdoms of thousands of km².

FEUDALISM

land and protection. A similar tie existed between the Germanic chieftains and their *comitatus* or companions, their captains, and warriors. Now, with danger lurking behind any contact with a stranger, freemen eagerly linked themselves with any lord who could provide protection. Weaker lords, in turn, associated themselves with more powerful lords in higher and higher positions of wealth and strength. The relationship between lords and vassals, those of higher and lower rank in the chain of association, provided the structure for what is known as **feudalism**.

The Dark Ages

A.D.

480–543	Dark Ages begin
	Saint Benedict revives the early Christian institution of the monastery
527–565	Reign of Justinian
	Golden age of the Byzantine Empire in the East
622	Hegira of Muhammad from Mecca to Medina
732	Charles Martel stops the Muslim advance into Europe at Tours
800	Charlemagne crowned by Pope Leo III
843	Treaty of Verdun divides kingdom of Charlemagne
800–1000	Muslims and Magyars threaten
	Vikings raid coasts of Europe from Ireland to Spain, and France, Russia, and Constantinople
1000	Old Western Roman Empire blossoms into a new civilization, Europe

Feudal conditions varied greatly throughout Europe. Yet, clearly, one who owned a horse was more desirable than a peasant who had virtually nothing to offer but his labour. The importance of the horse in battle had increased with the successes of mounted barbarians against the rather undisciplined legions of the late Roman Empire. Now the mounted soldier or knight, steadied on his steed by a stirrup, became the most sought-after military weapon. From the knight with a single horse rose a hierarchy of barons, counts, and dukes. Each had increasing numbers of fully equipped knights which he committed to the person who ranked immediately above. All men of rank were vassals to the king, who could command their services in time of need.

At the heart of the feudal relationship was the **feud**, or **fief.** This was usually a grant of land given by a lord in return for a vassal's military service and other duties determined by local custom. An oath of homage or personal loyalty was made in a formal ceremony in which the vassal knelt with his hands between his lords hands until his fealty (a promise to keep a promise) was accepted with a kiss. A symbol of the bond thus sworn was recognized in the form of a staff or a clump of earth given by the lord to the vassal.

At the lowest level of feudal society were the **serfs**, or **villeins.** These common peasants worked the land on the manors, or estates, owned by members of the titled nobility. The serf owed no military service to his lord. Instead, he

THE FEUDAL RELATIONSHIP

SERFS

A new vassal kneels before his lord to take his oaths of homage and fealty.

was obliged to till the lord's land, use the lord's mill, fish in the lord's streams, hunt in the lord's forest, and worship in the manor church. For each opportunity, the serf paid rent, tax, or a **tithe**. The serf was also subject to the **corvée**, a condition of unpaid labour occasionally required for maintaining roads and ditches on the manor. When he died, even a death tax or *mortuarium* had to be paid to the lord! A wealthy baron might own several manors, the care of which was entrusted to a lesser vassal known as an **overseer**. Each manor was directed by a **bailiff**, who reported to the overseer as he travelled about inspecting the manors of his domain. When disputes arose, cases were heard in the baron's court, and, yes, the serf again paid a sum for the privilege of its use.

Feudal society worked because of the voluntary co-operation given from the lowliest serf to the highest noble. A man's word was the cornerstone of his life. Social life, economic existence, and private law were only possible in a broken world without public law with the mutual obligation of feudal relationships and the kingdoms they held together. By the year 1000, feudal states, ranging in size from isolated castles to great kingdoms like Normandy, Burgundy, Saxony, and Bavaria, spread across Europe.

FEUDAL STATES

The Byzantine Empire

In contrast to the disintegration of Rome and its Western Empire, the Eastern Empire continued to flourish and survive under the rule of emperors until 1453. Referred to as the Byzantine Empire because Constantinople, the magnificent capital established by Constantine, was founded on the site of the earlier city of Byzantium, it developed a blending of Hellenistic and Asian culture. The ideal location of Constantinople, at the mouth of the Bosporus, was a natural crossroad for trade routes by land and sea. The golden age of the Byzantine Empire was ushered in with the reign of Justinian (527–565).

THE EASTERN ROMAN EMPIRE

Justinian's ambition was to restore the glory of the old Roman Empire and maintain the unity of the Christian Church. No man was more vigorous in pursuit of his ambition. In the West, North Africa, part of Spain, Italy, Greece, and the Mediterranean islands were reconquered from the barbarians. The collected treasure of generations and continued heavy taxation enabled Justinian to lavish such wealth on Constantinople that it became the greatest city in the world. Chariot races in the sixty-thousand seat Hippodrome became the main attraction for public entertainment, but the architectural and spiritual wonder was the great basilica of Hagia Sophia or "Holy Wisdom." Within its walls, originally decorated with brilliant mosaics, gold leaf, coloured marble, silver, and ivory, emperors were baptized, crowned, and married.

JUSTINIAN

HAGIA SOPHIA

Of perhaps even greater importance was Justinian's decision to establish a commission of ten jurists to study and clarify the confused mass of custom, statute, decree, and judicial ruling that made up Roman law. The product of their efforts was the Body of Civil Law. This work was important for the principles it established for the practice of law in Western civilization. The Romans clearly recognized that the principles of justice should be applied without prej-

THE BODY OF CIVIL LAW

Hagia Sophia. Completed in five years with the labour of ten thousand men, the church is dominated by a central dome 32 m wide and 49 m high and lighted by a base of arched windows that rest upon a second dome which stretches to the ground. Hagia Sophia served as a basilica for 916 years and as a mosque for 477 years before being converted to a museum in 1930.

udice to all cases; that the accused person had a right to defend her or himself before he could be convicted; that the prosecution must prove guilt rather than the accused person prove his or her innocence; and that the spirit is more important than the letter of law. Roman law was not only preserved in the Eastern Empire, but remains as the basis of legal codes in many modern societies including France, Spain, Latin America, the state of Louisiana, and the province of Québec.

The majesty of Justinian did not long survive his death. Gains in the West were completely lost by the eighth century, while pressure from Persians, Slavs, and Bulgars threatened closer to home. Nevertheless, the values of Greek and Roman civilizations were sustained while the chaos of barbarian invasion crippled most of Europe for five centuries.

Islam

In the seventh century, however, a force emerged from the life of a single person that changed the course of the Empire. An orphaned Arab named Muhammad became a shepherd boy, then a servant and caravan agent for a wealthy and somewhat older widow whom he eventually married. Until he was forty, Muhammad led an unaccomplished life in Mecca; then, on his caravan journeys to the Yemen and Syria regions of the Arabian world, he became greatly impressed by Jewish and Christian faith in one God. His intensity of thought led to visions, shared initially only with his wife and friends, in which the angel Gabriel spoke to him in the name of Allah whom Muhammad took to be the

MUHAMMAD

God of all people. Muhammad saw himself as a man, but a special man chosen by Allah to be his prophet. Unfortunately for Muhammad, Mecca was a desert city recently settled by Bedouin tribes who worshipped a seemingly endless number of pagan gods. When Muhammad began to preach in such an environment, he was persecuted for his faith and forced to leave the city.

Muhammad and his loyal followers wandered the desert in desperation until they received an unexpected invitation from the religiously divided city of Medina. Uncertain of his future, Muhammad sent his disciples to Medina for two years before he went to the city in triumph in 622. The flight from Mecca to Medina is called the **Hegira**, an event so significant to the Muslims who follow Muhammad and his religion of Islam that it marks the beginning of their calendar. The teaching of Muhammad now spread so rapidly that, after a series of brief hostilities, he returned as master to Mecca in 630. Following Muhammad's death, his revelations–taken as the word of Allah–were collected into a work known as the **Koran** which has become the central guide for the Islam religion.

The success of Islam was based on its rather simple and unswerving set of beliefs in an Arab world that could not relate to other major religions of the day. Islam was the third great religion, after Judaism and Christianity, to adopt **monotheism**, the belief in one God. Muslims promised equality to all people who accepted Islam. They were required to pray five times daily, kneeling and facing the Holy City of Mecca, where the Hegira began. In addition, Muslims had to give alms to the poor, observe a daily fast during the month of Ramadan, and, where possible, make at least one pilgrimage to Mecca during their lifetimes. Idol worship, gambling, and the consumption of alcohol and pork were prohibited.

Islam had no priests or ministers or complicated symbolism–only an often-kind and considerate appeal to humanity. Following Muhammad's death in 632, however, Islam united the Arab world. The idea that Muslims ought to wage holy war against unbelievers became the motivating force for territorial expansion. Always fierce fighters, the Arabs built a Muslim Empire in one hundred years that stretched from the steppes of Russia to North Africa and Spain. Their advance, comparable in scale to that of Alexander, was stopped only by the able leader of the Germanic Franks, Charles Martel, at the Battle of Tours in 732. Arab civilization did, however, leave its cultural imprint on the lands it conquered through the advanced use of the dome in building, and of the sciences of algebra, astronomy, and medicine.

The Christian Church in the Dark Ages

Christianity, as practised and organized by the Church, had come a long way since Jesus journeyed the lands about Judea as a charismatic preacher. After his crucifixion, the Apostles presided over the Christian groups they had founded and were helped in their work by respected Christians known as bishops. The

This partial mosaic of Jesus Christ, found in the Hagia Sophia, was one of many from the Byzantine era that were discovered underneath layers of paint applied by the Muslims.

THE SPREAD OF ISLAM

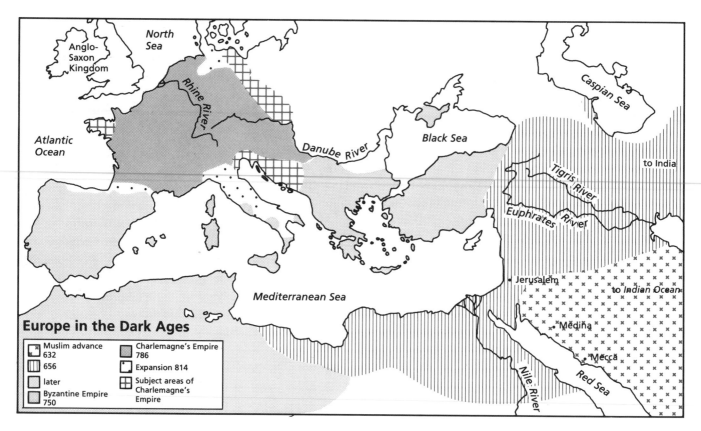

Europe in the Dark Ages

Muslim advance 632		Charlemagne's Empire 786	
656		Expansion 814	
later		Subject areas of Charlemagne's Empire	
Byzantine Empire 750			

prestige and power of the bishop increased with the size of his church congregation. As a result, the bishops who headed churches in large cities exerted dominant influence over those in local communities. By the fourth century, five metropolitan bishops who headed churches in the capital cities of the Roman provinces had become the most important and were known as patriarchs.

To avoid a regional split over doctrine, ceremony, and authority, Constantine, the first emperor to support the Christian religion, called a Universal Church Council at Nicaea in A.D. 325. Over three hundred bishops attended. Those from Rome insisted on their supremacy, basing their claims on Christ's words to Peter, who later became the first Bishop of Rome. In Matthew 16:18–19, Christ had identified Peter as his successor on earth with the final authority in all religious questions. Each succeeding bishop of Rome assumed the same power. The fact that Rome had been the capital of the Empire for so long and continued as the capital of the West helped support their position. By the fifth century, the bishop of Rome had assumed the title of pope or "father of the Church." Although the supremacy of the Roman bishop was denied by certain bishops of the Eastern Orthodox Church, the Church in the West became wealthy and strong.

POPE

Indeed, the growing worldliness of the Church was criticized by some who felt that a meditative life organized under strict regulations of silence, obedience, labour, and religious practices was closer to the real meaning of Christian faith. Such men were housed in monasteries that contained only the necessities of life. The most influential figure in Western monasticism was Saint Benedict. By following a rigid but reasonable set of regulations called the **Rule**, he established a code that encouraged the spread of monasticism throughout Europe. In fact, some isolated monasteries in France and Corfu still observe the rules laid down almost fifteen hundred years ago.

MONASTICISM

The moral direction of Christianity from the fifth century onwards had been charted by Saint Augustine of Hippo in his most famous work, *The City of God*. Written in response to the sacking of Rome in A.D. 410, Saint Augustine was inspired by the need to defend against charges that Christianity was responsible for the decline of Rome. In addition to arguing that events unfolded according to God's will and that non-Christian empires had fallen in the past, Saint Augustine asserted that the fall of Rome was unimportant! What counted was the city of God and its immortal citizens on earth and in heaven. The need to live out life here and now as a preparation for everlasting life after death anticipated the particular lifestyle of later medieval monks and provided general direction for the life of all Christians.

SAINT AUGUSTINE

As a formal organization, however, the unity of the Church was superficial. Long-running disputes over the nature of the Trinity, the dates of key religious events, the use of icons or images, and the extent of celibacy practised by the clergy resulted in regional centres of Christianity in practice. Not surprisingly, the major divisions of the Church reflected the political divisions of the Empire. Just as Roman Catholicism dominated the faltering Western Empire with Rome as its centrepiece, so the Eastern Orthodox Church, with its capital at Constantinople, dominated the Eastern and Byzantine Empires that followed. The official split between the two Churches occurred in 1054, but other localized branches of Christianity already established in Syria, Egypt, Armenia, and Ethiopia have continued to the present.

DIVISIONS IN THE CHRISTIAN CHURCH

Centuries of invasion and conquest have left only Greece and part of Cyprus as today's remnants of the original Eastern Orthodoxy. Yet in the tenth century, the Russian grand prince Vladimir was converted and took his Orthodox outlook to the unlikely setting of Moscow. The fall of Rome, then Constantinople, left Muscovites with the conviction that their city was the new centre of Christendom. The sixteenth century Byzantine domes of St. Basil's in Moscow, so familiar to twentieth century tourists, are a vivid reminder of the historic roots of Russian Orthodoxy.

Meanwhile, in the crumbled Western Empire, the Roman Catholic Church was the only bond of unity that survived the barbarian advance and the subsequent political and economic disintegration of the Roman world. Church organization mirrored, to some extent, the hierarchy of imperial Rome, but, with an established system to transfer authority, the Church became more efficient.

THE ROMAN CATHOLIC CHURCH

The eagles and fleur-de-lis represented on the cloak of Charlemagne became the symbols of Germany and France. Both countries claim Charlemagne as their founding father.

CAROLINGIAN LEADERS

CHARLEMAGNE

Rome had its emperor; the Catholic Church had its pope; for Rome, an emperor's death often resulted in chaos that could only be resolved by the army; in contrast, the pope was advised by assistants in the Curia, the leading members of which formed a College of Cardinals that elected a new pope upon the death of the old, as it does today. The Roman Empire was divided into provinces administered by governors and cities run by magistrates; the Roman Catholic world of the West was organized into provinces, dioceses, and then parishes under the respective responsibility of archbishops, bishops, and parish priests. The intimate contact of the parish priest with his parishoners, through work and prayer, made him their teacher as well as their spiritual leader.

Indeed, the Roman Catholic Church, through its universal vision in the Western Empire, consciously maintained a unity throughout Europe that had been the essence of imperial Rome. During the Dark Ages, the few men who received formal education were usually trained in a monastery (by the sixth century) or in a cathedral school (by the eighth century). The Catholic Church continued to teach Latin, the language of the Western Empire, and actively studied the major works of Roman literature. In the damp cold of dimly lighted rooms, monks spent countless hours hand copying classical manuscripts that preserved much of the Roman heritage handed down to the present. Above and beyond education, the Church also administered its own law known as **canon law**, which was strongly influenced by Roman precedent and jurisprudence. Many of the day-to-day matters that are now settled in civil courts were handled by the Church, the influence of which touched almost every part of a person's life.

Charlemagne

Since the days of Clovis, at the turn of the sixth century, Frankish leaders in Gaul had assisted the Catholic Church, encouraged conversion to Christianity, and became, at times, the only strong Christian community that supported the papacy. A series of weak, often corrupt rulers in the seventh century–when the country was run by a court official known as the "mayor of the palace"–resulted in more power and prestige for the papacy in everyday affairs.

The Carolingian leaders, however, began to redress the balance between Church and state, beginning with the rule of Charles Martel in the eighth century. Charles introduced the feudal concept of land grants in return for military service and used his military genius to fight back the Muslim advance into Europe at the Battle of Tours in 732. His son, Pepin the Short, was more co-operative with the Church and even protected the pope from attack by the Lombards. In return for a donation of Lombard land, known to history as the Papal States, Pepin was recognized by the Church as the king of the Franks. This blending of Christian authority with the traditions of the Germanic Franks paved the way for Pepin's son Charlemagne to attempt to reestablish the old Roman Empire.

Charlemagne's favourite book was Saint Augustine's *City of God*, and no doubt he saw himself as the city's architect here on earth. A natural leader and brilliant military strategist, Charlemagne waged at least fifty-three campaigns against pagan nonbelievers, although his methods would have been questioned by many Christians. The troublesome Saxons, like other pagan peoples he conquered, were offered the choice between baptism and death. Their failure to make the proper choice led to forty-five hundred executions in a single day. Between 768 and 814, Charlemagne gained control over a territory that stretched from the Baltic to the Pyrenees and from the Balkans to the Atlantic. State and Church marched together throughout the realm in Charlemagne's scheme of operations. He shrewdly administered his lands by dividing territory into counties run by counts and bishops. Special agents were sent annually to inspect local operations.

Treaty of Verdun, 843

The knowledge that the pope needed his protection against possible attack from the Lombards and Islamics gave Charlemagne considerable influence and supervision in Church affairs. In return, Charlemagne sent money to Christians in other lands and enforced the collection of tithes for the Church. During the mass of Christmas Day in the year 800, Pope Leo III suddenly placed a crown on Charlemagne's head while the large congregation cried out, "Long life and victory to Charles Augustus, great and peace-making emperor of the Romans, crowned by God!" The chorus was repeated twice more in ancient Roman fashion. Although Charlemagne acted surprised, it is quite likely that Charlemagne and Leo had arranged the event when they met at Paderborn the previous year.

"EMPEROR OF THE ROMANS, CROWNED BY GOD!"

Although this coronation recognized Charlemagne as the most powerful king in Europe, the fact that the crown was received from the pope implied a supremacy of spiritual authority that Charlemagne did not accept. To avoid any future doubts about the relationship between state and Church, Charlemagne instructed his son to crown himself when the time came.

The phrase "Holy Roman Empire" was not used until later, but Charlemagne successfully embodied the traditions of the Christian Church, Germanic kings, and Roman emperors. Such claims were initially resisted by the Roman emperors in Byzantium, but in 812, after years of turmoil, Charlemagne was accepted as co-emperor in the West.

Muslims, Magyars, and Vikings

After Charlemagne's death in 814, the Carolingian Empire began to dissolve as his less-able grandsons fought over their inheritance. The Treaty of Verdun, in 843, divided the kingdom into sections from which the modern states of France and Germany eventually emerged. This division, however, came at an unfortunate time as Europe was once again under siege from almost every quarter. While the Muslims threatened in southern Italy and France, and the Magyars–a Turkish people–moved across the Danube into Germany, the most destructive force were the Norsemen or Vikings, Germanic peoples from Scandinavia.

TREATY OF VERDUN

EUROPE INVADED

THE VIKINGS

Inspired partly by the love of adventure, exploration, and the desire for booty, the Vikings were also forced to expand beyond their limited homeland. A growing population in the eighth and ninth centuries could not be fed from the small amounts of arable land available in the Scandinavian countries. Expert seamen who sailed on speedy, shallow-drafted ships, some Vikings went westward to Iceland, Greenland, and the coast of North America, while others terrorized Europe on several fronts. The monasteries of Irish monks were obvious and easy targets, but the coastal regions of England, France, and Spain were also at bay to Viking raiders for nearly two hundred years. The name of the modern French province of Normandy, on the English Channel, can be traced to a land grant forced by the Vikings from a Frankish king in 911. To the east, the Vikings moved across the Baltic into Russia and then moved south as far as Constantinople!

THE EMERGENCE OF EUROPE

At first, it might appear that the barbarian invasion of Europe in the ninth and tenth centuries was similar to the onslaught that hit the Western Empire five hundred years earlier. There was, however, a crucial difference. Where the military and political resistance of Rome had simply faded away, the Germanic kingdoms of Europe by A.D. 1000 had gradually organized their own defences and survived the storm. Feudal obligations had strengthened local kingdoms to the point where peasants were offered protection from barbarian attack and a system of justice in feudal courts.

As the Vikings settled in the lands they had formerly raided, many became Christians and adapted to Christian ways. In so doing, they became part of the mainstream of a new life and order that was emerging on the continent. Europe in A.D. 1000 was still violent and lawless by modern standards, but the groundwork for a new civilization had been established. As Europe moved from the Dark Ages into the medieval period, this civilization would blossom as an extension of the blending of Roman, Christian, and barbarian tradition.

COMMENT

Roman culture owed so much to the Greeks that historian Arnold Toynbee viewed the Roman experience as the last stand of Hellenic civilization. Certainly, the debt is a heavy one. The Roman writer Virgil's greatest work, the *Aeneid*, is very similar to the epic poems of Homer, while the major Roman gods were often renamed after Greek originials. In art, the Romans not only borrowed Greek ideas but stole many statues and columns for use in their own buildings. Rome did develop fine sculpture in bas-relief, such as that showing military campaigns on the Arch of Titus and Trajan's Column, but Roman artists were often content to copy Greek productions. Though not creative, this practice at least preserved the form of many lost originals. In architecture, the Roman engineers used the column and lintel developed by the Greeks and Egyptians and made extensive application of the arch and the dome, first developed in the Middle East.

Yet the Romans were a very practical people who had a knack for taking an idea or a technique and using it in a way that was uniquely their own. Aided by the discovery of concrete, the Romans took contributions from Egypt, Greece, and the Middle East and built extensive systems of aqueducts, bridges, public baths, and temples that were unprecedented in size, variety, scale, and purpose. For all of their remarkable achievements in philosophy and politics, the attachment of the Greek individuals to their tiny city-states left the country sorely divided. Alexander of Macedonia, through his conquests, introduced a vision of a continental empire, but it was the Romans who eventually made it work. Enjoying the protection of the Roman legions, the strongest fighting forces of their time, Rome administered an Empire that was unified by law, custom, and toleration, and which lasted without challenge until signs of decay began to surface in the third century.

It has often been said that of all the people of the ancient world, the Romans were the most like ourselves. Seen in historical perspective, this notion is really a tribute to the lasting influence of Roman civilization. Merchants were supplied with merchandise from the corners of the known world. Busy shops that opened with sliding doors onto sidewalks raised above the level of paved streets jammed with traffic were as common then as they are now. Public monuments, statues, theatres, stadiums, and race-tracks were, and are, taken for granted. Politicians ran for election and catered to the masses, while the unemployed collected the dole (welfare).

The parallels are not exact but it is the general similarities that usually capture people's attention. Perhaps the twentieth-century challenges to Western leadership in world affairs have made it necessary to understand fully the reasons why other empires have crumbled if our own civilization is to avoid the same fate. Of key importance in this regard is the fact that each historical issue is set in its own time, place, and circumstance, a situation that requires foresight as well as hindsight if progress is to be made.

Why, then, does a civilization collapse given a series of remarkable material achievements under a unified political system with a common code of laws? With hindsight, almost every negative or unsuccessful element in Roman life has been used as a partial explanation of decline. Beyond the factors specified in the alternatives, exhaustion of the mines and the soil, a self-indulgent lifestyle, and poor leadership are most commonly sighted. Separately, any one of these could have been overcome; collectively, perhaps not.

As a group it is unfair to say that the Roman emperors were not capable leaders. At the outset of the Empire, Augustus proved to be a masterful organizer while in the fourth century Diocletian and Constantine were exceptional men who might well have arrived too late to reverse the tide of events already set in motion. Other emperors, whether ascending to office by hereditary right or at the whim of the military, did little credit to their position. Caligula was probably insane, Nero and Tiberius were eccentric, while several later emperors were simply incompetent.

ARCHITECTURE TIME LINE

Megalithic 5500–1500 B.C.
Stonehenge c.2400 B.C.

Egypt c.2700 B.C.
Karnak c.1200 B.C.

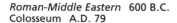

Minoan c.2200 B.C.
Knossos 2000 B.C.

Mycenaean 1500 B.C.
Mycenae c.1300 B.C.

Greek 750 B.C.
Parthenon 438 B.C.

Roman-Middle Eastern 600 B.C.
Colosseum A.D. 79

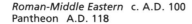

Roman-Middle Eastern c. A.D. 100
Pantheon A.D. 118

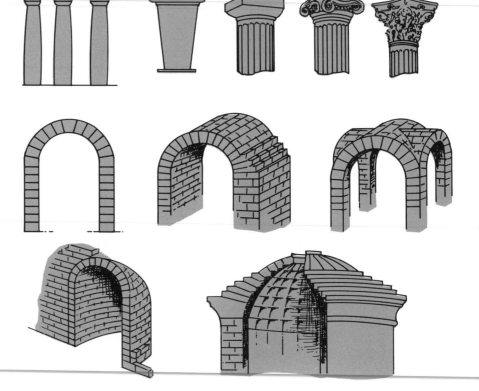

One bizarre explanation about the number of emperors who exhibited unusual behavior rests with the possibility of lead poisoning. By the first century B.C., lead and terra cotta pipes had replaced hollowed tree trunks and stone blocks cut with channels as the conduit for water within city limits. The pipe was made from sheets cast in 3-m lengths that were wrapped around a pole of desired thickness and soldered at the joint. Pipes made in this fashion can still be seen in private homes of Pompeii. The Romans, however, were well aware of the effects of lead poisoning, a condition characterized by a dark line along the gums, local muscular paralysis, and pain. The additional suggestion is that it not only shortened life span but affected the mental stability of those afflicted. Despite the potential danger, the demand for lead was so great that it could not be satisfied. By good fortune, the water used by the Romans was so hard that the encrustation of minerals on the pipes offered natural protection against the lead itself.

No doubt there were many who endured the effects of mild lead poisoning in varying degrees. However, it cannot be considered as the factor affecting the decisions made by emperors. In the half century before Diocletian came to power, twenty emperors had ruled for fragmented periods. Clearly the instability and the lack of continuity had a greater influence on the political leadership of the empire than the possible negative effects of water quality.

The very existence of Rome as a worldwide state was a magnificent accomplishment. Today, Roman architecture can be found in many public buildings, but it is the spirit of the Roman achievement through its approach to law and the Empire that deeply affects Western civilization. Ironically, the peace of *Pax Romana* enabled the Christian Church to grow and flourish and to develop an organization that mirrored that of the Empire. Through its use and study of Latin in learning, law, and theology, the Church preserved the record of Rome as the military and political forces of the Empire withered away. By understanding the world when it was Roman, our progress can be measured. By understanding ourselves, a successful future can be planned.

Date A.D.	Event
800–1000	Old Western Roman Empire blossoms into a new civilization, Europe
1054	Great Schism–Christendom is divided between the Roman Catholic Church of the West and the Greek Orthodox Church of the East
1066	Battle of Hastings–William of Normandy conquers England
1071	Seljuk Turks defeat the Byzantines and begin the conquest of the Holy Land
1076	Pope Gregory VII asserts papal authority over Henry IV of Germany
1095	Pope Urban II calls the Crusades to win back the Holy Land for Christendom
c.1100	Growth of towns and cities and the expansion of trade and commerce mark the rise of middle-class merchants
c.1150	Cathedral crusade–wealthy towns and cities build impressive Gothic cathedrals
1215	Magna Carta outlines existing relationship between the king and his feudal barons in England
1271	Marco Polo begins expedition to the court of Kublai Khan
1302	King Philip of France arrests the pope Babylonian Captivity–seven consecutive popes are forced to live at Avignon Church prestige declines
1337	Hundred Years' War begins between England and France
1347	Black Death devastates Europe killing between one-quarter and one-third of the population
1453	Islamic Ottoman Turks conquer Constantinople
1488	Bartolemeu Diaz rounds Cape of Good Hope
1492	Christopher Columbus reaches San Salvador in the Bahamas
1519	Cortes begins conquest of Mesoamerica
1531	Pizarro begins conquest of South America Was the New World discovered by fifteenth- and sixteenth-century Europeans or had visitors from several continents arrived hundreds and even thousands of years earlier?

8

Europe and the Pre-Columbian Discovery of America

BACKGROUND

The European Revival

With the emergence of law and order, the population of Europe steadily increased from 35 million in the tenth century to about 80 million by the end of the thirteenth century. More intensive methods of agriculture were needed to feed this growing population. In response, much of Europe, particularly the manors of the north, adopted the three-field system of crop rotation: one field was planted in the fall and one in the spring, while one lay fallow for an entire year. More land was cultivated than in the older two-field system, vastly improving yields. Even the wasteland at manor's edge and reclaimed land from drained swamps now fell under the plough. And what a plough it was! The traditional single-pronged scratch plough, used since Roman times, required at least two passes to prepare the soil. The heavy-wheeled plough that replaced it had a mouldboard that overturned the soil in a single pass.

THE AGRICULTURAL REVOLUTION

The most revolutionary change, however, was a series of inventions in the early tenth century that led to the widespread use of the horse, rather than the slower-moving ox. The introduction of the horseshoe gave the horse better traction, protected the hoof, and extended the working life of the animal; the tandem harness lined up teams behind each other and gave a more efficient use of their pulling power; while the horse collar enabled the animal to pull without the strangling effect of a yoke.

Still, it was the serf's sweat and backbreaking toil from dawn to dusk that produced grain surpluses and gave the nobility its leisure time. The use of the ancient water mill, the newly invented windmill, and the development of iron, rather than wooden hoes and pitchforks did not lighten the burden of the dull, dreary life of about 90 percent of Europe's population. Accident, injury, and illness always threatened at a time when medical aid was virtually nonexistent and when nourishment was provided by a breakfast and dinner of only black bread and ale.

PEASANT LIFE

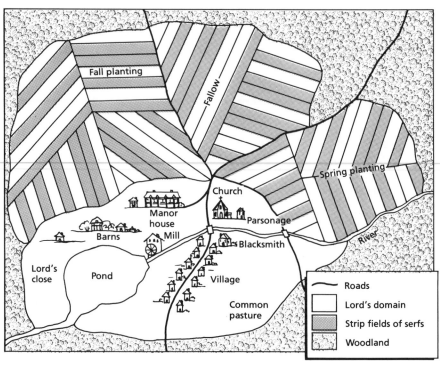

The Three-Field System of Agriculture.

GROWTH OF TOWNS

There was, however, an escape from this monotonous existence. The stable atmosphere of the feudal world led to the revival of trade and, with it, the growth or rebirth of towns that had been idle since the last days of Rome. At the end of the tenth century, Europe contained only a handful of what were really local villages, none with a population of ten thousand. By the end of the eleventh century, there were dozens of towns, some with populations of over twenty thousand. This represented the start of an urban expansion that would continue until the fourteenth century. Manor lords were hard pressed to keep their serfs tilling the soil. Many serfs simply left to seek out new lives in the nearest towns. Those who remained had often saved enough money to buy their freedom, which meant that they paid a fee in place of feudal obligations and then sold their produce for profit in the closest urban market.

In the north, many towns developed when wandering merchants, often in search of the trade fairs held throughout Europe, sought protection in a fortified castle or monastery. If the walls overshadowed the junction of two navigable rivers or some other transhipment point, the merchants occasionally decided to stay and set up stands for their wares. As trade expanded, people began to move to the town for commerce and work. The urban community became more than simply a religious or political centre.

The merchants soon set up shop outside the castle creating a **suburb**, which was, in turn, enclosed by a new wall. As the suburbs continued to grow,

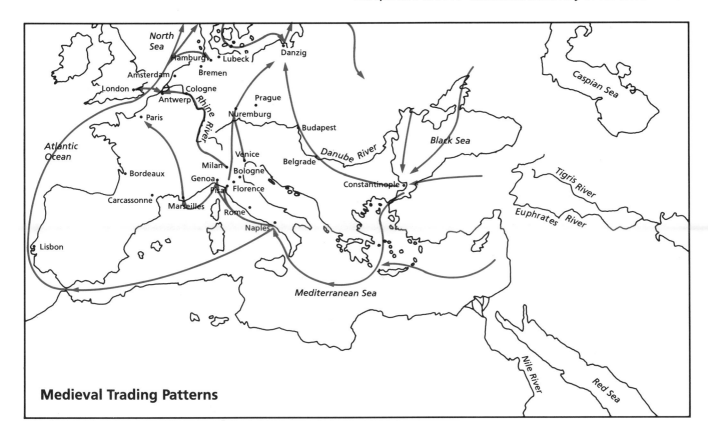

Medieval Trading Patterns

additional new walls had to be added about every fifty years or so with each one overshadowing the older walls it encircled. The French community of Carcassonne is the best surviving example of a medieval walled town.

The growth of trade in the eleventh century brought prosperity to Paris and Rouen in France as well as to Hamburg and Cologne in Germany. The Italian city of Venice, with its great fleet, cleared the Adriatic Sea of pirates, and became a major force in the trade between the Muslim and Byzantine empires. Venice became the first commercially independent city of the medieval world. Genoa and Pisa entered the competition for commercial supremacy shortly afterwards. Merchants from all parts of Europe met at the famous trade fair held six times a year in the French state of Champagne. Here, highly valued Flemish cloth and British wool were exchanged for spices, silks, and jewellery that funnelled through the Italian ports from the Byzantine and Muslim worlds.

Feudal life had known only two major classes, the nobility and the serf. By the end of the eleventh century, the **burgers** of Germany, the **burgesses** of England, and the **bourgeoisie** of France had emerged as a new **middle class** of merchants. The driving force of a new economic life, they organized them-

GROWTH OF TRADE AND COMMERCE

RISE OF THE MIDDLE CLASS

*In this medieval painting the work
of a carpenter and a stonemason are
judged by a guild master.*

GUILDS

selves into **merchant guilds** to control prices, to maintain local monopolies,
and to guarantee the quality of the items they sold. Most of the townspeople,
however, were engaged in the production of goods and support services that
were organized into **craft guilds**. Here, a **master craftsman** would train an
apprentice for up to seven years to learn a trade or business. Only when he

became a **journeyman** did the apprentice receive a wage. To become a master craftsman himself, the journeyman had to complete a **masterpiece** of work that was acceptable to his superior. Then, if he had the money, he could open his own shop. Each occupation, butchers, bakers, dye and candle-stick makers, among countless others, had its own guild. In time of need, guilds cared for the sick and widowed families of their members.

At the outset, the workshops of craft guilds were usually located in the masters' houses. This often meant that the wives of the guild masters were involved either in the actual production or the sale of the products. Some of the early textile guilds were mixed guilds. Women and men had equal positions. As guilds expanded and most of the home workshops disappeared, however, quotas and regulations restricting women began to appear, until women were eventually excluded altogether.

Although towns were originally owned by the nobility, the close-knit ties of commerce and trade were a world apart from life on a feudal manor. To gain the independence needed to run their own affairs, the townspeople purchased a **charter** from a king or noble, usually at a terrible price and after much bargaining. This charter freed the townspeople and allowed them to set up their own government. Many nobles living in the countryside became upset when the peasants who worked their fields left for the new opportunities that a town could offer. For nobles living in the towns, however, the increased income from rents and tolls, made possible by commerce, was easy to accept. Squabbles between nobles and merchants over town-council appointments, however, were frequent. Resentment of wealthy merchants, who always seemed to have more cash on hand than either the nobility or upper clergy, became commonplace. Throughout the medieval era this transition from the old feudal order to the increasing prosperity and power of the new middle class was an uneasy one.

TOWN CHARTERS

The Relationship between Church and State

By the middle of the eleventh century, Europe had not only undergone a rapid population increase, economic revival, and the growth of towns, it had also experienced complete conversion to Christianity. As the countries of England, France, and Germany began to take shape out of the many local kingdoms, a harmony of interests developed between the individual states and the Church within their borders. The Benedictine monks often responded to the local needs of princes and kings. Even the prestigious French monastery of Cluny, responsible only to the papacy, endorsed the co-operation of Church and state.

CO-OPERATION OF CHURCH AND STATE

Pope Gregory VII upset this relationship with an assertion of papal power in 1076. Gregory insisted that the Church, not the kings, should control the appointment and election of archbishops, bishops, and other clergy. Henry IV of Germany disagreed and, after a bitter exchange of letters, Gregory excommunicated him and threatened to excommunicate any German clergy who did

Queen Mathilda is credited with having designed and supervised the execution of the Bayeux Tapestry *depicting the events relating to the Norman Conquest in which her husband, William the Conqueror, played a strategic role.*

not follow the pope's wishes. Since much of Henry's army came from lands administered by the Church, he was now exposed to the ambition of the power-hungry nobles. There was a shocking collapse of royal power. All of Europe watched as Henry journeyed in haste to Italy to seek forgiveness, while Gregory, in a slower, stately fashion headed toward Germany to oversee the election of a new German king! Henry encountered the pope at a castle in Canossa where, after he stood in the snow with deep humiliation for three days, Gregory reluctantly forgave him his sins.

THE ROAD TO CANOSSA

WILLIAM THE CONQUEROR

The Church had also hoped to improve its authority and prestige by supporting the Norman invasion of England. William, duke of the feudal duchy of Normandy, won a decisive victory at the Battle of Hastings in 1066, but he proved to be a strong king with no thought of playing second fiddle to the papacy. William feudalized the entire country (as he had Normandy), including bishops and abbots. In contrast to the German monarchy, he made every noble swear a personal oath of loyalty to him. When Gregory tried to intervene in the operation of the Anglo-Norman Church, William forbade all English clergy to go to Rome. There was little that Gregory could do.

UNITY OF FAITH

The rivalry between Church and state continued in varying forms throughout Europe without final resolution. There was no question, however, that Europe was united in its Christian faith. Should that faith be threatened from any quarter, it was up to the Church to assume the spiritual leadership to right the wrong, an action that could only increase its power and prestige.

The Crusades

PILGRIMAGES TO THE HOLY LAND

The Muslim Arabs (or Moors as they were called in Spain) who held the vast territory that was once the southern Roman Empire, were a military threat to Europe. During their centuries of civilized life, however, they had learned tolerance and allowed Christians to make journeys known as pilgrimages to Bethlehem and Jerusalem. The Arabs were too independent minded and their territory was too extensive to be ruled from a single centre, but even as division set in, Christian pilgrims were left to go their own way with little interference. By the middle of the eleventh century, thousands of pilgrims each year made the long and difficult trek to the Holy Land. Those who completed the pilgrimage became known as "palmers" because of the palms they wore on their clothes.

In 1071, however, the aggressive Seljuk Turks, recently converted to Islam and led by the able Alp Arslan, defeated a Byzantine army at Manzikert and even captured the emperor. Arslan generously released his captive, but the victorious Seljuks quickly overran much of Anatolia and the Holy Land. Horror stories of pilgrims slaughtered or seized for slavery or ransom filtered back to Europe. The Byzantine Empire, which had protected Europe from Asian armies since the days of ancient Rome, seemed powerless to react and appeared to be in danger of collapse in the face of Seljuk power. The Great Schism of 1054 had divided Christendom between the Catholic Church of the West and the Orthodox Church of the East, but the Byzantine emperor, Alexius Comnenus, was so concerned that he appealed to the papacy for assistance on several occasions.

Pope Urban II finally gave Alexius the response he desired. Clearly, Urban wanted to win the Holy Land for the Cross and to oust the infidel from the birthplace of Christ, but there were other advantages. A holy crusade would draw attention away from the dispute between Church and state that had dominated the papacy of Gregory, and, with good fortune, would unite Europe in a cause that enhanced the reputation and strength of the Catholic Church. There was even the possibility that the split between Western and Eastern Churches could be healed on terms favourable to the pope. The eleventh century had witnessed the successful start of the reconquest or **Reconquista** in Spain where Spanish Christians had already regained about one-quarter of the country from the Muslims in what amounted to a holy war. Urban hoped for even more success in the East where the Seljuk Empire began to crumble as a result of internal squabbles after 1091.

The call to the Cross, delivered by Urban in 1095, was one of history's great orations and was carefully planned for maximum emotional impact. Aware that past difficulties with Germany and England would reduce enthusiasm for the project, Urban selected Clermont in central France as the site for his speech. This choice was heartily approved by the large numbers of landless French knights who had no outlet for their energies now that their country had become stabilized under the rule of feudal princes. When Urban began his appeal with "Oh, race of Franks" and then went on to speak of the spoils that could be won in a land of "milk and honey," he knew he was preaching to the converted and the passion of his plea was equal to the occasion. At the conclusion of the address, the audience shouted "God wills it" and many knights cut their red cloaks into the shape of crucifixes, which were later sown on their tunics.

The response to Urban's cry to take up the Cross, which the pope himself did not entirely understand, reflected the depth of religious feeling that touched

---

Moments in Time

Eleanor of Aquitaine (1122–1204) was raised in a royal family where women had considerable power. It was not surprising that she brought the liberal ideas of her childhood to her marriage with Louis VII of France. When her husband announced he was joining a crusade, Eleanor not only insisted on accompanying him but she also organized and led her own force of three hundred women. The Amazonian corp, as it was called, tended the wounded and fought when it could. This crusade, like the others, failed.

THE PEOPLE'S CRUSADE

every element of European society. The first move eastward came from the throngs of believers who joined the "People's Crusade." They were led by the barefooted monk, Peter the Hermit, who crossed Europe on a donkey with cross in tow, and his knight, Walter the Penniless. It was a misguided adventure. One advance guard so offended the Hungarians that the locals turned on them, killed many, and ended their existence as a unit. Another group, with Christian passion out of control, slaughtered the Jews in the Rhineland. Other followers eventually made it across the Bosporus only to be massacred by the Seljuks. Such was the tragic fate of the first appearance of the "people" as a distinct, though sadly undisciplined, group in modern European history.

THE FIRST CRUSADE

When the main force of organized knights, made up largely of Norman and Frankish stock, finally set out on the First Crusade in 1096, they, too, ravaged the lands they crossed in Europe and the Balkans. This thirst for adventure, sincerely begun on behalf of the Cross, finally led the Crusaders to Constantinople, which was still a city of wealth and grandeur in an otherwise-decaying Byzantine Empire. A sudden and unforeseen weakening of Seljuk power, however, made the emperor Alexius less anxious to receive European assistance. The historic meeting of the Western and Eastern Christian worlds quickly fell into mutual suspicion, broken promises, and the withdrawal of the Byzantines from the crusading effort after a few minor victories. With a total force of under ten thousand, the feudal knights of Europe and their companion infantry pushed onward with high emotion and not only took Antioch in 1098, but slaughtered thousands of people in the capture of Jerusalem the following year.

THE CRUSADING STATES

The Holy City became the most powerful of the four Crusading States that were established in the subsequent conquest of Syria. To protect the gains that were made, a series of castles, among the greatest of any built in the medieval period, were constructed overlooking strategic valley passes and communication routes. Following the First Crusade, many of these castles were either built or manned by the two great military orders of the Holy Land, the Templars

MILITARY ORDERS

and Hospitallers. Like the monks of the monasteries, the military orders took vows of poverty, chastity, and obedience. Their solemn duty, however, was to defend the Holy Land. Identified by a red cross on a white mantle for Templars and a white cross on a red mantle for Hospitallers, their organizations spread into England, France, Portugal, Spain, Italy, and Hungary.

FAILURE OF THE CRUSADES

Three major and several minor crusades followed the initial attempt to secure the Holy Land. Each one failed. The papacy had achieved moral leadership in 1095, but later invoked crusades too frequently over trivial matters with secular kings to rekindle the emotion of the original effort. As the leadership of the Crusades at times passed to prominent rulers and became more worldly and less spiritual in purpose, the reputation of the papacy suffered. When the pope raised taxes for a crusade, people understood. When the taxes continued as a normal part of papal revenue, people became resentful. Collectively, the Crusades left a mixed story of courage, destruction, often disgrace, and little understanding.

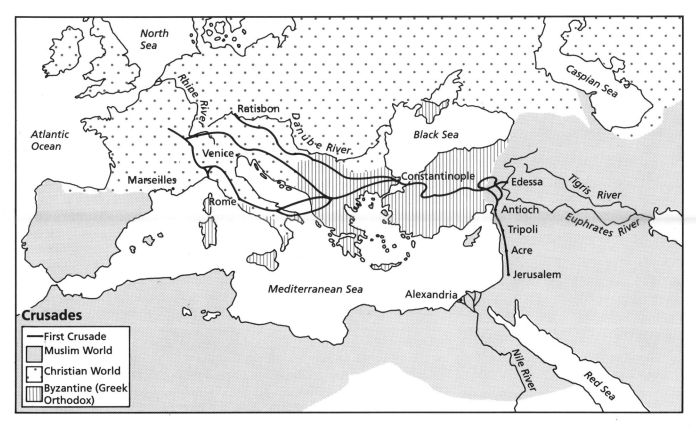

Crusades
— First Crusade
▨ Muslim World
▫ Christian World
▥ Byzantine (Greek Orthodox)

What did the Crusades achieve? The direct results were extremely limited since the Holy Land was brought under Christian control for only a short period of time. Clearly, the Byzantine Empire lost more than it gained. When the Franks of the First Crusade encountered the Byzantine world in Constantinople, they were overwhelmed by what they saw. Indeed, they were treated as and felt themselves to be members of an uncouth and inferior culture. The Byzantine court, however, was a mask of pomp, ceremony, and sophistication over a decaying world while the Franks were the enterprising edge of a new and vigorous civilization. When the Byzantine Empire wilted in the Fourth Crusade, the way was paved for its complete overthrow by the Turks. This left Europe as the central driving force of the Christian message.

Most of the changes that were reshaping Europe from the eleventh to the thirteenth centuries would have taken place with or without the Crusades. Nevertheless, even for trends that began before Urban launched the crusading era, the pace and emphasis of their development was certainly increased. The temporary conquest of Syria gave Westerners an inviting taste of Eastern luxury goods on a much bigger scale than ever before. Spices, valued fabrics, rugs, tapestries, glass mirrors, precious metals, and enamels found their way into

MEETING OF WEST AND EAST

THE PROSPERITY OF ITALIAN CITIES

castles and manor homes of the rich. The trade came to Europe by way of the Italian cities of Venice, Genoa, and Pisa which, largely as a result of their role in the Crusades, emerged as great trading republics that monopolized Mediterranean commerce. Venetian fleets had taken reinforcements to the Holy Land as early as 1100, and all crusades from the Third to the Eighth were transported by sea, usually on Italian merchant ships. The Venetians and Genoese had set up trading posts in Syria and retained many of the Aegean islands taken from the Greeks until the seventeenth century. The need for cash to buy luxury goods available from the Italian traders led to the development of international banking, including loans for trade and the transfer of money by credit note throughout the Mediterranean. The commerce of Venice, in particular, slowly moved northward through the Brenner Pass into the Rhineland and to the medieval towns that were thriving in Flanders and northern Germany.

Crusades to the Holy Land gave Westerners a first-hand look at the geography of the East and an interest in new lands and peoples. During this time, the West became aware of Arab scholarship and science, but few of these advances came from contacts with Syria. The possible exception is the introduction of

ARABIC NUMERALS

Arabic numerals which may have reached the West through commercial relations with Eastern ports. The Venetians minted a gold coin with Arabic inscriptions for Eastern trade. Merchants relying on the cumbersome recording system of Roman numerals probably adopted the more efficient Arabic system as its advantages became clear.

ARAB LEARNING

Most Arab learning, however, reached Europe from the high Islamic culture in Spain. Here, Muslims taught Christian scholars the Greek language which had been virtually unknown in the West since the fall of Rome. Westerners could now study the work of Greek philosophers on a first-hand basis rather than through Arab translations. Such co-operation was not easily achieved since Christian warriors of the Reconquista were trying to rid Spain of Muslim domination! In Sicily, the same process of study was applied to the more technical subjects of medicine, mathematics, and the natural sciences. The achievements of Arab and Greek learning in the arts and sciences became a stimulus for the Renaissance (rebirth) of the twelfth century, in which Europe sought to create a cultural image of its own making.

Cathedrals

ARCHITECTURE

Architecture is the physical imprint that a civilization leaves on the mind. To think of Egypt is to visualize the pyramids, of Greece the Parthenon, and of Rome the Colosseum. Each civilization had much more to offer, but these images capture our attention and raise important questions about the people who built them. The physical imprint of high medieval Europe is the architecture of the great cathedrals.

EARLY BUILDINGS OF CHRISTIAN WORSHIP

Buildings for worship were first built in the third and fourth centuries. The number of Christian converts was growing so rapidly that services could no longer be held in private homes. The Roman basilica had a long, high **nave**, low side aisles, and a semicircular **apse** at the end to accommodate larger numbers. When the Western Roman Empire declined, cities fell into ruin, building skills were lost, and the grandeur of the past became a memory.

Most of the churches constructed during the Dark Ages were simple, rectangular buildings with wooden roofs that frequently caught fire. Charlemagne's Palatine Chapel, built at Aachen in an impressive, octagonal plan, was the exception rather than the rule.

By the eleventh century, with the return of peace and stability, a clear but short-lived, Roman-like style of architecture emerged that became known as **Romanesque**. This was the style used in the mother church of the Clunaic Order and in the hundreds of monasteries sprinkled throughout Western Europe. The old form of the basilica was used to give a long perspective on a raised altar, while a **transept**, which widened each side of the building in front of the apse, gave the ground plan the shape of a Latin cross. From the outside, a Romanesque church appeared as a massive, solid building with heavy, horizontal lines. The nave was covered in a fire-resistant barrel vault of stone, supported by ponderous pillars and thick walls. Little space was left for windows, which often had to be placed near the top so that the strength of the walls would not be weakened. Whether wheel shaped or in a tightened Romanesque arch, windows provided little light. In an age of dim candlelight, the total impact of the interior was gloomy, even depressing. Sculptors and artists attempted, rather unsuccessfully, to brighten the atmosphere with religious carvings on columns or walls and with biblical scenes painted on the ceiling.

Advances in building design, first brought together in 1140 under the guiding inspiration of Suger, Abbot of St. Denis, resulted in a dramatic, new style of architecture known as **Gothic**. Gothic architects were master masons. They developed the **ribbed vault** in which stone ribs, radiating from slender columns like the spokes of an umbrella, spread the weight of the roof from column to column toward the walls. To prevent the cathedral from collapsing outward, **flying buttresses** braced the stress from the outside by spanning a space to the side of the building. The exterior support allowed larger open spaces inside and larger windows that brightened the interior. Indeed, as the **pointed arch**, which could be varied in size, replaced the more limited rounded arch, and as rose windows replaced the more simple wheel, the Gothic cathedral became a storehouse of light that was pleasing to the eye. In contrast to the spiked spires and towers of different shapes and sizes often found in Romanesque buildings, the Gothic cathedral soared towards the sky in total grace and harmony. Every arch and tower on one side had a mirror image on the other. The effect was visually, and, of course, spiritually uplifting. It made everything about the building seem higher than it really was.

Clearly, it was the religious faith of the medieval period that provided the thrust for the "Cathedral Crusade" of Gothic architecture that spread from

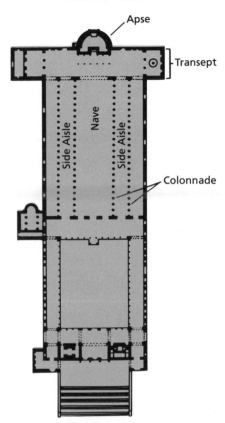

Roman Basilica

The Roman Basilica.

A flying buttress.

CATHEDRAL CRUSADE

The Romanesque Cathedral. A transept, which widens each side of the building in front of the apse, gives the ground plan the shape of a Latin cross.

The Gothic Cathedral. Notice the ribbed vaulting, pointed arch, and flying buttresses typical of this architectural style.

France across Europe until it peaked in the thirteenth century. The Gothic cathedral is a fitting medieval symbol because it harnessed many of the new forces at work in European society. Gothic cathedrals represented the largest economic enterprise of the day, utilizing the skills of master masons, stonecutters, glass makers, metal smiths, carpenters, plumbers, and endless numbers of manual labourers.

Where did the money come from to proceed on such grand projects? Above and beyond the considerable resources of the Church, independent cities of great commercial strength again provide an important answer. The rise of the middle-class merchant marked a shift in medieval wealth from the land and the feudal system to the trade and commerce of the city. In a religious age, nothing could be a greater source of civic pride than to have a grand cathedral. Such a building would dominate the skyline, attract strangers, improve commerce and, for the merchant who contributed to its construction, move his soul one step closer to heaven! Having a magnificent cathedral meant so much that competition in building became a serious undertaking. Architects and designers moved from city to city to learn the latest techniques, see the largest cathedral, and then plan one bigger than anything that had been built before.

The first record construction began in 1163 at Notre Dame in Paris, where the nave reached about 35 m off the floor. After careful measurement and planning, Chartres outdid Notre Dame with a nave height of 36.5 m. In 1212, the cathedral at Reims peaked at almost 38 m, while Amiens boasted a cathedral nave of 42 m within the next decade. Finally, in 1247, the apse at Beauvais soared to almost 48 m, the highest ever achieved by a Gothic cathedral. Unfortunately, it collapsed twice after 1284.

By the middle of the fourteenth century, building enthusiasm began to lessen noticeably. Fewer cathedrals were started, fewer were finished, and most were conceived on a smaller scale.

The Gothic cathedral was more than just a church. Merchants, barons, pilgrims, and travellers contributed their personal sweat and toil as they lifted blocks into place under the guidance of a master mason. In most ancient religions, the people did not have access to their religious sanctuary, but the cathedral, by design, was built to house much of the city's population and became a social centre. Without chairs, people could move about freely. They often brought animals with them, talked openly, and even held town meetings in the cathedral. In some cases, towns did not build city halls because the cathedral provided such an excellent civic meeting place!

Castles

The medieval castles often found beside the churches also bring to mind bold and splendid images. Whereas the church symbolized the power of the divine spirit, the castle represented the position and authority of the feudal lord who wanted to impose local order on an otherwise-lawless countryside. As watch-

The cathedral of Notre Dame in Paris. Note the pointed arches, high proportion of window space, and soaring towers typical of the Gothic style.

SOCIAL ROLE OF THE CATHEDRAL

FEUDALISM AND CASTLES

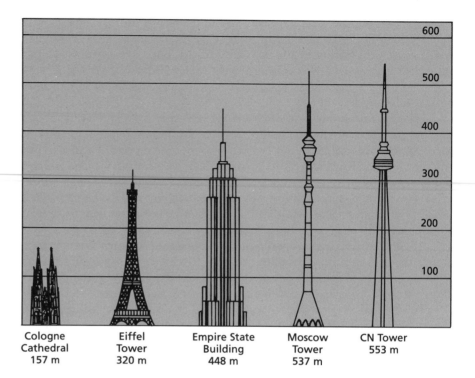

Cologne Cathedral 157 m	Eiffel Tower 320 m	Empire State Building 448 m	Moscow Tower 537 m	CN Tower 553 m

Competitive building was not a purely medieval phenomenon. The practice continues to this day. The Cologne Cathedral, which stands 157 m high, was begun in 1248 and was completed 632 years later in 1880; the Eiffel Tower, built in Paris in 1889, tips at over 304 m; while New York's Empire State Building, completed in 1931, stands at 448 m. More recent constructions, the Moscow Tower and Toronto's CN Tower, soar to 537 and 553 m respectively.

MILITARY ROLE OF THE CASTLE

towers surrounded by wooden palisades developed into massive fortresses with thick stone walls, deep moats, and protected entrances, the castle emerged as the fortified residence of knights, princes, and kings.

As feudalism spread outwards from France, so did the presence of castles. When William conquered the Anglo-Saxons at Hastings, the feudal approach used successfully in Normandy was transferred to England. The building program that followed in the first century after the Norman Conquest gave England more castles than it ever had before or since. It was also the Frankish knights who led the First Crusade, set up feudal kingdoms in the Holy Land, and left a magnificent series of fortified castles for local defence against the infidel. Krak des Chevaliers in Syria, with walls over 24 m thick, immense towers, and facilities for two thousand men, represented the crowning achievement of military architecture. In Germany, castle building was not widespread until feudalism became firmly established in the twelfth century.

CASTLE LIFE

Feudal society, with reciprocal obligations from serf to lord to king, was organized for war. The castles it fostered were not only defensive strongholds commanding a dominating position over hilltop and valley, but were an aggressive extension of military operations. Mounted knights organized into cavalry, when properly used with supporting infantry, were the most effective fighting force of the day and the castle provided a secure home base for their daily adventures. Ironically, the castle was also the only real defence against a strong cavalry charge! Even with the later inventions of guns and gunpowder, it was discovered that the new weapons made the castle easier to defend than to attack.

RESIDENTIAL ROLE OF THE CASTLE

The castle was also the residence of the feudal lord, his vassal knights, and a garrison of soldiers. Although private apartments had some comforts, life in the castle was hardly luxurious. Sanitation was poor, halls were drafty, and the limited heat provided by fireplaces and inefficient stoves could not warm the dampness of an earthen or stone floor. Odours from the knights' horses and other animals were always present and ventilation was such that smoke-filled rooms were slow to clear. The efforts of a supporting staff of artisans, cooks, and household servants to complete the daily chores made the castle a busy place. When rent had to be paid, services rendered, or lawsuits pleaded, it was to the castle that people came. Jousting tournaments that prepared the knights for the ordeal of battle were usually held at or near the castle grounds. On special occasions, serfs even ate in the great hall that was a common feature of most castles, and they were entertained by troupes of acrobats and jugglers.

Castles were relatively small in area. The Tower of London, for example, occupied only a corner of the English town that grew within the walls of an ancient Roman city. Its impressive position on high ground, however, accurately reflected the castle's influence as the grandest residence in medieval life.

THE CASTLE AS A PRISON

The dual role of the castle as fortress and residence was accompanied by its use as a prison for men and women of political importance or high social rank. Not only were the castles secure, but they provided a surrounding that matched the status of those detained. Prisons did not reflect the picture painted by folklore and tourist pamphlets of cold, damp, rat-infested dungeons until the sixteenth and seventeenth centuries.

The multipurpose role of the castle began to decline with the emergence of the middle class and its strong, central government in the cities. As the castle's military value lessened, it became simply a stately manor residence.

The Power and Decline of the Medieval Church

The thirteenth century, often referred to as the "High Middle Ages," saw the flowering of medieval civilization. Church reform continued in both traditional and new directions as the papacy reached the zenith of its power. Human knowledge, now greatly increased through contact with the Muslim world, seemed to be in perfect harmony with heavenly wisdom.

NEW RELIGIOUS ORDERS

In the twelfth century, many new religious orders, including the Cistercians, Carthusians, and Carmelites, devoted themselves to a stricter Christian life in isolated monasteries when the Church became too worldly in its affairs. The prestige lost by the papacy in calling crusades of questionable purpose was regained by Pope Innocent III (1198–1216). Like Gregory VII, Innocent believed in the supremacy of the pope not just in the Church of Rome, but over the secular world as well. Innocent, however, proved to be a more capable

INNOCENT III

Christ's ascension to heaven is typical of the themes found in medieval art.

THE FRANCISCANS

THE DOMINICANS

ABELARD

THOMAS AQUINAS

leader. He successfully intervened in a feud over the German throne, settled a marriage dispute involving Philip Augustus of France, and forced King John, upon threat of invasion, to accept papal nomination within the English Church. At the same time, Innocent introduced the first of many thirteenth-century taxes on the clergy and tightened the administrative system of the Church. This increased papal revenue and improved the quality of Church representatives in the eyes of the people. Under Innocent, the Church was as effective as any medieval monarchy.

The growth of towns, however, posed new problems and made it necessary for the Church to adapt to changing times. Rural monasteries were ill suited to the purpose. The answer came from the son of a wealthy Italian merchant from the town of Assisi. A spoiled and carefree young man, Francis experienced a sudden conversion and determined to live his life as Christ had done, tending to the needs of the poor, the sick, the downtrodden, and even the lepers who were quite numerous in the Italian countryside. During the Fifth Crusade, he carried his service to Egypt and Palestine where he preached the love of God. Francis's example attracted disciples who dutifully followed his truly Christian existence. Their simple and emotional appeal proved so successful that Pope Innocent III recognized them as a new mendicant order that became known as the Franciscans or Grey Friars. In contrast to the monks of the monasteries who devoted their lives to personal salvation, the Franciscan friars travelled to the towns and cities of Europe bringing their message to the people. Their work kept in the fold those who were unhappy with the Church but who still held sincere Christian beliefs.

The papacy attempted to win the minds of the educated classes by authorizing a second mendicant order known as Dominicans or Black Friars after the Spaniard Dominic. Their prime concern was the growing number of **heretics** who had became disillusioned with Church practices and were swayed by new ideas contrary to Church doctrine. As the texts of Aristotle entered Europe from the Muslim world, the Church faced a serious intellectual challenge to its teaching. Many of Aristotle's scientific views conflicted with those of the Bible. The French philosopher Abelard startled his fellow Christians in the twelfth century by arguing that by studying both sides of an issue, a deeper understanding and stronger religious faith could be achieved. The Dominicans continued this study by recruiting the brightest minds available with the intent of showing that one truth formed the foundation of both the new science and religion.

In the late thirteenth century, Thomas Aquinas, the greatest scholar of his time, joined the Dominican order and produced his famous work, *Summation of Theology*, in which he attempted to answer every possible argument that a nonbeliever could raise against Christian beliefs. For Thomas, there was no conflict between faith and reason. If a question could not be resolved, it meant that human reason was imperfect and that one therefore should rely on Christian faith for the answer. In this way, Thomas felt that Aristotle and Christianity were quite consistent.

Meanwhile, the intellectual training of the Dominicans made them a natural choice to direct a special court called the **Inquisition**, established in 1233 to combat heresy. The Church demanded total obedience to its teaching and the inquest marked an attempt to stamp out unacceptable ideas before other Christians were led astray. It also represented a sincere attempt to reclaim the soul of the accused. If the heretic admitted error and sought reconciliation with the Church, the trial ended after a suitable penance was administered. If the heretic was slow to confess, s/he was tortured. A convicted heretic was usually burned at the stake. The sight of charred bodies in the marketplaces of Europe certainly created fear, but it won little respect and few sincere converts to the Christian cause. No doubt the inquisitors felt they were performing a necessary service, but in the long run the Christian Church could not be held together by such extreme measures.

THE INQUISITION

By the early fourteenth century, papal prestige and influence began a rapid decline. When Pope Boniface VII proclaimed papal supremacy in 1302, King Philip of France had him arrested! Philip then secured the election of the first of seven consecutive French popes who took up residence at Avignon, where they were subjected to French pressure. Although the English and Germans were upset, popes lived at Avignon until 1378. This period is known to history as the "Babylonian Captivity" because of the corruption it produced. Cut off from most of the normal Church revenue because of frequent rebellions in the Papal States around Rome, popes issued indulgences for money, sold offices, and even auctioned off an "expectancy" which gave the next vacant post after all regular offices were gone to the highest bidder.

THE BABYLONIAN CAPTIVITY

To make matters worse, rival factions of cardinals elected two claimants to the papal throne in 1378 only to be followed by a third candidate in 1409! The Church thus had three popes, each with his own set of cardinals and bureaucracy. Although the **Great Schism** was ended by the General Church Council of Constance in 1418, the respect given to the papacy was at an all-time low. Failure to see the need for reform in the face of mounting criticism eventually divided Christian Europe into the Roman Catholic and Protestant faiths in the course of the next century.

THE GREAT SCHISM

Prosperity and Depression

During the High Middle Ages, cities increased in size, became more numerous and even banded together for their mutual protection against a local prince or lord. The prosperity of the middle-class merchant steadily broke the bonds of feudalism which had held medieval society together for so long.

PROSPERITY OF THE MIDDLE CLASS

Although several trading associations developed in various regions of Europe, the most important was the collection of north German cities known as the **Hanseatic League**. Formed to combat the revived strength of the Ger-

THE HANSEATIC LEAGUE

man nobility, the Hanseatic League included the major centres of Lubeck, Bremen, Cologne, Hamburg, and Danzig, and almost one hundred smaller towns and villages. Members abided by a common set of rules for trade, enjoyed economic concessions, outfitted a navy to protect themselves from pirates, and had an army strong enough to win trading privileges from unwilling nobles and kings. By the beginning of the fourteenth century, the axis of trade moved eastward from the Champagne country of France to the German cities of northern Europe.

ECONOMIC STAGNATION AFTER 1300

After three centuries of steady economic progress, however, in about 1300 the European economy began to stagnate for reasons that are not entirely understood. Agricultural production dropped partly because there was no new land to be brought under cultivation and because existing soil was becoming exhausted. No technological advances were developed to meet the problem of declining yields. At the same time, the climate of Europe cooled noticeably for much of the next century and widespread famine struck hard in 1315–1317, 1333–1334, 1337–1342, and 1345–1347. Population growth not only levelled off but began to decline.

EUROPEAN EXPANSION STALLED

In addition, the geographical expansion of Europe was halted and even reversed. All of the territory won by the Crusaders in the Holy Land was now lost; the Scandinavians abandoned their outposts in Greenland and stopped their voyages to the New World; the Moors stalled the reconquest in Spain; the Russians prevented any further advance in Eastern Europe; the break-up of the Mongol Empire in Asia ended the few ties established with the Far East; while the Ottoman Turks, a Muslim tribe from Asia, threatened the Balkans. Without new markets to compensate for a declining population, the production of goods fell and the trade that had encouraged the growth of cities decreased. It became increasingly difficult to obtain money, which had replaced feudal loyalty as the basis for relationships in all walks of medieval life. Vassals of the king increasingly paid **scutage** fees in place of military service, while nobles concentrated on the production of cash crops for profit. As production slowed, guild membership in the towns became more restrictive, and wages often fell behind the rapid rise in prices. Tension between journeymen and the wealthy city merchants, who had large sums of money or **capital** for investment in trade and industry, became frequent. Usually, it was the peasants who were squeezed the hardest since their only choice was to work in the city for a low wage or return as lowly serfs to the feudal countryside. Peasant suffering became so extreme that serious peasant revolts occurred in Flanders, France, and England.

THE BLACK DEATH

Any hope for improvement fell to despair with the arrival of the bubonic plague, better known as the Black Death because of the dark spots that appeared on the victims' skin. The disease, carried by fleas on black rats, was brought on trading ships from the Black Sea ports of Asia to the Italian city of Genoa in 1347. The narrow, winding, sewage-laden streets of medieval towns were poorly drained and filthy, natural breeding grounds for the killer rodents. In three years, the highly contagious disease spread throughout Christendom, from the Mediterranean to Scandinavia, bringing horror and death to every village and town in its path. Characterized by high fever, inflammation of the throat, swelling in the groin and armpits, stabbing chest pain, and the vomiting and spitting of blood, death brought the suffering to a merciful end within three days. Panic-stricken officials fled from their cities as the plague approached, while parents abandoned infected children and physicians and clergymen left the sick to fend for themselves.

It is hard to grasp the scale of the disaster. No calamity in history, from the plague of Pericles in ancient Athens to the slaughter of civilian populations in World War II, has been as severe. Between one-quarter and one-third of Europe's population, about 25 000 000 people, died from the onslaught of the Black Death. Florence had a population of 114 000 in 1338, but only 50 000 were left when the plague had passed. The tiny village of Givy in Burgundy lost almost half of its 1600 people within five months. England had a population of 3 700 000 before the plague struck but only 2 100 000 a half century later.

POPULATION DECLINE

The Black Death intensified the dislocation of the medieval economy that had already been hard hit by famine and would continue to be ravaged by war. The old order seemed to collapse and it was not until the beginning of the fifteenth century that Europe began to recover.

Emergence of the Nation State in England and France

While Germany remained divided by the power of feudal princes and Italy became dominated by rival city-states, England and France grew into national monarchies with centralized governments that attracted the loyalty and support of their subjects. In the twelfth and thirteenth centuries, the Church was often a serious rival for power and influence. But the decline of the Church during the ''Babylonian Captivity'' and the Great Schism opened the way for the strengthening of national feeling under the leadership of the nation state.

In England, strong kings like Henry II (1154–1189) considerably enhanced royal power. Through Henry, the king assumed more responsibility for civil law by giving royal courts jurisdiction over appeals from local courts and in questions of land tenure. By expanding the use of the jury system in royal courts, the traditional fate of trial by ordeal and the great variety of practices in feudal customs were slowly replaced. Henry had thus laid the foundation for English common law which would be applied equally to all individuals throughout the kingdom, and which made the people look to the king rather than to the nobles for justice.

HENRY II

Henry was equally concerned that the king should control the Church. He secured the appointment of his friend Thomas Becket as the Archbishop of Canterbury in 1162 to help achieve that goal. Becket turned the tables on his

THOMAS BECKET

sponsor, however, by insisting on special privileges for the Church in cases concerning the clergy. Not surprisingly, this led to a clash with Henry, followed by a six-year exile for Becket in France, and then a pardon which did not conceal the fact that neither man had changed his mind. When Becket was assassinated in Canterbury Cathedral by some misguided knights who thought they were acting out the king's wishes, Henry was genuinely crushed and in despair. He was also forced to give in to the demands of an outraged Church to secure his repentance. Although Henry lost this dispute, he was able to dominate Church life by ensuring that the election of bishops take place in accordance with the king's wishes.

MAGNA CARTA

Later attempts to wield royal power by less able kings contributed to England's unique political character. In a desperate effort to raise money for a war against France, King John (1199–1216) resorted to excessive taxation that weakened his support throughout the country. When defeat on the battlefield also brought the king's military leadership into question, the English barons plotted a revolt and forced John to accept the Great Charter or **Magna Carta** of 1215. Often misquoted and misunderstood, this famous feudal document outlined the existing relationship between the king and his feudal barons. In practice, it meant that the great council, made up of the king's leading vassals, must give its approval before any taxes could be raised beyond the king's personal or normal revenue. In theory, it established the principle that the king was beneath the law of the land and bound by its provisions.

PARLIAMENT

As the thirteenth century progressed, kings continually needed more money. The great council, which became known as **Parliament**, after the French word *parler*, to speak, allowed the king to raise taxes on terms that increased its power. When Henry III resisted Parliament's attempt to extend its influence, a rebellion led by the king's brother-in-law, Simon de Monfort, virtually took over the state on behalf of Parliament. Membership in Parliament was granted to knights and to representatives from every borough, which at least gave the people who were most likely to contribute a say in the passage of future taxes. In the reign of Edward III in the fourteenth century, Parliament not only approved new taxes, but signed laws debated in open parliamentary sessions. Parliament was limited by the short length of its sessions, and the king remained a powerful figure who ruled most of the time by royal decree. Nevertheless, laws were now passed by the **King-in-Parliament**, a term which accurately summed up the fact that power was shared and needed the approval of those who were governed.

THE KING-IN-PARLIAMENT

HUGH CAPET

France took much longer to unite under the control of one government. When Hugh Capet was selected in 987 by an assembly of nobles and bishops to become king, France was really a collection of almost independent territories that included Flanders, Normandy, Burgundy, Toulouse, Anjou, Champagne, and Aquitaine. Royal authority was limited to the Île de France in the Seine Valley and focussed on the cities of Orleans and Paris. In the territories, it was the members of the nobility who ruled, and for two centuries their allegiance to Capetian kings was token at best. William the Conqueror, as duke of Normandy, had been a vassal to the French king in this limited sense, but he kept Normandy after his victory at Hastings. Later English kings, through a series of marriages, claimed authority over about half of France.

Under the skilled military leadership of Philip II, better known as Philip Augustus (1180–1222), most of these English feudal kingdoms were brought under French control. Stalled at first by Richard the Lionhearted (1189–1199), Philip did much better when Richard's brother John came to the throne. After Philip won all of northern France from John and his German allies, the English king attempted to regain his former possessions, but was crushed at the Battle of Bouvines in 1214. At home, this forced John to accept the Magna Carta thrust upon him by the English barons, while in France it weakened any English claim to French territory. Military success enabled Philip to tighten his grip over the French nobility and his successors built on the foundation that he established.

PHILIP AUGUSTUS

By the reign of Philip IV (1285–1314), France had become the most powerful state in Europe. Philip, known as "the Fair," because of his blond hair and light skin, called the first meeting of the Estates General, a council similar in appearance, but not in operation, to the English Parliament. The Estates General consisted of representatives from each of the three major classes in France–the nobles, the clergy, and the commoners–and was directly under royal control. Where the English Parliament acted as a partner in running the country with the king, each of the three estates in the Estates General met and voted separately, which weakened their influence. The French king could raise taxes on his own authority and, as a result, the Estates General seldom met and provided little advice. As ties between the king and wealthy trading towns increased, a royal army was created that could defeat any rebellious baron, a fact which made it clear that in France the king was supreme. While England followed a path leading to parliamentary government, France was headed towards absolute rule with the king responsible only to himself.

PHILIP THE FAIR

THE ESTATES GENERAL

In 1337, when Edward III landed in Normandy to claim the French throne, a series of intermittent wars, known as the Hundred Years' War, began between England and France. Economic depression and the onslaught of the Black Death occurred during the same era, which meant years of hardship and exhaustion for both countries. Although more time was spent seeking out the enemy than in actual fighting, England won most of the major battles in the war largely because of better tactics and co-ordination of their smaller military forces. The French relied on the charge of the mounted knight, but did not reckon with the devastating impact of the 2-m English longbow and, later, the thunderous cannon, which marked the beginning of the end for the feudal knight and his castle as the cornerstones of war.

THE HUNDRED YEARS' WAR

Despite its military success, England had become a divided nation at home. The death of Edward's son, the Black Prince, opened the door to rival claimants to the throne. England did not have the resources to conquer a country

At Crécy in 1346, a hail of 75-cm arrows from the 2-m English longbow greeted the French charge. Horses were felled at 200 m, armour was pierced at 50 m, and the battlefield was littered with the dead and the pride of French chivalry.

JOAN OF ARC

with four times its population, and the lack of a united war effort slowly took its toll. As the French army became better organized and better supplied, the tide of the war began to turn in favour of France. In 1424, a young peasant girl from Domremy, known as Joan of Arc, travelled 500 km to tell the king that angels had chosen her to save France from the English invaders. Although she had no military knowledge, she was given a minor post in the French army. Her bravery and self-sacrifice inspired enthusiasm in the French troops and fear among the English who believed that she was responsible for many of their misfortunes in battle. When Joan of Arc was captured by the English and condemned by the Church as a heretic and a witch, she was burned at the stake and became a martyr for the French cause.

Under the peace concluded in 1453, England lost all of its territory in France except the port of Calais. Nevertheless, the wars stimulated a sense of national feeling and purpose that focussed attention on the central government in each country. Within England, the struggle for the throne, which had weakened the country during the Hundred Years' War, continued for another three decades. The king's supporters fought on behalf of the red rose of the house of Lancaster while their opponents wore the white rose of the house of York. When Henry Tudor assumed the leadership of the Lancastrian forces and won a decisive victory at the Battle of Bosworth in 1485, few people realized that a new era had begun. Henry's victory ended the instability of the medieval period and marked the beginning of prosperity for England under Tudor leadership. The wars of the fifteenth century had rendered the feudal knights less valuable in war and reduced their power as a political force while the central governments in the nation states of England and France emerged as the focal points of power. Relations between the two countries, however, remained bitter and hostile for centuries until the threat of German might drew them together in an entente (understanding) prior to World War I.

BATTLE OF BOSWORTH

The Fall of Constantinople and the Ottoman Turks

The shifting tides of war and politics were gradually overshadowed by the increasingly serious threat posed by the Ottoman Turks to the eastern borders of Europe after 1350. An obscure Asian people who finally gained their independence from the Seljuks, the Ottoman Turks crossed the Dardanelles from Asia Minor in 1356 and ravaged their way through much of Greece and Bulgaria. In the process, the shrinking and decaying Byzantine Empire, with its ancient capital of Constantinople, was hemmed in at every turn. The city was saved from invasion only when the Turks were defeated at Ankara in 1402 by the ruthless Mongolian warrior Tamerlane, who extended his short-lived empire from India to the Mediterranean. When the highly skilled Muhammad II came to the Ottoman throne in 1451, however, the Turks were ready for a final siege against the last great city of Christendom.

THE OTTOMAN TURKS

TAMERLANE
MUHAMMAD II

Constantinople was not the magnificent centre of former ages. The Black Death had been devastating and, by the fifteenth century only about one hundred thousand people were left in a city where over half a million had lived two centuries before. Nevertheless, Constantinople had stood for over a thousand years as the guardian of Greek, Roman, and Byzantine culture and tradition through peace and war. Of direct importance to Muhammad was the city's incredible defences which were the most formidable in all Christendom. Set on a wedge-shaped peninsula that jutted into the Bosporus, Constantinople was protected on the landward side by a moat and triple walls over 6 km long and 10 m high that were spiked with ninety-six fortified towers. An additional 14 km of walled harbour and a floating boom across the mouth of the Golden Horn prevented assault from the sea.

THE DEFENCE OF CONSTANTINOPLE

Muhammad planned the siege of Constantinople very carefully. The city had survived even in the centuries of Byzantine decline, not just because of its impregnable walls but because it could be supplied by ship from the Bosporus.

THE SIEGE OF CONSTANTINOPLE

Part of the waterway could be controlled from the small fourteenth-century fortress of Anadolu on the Asian side. In 1452, Muhammad organized and completed construction of the great Remuli fortress on the European side with a 3-t cannon that effectively halted any ship heading toward Constantinople from the Black Sea. With a force of at least eighty thousand soldiers and huge cannons upwards of 9 m in length that could shoot a 500-kg ball, Muhammad began his attack in April of 1453. Despite continuous bombardment and repeated military assault, the Turks were repulsed for six weeks through a heroic defence by only nine thousand able-bodied citizens.

Muhammad's failure to break the floating boom that blocked the entrance to the Golden Horn inspired an impressive engineering feat. A roadway of almost 2 km was laid overland from the Bosporus, across ridges 60 m high, to the shore behind the boom at the harbour entrance. Through an exhaustive effort of oxen pulling and men pushing to the rhythm of fife and drum, seventy Turkish ships, braced on wheeled cradles, reached the Golden Horn. Muhammad now surrounded Constantinople on all sides by land and sea. Even in this seemingly impossible situation, the Byzantines valiantly beat off two Turkish assaults. With frustration rapidly setting in, Muhammad launched yet another attack during the night of 29 May. He finally won a hard-fought victory when the Turks discovered a small gate that gave them direct access to the inner city had been carelessly left open. Muhammad's specially trained regiment of Janizaries escorted him to the city centre and his men were allowed to pillage for three days as was the Muslim custom. The great Christian church of Hagia Sophia was converted into a mosque, and when minarets were added later, it became the prototype for all Islamic places of worship.

THE OTTOMAN EMPIRE

Muhammad proved to be an able statesman who consolidated the territory won from the Byzantines, and, through additional conquest, helped to make the Ottoman Turks the strongest force in the eastern Mediterranean. Under Suleiman the Magnificent (1520–1566), the Ottoman Empire reached its zenith, encompassing territory from the Persian Gulf, North Africa, Anatolia, the Balkans, and even much of Hungary. The limit of its westward expansion was reached only after Suleiman's force of two hundred fifty thousand men withdrew from the siege of Vienna in 1529, in the face of a gallant defence by the local garrison. For much of the fifteenth and sixteenth centuries, however, the Ottoman Empire, as leader of the Muslim world, appeared ready to seize Eastern Europe at any time.

Discovering "New" Worlds?

IMAGES OF DISTANT LANDS

Medieval Europe was fascinated by Asia and Africa, even though little was known about them. In popular stories, they became the homes of legendary dragons, legless birds, and giant animals and sea creatures who would sink any ship that came too close. They were lands of magic, wealth, and danger, where a river of gold flowed into scorching seas too hot for any human to survive. Lack of

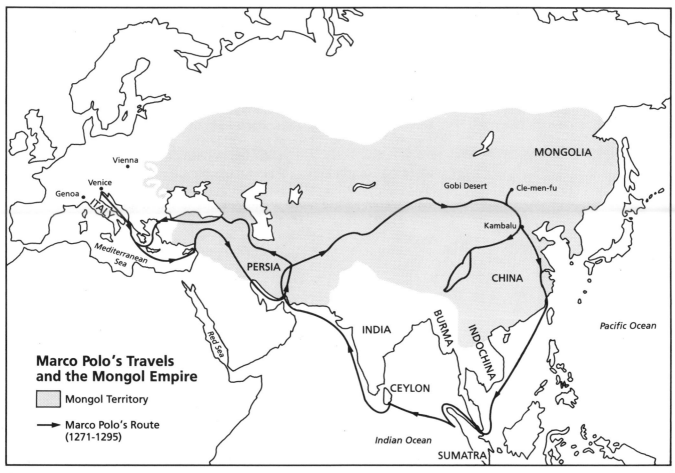

Marco Polo's Travels and the Mongol Empire

Mongol Territory

Marco Polo's Route (1271-1295)

first-hand knowledge fuelled the imagination when there was no way to prove or disprove the claims that were made. In the thirteenth century, however, the mighty Genghis Khan (1206–1227) conquered the Asian tribes from China to southern Russia and created the colossal Mongol Empire that was even more extensive than the world subdued by Alexander the Great. After 1250, Christian travellers were allowed to pass unmolested through these lands and Kublai Khan (1257–1294) requested that the "Latin" people send him one hundred teachers who could prove the virtue of Christianity. At that critical moment, when a bridge between East and West might have been built, a troubled papacy sent only two Dominican friars! And they abandoned their task when the hardships of their journey became apparent!

In 1271, however, Marco Polo, the son of a Venetian businessman who traded at Constantinople, accompanied his father on a three-and-a-half-year expedition to the court of Kublai Khan. Here, Marco Polo's quick wit and

GENGHIS KHAN

KUBLAI KHAN

MARCO POLO

mastery of the Tartar language won favour with the emperor, who gave Marco an official position and sent him on numerous missions in southwestern China over a seventeen-year period. Kublai Khan wanted the Polos to stay, but they eventually made their way out of China after serving as travel guides for a Mongolian princess.

POLO'S PICTURE OF THE EAST

Upon their return to Europe, Marco Polo was taken prisoner by the Genoese during a naval battle with Venice in 1298. While in prison, he told his story to a writer named Rusticciano and the result, *The Travels of Marco Polo*, opened the eyes of Europe to the world of the Orient. Descriptions of untold wealth in gold, silks, and jewels, and populations numbering in the millions led many to conclude that Polo was exaggerating, and he was ridiculed as "Marco Millions." Nevertheless, his tale about a powerful, Christian king named Prester John, whom he had heard of but not met, inspired hope that these distant lands could be converted to the Cross. Chinese records of the day confirm that a certain Polo was a member of the imperial court of 1277, which suggests a general truth to Marco Polo's story, if not to all of the specific details.

TRADE WITH THE EAST

As the Ottoman Turks gradually ended safe Christian travel to the East, the images of Asia and Africa again became a mixture of legend and the startling reports of Marco Polo. The spices, silks, perfumes, and jewels that arrived in Europe by way of overland caravan routes across Asia to Constantinople and Levantine ports, however, had to be paid for with dwindling supplies of gold. Trade in the Mediterranean was dominated by Florence, Milan, and, particularly, Venice who, as intermediaries, profited from the mark-up on the oriental products they funnelled into Europe.

Those developing nation states that did not profit from Mediterranean trade were encouraged by improvements in navigation and shipbuilding to search for sea routes to establish their own trade links with fabled Asian lands. Not only did they hope to reduce the cost of the luxury goods, they also hoped to conquer new lands that could provide gold and precious stones.

PRINCE HENRY THE NAVIGATOR

It was the leadership of Prince Henry the Navigator (1394–1460) that made Portugal a world leader in exploration. Although Henry did not go on any of the voyages that made him famous, he gathered together at Sagres geographers, map makers, and sailors who systematically collected evidence, improved charts, and extended the limits of human knowledge about open sea navigation. As the Moors were driven out of their homeland, the Portuguese became aware of the gold, ivory, and slaves brought by Muslim caravans to the coast of Africa. Henry intended to seize these riches for Portugal, find a route around Africa, and meet the legendary Prester John, whom he hoped would join in a crusade to rid the Holy Land of Muslims once and for all. During Henry's lifetime, the coastal islands of the Madeiras, the Canaries, and the Azores were secured, but Africa proved to be a much larger continent than anyone imagined. The work and inspiration that Henry provided, however, were responsible for the later success of Bartolemeu Diaz, who rounded the Cape of Good

Hope in 1488, and for Vasco da Gama, who reached India by way of the Cape in 1498. Da Gama returned to Lisbon with a cargo valued at sixty times the cost of the voyage, but, by this time, another explorer, largely by luck and courage rather than systematic planning, had opened new horizons in another direction.

VASCO DA GAMA

In 1484, a Genoese Italian named Christopher Columbus had approached King John of Portugal with a plan to reach Asia by sailing west. Columbus was turned down, probably because his estimate of the size of the earth and, therefore, the length of his voyage, seemed too short. Throughout history, the size and shape of the earth had been a subject of keen interest and discussion. By the fifteenth century, however, most informed thinkers believed that the earth was a sphere. The revived work of the ancient geographer Ptolemy was used to calculate the distance across the ocean from Europe to Asia. No one had any conception of the continents of North and South America. The Viking voyages of the tenth and eleventh centuries were either unknown or ignored, and if Columbus had heard of them when he travelled to Iceland, they played no part in his quest for Asia.

CHRISTOPHER COLUMBUS

Columbus greatly underestimated the distance from Europe to the fabled wealth of Cathay (China) and Cipangu (Japan) that he had eagerly read about in *The Travels of Marco Polo*. With the assistance of the Italian physician and part-time geographer Paolo Toscanelli, Columbus studied Ptolemy (whom he doubted), Marines of Tyre (whom he believed), and the first-hand calculations of Marco Polo about the size of Asia. Columbus concluded that the distance from the Canaries to Japan was about 3900 km. The real distance by air is over 17 000 km.

THE CALCULATIONS OF COLUMBUS

Absolutely convinced he was right, Columbus went to Spain and presented his project to King Ferdinand and Queen Isabella in 1486. After six years of waiting and ridicule at the hands of those who thought he was mad, Columbus was given a chance to prove his boastful claims. Columbus left on his voyage with the same motivations that spurred his many followers: hopes of glory and wealth, and curiosity combined with a sense of Christian mission. Spain, in the same year, climaxed the centuries-old Reconquista with the final expulsion of the Moors from Granada. The religious zeal that saw the creation of the Spanish Inquisition at home now received a possible outlet overseas should new lands be discovered.

THE LONG WAIT

Columbus's epoch-making, thirty-five-day voyage that reached the shores of San Salvador in the Bahamas on 12 October 1492, was long regarded as the first discovery of America. Nevertheless, sagas passed by word of mouth and recent archaeological evidence have since revealed that the Vikings made earlier voyages to the New World. The Aztecs believed Cortes's arrival in 1519 was the promised return of the legendary, white, red-bearded god who had once lived among them. Was the conquest of Mexico made possible by the arrival of a wayward Viking from an earlier age? Other questions raised from a

SUCCESS?

variety of sources suggest that contacts could have been made by the Egyptians and Phoenicians and even from oriental cultures that somehow crossed the Pacific Ocean long before Columbus approached America from the opposite direction. When was the first transoceanic crossing completed?

PROBLEM QUESTION

When the issue of the earliest pre-Columbian discovery of America is examined in terms of archaeological evidence and logical speculation, is the most convincing view expressed by Casson, who favoured the Viking landings, Heyerdahl, who stressed the role of the Egyptians and Phoenicians, or Hitching, who felt that prehistoric contact had been made?

ALTERNATIVE ONE

Who First Crossed the Oceans?—Based on "Who First Crossed the Oceans?" by Lionel Casson, 1977

Lionel Casson thinks the Vikings were probably the first to cross the Atlantic Ocean, and in his contribution to *Mysteries of the Past*, he explains why.

We know that all of the Vikings, and especially the Norwegians, were expert seamen. We also know that they had robust galleys for their voyages. The first we know from epic tales. For the second, we have evidence. Between 1867 and 1903, archaeologists discovered three Viking tombs in which the dead had been buried in their boats. But why does Casson think the Vikings crossed the Atlantic first?

The same sagas that tell of the Viking skill and daring at sea also tell about their adventures. It is on these poems, written by Icelandic bards, that Casson bases his text.

The story begins around A.D. 900, when a mariner named Gunbjorn was blown off his course to Iceland and sighted the coast of Greenland. For almost a hundred years, Gunbjorn's claim was little more than the subject of a saga. Then, a Norwegian living in Iceland named Eric the Red, decided to search for the site. As legend has it, Eric had committed murder and was banished from Iceland for three years. Looking for Gunbjorn's land was an adventurous way to fill the time.

With his family and some friends in tow, Eric set sail in A.D. 982, and landed on the southwest coast of Greenland. Apparently, Eric liked the country. When his exile was over, he returned to Iceland, not to stay, but to recruit settlers for his new colony near present-day Julianehab.

According to Casson, Danish archaeologists have evidence that verifies this part of the tale. The typical longhouse described in Viking legends has been found at the excavation site. The great hall with 3-m thick walls of solid earth measures 15 m by 5 m, and is claimed to be the home of Eric himself.

Trained as a missionary, Eric's son, Leif, abandoned preaching for exploring by about A.D. 1000. His father had been prompted by the tales of Gunbjorn's discovery and Leif was lured by a similar story. Some years earlier, another mariner, who had been blown off his course to Greenland, had reported seeing land three times. With a crew of thirty-five, Leif set sail.

Poems tell of Leif's successes. He found the rocky island, the wooded areas, and the grassy island just as the mariner had described. Leif named the mainland opposite Wineland, or Vinland, when grapes were discovered growing in the area. Leif and his crew were in for another surprise. Winter was very different from winters in Greenland or Iceland. There was no frost, the grass stayed green almost all year, and the daylight hours were longer.

Although Leif's party left in the spring, others ventured to the new land. Thorwald, another of Eric's sons, spent two years on Vinland before he was killed by an arrow during an argument with natives using skin boats. Two more expeditions followed, spent time, and returned home; there the story ends.

Just how much of the tale actually occurred and how much is poetic imagination? According to Casson, there is firm evidence of a Viking settlement in Newfoundland. Between 1961 and 1968, Danish archaeologists excavating at L'Anse-au-Meadow uncovered buildings and artifacts that were definitely Norse, dating about A.D. 1000. Could these be the remains of Leif's visit? Is northern Newfoundland Vinland? No one will say.

Casson begins his examination of the description of Vinland with the most obvious problem, the grapes. Yet, Casson points out that a sixteenth-century naval surgeon reports seeing "wild grapes incredible" in Newfoundland. If then, why not earlier? This could certainly be the case if there were warmer temperatures over the northern Atlantic, as many historians argue. Casson admits, however, that even warmer weather would probably not produce the abundant forests and green grass year-round as told in the sagas. Could this be the exaggeration of the bards?

If not Newfoundland, then where? According to Casson, a number of locations along the eastern seaboard as far south as Virginia have been offered at one time or another. A round tower at Newport, Rhode Island is one example. Some scholars credit it to the Vikings, others credit it to the colonials. The evidence tends to favour the colonials.

Perhaps the most interesting claim Casson describes involved the notorious Kensington Stone, found during the last century on a farm near Kensington, Minnesota. Apparently, the stone, which bore an inscription in the Viking script, was discredited as a forgery. Later, the stone was retrieved from the farmer's yard by Hjalmar Holland, a collector of Viking artifacts, who defended its authenticity for the next fifty years. However, the validity of other objects owned by Holland was also questionable. None was found *in situ*, and the three halberds in his collection were discredited when it was discovered that they were actually tobacco cutters made for the American Tobacco Company to advertise Battle Axe Plug Tobacco.

Although the exact location of Vinland has yet to be verified, Casson is convinced that the Vikings did indeed cross the Atlantic.

Questions

1. a) What is the source of our information about Viking voyages in the North Atlantic?
   b) How do we know what Viking ships looked like?
2. a) Why did Eric the Red set out in search of Greenland?
   b) What evidence has confirmed the presence of a Viking settlement on Greenland?
3. When Eric's son Leif was carried past Greenland in a voyage about 1000, he came upon a rocky island and a coastal area he named Vinland. What were the conditions like in this newly discovered area?
4. What archaeological evidence has verified the presence of the Vikings in Newfoundland at the time of the Viking sagas?
5. a) What areas have been suggested as possible locations of Vinland?
   b) Explain how evidence has been used and misused in an attempt to locate Vinland.
6. Should the Vikings, rather than Columbus, be regarded as the real discoverers of America? Explain your answer with evidence.

ALTERNATIVE TWO

The Ra Expeditions—Based on *The Ra Expeditions* by Thor Heyerdahl, 1971

Thor Heyerdahl, adventurer and author, is convinced that the influence of Mediterranean voyagers was the source of the advanced cultures found in the New World. To prove his theory, Heyerdahl and his crew of mixed nationalities made two journeys from Egypt in ships made of papyrus reeds—the *Ra I* and the *Ra II*. The second voyage landed in America. In *The Ra Expeditions*, Thor Heyerdahl explains the theory that prompted these adventures.

The day Christopher Columbus discovered America has long been regarded as 12 October 1492. In reality, it was the day Columbus "flung open the doors of America" to his fellow Europeans, since, as Heyerdahl points out, thousands of non-Europeans had already established great cultural centres in this land.

What Heyerdahl finds interesting about the native people is the reception they gave to conquistadores like Cortes and Pizarro. It was as though they were expected. According to Heyerdahl, the Spaniards were told legends of white-skinned, bearded men from across the sea who had brought with them the "secrets of civilization." Heyerdahl claims this is the reason neither the natives of Mexico nor Peru were surprised to see these new voyagers.

What is even more interesting is that these legends of early culture bearers were prevalent only in the areas of the three great kingdoms—Aztec, Maya, and Inca.

After the Spaniards arrived, it was only a few decades before these civilizations crumbled. Their ruin was due partly to annihilation, and partly to integration. According to Heyerdahl, this limited exposure left the unknown unknown, and made it convenient for Europeans to take credit for the positive aspects of New World culture. Had these civilizations survived for any length of time, we might have learned more about their heritage.

Of course, this raises the obvious question: What really happened in Mexico and Peru before the arrival of Columbus? Heyerdahl takes this question even further. "Had descendants of barbarians from Arctic Asia received voyagers who landed in the Gulf of Mexico in the morning of time, when civilization also spread from Africa and Asia Minor up to the coasts of barbaric Europe?"

In his attempt to answer these questions, Heyerdahl examines the possibilities. If these great cultures had developed locally from ancient civilizations, then there should be archaeological evidence of this development. Yet, excavations of sites in Mexico and Peru indicate that these cultures were already mature when they arrived. The only evidence of development is later variations of the mature form.

If these cultures had arrived in a fully mature form, then they must have been imported; imported from where, and how?

From his travels about the world, Heyerdahl recalls seeing papyrus-reed boats as the seagoing transportation method most frequently depicted in antiquities. In northern Peru, they were shown on ceramic pots; in Egypt, they were painted on tombs; and on Easter Island, they were part of both wall paintings and reliefs. Was this the transportaion method used?

There are other intriguing parallels among these three cultures. The scenes on Peruvian pots also show a sungod or priest-king, much larger than his subjects, and surrounded by bird-headed men towing a reed boat through the water. The same elements appear on the Egyptian tombs; the imposing figure of the priest-king, or pharaoh, is surrounded by his subjects with bird-headed men again towing the reed boat. There are slight variations in the Easter Island paintings. A mask represents the sungod, and the reed boats have sails, but the bird-headed men remain the same. Heyerdahl finds it fascinating that these people in the Pacific even called their sungod "Ra" just as the ancient Egyptians had done.

Another similarity is the giant monoliths that each civlization erected to pay homage to its sungod. Are the enormous statues of Easter Island and the pyramids of Peru and Egypt in some way connected, or are they coincidental?

Heyerdahl thinks there is a connection. But since ancient Egypt had ceased to exist about two thousand years before the appearance of these civilizations, the connection must have been an indirect one. Perhaps, another civilization such as Phoenicia or the island people of the Mediterranean had been the source.

According to Heyerdahl, this is a likely prospect. The ancient Egyptians were a dynamic people who travelled about the Mediterranean and beyond, visiting Mesopotamian and other Asian ports. Certainly, they were affiliated with the people from Phoenicia, and influenced many of the civilizations on the islands.

Although little is known about the first Phoenician ships, Heyerdahl believes there is sufficient evidence from their neighbours to the south, east, and west, to conclude that the Phoenicians would have used reed boats for transportation. Indeed, by the time their culture had spread beyond Gibraltar to Lixus, reed boats were definitely being used. Although numerous voyagers had ventured beyond Gibraltar, the first voyage that is documented, according to Heyerdahl, is that of Hanno, in the fifth century B.C. The event, which was recorded on a stele in Carthage, tells of sixty ships stocked with supplies and colonists of both sexes. Hanno sailed as far as Equatoria, west Africa, stopping at Lixus on the way for navigational advice. It was the "foreigners" at Lixus who also gave Hanno advice on how to handle primitive people, who could sometimes be quite hostile.

According to Heyerdahl, collaboration between different nationalities was not new. The first voyage to sail round Africa occurred about 600 B.C., and was a combined effort organized by the Egyptian pharaoh, Necho and undertaken by a Phoenician crew and ships. The story was recorded by the historian Herodotus almost two hundred years later.

The idea of an expedition of mixed nationalities intrigued Heyerdahl. If such a party found themselves among primitive people in the New World, what cultural patterns would they impose? Could such an expedition survive an Atlantic crossing in a reed boat? These were the questions that prompted Thor Heyerdahl to embark on the Ra Expedition.

Questions

1. What was the reaction of the native people to the Spanish conquistadores who followed Columbus?
2. What happened to both the Aztec and Inca empires within a short time after the arrival of the Spanish?
3. What important question does Heyerdahl ask about the New World before the arrival of Columbus?
4. a) If great civilizations had developed on their own in Mexico or Peru, what pattern should archaeologists be able to identify?
   b) Was this pattern present?
   c) What alternative thus seemed worth pursuing?
5. Why did Heyerdahl make a connection among the reed boats in Egypt, Peru, and Easter Island?

6. a) How does Heyerdahl know that Egyptian and Phoenician influence spread throughout the Mediterranean?
   b) Should the voyages of Hanno and Pharaoh Necho be believed? Explain your answer.
7. To what extent does Heyerdahl's theory about the spread of culture from Egypt throughout the Mediterranean to Africa and, eventually, to Mesoamerica and Easter Island seem convincing? Explain your answer with evidence.

ALTERNATIVE THREE

Early Cartographers and the Discovery of America—Based on "Early Cartographers" and "Who Discovered America?" by Francis Hitching, 1978

In *The World Atlas of Mysteries*, Francis Hitching delves into the mystery of who discovered America. The traditional account of development in the New World tells of mongoloid migrants from Asia making their way on foot across the Bering Strait land-bridge over thirty thousand years ago. As they moved southward, small groups broke away and established societies that were influenced by local conditions. The conventional explanation for their physical differences is one of genetics and natural selection.

Are we to believe this traditional account of isolated evolution, when an analysis of ancient maps, records of seafaring voyages in small craft, and archaeological evidence suggest otherwise?

In his attempt to convince us that America might well have been visited many times in the prehistoric past, Hitching examines the evidence. His first example is the map compiled by the Turkish admiral Piri Re'is in 1513. Piri Re'is himself felt that his map was unique since it was based on earlier charts and maps prepared at the time of Alexander the Great. They were stored in the vast collection of ancient knowledge found among the million books in the Alexandrian library before its final destruction by fire in the eleventh century. Piri Re'is had only leftover fragments of the originals to work with, and today only part of the admiral's world map is left to us for study. The puzzle is that the admiral's map shows a detailed knowledge of the world's geography dating back to the time before civilization.

The state of map making in Piri Re'is's day was generally very primitive. Although latitude (the distance from the equator) was established with considerable accuracy, longitude (the vertical lines that indicate east-west positions) was only guesswork. Most of the maps in the Age of Discovery made large errors in the east-west placing of land, as did Columbus in his calculations about the location of Japan. Some ancient maps used a system of *portolans*, grids that radiate like the spokes of a wheel. These can cause locations to be tilted at the wrong angle when converted onto a normal map. Allowing for this distortion, Piri Re'is's map becomes extremely accurate. The western coasts of Africa, and Europe, and the north Atlantic islands (with the exception of Madeira) are all in their correct longitude and are even in their proper longitudinal relationship with the coast of South America and Antarctica. The Caribbean also falls into place once the error in the use of portolans is corrected. The southern part of South America is drawn accurately to an average error of less than one degree while the Falklands are at the correct latitude even though they are misplaced by five degrees on the east-west plane.

As additional support, Hitching offers a second map, drawn in 1531 by Oronteus Finnaeus, which gives even more spectacular evidence. While Piri Re'is's map shows a small portion of the Antarctic coastline known as Queen Maud Land, the map of Finnaeus shows the Antarctic coastline in detail, with rivers pouring out to sea from mountain ranges and a central ice-cap in the interior. The catch here is that Antarctica has been covered with ice since at least 4000 B.C., and it was not officially discovered until 1818! For these maps to exist, ancient travellers must have explored the coast when it was free of ice.

If ancient mariners travelled these seas in the remote past, it seems likely they also arrived on the shores of America. Certainly, there was no problem in finding a suitable vessel. Today, hundreds of crossings in small boats of every description have been verified. The list includes rafts, dugout canoes, dories propelled by oars or fitted with sails, sailboats less than 2 m long, kayaks, folding boats, and even an amphibian jeep.

Hitching believes transoceanic contact took place. What he would like to know is how early, how often, and how influential were these contacts. For answers to these questions, he examines records and artifacts. One of these is a case of pottery dated to 3000 B.C. that was picked up on the coast of Ecuador. The engravings on these artifacts are identical to those on pottery from the Jamon area of Japan. Moreover, there is *no* evidence in Ecuador of earlier, more primitive pottery from which these may have evolved. Therefore, the pottery must have been imported. Were voyagers from Japan blown off course or caught in a storm that carried them almost 13 000 km to Ecuador?

Hitching points out that other transoceanic contacts have been suggested. A legend of the Hopi Indians in Arizona recalls their journey across the water by means of "stepping stones" or islands. A Chinese classic of 2250 B.C., *Shan Hai King* contains a description of what could be the Grand Canyon. Were the civilizations that developed in Middle America and Peru around 2000 B.C. influenced by the Chinese?

The currents and Gulf Stream in the Atlantic would have made crossings quite likely both in the northern areas—from Scandinavian ports to Nova Scotia—and to the south—between the Mediterranean and Central America.

Such crossings may have resulted in trading partnerships, which would account for fishing gear and woodworking tools in the Great Lakes area, and slate knives in Scandinavian and the Baltic countries, all of which appeared around 2500 B.C. It might also explain the disappearance of pottery of the Early Woodland period in America that closely resembled Baltic pottery around 1000 B.C.

Other transatlantic contacts Hitching mentions are those interpreted from the texts of Plato and Diodorus that indicate there was trade between Phoenicians and the New World about 1000 B.C.

Evidence suggests a variety of races visited Mesoamerica. Sculptured heads, ranging in origin from 1500 B.C. to A.D. 1500 show African Blacks, bearded Jews, and other racial types. Indeed, the similarities between Mesoamerican civilization and Egypt seem too numerous to be explained except by the influence of Mediterranean voyagers. In Hitching's view, the arrival of Columbus and the Spaniards who followed was not the first but rather the last in a long line of visitors over a long period of time.

Questions

1. What is the standard explanation for historical development in the New World?
2. a) Who was Piri Re'is?
   b) When were the earlier charts he used to construct his map produced?
   c) Why was Piri Re'is's map so puzzling?
3. What error was found on the vast majority of maps made when Piri Re'is lived?
4. a) How accurate was the map made by Piri Re'is?
   b) Why was the map made by Oronteus Finnaeus in 1531 truly remarkable?
   c) What do these maps tell us about the mariners of the ancient world?
5. Is it possible to cross the Atlantic in a small boat? Explain your answer.
6. Why is pottery found in Ecuador, dated to 3000 B.C., important in explaining pre-Columbian contact with America?
7. Hitching gives several examples of possible transoceanic crossings to America. Which three examples are the most convincing?
8. Has Hitching proved that America was discovered before Columbus? Explain your answer.

ANSWERING THE PROBLEM QUESTION

Trying to solve a problem that requires a reasonable balance between archaeological evidence and logical speculation is a difficult task, particularly when time and space relationships are so complex. Solid conclusions, however, rest most securely on physical evidence, and logical speculation should be used only in direct conjunction with basic facts. All too often popular writers use half-truths to tie together exciting theories that are interesting to read but do not reflect what really happened.

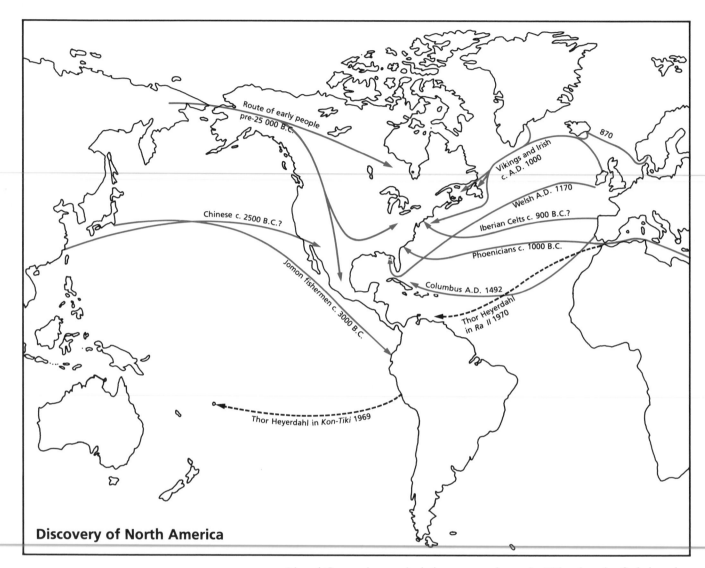

Discovery of North America

Lionel Casson is sceptical about most legends. Why does he feel that the Viking sagas are the most believable case for pre-Columbian discovery? Is the archaeological evidence of Viking presence in Newfoundland any more convincing than Heyerdahl's voyage across the Atlantic or the parallels between Old and New World culture? Casson, in other works, admires Heyerdahl's daring, but argues that the Egyptian papyrus-reed rafts were designed for river and coastal use rather than for sailing the rough waters of the open ocean.

Thor Heyerdahl, however, is one of those rare individuals who combines a credible academic approach with practical experience in areas related to his theories. Much of Heyerdahl's work depends on the cultural parallels that exist between Egyptian and New World societies. Are the similarities in buildings, pyramids, boats, and cultural practices precise enough to connect the two areas in question? It is possible that people can evolve independently in separate parts of the globe and simply go through the same stages of development? Crossing the Atlantic in a small boat would be difficult, though certainly possible, at any time. Did the success of *Ra II* prove that the same trip could have been made by Phoenicians centuries before the Roman Empire existed?

Francis Hitching uses elements of evidence and logic presented in each of the first two alternatives, but also provides the important consideration of ancient maps. The implication is that maps of unusual accuracy drawn in the Age of Discovery from charts dating to the pre-Christian era could have been produced only if the coastlines had been seen. Are his inferences from these maps sound enough to be persuasive? Are the similarities in artifacts between the Orient and the New World, and the New World and the Baltic, evidence of actual contact and influence?

Perhaps a critical consideration about pre-Columbian America is determining what makes up a "discovery." Are wind-swept seafarers, blown many kilometres off course to a place they were not looking for, reasonable candidates for a discovery? Or does the event have to be based on intent and appear in the record of European history to merit first claim in the finding of new lands? What, then, is the best explanation for the possibility of the pre-Columbian discovery of America once the criteria of archaeological evidence and logical speculation have been ranked and applied?

THE STORY CONTINUES . . .

Amerindians: Mesoamerica and the Aztecs

When Columbus died in 1506, after four voyages to the New World, he was convinced that his island discoveries were the gateway to Asia. Rumours of a wealthy land to the west inspired further exploration, first by Hernandez de Cordova, then Diego Velasquez, and finally Hernan Cortes, who came upon, not India, but the empire of the Aztecs in 1519. Little did the Spanish realize that civilizations had come and gone in Mesoamerica (Mexico and Central America) for over two thousand years before their arrival! Indeed, even the Aztecs had only hazy recollections of the distant past and shrouded their lack of direct knowledge with a series of legends.

MESOAMERICA

Archaeologists are still unfolding the complicated pattern of prehistory in Mesoamerica. Although each civilization focussed on a specific region, its influence usually spread throughout the low-lying and highland areas from the sea to the mountainous plateau of the interior. Therefore, each civilization was to some extent, a blend of new skills, lifestyles, and beliefs with those that had thrived before.

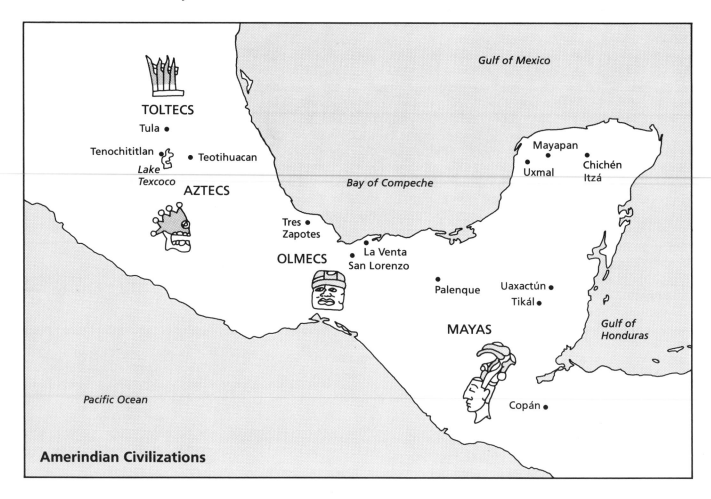

Amerindian Civilizations

THE OLMECS

The civilization that emerged from the hunter-gatherers who first populated the region was that of the **Olmecs**, beginning about 1200 B.C. and lasting for almost one thousand years. On the Gulf Coast of Mexico, the Olmecs built a series of ceremonial centres including La Venta, San Lorenzo, and Tres Zapotes. Each was a carefully planned community with raised platforms, courtyards, ball courts, artificial lagoons, and temples. The resident population was usually less than one thousand, but the lack of true cities did not prevent the development of distinct styles in pottery and architecture. Large and small sculpture, jade axes and pottery vessels showed a figure that was half woman and half jaguar, the focal point of their religion. Figurines of thick-limbed, paunchy bodies often displayed an almost oriental cast to the eyes. The Olmecs were also the first Mesoamericans to move and shape large masses of stone for buildings and monumental sculptures. Large chunks of basalt, weighing upwards of

Why did the Maya build central stairways with steep slopes on their ceremonial pyramids?

20 t, were hauled by rope and floated by raft for distances of 60 km and were used for the colossal stone heads almost 3 m tall that stood at each of the ceremonial centres. Some of the earliest evidence of ritual cannibalism can also be found at these sites.

It is likely that the Olmecs developed the carved figures known as **glyphs** and the calendar made famous by the Maya civilization that flourished in the lowlands of Yucatan from the third to the ninth centuries. The **Maya** were a people preoccupied with time and fascinated by numbers. Used widely throughout Mesoamerica by the fourth century, their time measurement system was based on a solar calendar of 365 days and a ritual calendar of 260 days in which each moment was watched over by one of their many gods. Every fifty-two years (365 × 260), the two calendars coincided in a cycle known as the **Calendar Round**. This was a year of great religous importance.

Like the megalithic builders of Europe, the Maya could predict the rising and setting of the sun and the eclipse cycle of the sun and moon, but Maya accuracy was virtually to the precise second. Their solar calendar estimated the length of the year at 365.2422 days, which is more accurate than either the Roman Julian or later Gregorian calendars introduced in Europe. The Maya system of counting, like all others in Mesoamerica, was based on twenty rather than on the ten used in Western mathematics. Through the use of symbols, the Maya could count forward or backward 400 million years. In addition, they invented the concept of zero for themselves long before the Arabs transferred it to Europe in the medieval period.

During their golden age, the Maya built extensive temple complexes with considerable skill. At Uaxactún, Tikál, Copán, and many other sites, temple

The basaltic Sun Stone of the Aztecs was carved about 1500 and depicts the sun at its centre. The presence of the twenty-day Aztec ritual cycle on the Sun Stone led many archaeologists to mistakenly conclude that the 26-t megalith was a calendar.

The crypt of the Maya prince of Palenque. Erich von Däniken believes that the lid of the sarcophagus shows an ancient astronaut poised at the controls of a space vehicle. Archeologists, however, believe the symbols, shapes, and hand gestures depict a scene common in Maya art that has nothing to do with ancient space travel.

platforms rose over 35 m off the jungle floor. Stepped pyramids, oriented towards the points of the compass, were constructed of stone cemented together with a strong lime mortar. The use of the corbelled arch, which narrowed at the top, allowed interior space. At Palenque, 24 m below the entrance to the pyramid tomb, a twisting, descending hall of steps ends at a crypt where a jade-and-jewel-covered "prince" was buried in the splendour of royalty. Coloured frescoes covered the walls of many public buildings and usually showed scenes of gods, priests, and religious rituals or wealthy merchants and nobles. Elaborate sculptures, which often appear overdone to modern eyes, show a masterful skill in achieving a three-dimensional quality and were found in every city.

UNANSWERED QUESTIONS

For all of their genius, the Maya have left several puzzling questions. Despite precise observation of heavenly bodies, they failed to realize that the earth revolves around the sun. They made toys with wheels, but never applied the

The structures in the Maya-Toltec centre at Chichén Itzá are noted for their massive grandeur and delicate relief. This observatory, which closely resembles its modern counterparts, reflects the Maya preoccupation with astronomy, time, and mathematics.

principle to construction, architecture, or everyday life. They built magnificent public temples but their tools were essentially those of the Stone Age. And they could develop advanced systems of mathematics and time while their hieroglyphic writing was based on symbols rather than on a phonetic alphabet. Perhaps the greatest mystery, often explained in terms of famine and war though never settled, is the sudden decline of the entire civilization in the ninth century. During that span of one hundred years, the Maya left their traditional strongholds and moved to colonial sites such as Uxmal, Mayapan, and Chichén Itzá. Here, the Maya experienced another era of prosperity that lasted until the arrival of the Spanish, but much of their lifestyle was changed by the influence of a culture that spread from the Mexican Plateau.

Upland Mexico was dominated by the grandeur and majesty of Teotihuacan from 100 B.C. to A.D. 750. It was the most impressive ceremonial centre ever built in Mesoamerica, but its people left no record of their way of life. When the Aztecs visited the site in ruins several centuries later, they were awed by what they saw and gave it legends of their own. The name, Teotihuacan means ''place of the gods'' and most of the buildings were explained as tombs for kings who became deities upon their death. The central avenue, 45 m wide and 4 km long, was known as the Street of the Dead and was flanked on the north by the Pyramid of the Moon, to the east by the 66-m high Pyramid of the Sun, and to the southeast by the temple of the feathered serpent Quetzalcoatl. As the city grew, it was divided into four large quadrants subdivided into smaller squares that accommodated two hundred thousand city residents in A.D. 600. This number must have swelled greatly when pilgrims

TEOTIHUACAN

The Street of the Dead in Teotihuacan. The Pyramid of the Sun (left background), like other structures in the city, is situated with precise geometric planning.

arrived to celebrate religious rituals. Trade in the volcanic glass obsidian, used in the Old and New Worlds for making sharp tools and weapons, appeared to be a major economic activity. Brightly coloured murals of mythical beasts, animals, and birds, painted on building walls, provided a cheerful atmosphere for all passers-by. The last stages of life at Teotihuacan show priests portrayed with weapons and shields that suggest the metropolis might have fallen victim to a series of wars. A full explanation of the fall of Teotihuacan, however, remains one of the mysteries of civilization in Mesoamerica.

THE TOLTECS

Another upland people who greatly influenced Aztec development were the imperialistic **Toltecs**, one of the wandering bands of Chichimec tribes. The Toltecs conquered much of civilized Mesoamerica and built their capital at Tula, which thrived from about A.D. 900 to 1200. The Aztecs believed the Toltecs were skilled artisans, possessed of great wisdom who lived in magnificent cities. Most Toltec buildings, however, reveal a hasty construction which suggests their main concern was military conquest, as symbolized by the 5-m high stone warriors resting on the temple platform at Tula. The Toltecs also preserved the worship of Quetzalcoatl who, though a god of legend, might also have been a man of exceptional accomplishment. Aztec priests would later take his name just as they continued the practice of human sacrifice demanded by other, less charitable Toltec gods.

THE AZTECS

As the Toltec Empire collapsed, many of its people intermarried with another Chichimec tribe, the **Aztecs** (who called themselves Mexica). After much wandering and strife, the Aztecs settled on a rocky island in Lake Texcoco

The Pyramid of the Moon, a triumph of stepped-pyramid construction, features a complex system of interior stone piers and walls filled with earth and rubble. It is faced with trimmed stone masonry. This and other stepped pyramids resemble the form and served the same ceremonial purpose as the mud-brick ziggurats from Mesopotamia.

in 1325. Here, their leader witnessed a sight predicted by their tribal god in which an eagle, perched on a cactus beside a rock, marked the spot of a great Aztec city that would rule all of Mexico. With their quest completed, the Aztecs began construction of Tenochititlan (Mexico City), which became a city of waterways, much like Venice. To increase the amount of arable land, islands of mud and fibre were built and joined by causeways. By 1375, as their military strength grew, the Aztecs subdued the tribes along the lakeshore and their city became a rich, commerical centre with enormous temples and palaces run by a chief whose successors ruled until the Spanish conquest. Although the Aztecs dominated the Valley of Mexico, many of the tribes they overran in outlying areas remained resentful and were always on the verge of revolt.

TENOCHITITLAN

    The Aztecs, like the Toltecs before them, were a religious and warlike people. According to their belief, there had been four previous worlds or "suns" that had been destroyed by jaguars, wind, fire, and water. After each disaster, a new sun was placed in the sky by the gods, and the present world would be ended by an earthquake that could be prevented only if the sun was fed continually with human blood. The military orders of the Aztecs, the Jaguars and Eagles, were constantly at war to gain the victims needed for sacrifice to the sun. In peacetime, ritual games served the same purpose.

RELIGION AND WAR

    The architecture of Aztec temples was designed for the religious ceremonies needed to keep the universe alive. Broad, impressive stairways with steep steps rose to a height that was imposing but which was low enough to provide a clear view of all of the sacrificial proceedings.

HUMAN SACRIFICE

Moments in Time

Although other crops such as beans, squash, and potatoes originated in Mexico, Indian corn or **maize** became the staple of the Amerindian diet. Tiny cobs a few centimetres long found at several cave sites have been dated to 5000 B.C. This type of maize grew naturally. Deliberate selection produced bigger and better varieties that were common staples by 1500 B.C. Maize proved to be very adaptable and could survive under a variety of conditions from the hot, steamy lowland forests to dry upland plateaus, and in mountain valleys found throughout the New World. Improvements in cultured varieties continued until the arrival of the Spaniards.

THE END OF AZTEC CIVILIZATION

SOUTH AMERICA

Sacrifice to the sun was considered a glorious death. Those so chosen were often treated to months of feasting and entertainment until the day of departure. When Cortes interrupted such a ceremony, the privileged youth protested that he was denied his right to an everlasting life! The scale of the carnage was usually low, but, at special events such as the opening of a new temple at Tenochtitlan in 1487, at least twenty thousand victims were sacrificed in a four-day period. Women were also sacrificed, but usually to the goddess of maize. Children were sacrificed to the god Tlaloc and their tears were regarded as the rain for which the Aztecs prayed.

The Aztecs developed a highly prosperous civilization that reached its peak at the very moment the Spanish arrived. Their textiles were beautifully made, as was their sculpture and pottery, which featured brightly coloured, floral patterns and animal designs. Although they developed no written script, they had a method of recording stories in pictures known as a "codex." Most were destroyed by the Spanish priests who regarded them as evil, but, fortunately, a few have survived. The splendour of the Aztec court befitted their famous monarch Montezuma II, who sat alone under a feathered canopy while others entertained and catered to his every need and long lines of nobles gathered to pay their sincere respects. From this court, priests and officials helped to organize a society geared for war, forcing those they conquered to pay taxes and tribute.

Aztec civilization came to an abrupt end. Cortes arrived in 1519 with eleven ships, about five hundred men, sixteen horses, and fourteen cannons. At first sight of a Spaniard riding a horse the Mesoamericans thought they were looking at one creature. The bearded Cortes was mistaken for the god Quetzalcoatl, who had left in disgrace from Tula in Toltec legend but who promised to return. Initial greetings were friendly and Montezuma showered the returning "god" with gifts of gold, jade, and jewels. Relations became strained as the early weeks passed, particularly when the Spaniards were horrified to discover they had been offered food soaked in blood from the human sacrifices of the Aztec religious practices that so appalled them. The Spanish seized the initiative by capturing Montezuma and, through the use of superior weaponry (cannons and guns against javelins), the assistance of tribes who resented Aztec domination, and the devastating effect of a plague (probably smallpox), the Aztec Empire was conquered within two years. To the Aztecs it seemed that their old gods had deserted them. In fact, the Age of Discovery was becoming transformed into the "Age of Exploitation."

Amerindians: South America and the Inca

South American prehistory, like its Mesoamerican counterpart, was a complex puzzle that featured the rise and decline of several cultures long before the arrival of the Spaniards. As in Mesoamerica, each culture centred on a particular area, but extended its influence throughout much of the territory inhabited

Atlantic Ocean

• Quito

• Chan Chan

Machu Picchu
• • Cuzco
↯ *L. Titicaca*
• Tiahuanaco

Pacific
Ocean

• Talca

Inca Empire

by its neighbours. Stretched along a Pacific coastal region from modern-day Ecuador to Chile, an incredible variety of geography from the ocean shores to the Andes was mastered through impressive agricultural and building techniques and, under the Inca, the most advanced political organization in the Americas.

CHAVIN CULTURE

The **Chavin** cult, dominated by the worship of a jaguar god, was the first to unite distinct regions under a common culture. From 1000 to 300 B.C., their main ceremonial centre was Chavin de Huantar, located above 3000 m in the eastern Andes and dominated by a temple known as the Castillo. Enlarged as Chavin influence expanded, the Castillo was originally a terraced platform that contained a maze of corridors, stairways, rooms, and even ventilator shafts. Sculptured heads projecting from the outer walls showed a snarling, jaguarlike mouth with canines bared and lips curled at the corners. Other sites have shown that Chavin pottery in red or black was decorated with designs of mythological creatures, as were the patterns seen on textiles woven on backstrap looms. Chavin styles also appeared on gold and copper jewellery, belts, and even tweezers. Burial chambers containing dozens of mummies, each wrapped in layers of cloth, have also been found.

TIAHUANACO

With the decline of Chavin influence by about 300 B.C., cultural development and power became fragmented as several nations evolved traditions of their own. At 3800 m in the high Andes near Lake Titicaca, an important centre emerged after A.D. 200 at Tiahuanaco. Entrance to the temple complex was made through a doorway, known as the "Gateway of the Sun," cut in a single block of stone. Atop the opening is the rigid form of the supreme god, Veracocha, who, like Quetzalcoatl of the Aztecs, was thought to have white skin. Inside, a stepped pyramid, resting on a natural mound faced with stone, rose to a height of over 15 m, while a lower temple platform with upright stones of 4 m may have supported a stone roof. Tiahuanaco greatly influenced the city of Huari, which grew into an empire that lasted until about the tenth century.

THE MOCHICA

The **Mochica** culture became dominant in the north. The Mochica built several pyramid centres of adobe brick fastened with cane and wood and covered with plaster. Their temple at Huaca de Sol contained 130 million bricks and measured 228 m × 137 m at the base, which made it the largest adobe structure built in the New World before the conquest. Irrigation systems, canals, and aqueducts turned desert into productive fields, while villages in the shadow of temple sites were built into terraced hillsides when level clearings were not available. Mochica pottery was produced in large quantities and characterized by a striking realism whether depicting animals, humans, or gods. Metalwork in gold, silver, and copper was superior to the earlier Chavin culture. Similar advances were made by the **Nazca** people to the south. They, too, built ceremonial centres, developed a distinctive pottery style, showing gods and scenes from everyday life, and, like the Chavins, mummified their dead. Deformed skulls suggest that these honoured victims may have been sacrificed for religious purposes.

From the eleventh to the fifteenth centuries, the coastal region from central Peru to Ecuador was dominated by the **Chimu** Kingdom, with its capital of Chan Chan. Estimates of the city's population often exceed forty thousand, which made it the largest city in South America before the conquest. Massive adobe walls, sculptured with outlines of sea creatures, gods, and decorative designs, enclosed a series of ten compounds. Each one had a labyrinth of corridors that led to the inner courtyards and burial compounds for the governing class. Connected to the coastal cities of the empire by roads, the countryside of the Chimu Kingdom was dominated by agriculture. Peasants worked on community irrigation systems, canals, and construction projects. During the 1470s, however, Chan Chan was overthrown by the Inca who had begun to spread outward from their capital at Cuzco in the early fifteenth century.

The word **Inca** was used to identify both the people of the empire and their king, who ruled by divine right as the sun's representative. Every Inca king, assisted by a court and high priests, governed from Cuzco where a palace was built for each successive monarch. The administration was efficient and tightly controlled and almost every aspect of an individual's life was subject to laws which were enforced by state officials. During the reign of Topa Inca in the late fifteenth century, the Inca Empire stretched 4800 km from Ecuador to Chile in a belt 320 km wide from the ocean to the jungle of Amazonia. Through exceptional feats of engineering, the Inca manipulated environments that ranged from coastal lowlands to deserts, moist uplands and the upper reaches of mountains, and encompassed a greater area than was held by all of their ancestors combined.

A marvellous system of stone and earthen roads covered the entire length and breadth of the Inca Empire. Where slopes were steep, switchback trails provided access to higher ground. Where roads ran into deep ravines and canyons, suspension bridges of twisted lianas anchored to blocks of stone on either side spanned the gap. When they first saw them, the Spaniards were terrified of the bridges that swayed back and forth over pounding river rapids far below. But just as the Inca army, wielding its slings, bolas, and swords had used the passages to subdue an enemy, so the Spaniards with horses and guns travelled the bridges in their conquest of the Inca.

The Inca developed no formal writing, but a specially trained group of **chasquis** runners transferred memorized messages in the commonly used language of **Quechua** over distances of 200 km on Inca roads in a single day. Numerical records, also carried by the chasquis, were kept by a **quipo** made of knotted strings. They were used by the administrators at Cuzco to keep track of the yearly tribute paid by all subject communities. Such tribute might include a quota of goods, of soldiers, or of workers to maintain community fields. In return, the people received military protection and food from state storehouses in

Fortress of Sacsahuaman. The biggest stones were placed at the bottom and the smaller ones were aligned to the irregular-shaped sides and higher elevations. The tight lines of contact, which appear only on the outside, were probably achieved by hours of pounding with a stone hammer on the face and adjoining edges, the mottled effects of which can still be seen on the rock surfaces. Behind the outward facade, the spaces were actually quite wide and usually packed with earth.

MACHU PICCHU

time of famine. Whether for tribute or commerce, transportation in such varied terrain was made possible only by the Inca roads and the willing backs of domesticated llamas to carry the goods, since the Inca had no wheeled vehicles.

Inca engineering was truly skillful. At the fortress of Sacsahuaman near Cuzco, 100-t megaliths were dragged and fitted into place within the thickness of a knife blade. Although such precision rightly impressed the conquering Spaniards, the Inca combined their ability to organize large masses of labour, unique building techniques, and a logical step-by-step approach to create such massive walls.

Similar stonework can be found throughout the public buildings in many Inca towns, including the foundation of the lost city Machu Picchu. Missed by the Spanish and unknown to the West until discovered by the American Hiram Bingham in 1911, Machu Picchu is situated at over 2700 m in the Andes and provides a stunning reminder of Inca ingenuity. Rock outcrops were incorporated into the design of buildings, while natural fissures or cracks in the rock were often sealed and used as burial caves. Such caves contained 173 mummies at the time of excavation even though the city had been looted. The steep slopes that led upwards towards the city were carefully groomed with supporting walls that braced garden terraces used for agriculture. These slopes, along with a series of fountains and baths, were fed water through stone aqueducts. Yet Machu Picchu was typically Inca in that it contained a central square surrounded by buildings with trapezoidal doorways, temples, defensive walls, and a palace. At one temple, stone posts used by Inca priests–quite clever astronomers–were aligned to predict the rising and setting of the summer sun on 21 June–the start of the Inca ceremonial year.

The Inca, like the Aztecs of Mesoamerica, had built an empire through political and economic organization, and skill in battle. They were no match,

Machu Picchu, a tribute to Inca genius in engineering and adaptability.

however, for the iron-clad Spaniards with their guns, horses, and the contagious diseases they unintentionally introduced. When Pizarro arrived in 1531 with only 62 horsemen and 102 foot soldiers, he was able to take advantage of a political struggle over the succession to the Inca throne. Pizarro seized the strongest claimant, Atahuallpa, who tried to buy his freedom by ordering the gold stripped from the Temple of the Sun at Cuzco for the Spaniards to melt down. Atahuallpa was eventually executed despite the payment, and the Spanish took control of the highly centralized Inca political system. Although isolated pockets of fierce resistance held out in the mountains until 1580, the sun had set on the native civilization of South America just as it had in Mesoamerica to the north.

PIZARRO AND ATAHUALLPA

COMMENT

The mariners who searched for new worlds in the fifteenth and sixteenth centuries have often been compared with the astronauts of the twentieth century. As individuals, the adventurers of both ages were daring and brave, in search of knowledge, personal glory and wealth. Explorers in the Age of Discovery were also possessed by a sense of Christian mission to convert any new peoples who might be discovered. The astronauts of the space age, certain there will be no one to greet them, often align God with their sense of national purpose and, from their viewpoint, the welfare of the human race.

Yet, in other ways, there are important differences. Limited by the technology of the day, explorers had either a general or inaccurate understanding of where they were headed and what they might find once they lost sight of land. In contrast, astronaut voyages are a product of technology in which every step from beginning to end is precisely understood, calculated, and planned to the smallest detail. The major suspense lies in waiting to see if the technology works rather than in what might be found since they know exactly where they are going. Most of the new "discoveries" are made when the results of an entire trip are analyzed at home base.

But what about possible pre-Columbian discoveries of new lands in the Americas that happened by chance, that were not followed by permanent settlement, and that were eventually forgotten? Potential sources of discovery have been many. The break-up of Atlantis, *if* it existed, and *if* it existed in the mid-Atlantic, has left a popular picture of survivors fleeing in all directions to Europe, Africa, and the Americas, spreading a common culture in the process. Cultural similarities in building skills, inscriptions, and artifacts, each subject to interpretation, have also suggested that megalithic seafarers from Europe crossed the ocean to New England as far back as 2000 B.C. It is possible that Saint Brendan of Ireland sailed the Atlantic in an ox hide boat in the sixth century, but no trace of his voyage has been found. The Pacific has been crossed with equal regularity in legend if not in life. The lost continent of Mu, the Pacific counterpart of Atlantis, was once thought to have spread the gift of civilization to Asia and America. Kublai Khan's great fleet of one hundred forty-two thousand sailors and warriors was dispersed in 1281 by a "divine wind," or **kami-kaze**, en route to invade Japan, and survivors might have drifted to America. Even the lost tribes of Israel, who moved on the order of Tiglath Pileser to Media in the eighth century B.C., but whose final destination remains unknown, may have ended up on American shores!

Columbus, rather than the Vikings, was long credited with the discovery of America. Although they had landed and settled in the New World, the Vikings had abandoned their outposts just prior to the Age of Discovery. Archaeological evidence, as Casson persuasively argues, has verified the story of discovery as described in the oral tradition of the Viking sagas. Heyerdahl's claim that the Egyptians and Phoenicians were even earlier travellers to America is possible, but it does rely on a greater degree of speculation. The fact that he and his inexperienced crew crossed the ocean in a papyrus-reed boat demonstrated that the voyage *could* be done, but did not prove that it actually *was* done by an Egyptian or a Phoenician expedition. The existence of papyrus-reed boats in locations as distant as the Nile River and Lake Titicaca, however, at least suggests that cultural contact between the two civilizations was made.

Two key questions must be considered. Were the common cultural practices found on both sides of the Atlantic developed independently? Or were they so special that there could be only one point of origin from which they were spread by ancient mariners to different parts of the world? The sun as the source of light and heat is so vital that it is not surprising to find that it is worshipped by cultures living far apart. Pyramid cultures are another matter. The stepped pyramids of Mesoamerica contained different material and were a different shape than those built in Egypt. Yet the discovery of the "Prince of Palenque" showed that Mesoamerican pyramids had interior chambers for burial like their Egyptian counterparts, even though the practice was more common in the Nile Valley. Most Mesoamerican pyramids had steps built into platforms that were to be climbed as part of a public ceremony on special occasions. In Egypt, most pyramids were smooth faced and provided the final and private sanctuary of the dead pharaoh. Are these differences the results of a mixed tradition that followed a transatlantic voyage? Or are they so great that they illustrate two unique cultures that show general similarities only by coincidence?

Hitching's view delves even more into the realm of speculation, but it is intriguing. Piri Re'is's maps, though open to interpretation, seem to show a remarkable accuracy about coastlines in the Western Hemisphere and Antarctica. Erich von Däniken was so impressed that he related such views of the earth to a satellite photo focussing on Cairo and suggested that such ancient maps could only have been made by a prehistoric space traveller. Von Däniken argued further that the monuments and buildings of Mesoamerica and South America were so exceptional that only ancient astronauts could have supervised the construction of such projects. Wonderful as they are, however, the pyramids and palaces of the New World should be compared with the public buildings of Rome and the cathedrals and castles of medieval Europe, none of which has ever been credited to an ancient extraterrestrial! It is certainly possible that isolated mariners did reach the shores of America, but it remains an unanswered question how much influence limited contact might have had. The word "discovery" as it is usually used, refers to the first contact and awareness of fifteenth- and sixteenth-century Europe. The native populations of Mesoamerica and South America, however, had distinct identities of their own and did not feel that they were being "discovered." Even if earlier, unrecorded voyages did occur, the native Americans probably felt it was they who had "discovered" a new race!

Date A.D.	Events
1300	Church prestige declines
1337	Hundred Years' War begins between England and France
c.1400	The Renaissance period (c.1400–1550) is expressed in works by Ghiberti, Leonardo da Vinci, Michelangelo, Erasmus, Dürer, et al.
1444	Portugal begins importing African slaves
1446	Gutenburg of Mainz and Coster of Haarlem print with movable type
1453	Islamic Ottoman Turks conquer Constantinople
1492	Christopher Columbus reaches San Salvador in the Bahamas
1517	Luther nails his list of Ninety-five Theses to the door of Castle church in Wittenburg
1529–1555	Catholic and Lutheran states wage intermittent wars Peace of Augsburg gives each ruler choice of religion for his state
1588	English navy defeats Spanish Armada
1598	The Edict of Nantes introduces a period of toleration in France
1602	Dutch East India Company, with its worldwide network of trading factories, is formed
1618–1648	Thirty Years' War Religious motives give way to the power of the nation state
1651	English Navigation Acts reflect the mercantilist goal of self-sufficiency
1661–1715	French civilization sets the standard for Europe during the reign of the Sun King, Louis XIV
1713–1740	Hapsburg or Austrian Empire reemerges under the leadership of Charles VI Frederick William, the first king of Prussia, builds his kingdom into a military state Peter the Great continues the Westernization of Russia, including the modernization of military forces England develops as a limited monarchy following the Glorious Revolution of 1688 France and England compete for colonial and naval supremacy European conflicts involve colonial empires

9

Europe and the Sun King

BACKGROUND

The Renaissance and Humanism

About the time that the Aztecs and Inca were building their cities and creating empires, medieval Europe was evolving into a new age. Known as the **Renaissance** because it was thought to represent the rebirth of the classical learning of Greece and Rome, the label provides an important half-truth. It was misleading in the sense that no single, dramatic event ushered in great change. The West had always maintained some awareness of classical writers throughout the medieval period even though such knowledge was limited to a handful of scholars. Christian contact with Moorish centres in Spain had introduced Islamic science and had revived Greek philosophy, and attempts were made to reconcile them with the teachings of the Church. A decline of interest in the classics during the thirteenth century was followed by a renewed enthusiasm in the fourteenth century and it was this "rebirth" that gives some strength to the term Renaissance.

CLASSICAL LEARNING

The era of the Renaissance was more than the outgrowth of medieval Europe. It combined a heightened awareness of the Greek and Roman heritage of the West with a clear understanding that Europe was, in its own right, something special. This dual recognition of past and present unleashed a wave of creative genius and accomplishment in writing, painting, sculpture, and architecture that the world has marvelled at ever since. Historical circumstances cannot account for the genius of an individual, but it should be stressed that the people of the Renaissance were no more or less intelligent than those of any other age. The extraordinary number of accomplishments that could only be ascribed to genius, however, strongly suggest that the environment encouraged those gifted individuals to maximize their talents.

NATURE OF THE RENAISSANCE

Italy provided such an opportunity, and it was here that the Renaissance began. Fragmented by geography, the Italian peninsula had never been unified under a single ruler after the decline of the Western Roman Empire and the chaos that followed. Throughout much of the medieval period, Italy was a

THE ITALIAN SETTING

land of shifting loyalties divided between the claims of the Holy Roman Empire and the papacy. Instead of the feudal existence that dominated northern Europe, Italian life was politically organized around a series of independent states including Venice, Florence, Milan, Naples, Genoa, Pisa, and Bologna. Bearing a curious resemblance to the city-states of ancient Greece, there was no thought of a political unit on the scale of a nation. Instead, each city-state developed its own government and controlled its own hinterland. The type of government varied in time and place. Most of the early democracies, however, gave way to the influence of powerful merchants, aristocratic families, and dictators who could offer protection against external threats to commercial enterprise. Landowners lived in the cities and participated in the economic, political, and social life of the day alongside prosperous middle-class merchants, a condition that reorganized society according to wealth and power rather than by birth. The cities became a stimulating combination of gossip, discussion, and intrigue as the tension between rival groups reaching for power provided almost daily excitement.

PROSPERITY

Although there was constant friction between Italian city-states, they were spared the political and economic turmoil and distraction of the Hundred Years' War endured by England and France. Situated on trade routes that gave access to luxury goods and cultures from the East, and with direct links to northern markets through selected Alpine passes, Italian cities, like Athens in Greece's Golden Age, developed a cosmopolitan outlook and accumulated wealth and capital. The Italian middle class used its financial resources to either acquire valued objects or, more importantly, to sponsor the budding talent of young painters, sculptors, and writers. While their patrons provided food, clothing, and comfortable lodging, those with exceptional ability were given the time and opportunity to realize their potential. It was not surprising that the atmosphere of involved city life, and the wealth provided by a flourishing economy based on extensive foreign contact, inspired cultural achievement. Although not every artist had a patron, Italy was the stage on which genius could be recognized and encouraged.

HUMANISM

While there were splendid achievements in architecture and learning, medieval society had not generally provided such an opening. The best talents of the period brushed paintings, chiselled sculpture, carved wood, and stained glass to glorify God, the focal point of their purpose. Living a good, Christian life according to the teachings of the Church was regarded as necessary preparation for paradise after death. The **humanism** of the Renaissance, which admired the beauty of the body, the intelligence of the mind, and the unrivalled levels of accomplishments that were possible, shifted the emphasis in a secular direction to life here and now. Though people continued to praise God and hoped to enter heaven, what mattered most was an *individual's* relationship to society rather than to God and the afterlife. The wealthy Italian trading cities provided the most wordly setting imaginable in their unharnessed pursuit of material

This Romanesque campanile (bell tower), situated in the Piazza del Duomo, is better known as the Leaning Tower of Pisa. The 3-m foundation was constructed in soil that was too soft to support the heavy marble used for the building. As a result, the 55-m structure now leans about 35 cm from the perpendicular.

goods. Artists and composers began to leave signatures on their work, while bankers and popes ordered busts, portraits, and monuments created in their honour. Indeed, the Church commissioned some of the finest works of the Renaissance as it became clear that individuals in every walk of life developed a heightened sense of self-awarenesss. Now, the excellence of the artwork itself, and the talent that created it, received as much and often more attention than the purpose for which it was created. People of the Renaissance valued and celebrated their individualism and abilities in all fields of human activity.

The Italian Renaissance was also inspired, understandably, by the magnificence of ancient Rome which, even in ruin, reminded every onlooker of its former glory. For the first time since antiquity, the Roman forum, known locally as the "cowfield" had its treasures catalogued and excavated for study. As scholars sifted through long-forgotten Roman manuscripts, they discovered their ancestors and came to admire what they found. It seemed as if the ancients had reached a peak of human accomplishment in almost all of their endeavours and that their Renaissance descendants should strive to follow their example.

THE GLORY OF ROME

COMMUNITY SERVICE

From Rome, the Renaissance ideal of using learning to service the community provided a refreshing change from the immediate past. Medieval scholars had been associated with isolated monasteries, halls of private study, and meditation in which the way of the world was passively accepted. Renaissance scholars, however, were more apt to be public figures eager to transform the world to fit their new-found ideals. Although new to the era, the changes often represented patterns previously established by the ancients. Similarly, Renaissance "science," which focussed on the practical, relied on the ancient Greeks to deal with questions about universal laws and principles. Nevertheless, an awareness of the commitment to truth, the role of the individual, and the contribution that an individual could make signalled a new era in human development.

All of this was greatly stimulated by the invention of movable block type and the appearance of printed books. Throughout history, the record of human experience had been painstakingly copied by hand as Sumerians etched clay tablets, Egyptians marked papyrus, and medieval monks inked their messages on vellum or parchment. The hours of production limited the amount of knowledge that could be accumulated and preserved, and led the Greeks and their medieval admirers to group several areas of study under the heading of "philosophy." There were only a few thousand manuscripts in all of Europe prior to the printing press and they were the cherished possessions of church libraries and upper classes. Reading and study had been a privileged option, not a public practice.

PRINTING

With the discovery of movable type, the number of books available skyrocketed to a minimum of 6 million by 1500. Although it would take significantly longer for the uneducated peasants to appreciate the change, the literate and wealthy middle classes, who began to stock their libraries, were quick to realize its importance. New horizons of thought opened everywhere in the Renaissance as the mystery of knowledge, long preserved but rarely seen, was unveiled. Information, ideas, scientific knowledge, and discoveries could be recorded and distributed to the far corners of Europe, and the knowledge of one generation could be preserved and built upon by the next. Never again would society enter a "Dark Age" of lost or forgotten accomplishments.

The Italian Renaissance

THE IMPORTANCE OF FLORENCE

Although Venice was Italy's wealthiest city and Rome the most prestigious, the heart of the Renaissance was Florence. The rich, luxury-loving atmosphere of worldly pleasure and civic pride inspired the highest degree of daring, creativity, and achievement. A roll call of select Florentines, among others who could be mentioned, reads like a who's who of the Renaissance: Dante, Boccaccio, Machiavelli, Giotto, Masaccio, da Vinci, and Michelangelo. In addition, non-Florentines like Raphael came to the city and had their work greatly influenced by what they saw.

City dwellers were concerned with new ideas and with the freedom of the individual. They were intensely interested in politics and, just as they did in business, looked to the most practical solutions to political problems. After brief experiments with dictatorship in the fourteenth century, the city adopted a republican government and tried to live in the spirit of ancient Rome. In the fifteenth century, Florentine politics came to be dominated by the Medici family, the greatest bankers in Europe. Their rule saw continual controversy among various factions within the city. Three times they were expelled only to return with greater power, and for the sake of the Renaissance spirit it was well that they did.

Largely through the influence, wealth, and values of the Medici family, Florence gathered the great talents of the Renaissance whose achievements seemed only to be heightened by the tensions of city life. Cosimo de' Medici was criticized for building a private palace in 1444, but by that time his family had spent millions of dollars on public as well as personal work in the arts and architecture. Lorenzeo de' Medici was a man of many talents who lived the Renaissance ideal as he excelled as a poet, statesman, scholar, economist, and military planner. But his lavish spending on behalf of the arts, which he regarded as a public duty, weakened even the Medici fortune. His vast personal collection of books became the first public library in Europe and he sponsored attempts to secure ancient manuscripts from all over Europe and the East. During his lifetime he assisted, employed, or gave lodging to about every talent in Florence including Botticelli, da Vinci, and Michelangelo. A later Medici, Pope Leo X, continued his family's tradition in the arts in the most famous court of Europe.

THE MEDICI FAMILY

The earliest impulse towards the Renaissance sprang from the pens of three Italian writers. Dante Alighieri (1265–1321) was the key transitional figure. Medieval writers in the universities, the Church, and the state wrote in Latin and recognized Greek (which they knew little about) as the only other language worthy of cultured people. Dante, however, did some of his writing in Italian, the vernacular language of the common classes, and thereby became the father of Italian literature. Like the medieval world in which he lived, Dante was preoccupied with religion and the afterlife. In his most famous work, *Divine Comedy*, however, Dante, as a man in search of ''Truth,'' struggles through ''Hell,'' ''Purgatory,'' and ''Paradise,'' is critical of the Church, and shows an individualism that would become characteristic of the Renaissance.

DANTE

Petrarcha Francesco, better known as Petrarch (1304–1375), followed Dante's lead by writing in Italian, but he was less concerned with religion and more interested in fame and fortune on earth. Later, his attention turned to the pagan past of Greece and Rome as he wrote letters in Latin to the ancients and encouraged others to locate classical manuscripts from the libraries and monasteries of Europe. By 1400, Greek scholars had begun to arrive from the East, and they revived an interest in the study of the Greek language. When Constantinople fell to the Turks in 1453, the arrival of even greater numbers of Greek-refugee scholars hastened a process that had been under way for nearly a century.

PETRARCH

BOCCACCIO

Certainly the most worldly in his personal life, and therefore the most typical of the Renaissance, was Giovanni Boccaccio (1313–1375). His books, usually written in Italian, reflected the enjoyment of the life he pursued, and his collection of short stories in the *Decamerone* focussed on ordinary people and ridiculed the Church. Boccaccio's work became one of the earliest "best sellers," and his approach influenced many writers throughout Europe, including Geoffrey Chaucer and William Shakespeare. On the suggestion of Petrarch, Boccaccio became interested in the Greek classics as the Italian writers provided the inspiration for the humanist movement of the Renaissance in scholarship, painting, sculpture, and architecture.

Humanist scholarship excelled in its technical approach and in the study of human actions. Lorenzo Valla (1407–1457) of Naples and Rome used his expertise in Latin and history to show that the Donation of Constantine, claimed to be a fourth-century document in which the emperor recognized the superior authority of the pope, was an eighth-century forgery. He also did an unpublished criticism of Saint Jerome's Vulgate translation of the New Testament, which demonstrated mistakes and questionable phrasing in what had been an unchallenged source of Christian truth.

Later, Niccolo Machiavelli (1469–1527), a Florentine diplomat and soldier educated in the classics, wrote a revealing humanist study called *The Prince* in which he attempted to show how politicians really thought. In 1502, Machiavelli had met and been greatly impressed with Cesare Borgia, son of Pope Alexander VI. A ruthless man, Cesare engineered the deaths of his elder brother and the second husband of his sister, Lucrezia, and he developed a reputation for kidnapping and torturing his enemies in castle dungeons, and murder. Nevertheless, his unscrupulous methods led to a remarkable career in Romagna. Machiavelli, who felt that Cesare represented the highest ideals of the successful prince, made him the model prince for his study. According to Machiavelli, a ruler could not afford to worry about right or wrong but had to use any means to secure the safety of the state. Upset by the bands of foreign mercenaries making war in the Italian countryside, Machiavelli felt that a state must have a fully equipped army at its disposal. Since one prince could not trust another, the army should be used to attack when it was least expected. Even the followers of a prince should be kept divided so they could not overthrow his crown. Machiavelli's defenders argue that he was simply analyzing the "mechanics of statecraft" and that he should not be condemned for the deceit and treachery of the Renaissance world. Critics feel that his book, written a year after his dismissal from public service by the Medici, reflected a callous and bitter attitude about a world from which he was now excluded. Of key importance to the Renaissance, however, was that Machiavelli had abandoned the medieval practice of writing about the ideal world by stressing the real-life methods rulers actually used to ensure their survival.

Perhaps no contrast with the medieval period was clearer than in painting. Medieval figures appear stiff, flat, and unreal, devoid of muscle and emotion.

Moments in Time

Vittoria Colonna (1490/92–1549) was one of the most influential women of the Italian Renaissance. Her writings dealt with religion, nature, patriotism, and the human condition.

The Colonna castle was a gathering place for the greats of the Italian Renaissance. The most distinguished of these was Michelangelo. Of Vittoria Colonna he wrote, "Without wings, I fly with your wings; by your genius I am raised to the skies; in your soul my thought is born."

MACHIAVELLI

MEDIEVAL AND RENAISSANCE
PAINTING

This allowed the worshipper to concentrate on the religious story being told. While Renaissance painting retained religious themes, the focal point of attention was on the human form, whether commoner, saint, or angel, and the *way* it was portrayed. The goal of the Renaissance artist was to illustrate nature as s/he saw it, unhindered by conventions of the past. To achieve this end, techniques of shading, colour, and above all, perspective–that quality that gives depth to the image–had to be pioneered and perfected. Giotto (1267–1336), a contemporary of Dante and, like him, a transitional figure towards the Renaissance, was the first to portray the human form in a more natural, three-dimensional manner. Another Florentine artist, Masaccio (1401–1428), would later demonstrate the reality that Giotto had only attempted, particularly in his emotion-filled *Adam and Eve Expelled from Paradise*. In other works, Masaccio's sense of colour, depth, and movement anticipated the genius in painting that was to follow.

GIOTTO

MASACCIO

One of the greatest masters of the High Renaissance, and perhaps of all time, was Leonardo da Vinci (1452–1519) whose genius in so many fields of study was rivalled only by Michelangelo. As an apprentice of the most famous artist in Florence, Andrea del Verrocchio, Leonardo was allowed to paint an angel in the left-hand corner of his teacher's mural, the *Baptism of Christ*. When Verrocchio saw the result in comparison with his own blankly staring figures, he realized that Leonardo, at age twenty, had surpassed his own talent. Leonardo became a master of proportion and perspective, but there was much more to his painting than this. Throughout the extensive notes made in his career, Leonardo's references to nature were many, to God few, and to the classics not at all. The only authority he recognized was the eye which, as the "window of the soul," could be used by the artist to capture not just the physical appearance of the subject but the range of human emotions within. It is the essence of being, physical and emotional, that Leonardo embodied in his world-famous *Mona Lisa* and lesser known but equally impressive *Virgin of the Rocks*. In his renowned mural, *The Last Supper*, painted on the dining room wall of the monastery of Santa Maria delle Grazie in Milan, Leonardo chose as his subject the dramatic moment when Jesus told his disciples that one of them would betray him. The serenity of Jesus, the centre of attention amid clusters of agitated disciples, brings together all of Leonardo's extensive study of human psychology and practical technique. Rather than the traditional fresco method on wet plaster, Leonardo used an experimental oil and tempera emulsion on dry plaster which allowed him hours of meditation and study of the mural as he progressed.

Precious few of Leonardo's paintings were left or even completed, but his reputation as an artist would have been secure if only his sketches of humans, animals, and anatomical studies had survived.

The sixteenth-century High and Late Renaissance were dominated by the towering genius of Michelangelo Buonarroti (1475–1564). He was almost Leonardo's equal in versatility and influence, shared Leonardo's peak of accom-

LEONARDO DA VINCI

MICHELANGELO

Moments in Time

Isabella d'Este (1474–1539) is one of a few female examples of the true Renaissance ideal. A student of literature, theology, music, and linguistics, as well as the more "traditional" female subjects, needlework and art, d'Este also became proficient in the affairs of state. She ably ruled the duchy of Mantua during her husband's frequent absences. D'Este won lasting renown as a patron of the arts, and her private museum contained one of the best collections of its day.

After five hundred years of abuse, Leonardo da Vinci's Last Supper *is being reborn patch by patch. Dr. Pinin Brambilla Barcilon began the painstaking restoration of this masterpiece in 1977. She first examines the paint fragments through a microscope, enlarging the small area forty times. Once she has*

determined the amount of impurities to be removed, she applies a solvent,
blotting quickly before the chemicals reach Leonardo's colours. It takes
Dr. Brambilla a week to clean an area the size of a postage stamp. Estimates
for completing the work range from three to five years.

Michelangelo's technical mastery is revealed in his Creation of Adam. *The simplicity of the earth scene focusses attention on the perfect human form as Adam's lethargic body is animated by the impulse of life passing down his arm.*

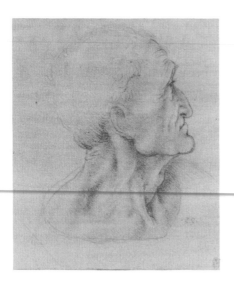

This chalk portrait of Judas is only one of the meticulous studies Leonardo drew as preliminaries for his Last Supper. *The few sketches still in existence help guide today's restoration of the masterpiece.*

plishment, and surpassed his number of completed projects. These two men, so close in talent, provide an important contrast based on attitude, inclination, and probably ego. Leonardo's scientific mind and personal scepticism thrust him towards a lifelong inquiry into the world of nature. Michelangelos' deep faith led to a search for God and the divine intention of artistic expression that he believed sprang from the human body. For Leonardo, it was the artist who created, but for Michelangelo, the artist's craft was an extension of divine will.

The soul of Michelangelo's work, and perhaps the Renaissance, was clearly portrayed on the famous ceiling and altar wall of the Vatican's Sistine Chapel. Although Michelangelo protested that he was not a painter, in 1508 he accepted the commission from Pope Julius II and began his task on the ceiling, 18 m above the floor. Working up to fourteen hours a day in dim light, Michelangelo repeatedly had to lie on his back in an awkward position while his legs hung loosely over the scaffolding to complete the smallest detail. At day's end he often slept on the platform only to begin another day totally absorbed in his divine art. On the floor below, an impatient Pope Julius kept asking when the painting would be finished. Michelangelo, as quick tempered and quarrelsome as he was talented, replied that it would never be done if the pope kept interrupting. After four agonizing years, Michelangelo completed his eternal drama, the *Creation and Fall*. It seems that all conflict served only as an inspiration, for the ceiling fresco is overpowering in scale and impact. A stunning achievement, covering over 900 m², biblical scenes unfold with 343 larger-than-life human figures dazzling the eye and imagination.

Raphael's School of Athens.

THE LAST JUDGEMENT

Twenty-four years later, at age sixty-one, Michelangelo began another commission for another pope to paint the *Last Judgement* on the altar wall of the Sistine Chapel. Greatly weakened and less agile, Michelangelo ended many days too weak to hold a brush. He once fell to the floor from the scaffolding, injuring a leg that left him with a permanent limp. After almost six years, a colossal scene with over three hundred human figures was unveiled, overwhelming onlookers with its unrivalled strength. God occupied the centre stage, surrounded by those who had been judged. At the bottom, the wicked, condemned to hell, suffered their fate. Another artist later painted garments over Michelangelo's nude figures, and centuries of candle smoke have blackened the entire wall. Nevertheless, even today, those who see it cannot help but be moved by the impact of such genius.

TITIAN

RAPHAEL

In painting, the Renaissance spotlight had to be shared with Titian (1490–1576) and Raphael (1483–1520). Titian was a portrait painter for the wealthy in the prosperous city of Venice, and his work reflected the atmosphere of his surroundings. His use of form and striking colours earned him respect and a fortune large enough to sustain a princely existence. Raphael, also a master of colour, went to Florence in 1504, where he was greatly impressed by the work of Leonardo da Vinci and Michelangelo. Yet Raphael developed a serene, emotional feeling and skill in composition that was original and, although he was primarily a painter of portraits like Titian, his best-known work is the mural-sized *School of Athens*. Considered by many to be the greatest painting of

"The Story of Jacob and Esau" from the second set of Ghiberti's bronze doors, **The Gates of Paradise.** *Notice the impressive use of space, perspective, detail, and motion.*

the Renaissance, it shows Greek philosophers from all periods of history, including Plato, Aristotle, Socrates, and Pythagorus, set in a circle against a backdrop of perfect classical architecture. Although he died before he was forty, Raphael achieved the fame and riches that his talent so deserved.

RENAISSANCE SCULPTURE

Medieval sculpture had been regarded as decoration for the great churches of the period, but during the Renaissance, sculpture took on a new importance. The vitality and movement of the human form, so typical of Renaissance painting, enabled sculpture to be commissioned for its own sake as in ancient Greece and Rome. Leonardo da Vinci believed that painting was superior to architecture, but Michelangelo argued that sculpture was to painting what the sun was to the moon. The former was the source of all light, while the latter shone by virtue of light that was reflected. For Michelangelo, the figure lived in the stone and he only sought to free it with his chisel.

GHIBERTI

The transition to Renaissance sculpture began with the work of Lorenzo Ghiberti (1378–1455). In 1402, he won a competition for the contract to carve and cast in bas-relief the panels on the bronze doors of the baptistery in Florence. Although this project still linked sculpture with architecture, Ghiberti laboured for twenty-four years and produced a result worthy of a new art form. His fellow citizens were so impressed that Ghiberti was rewarded with a commission for a second set of doors which also took over two decades to complete! The lifelike figures in the Old Testament scenes leave a feeling of space, not just *behind* them but also *around* them. Even Michelangelo felt that the gilded doors would make a fitting entrance into heaven, and they last as the ultimate tribute to Ghiberti's skill.

Michelangelo's Moses, the most famous of his remaining statues, was originally intended for the tomb of the warrior pope, Julius II. The massive power of the 2.5-m work had not been achieved since the days of ancient Greece and Rome.

Yet, the greatest sculptor of the Renaissance was Michelangelo himself, who consistently achieved artistic peaks that others reached only occasionally. He considered himself first and foremost a sculptor. His themes were universal, their impact timeless, and their strength unrivalled. As a relative unknown, Michelangelo had boasted that he would create the finest work in marble of his day. At age twenty-five, his ambition was realized when he finished the moving and eternal *Pietà* of Christ lying broken across his mother's lap after his

THE PIETÀ

Michelangelo simplified the design of the dome of St. Peter's Basilica by combining the vertical lines of Brunelleschi's ribbed dome with the features of Bramante's original form.

DAVID

MOSES

RENAISSANCE ARCHITECTURE

ST. PETER'S

ordeal on the cross. Aware of what he had achieved, Michelangelo carved his name on the ribbon which lies over the Virgin's left shoulder. Today, behind glass, the *Pietà* glows in one of the side chapels in St. Peter's. The heroic style of Michelangelo was later demonstrated when he completed a magnificent 4.3 m statue of *David* from a huge block of marble quarried and loosely worked by another Florentine sculptor in the 1460s. No vision could be more powerful than the twisting pose of *Moses*, carved for the tomb of Pope Julius in 1513.

It has been argued that the Renaissance achievement in architecture did not live up to that of the medieval period. While such a conclusion will vary with personal taste, there is little doubt that it can be misleading. The soaring lines of Gothic architecture were largely a development of northern Europe and had only limited success in the Italian peninsula. With the humanist emphasis on ancient Greece and Rome, it is perhaps not surprising that Renaissance architects were more influenced by classical styles.

The planning and construction of St. Peter's Basilica, initiated by Pope Julius to replace an existing twelve-hundred-year-old church, illustrate the promise and problems faced by Renaissance planners. The original design submitted by Donato Bramante was circular in shape and dominated by a dome without ribs, in the tradition of the ancient Roman Pantheon. Following Bramante's death in 1514, construction halted and several other architects recommended drastic changes. When Michelangelo took over the commisison in 1546 at age seventy-one, the building had been abandoned for so long that trees were growing out of the arches built in Bramante's day. Michelangelo had been impressed by the ribbed dome designed by Brunelleschi in the cathedral in Florence. Instead of sweeping alterations, Michelangelo simplified the design by combining the vertical lines of Brunelleschi's ribbed dome with the basic features of Bramante's original form. After Michelangelo's death, other architects made additional alterations, including an elongated nave and a massive facade that blocks the dome almost completely when it is approached from the front. Upon its completion in 1626, St. Peter's became the largest church in the world, but the succession of planners and design changes left a heavy and ponderous building that lacks visual unity. In the process, the original Renaissance architecture had evolved into the new style of **Baroque**, which stressed the control that human beings could now exert over nature.

Despite outstanding individual achievements in particular fields, it was the ideal of all-round competence in several areas that made up the true Renaissance personality. Leonardo da Vinci embodied this ideal in a scope of achievement that was truly astounding. Moved by a desire to know how the body worked so that it could be painted with greater effect, Leonardo dissected over thirty cadavers before he was denied access to the mortuary in Rome. Leonardo's findings were recorded in a series of notebooks written in "mirror writing" from right to left on the page. He speculated about blood circulation, the nervous system, the operation of the eye, and drew superb sketches of body and muscle functions that remain striking in their realism. The man whose talented touch painted the *Mona Lisa* was also a gymnast who had the hand strength to bend a horseshoe. While under the patronage of Duke Ludovico Sforza, Leonardo sculpted the famous equestrian statue of the first duke of Milan and, as a military engineer, enquired into the potential of gas bombs, cannons, and exploding and conical shells, among other projects. In architecture, Leonardo's circular, central-plan schemes influenced Bramante's original plan for the rebuilding of St. Peter's. Leonardo went on to build water mills, aqueducts, and irrigation canals. He is often cited for his drawings of flying machines that were aerodynamically correct, but he also worked on balloon flight and parachutes. He described fossils on mountain tops and suspected that the sun did not move as ancient authorities had usually argued.

> ## Moments in Time
> Artemisia Gentileschi (1590–1652) is one of the few women artists of note in the seventeenth century. Artemisia developed her talent under the supervision of her father, an Italian painter. Her portraits and historical and religious paintings eventually gained her admission to the Academy of Design in Florence.

Most of Leonardo's attention, like that of Renaissance thinkers in general, was in the area of what is now called **applied** science. There was little interest in looking at the underlying principles of the natural world in terms of natural laws or theories. The genius of the Renaissance was a visible, concrete achievement that was recognized and celebrated by an informed public that was eager for glory. Yet the spirit of inquiry laid the foundation for the breakthroughs in **pure** science that began in the seventeenth century.

Northern Europe and the Renaissance

North of the Alps, the feudal system had not encouraged artistic development. As feudalism declined, however, the rise of the nation state and the commercial wealth of middle-class merchants and financiers gradually signalled a change. Increasing exchanges with Italian traders, diplomats, and even tourists brought back the exciting news of Renaissance achievement. The prosperity of trading cities in Europe now made patronage of the arts possible, just as it was in Italy. Although the "Northern Renaissance" owed much of its character to its Italian counterpart, several aspects were unique to the local environment.

CHAUCER

The impact of Italian writers is clear in the emergence of northern literature. Among the best of several northern writers that could be mentioned was the civil servant Geoffrey Chaucer (1340–1400), who represented a clear transition from the medieval period to the Renaissance. In his famous work, *Canterbury Tales*, Chaucer tells the stories of thirty pilgrims on their way to visit the shrine of Thomas à Becket, an approach used by Boccaccio in the *Decamerone*. The scene is medieval, but the characterizations of real people, like the very human and earthy "Wife of Bath," mirror the Renaissance tradition pioneered by Dante in his *Divine Comedy*. Chaucer wrote in the vernacular English of the fourteenth century, just as his Italian predecessors had popularized their native tongue. Nevertheless, the range of characters is so wide that their stories provide a cross section of how the English people felt, thought, and reacted to the problems of their world.

ERASMUS

The humanist writers of the north set their own direction and became prominent throughout Europe. Clearly among the most respected and widely read of classical scholars was Desiderius Erasmus (1466–1536) of Rotterdam, known as the "Prince of Humanists." In his travels to Germany, France, Switzerland, England, and Italy, Erasmus developed an international reputation for learning and reform. His influence in Italy, home of the Renaissance, led to the formation of the Oratory of Divine Love, an intellectual association that attempted to upgrade the clergy through improved education. Emphasis on quality scholarship led Erasmus to publish Greek and Latin translations of the New Testament that brought into question the accuracy of the Vulgate Bible used by the Church. Erasmus also felt that the Bible should be published in popular languages for all to read and interpret rather than to remain the private domain of a select few theologians. Although this appeared to be a direct challenge to Church authority, Erasmus remained a priest and devout Catholic who believed in tolerance and education. For Erasmus, intelligent discussion raised the dignity of the individual in a way that was in harmony with the Christian spirit.

SIR THOMAS MORE

Erasmus was in correspondence with many of the great thinkers of Europe, including the famous English humanist Sir Thomas More (1478-1535). More gained lasting fame with his book *Utopia* (Nowhere), which realistically described an ideal society that shared the wealth it produced. According to More, this was the kind of world that people could build if they chose and it represented a criticism of the greed and wars of Europe from a Christian perspective.

MONTAIGNE

SHAKESPEARE

Several literary masters emerged in northern Europe just as they previously had in Italy. In France, Michel de Montaigne (1533–1592), a religious sceptic who loved the classics, wrote serious essays about the need to be open-minded. William Shakespeare (1564–1616), with "little Latin and less Greek," became the greatest writer in the English language, excelling in every facet of drama and the study of human nature. His admiration and debt to the classical world

This woodcut by Albrecht Dürer, entitled Christ before the People, *is from the* Large Passion, *c. 1498.*

CERVANTES

of Greece and Rome was evident in such plays as *Antony and Cleopatra* and *Julius Caesar*, but it was his precise and imaginative use of words, many of them adapted to English for the first time, that forever enriched the language. Meanwhile, the Spanish novelist, Miguel de Cervantes (1547–1616), wrote the brilliant and entertaining *Don Quixote*, that criticized the improbable excesses of medieval chivalry. The comic figures of the lean, half-crazed knight Don Quixote and the donkey-riding Sancho Panza cleverly betray the folly of the era without losing sight of the author's serious purpose.

The free interpretation and range of colour found in Italy–indeed, the entire classical outlook of Greece and Rome–never rested easily with the artists of northern Europe. This, however, was a matter of tradition rather than talent.

JAN VAN EYCK

The works of Belgian painter Jan van Eyck (1380–1441) equalled the high achievements of the Italian Renaissance. Van Eyck's *Man in a Red Turban* is the earliest-known example of the subject looking at the spectator. His minute detail, typified in the famous work *Arnolfini Wedding*, captured a greater reality than a modern photograph.

DÜRER

Albrecht Dürer (1471–1528) has often been described as Germany's answer to Leonardo da Vinci because of his achievements in a variety of fields. Dürer was the first painter to use himself repeatedly as a model in a series of portraits and his black and white designs have never been excelled. Nevertheless, Dürer was also inspired by native German tradition in his use of woodcuts and copper etchings, which were reproduced and distributed in great quantity.

HOLBEIN

Hans Holbein (1497–1543) was also a German portrait painter of the highest order who became famous for a series of paintings completed for his patron, Henry VIII of England. Generally, northern artists avoided the universal Christian themes of an all-powerful God and concentrated on individual scenes of Christ on the cross, the Virgin Mary and child.

The almost perfect world within the grasp of Renaissance genius, however, was about to be exploded by an obscure German monk.

The Protestant Reformation

THE CHRISTIAN WORLD

Following the decline of the Roman Empire, the Roman Catholic Church was the cement that united the Christian world. While regional differences had always existed, it was not until 1054 that Christendom officially became divided between the Catholic and Orthodox churches of Rome and Constantinople. Although the attempts to breach the gap and permanently secure the Holy Land in the grasp of crusading Christians had been unsuccessful, there was no question about the spiritual and economic power of the Roman Catholic Church in Europe. From the pope to the parish priest, the spiritual impact of the Church was relayed with the same universal message. A person could find eternal salvation only by accepting the seven sacraments which could be administered only by the clergy. In addition, the Church was among the largest landholders in Europe and played a pivotal role in education, as a patron of the arts, and as a social focal point in every community. The pope ruled outright in the Papal States and was a maker and breaker of emperors.

Nevertheless, the prestige of the Church had been battered on several occasions. Crusades invoked too frequently for questionable purposes and paid for by regular collections drew widespread resentment. The Great Schism, during which three popes briefly ruled simultaneously, split the direction of the Church and weakened claims to spiritual leadership. By 1500, corruption of wealth and power had filtered from the papacy to the parish, although there were dedicated members of the clergy who continued to perform many good works. For a pope like Alexander VI (1492–1503), human salvation seemed less important than helping his son Cesare Borgia gain prosperity and dominance in the provinces of Italy. Pope Julius II (1503–1513), patron of Michelangelo, was a military man with great political ambition. His successor, Leo X (1513–1521), son of Lorenzo de' Medici, was also a patron of the arts who was driven by a desire to build St. Peter's Basilica in Rome. In his quest to raise money, Leo was not above selling statues of the apostles, papal jewellery, plates, and furniture. He also accepted payment for the appointment of a new bishop to a diocese and the annulment of marriages and other vows.

DECLINE OF CHURCH PRESTIGE

The practice of **simony**, the buying and selling of Church offices, earned Leo his greatest reputation for financial abuse as he maintained an annual income of over a million dollars from the sale of over two thousand such appointments. Many bishops were nobles, interested in prestige and money rather than God's work, and they engaged in immoral private lives. They often received incomes from dioceses they had never seen. Local clerical positions were often given to relatives and friends and many priests did not even know the Latin required for the Mass.

SIMONY

As the quality of the clergy declined, the moral fibre of the Church was extensively criticized for exploiting papal letters of indulgence. The idea of an indulgence sprang from the belief that Christ and the saints were more worthy than was necessary for their own salvation and that the Church could shift this surplus merit to the deserving. An indulgence ended all or part of the punishment that faced a confessed and repentant sinner, and, in its extreme sixteenth-century form, could even be obtained for the dead. At first, indulgences were issued to pilgrims, crusaders, and those who did "good work" at home. Eventually, a cash payment replaced the need for good work, and it became obvious that the papal motive was money rather than the forgiveness of sin.

LETTERS OF INDULGENCE

Many recognized that reforms were needed to stem this growing worldliness and immorality of the Church. The English theologian John Wycliff (1320–1384) argued that the low morality of the clergy could be corrected by allowing them to marry. He criticized indulgences and the veneration of the Church hierarchy, including the pope, and insisted that the only requirement for individual salvation was to read the Bible and follow the word of God. To assist the people of England, Wycliff translated the Bible into English. John Hus (1369–1415) of Prague later translated some of Wycliff's writing into Czechoslovakian. For supporting such radical ideas, however, Hus was eventually excommunicated and burned at the stake. In Italy, Girolamo Savonarola (1452–1498) of Florence, a spellbinding preacher, attacked the lack of virtue and excess of vice in his prosperous city, was critical of the worldly ways of the

WYCLIFF

HUS

SAVONAROLA

pope, and argued for a simpler, stricter Christian life. The fanatical Savonarola became a leading political force in Florence, but he, too, was excommunicated and burned at the stake for heresy.

Beyond reviving an interest in the classics, Renaissance humanism released an intellectual inquiry into and reexamination of the practices of the Church with the aim of reform and improvement. Erasmus personified this sincere concern as he joined his reform-minded predecessors in condemning the abuse of indulgences, the low quality of the clergy, the secular preoccupation with wealth, and the power evident in the Church in Rome. Somehow the Church had drifted away from the cleansing simplicity of the original Christian values. The key to salvation, according to Erasmus, lay in rediscovering those values and living a humble life in the tradition of Christ, rather than emphasizing the sacraments of the Church and the veneration of saints and relics. As a respected scholar and faithful Catholic, who personally knew the popes and kings of his day, Erasmus had unlocked the door to reform. It would remain for another to open it and walk through.

Unwilling or unable to listen to the genuine voice of reform from within, the Church was now beset by uncontrollable pressures from the secular world. The Roman Catholic ideal of Christian universality was now threatened by the growth of nation states and the nationalism they encouraged. Monarchs in France and England were jealous of Church wealth and resented the way that papal revenue was siphoned from their domain whether for religious purposes or war. Although landless peasants eyed the extensive landholdings of the Church, it was the middle-class merchant who had made his way through private enterprise. The Renaissance had given new dignity to the individual and now reformers argued for changes that would allow the individual to obtain salvation by personally reading the scriptures.

The crosscurrents of European civilization crystallized in the life of Martin Luther (1483–1546), the eldest son of a German peasant family, who ultimately walked through the door of reform opened by Erasmus. Born in Eisleben, the gradual success of his father in copper mining enabled Luther to attend the respected University of Erfurt, where he eventually settled on the study of law. Then, one July day in 1505, Luther was struck by lightning in a violent storm and survived. He attributed the event to the power and anger of God. People of the sixteenth century believed that God communicated to them in such dramatic moments and Luther was so moved that he vowed to seek his own salvation and become a monk. At the local Augustinian monastery, Luther tried the normal Church procedures to gain salvation, including rigorous fasting, prayer, the visitation of relics, and particularly confession. Nothing seemed to help. With the hope that change might do him some good, Luther's confessor sent him to the University of Wittenburg where he became a professor of philosophy and a priest. Luther visited Rome in 1511 only to discover that many Italians, even on the holy ground of the Christian capital, were less earnest about their religion than he was. Disillusioned, he returned to Wittenburg.

M. LUTHER.

Luther remained burdened with guilt and obsessed with the need for salvation. Suddenly, in reading a familiar line in Saint Paul's *Epistle to the Romans,* "The just shall live by faith," the answer came to Luther like a bolt from heaven. Not good works, not fasting, not pilgrimages nor indulgences, but *faith* in God's redemption was the road to salvation. The idea was not new, but Luther gripped it, after years of inner turmoil, with a single-minded purpose that waved aside all other obstacles. The entire ritual of the Church was unnecessary–faith in a loving and merciful God was the key. With the path to salvation now clear, Luther was about to become the focal point of a controversy much larger than he ever imagined.

MARTIN LUTHER

Lacking a centralized national government like England and France, German princes often felt the heaviest weight of papal demands. In 1515, Pope Leo X proclaimed an indulgence primarily to raise money for the construction of St. Peter's in Rome, but also to help Albert of Brandenburg with the financial obligations of holding three bishoprics at the same time! The seller of the indulgence was the Dominican friar John Tetzel who made his pitch to a largely superstitious community with the fast-talking panache of a modern swindler. Throughout the German states, Tetzel passionately claimed that each time money hit the box a soul jumped from purgatory into heaven. What a deal! This was too much for Luther, who objected on nationalistic grounds that German money should not be used to build a Roman church and on religious grounds that salvation depended on faith *alone* rather than indulgences. With the hope of engaging a public debate, Luther nailed a list of Ninety-Five Theses (statements) that condemned the value of indulgences to the door of the castle church in Wittenburg on 13 October 1517.

POPE LEO X

JOHN TETZEL

THE NINETY-FIVE THESES

Luther's statements, much to the author's surprise, were translated from Latin into German, printed, and circulated throughout the countryside. Luther had no intention of breaking with the Church, however, circumstances now demanded that the implication of his ideas be carefully thought out. He challenged the supremacy of the pope and Church councils. Of the seven sacraments, only baptism and the Lord's Supper were acceptable because they were the only ones directly implemented by Christ. Luther argued, as did others before him, that the clergy could marry and felt that the priesthood included all who believed rather than the select few ordained by the Church.

LUTHER'S CHALLENGE

Luther spread his views through a series of sermons and tracts, regarding himself as a son of the Church who was purifying Christianity, rather than as a heretic. Pope Leo X saw it differently, particularly as the sale of indulgences fell, and in 1520, issued a papal bull (decree) of excommunication. Luther was given sixty days to reconsider his position. On the final day, in front of his students and the citizens of Wittenburg, he threw the decree into a bonfire. At that moment, Luther was a national hero to many of the peasants and princes of Germany. He had defied what they regarded as the foreign authority of Rome. Although not everyone agreed or even understood him, the German princes had been whittling away at papal authority since the fourteenth century. When

Luther went on to argue that civil authority had a duty to reform the Church, many German princes saw a chance to control Church lands and the revenues that flowed to Rome.

THE IMPERIAL DIET OF WORMS

Excommunicated a second time, Luther was summoned to the Imperial Diet (parliament) in the town of Worms in 1521 with a guarantee of safe-conduct to see if he would recant. At the Diet of Worms, Luther refused to admit the error of his ways. He was declared a heretic, denied help of any kind, and his books were not to be bought, sold, or read. Although it appeared his fate was sealed, Luther was taken by Frederick III, the elector of Saxony, to Wartburg Castle and given the protection needed to continue his work.

During the next decade, Luther translated the Bible into German and formulated the main elements of his own Church. By following this path, he lost the support of many humanists, including Erasmus, who may have desired reform but did not want to revolt against the foundation of Catholic authority. Luther's heresy, however, was not the Church's most pressing problem of the moment.

The Ottoman Turks were moving towards the Danube and had infiltrated parts of the western Mediterranean, while hostility with France threatened in Italy, the Netherlands, and Spain. When Pope Clement VII allied the papacy with France against the Holy Roman Emperor, the conflict that followed resulted in the sacking of Rome in 1527. Meanwhile, within the German states, a rebellion of feudal knights in 1522–1523 was followed by the more serious Peasants' War in 1524–1525. Luther, though radical in thought, was essentially conservative in his attitude towards social order. He supported the German princes against the knights and the peasants. Rapid implementation of his ideas had led to violent raids on churches and the needless destruction of art objects, a practice that Luther strongly opposed. The champions of his Church, for reasons of religion and politics, were the German princes. When the emperor

THE PROTESTANTS

called the Imperial Diet of Speyer in 1529, it was the princes who protested (hence the name **Protestant**) when Charles proclaimed they did not have the right to determine the religion of their subjects.

Attempts by the emperor to reconcile the differences between Luther and the Catholics failed, and for twenty-five years an intermittent war between

THE PEACE OF AUGSBURG

Lutheran and Catholic states dragged on. With the Peace of Augsburg in 1555, the war ended with the agreement that the religion of each state could be determined by its ruler. Northern Germany and all of Scandinavia had become Lutheran, while the southern German states remained Catholic. Each religion was given equal recognition, but no thought was given to religious freedom. For the next century, Europe would be seriously divided by religion as well as politics, and a country's faith would often determine its alliance in war.

The Reformation Spreads

While Lutheran Protestantism dominated much of Germany and Scandinavia, other forms of Protestantism emerged elsewhere in Europe. Ulrich Zwingli

(1484–1531) of Switzerland, influenced by Luther, rejected the authority of the Catholic hierarchy and associated rituals, and accepted only two of the seven sacraments. Unlike Luther, however, Zwingli substituted a Communion service for the Mass that was mainly a symbolic representation of Christ's last supper with the disciples. He argued that the body and blood of Christ were not really present in the bread and wine used in the proceedings. Zwingli also believed in the use of force to convert religious adversaries, and, while fighting for a cause he believed to be just, was killed in a religious war with Swiss Roman Catholics. Although he established no church, Zwingli partly influenced the development of the Anabaptists. They believed that the key to salvation lay in a simple and strict morality accompanied by adult baptism. In their opposition to the worldliness of the state, the Anabaptists agreed with Zwingli, but in their total opposition to war of any kind, a new direction had been set. One surviving group of Anabaptists, the Mennonites, fled to Pennsylvania to avoid persecution. Some of their descendants, the "Pennsylvania Dutch," came to Canada during the American Revolution to start a new life in what is now Kitchener, Ontario.

The greatest impact on the Protestant Reformation was made by the French humanist, John Calvin (1509–1564). Converted by the works of Erasmus and Luther, Calvin brought a reasoned approach and masterful organization to the Protestant cause. While in Basel, he wrote his famous work, *The Institutes of the Christian Religion*, which gave a summary of basic beliefs that became the guideline for the faithful. Although Calvin shared some of Luther's views, he emphasized that God was all-knowing and all-powerful, and that it was a person's duty to serve God. Luther had gone beyond good works to faith in search of salvation, but Calvin went beyond faith to a doctrine known as **predestination**. God had already decided one's fate and there was nothing that could be done about it. Evidence of those **elected** or saved was seen to be a life of high Christian morality and faith, while those who lived a sinful existence were certainly headed for hell. It was a moral obligation to convert the wayward, a motivation that made the Calvinists a dynamic force in European life.

In Geneva, Calvin put his talent for organization to work and tried to create the perfect Protestant city. Calvinists regulated the economy, education, and the council that visited homes to judge the lives of the occupants. Everything was governed by the Scriptures and the word of God with no deviation. Taverns, card games, dancing, drinking, and profaning, among other abuses, were criticized and penalized. Simplicity, with a focus on sermons, Bible reading, and hymn singing, was essential for all religious services, while the trappings of images, candles, and even bells were condemned.

Visitors were often deeply impressed by the stern quality of life they saw, and they returned to their homelands filled with Calvinist ideals. As leaders were trained, Calvin established churches throughout northern Europe that echoed the philosophy of the Geneva model. In Scotland, John Knox (1505–1572), after spending time in Geneva, laid the basis for a form of Prot-

ZWINGLI

ANABAPTISTS

MENNONITES

JOHN CALVIN

THE "PERFECT PROTESTANT CITY"

KNOX

estantism known as **Presbyterianism** that would eventually dominate his homeland. Calvinist influence in the Netherlands, along with the heavy taxes imposed by Philip II, played a large part in the revolt against Catholic Spain that resulted in the independence of Holland in 1581. French Calvinists, known as **Huguenots**, were regarded as a threat to political as well as religious unity, and they were subsequently persecuted by both the Catholic Church and the French government. The climax of the suppression was the St. Bartholomew Massacre of 1572, when the great nobles of the Huguenot party were slaughtered while attending a royal marriage. The Edict of Nantes, in 1598, introduced a period of toleration, but France remained a Catholic country.

HENRY VIII

Henry VIII (1509–1547) launched the Reformation in England mainly for personal and political reasons. Criticism of Luther had previously won Henry the title ''Defender of the Faith'' from Pope Leo X, but when another pope would not grant Henry a divorce so he could marry Anne Boleyn, his priorities became clear. Henry would not allow this affront to English sovereignty, particularly if it spoiled his plans for marriage! There were several reasons why Henry could expect to get his way. Nationalism spurred a commonly held resentment of papal revenue draining from England to Rome, and there was little sympathy for the wealth and materialism of the clergy. People no longer thought monasteries provided an essential service, and many were eager to share in the sale and distribution of large tracts of monastic land. A few people even had genuine support for the views of Luther. By several acts of Parliament, payments to Rome ceased, the king was given the right to appoint bishops, and then finally was recognized as the supreme head on earth of the Church of England.

It did not pay to quarrel with a man as determined as Henry. When Thomas More, the famed humanist, refused to support Henry's claims against the pope, he was executed. At the expense of his most outspoken opponent, Henry had thus enhanced national pride, increased royal revenue, and entered another of his six marriages, even though the Church remained Catholic in doctrine. Nevertheless, by establishing a national Church headed by the English king, Henry had also begun his own version of the Reformation.

EDWARD VI

Under Edward VI (1547–1553), several changes were made in the direction of Protestantism. The Church of England, or Anglican Church, recognized baptism and Communion as the chief sacraments and allowed priests to marry. Anglican doctrine was outlined in the first version of *The Book of Common Prayer*, which, though altered on several occasions, came into the posses-

MARY

sion of most English-speaking Protestants. The reign of Mary (1553–1558) marked an attempt to turn the clock back by reestablishing Roman Catholicism in England. About three hundred Protestants, including Archbishop Thomas Cranmer, were burned at the stake, and the nation was divided. Eliza-

ELIZABETH I

beth I (1558–1603), a ruler capable of effecting a badly needed compromise, appeared at the right moment. Working with Parliament, she established a

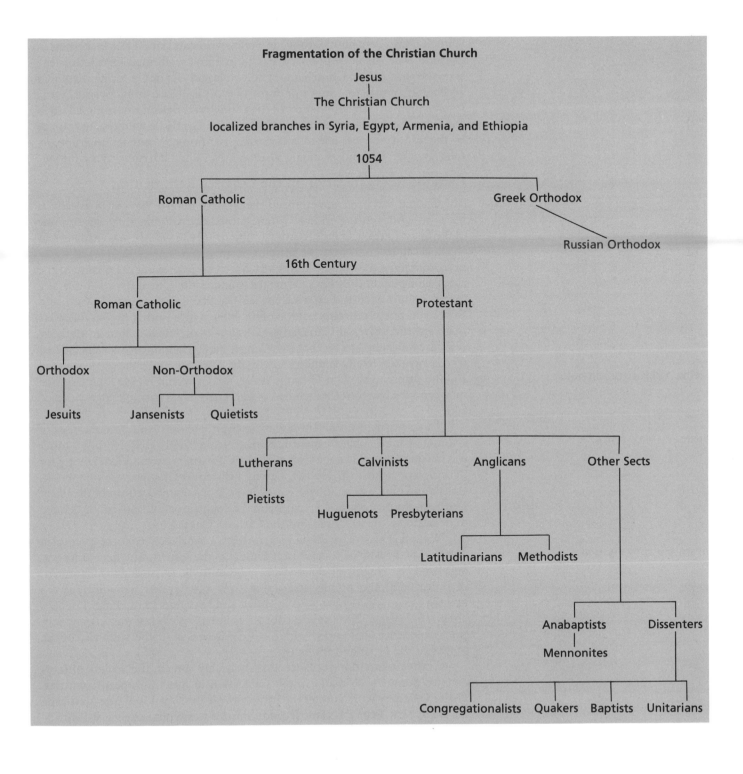

Church that was mainly Catholic in organization and ritual but Protestant in doctrine. The Act of Supremacy, passed in 1559, reaffirmed Elizabeth as the supreme authority in Church and state, while and Act of Uniformity required all English people to adopt one form of worship based on a revised *Book of Common Prayer*. The foundation of the Church of England was summed up in the Thirty-Nine Articles. Although England was regarded as a Protestant country by the rest of Europe, religious controversy at home threatened to erupt any time a weaker, less understanding sovereign than Elizabeth came to the throne.

Catholic Reorganization in the Counter Reformation

XIMENES

The Church had been slow to heed the cries for reform that began as early as the fourteenth century and had often ignored the recommendations of some of the finest Catholic minds. Cardinal Ximenes (1436–1517), who had been in the final campaign to oust the Muslims from Granada in 1492, worked vigorously to reform the Spanish Catholic Church by improving the quality of the clergy along traditional lines. Ximenes founded the University of Alcala as a centre for humanist studies, which he felt would only strengthen the faith, and worked on a new, scholarly edition of the Bible. Once Luther and his followers shattered the universal Christian establishment of Europe, Roman Catholic response quickened to meet the challenge. New religious orders were created whose members lived a simple, less worldly, Christian life in the service of God

NEW RELIGIOUS ORDERS

and the community. The Theatine order, the Capuchin monks, the Ursuline nuns, and the barefoot Carmelites were among the best examples of revitalized faith.

IGNATIUS LOYOLA

The most successful and important attempt at reform came from the work of a young Spanish soldier named Ignatius Loyola (1491–1556). While Luther was making his stand at the Diet of Worms, Loyola was wounded fighting for the emperor against the French. During his recovery, he read the only books available to him, a biography of saints and a four-volume account of the life of Christ. In the process, Loyola experienced a dramatic conversion and he decided to dedicate his life to Christ and the Catholic Church.

THE SOCIETY OF JESUS

Beginning his work with only six students, Loyola received papal approval in 1540 for a ''Society of Jesus,'' later known as the Jesuits. The new order was organized like a highly disciplined army committed to restoring the Church to its former position of prestige and power. To become a priest, a candidate served two years as a novice, nine years in study, and two years in teaching. Loyola's book, *The Spiritual Exercises*, described this intense period of training and religious experience that ended with a sincere devotion to the authority of the general of the order and the pope.

As their reputation for faith and scholarship spread, the Society of Jesus came to dominate Roman Catholic education in most European countries. Their missionary work among the native people in the wilds of Canada during the era of New France became legend, but this was typical of their worldwide efforts in India, Ceylon, the East Indies, and Japan. Clearly, the Society of Jesus was the spearhead of a reformed and reinvigorated Catholic faith.

Between the enthusiasm of new orders and the spread of Protestantism, the Church decided it was time to give direction to the Catholic world. When Pope Paul III came to office in 1534, the Church finally had a pope that was genuinely interested in reform, and he called a general council of the Church to meet in the German town of Trent to examine Catholic beliefs. The Council of Trent met in three sessions between 1545 and 1563, and the result clarified the basic foundation of Catholic faith with reforms intended to improve the quality of the clergy. Authority in religion stemmed from the Vulgate Bible and the tradition of the Church, and on earth this power was embodied in the pope. The importance of the seven sacraments, the priesthood, the need for good works as well as faith to achieve salvation, veneration of saints and relics, and transubstantiation in the Mass were reaffirmed. Protestant notions of predestination, faith alone, and the priesthood of all believers were rejected. At the same time, the council eliminated the sale of indulgences and Church offices, insisted that bishops be better trained, less worldly, and live in their dioceses, and that every diocese must have a seminary to train priests. Celibacy was to be strictly enforced and every member of the clergy now had to be a model of Christianity in his private and public life.

With rejuvenated faith and a better-trained clergy, the Church was prepared to roll back the gains made throughout northern Europe by Protestantism. To prevent the spread of heretical ideas that might lead the faithful Catholic astray, an *Index of Prohibited Books* was published to identify those authors who were not to be read. Even the role of the medieval Inquisition was again recognized to combat heresy. The line between Catholic and Protestant was now unmistakably drawn, with each intolerant of the other and voicing no interest in reconciliation. Europe now had to prepare for a power struggle between competing religions in addition to the secular conflicts of kingdoms and nation states that had become all too familiar.

THE COUNCIL OF TRENT

CATHOLIC VERSUS PROTESTANT

The Golden Century of Spain

Two years after Columbus's historic voyage, Pope Alexander VI sanctioned the Treaty of Tordesillas that divided the New World between Spain and Portugal along a north-south line 1600 km west of the Azores. In practice, this eventually gave Brazil–discovered in 1500 by Pedro Cabral when his ship was blown off course–to Portugal, and the rest of the New World to Spain. The Christian zeal that expelled the Muslims and supported the Inquisition propelled Spain into the exploration and exploitation of new lands once the path was cleared by the conquistadores. This gave Spain an important head start in commercial development that was not overcome by its European rivals for almost a century.

THE TREATY OF TORDESILLAS

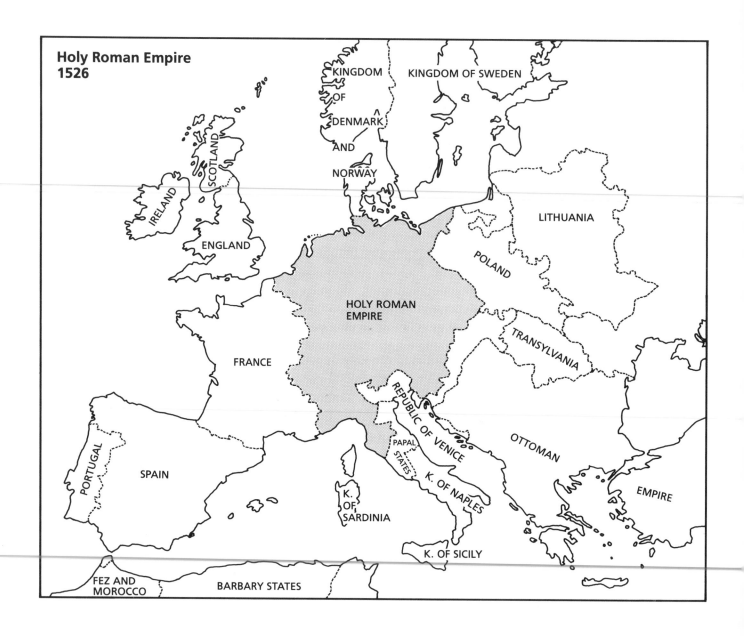

**Holy Roman Empire
1526**

KINGDOM OF DENMARK AND NORWAY

KINGDOM OF SWEDEN

IRELAND

SCOTLAND

ENGLAND

LITHUANIA

POLAND

HOLY ROMAN EMPIRE

FRANCE

TRANSYLVANIA

REPUBLIC OF VENICE

PAPAL STATES

OTTOMAN

PORTUGAL

SPAIN

K. OF SARDINIA

K. OF NAPLES

EMPIRE

K. OF SICILY

FEZ AND MOROCCO

BARBARY STATES

The firm rule of Ferdinand and Isabella gave more unity to the administration of Spain than it ever had before. This encouraged a prosperous economy which focussed on handicrafts and the production of wool, wine, and olive oil. Upon Ferdinand's death in 1516, his grandson Charles inherited the throne, and the history of Spain soon became tangled with that vague political expression known as the Holy Roman Empire. Developed after Charlemagne as a confederation of German principalities, the Holy Roman Empire disintegrated in 1250 only to be revived in the fourteenth century with territorial claims extending as far as Italy. An emperor and a diet were selected by seven electors who were German princes and archbishops, but local units known as ''circles'' retained considerable independence. While the prestige of the emperor was recognized by all, it was difficult to control and direct such a vast collection of semi-independent states. When Charles von Hapsburg bribed the electorate in 1519 to become Holy Roman Emperor Charles V, he had titular control over the largest territory under a single prince since the days of Charlemagne. Spain was the key to Charles's power, but he also ruled over most of Germany, the Netherlands, Bohemia, Milan, and Naples.

Throughout his reign, Charles was caught up in a series of conflicts with the Turks in eastern Europe and the Mediterranean, and with France over disputed territorial claims in the Rhineland and Italy. To rival nation states, such military action often appeared to be an attempt by Charles to dominate Europe, a real possibility since the Spanish soldiers hired as mercenaries were among the best fighting men on the continent. Their services were paid for by the huge quantities of silver and gold that began to arrive, first from collections of Amerindian jewellery, and later from the mines of Mexico and Peru. Increasing amounts of silver were imported to Spain each decade after the conquest, peaking between 1591 and 1600 when 2 707 626 kg arrived. Spanish galleons also brought back almost 900 000 kg of gold before supplies were gradually exhausted. While Spain restricted trade between the colonies and other countries, her ships, laden with precious metals, became inviting targets for British, French, and Dutch pirates on the high seas.

Spaniards had flocked to the New World on behalf of God, with hope of finding both glory and gold. Their success in securing the latter was assisted immensely by the exploitation of the Amerindian population through a grant of *encomienda*, in which natives were forced to provide food, labour, and tribute to their conquerors. The natives, who had been successful farmers and traders, had their homes looted and were forced to carry heavy loads long distances. They were tortured and, in extreme cases, murdered when they did not comply. The Spaniards did not intend to destroy the native population that supplied their labour. Their careless pursuit of riches, however, depopulated many of the towns scattered over the countryside of the New World. Bartolome de las Casas, a former colonial who became a bishop, argued that *encomiendas* were contrary to the moral laws of God and country. Although

FERDINAND AND ISABELLA

THE HOLY ROMAN EMPIRE

CHARLES V

BULLION FROM THE NEW WORLD

ENCOMIENDA

Mary I, or Mary Tudor, the Roman Catholic daughter of Henry VIII by his first wife, Catherine of Aragon, became known as "Bloody Mary" because of the large number of Protestants condemned to death during her reign.

reforms were passed, they were soon ignored to acquire more silver and gold. Charles V, to his credit, did suspend the exploration and conquest of new territory for a decade until a more humane approach could be developed.

The fate of Spain took another turn in 1556 when Charles abdicated his throne and divided his holdings. His younger brother, Ferdinand I, became Holy Roman Emperor and laid the foundation for the Hapsburg state on the Danube. His son Philip II (1556–1598) of Spain became ruler of the Netherlands, northern Italy, Naples, and a colonial empire that was the envy of Europe.

SPAIN AND THE NETHERLANDS

PHILIP II

This left Philip as the main political force behind the Catholic Counter Reformation, a task already begun when Charles arranged a marriage between his son and Mary Tudor of England, in 1553. Although the eighteen-year-old Philip was not inspired by thirty-nine-year-old Queen Mary, her rule cemented a traditional friendship with England and marked an earnest attempt to reestablish the Catholic faith on the island kingdom. The marriage was childless and, after Mary died in 1558, Philip continued his pro-English policy by offering his hand to Elizabeth. As the shrewdest of the Tudors, Elizabeth realized that England needed stability rather than the religious conflict of Mary's years. She initially dodged the offer from Philip and would later come to ridicule it.

Elizabeth I, daughter of Henry VIII by his second wife, Anne Boleyn, was an extremely popular, able monarch. England's Elizabethan Age was characterized by material prosperity, confidence in the government, and high national spirit.

Meanwhile, in the Netherlands, Philip attempted to centralize the authority of the Catholic Church in a country that jealously guarded its local autonomy and had a significant Protestant minority. The new administration would have clamped down on heresy, but Catholics and Protestants alike regarded such a measure as a threat to their freedom. When a petition of protest signed by five hundred prominent citizens was ignored, a wave of violence broke out, led by Calvinists who destroyed statues, paintings, and manuscripts in Catholic churches throughout the country. Philip sent in the duke of Alva to quell the unrest, but this only led to a struggle for independence that would not end until after Philip's death.

Philip's situation was complicated by his involvement on several fronts. Aided by the fleets of Venice and Genoa, Spain stopped the advance of the Turks in the Mediterranean with an important victory in 1571 at the great naval Battle of Lepanto off the Greek coast. Philip's success in harshly suppressing heresy at home drew resentment in England when escaping refugees arrived with their story. English money (as well as French) helped to fan the flames of discontent in the Netherlands while Elizabeth secretly commissioned Francis Drake and the English "sea dogs" to pirate Spanish treasure in the New World. Philip reluctantly determined to crush England, its wayward Church and, at the same time, gain the upper hand in the Netherlands by sending a great armada of 130 ships and thirty thousand men towards the Channel in 1588. An additional invasion force led by the duke of Parma waited in the Spanish-controlled coastal area of the Netherlands to be transported to England after the English navy had been swept from the sea. In one of history's most famous naval battles, however, the speed and manoeuvrability of the smaller English ships, the surprise arrival of fireboats at night while the Spanish anchored in Calais, and a great storm reduced the Spanish fleet to less than half its original size. Failure to control the sea lanes after the defeat of the armada resulted in broken supply lines and additional military losses against France on the continent during the final decade of Philip's reign.

Although Spain would remain a great power until the mid-seventeenth century, and enjoy artistic achievements like the paintings of El Greco and Velasquez, the die was cast. Philip's wars had been waged on a grand scale, yet Anglican England was more formidable than ever, the Dutch Protestants were in control of the northern Netherlands (Holland), and French Huguenot rights were guaranteed in the Edict of Nantes. The flow of silver and gold into Spain from the New World left as quickly as it arrived to pay for the burdens of war and the imported goods that Spain could not produce. Spain itself was essentially a poor country with few natural resources and limited human resources. When the supplies of precious metals began to dwindle in the seventeenth century following defeat on the battlefield, Spain quickly dropped out of the mainstream of European life with little to show for its efforts.

THE ENGLISH "SEA DOGS"

THE SPANISH ARMADA

THE EDICT OF NANTES

The Thirty Years' War and the Nation States of Europe

Although the hegemony of Catholic Spain was halted, Europe had not seen the last of wars that freely mixed religion and politics. In 1618, with Ferdinand von Hapsburg about to be elected Holy Roman Emperor, Bohemian Protestants feared that earlier practices of religious toleration would be withdrawn. A revolution was launched in Prague where the palace was stormed and two Hapsburg ministers were thrown out an upper window. They were saved from

REBELLION IN BOHEMIA

injury by a pile of manure that graced the royal courtyard, but Europe was not to be so lucky.

Ferdinand moved to crush the rebellion and to tighten control over the Protestant German states within the Holy Roman Empire. Spain came to the assistance of the Hapsburg emperor, but other European powers did not want to see the Holy Roman Empire become too strong. First Denmark, then Sweden, led by the colourful military genius of Gustavus Adolphus, entered the conflict against the forces of Spain and the emperor as the war became international in scope. In 1635, in the face of continued Hapsburg success, Catholic France came into the war *against* its religious brethren in Spain and the empire. This clearly showed that the religious issues associated with the earlier phases of the war had been replaced by political considerations. The French victory at Rocroi, in 1643, crippled Spanish military power, ending her days as a great European nation. With Spain humbled, the Hapsburg emperor opened peace talks five weeks later.

The technology and tactics of war had gradually become more destructive. The war that began in 1618, known to history as The Thirty Years' War, became brutal in the devastation it wrought, using refined tactics to sustain the war. Muzzle-loading muskets had abolished the individual knight, but a disciplined cavalry charge could reach the infantry before it had a chance to reload. Similarly, while a cannon could blow a hole in the line, it could not prevent the bulk of the charge from coming through. Only the wall of pikes held by an experienced force of well-drilled infantry could blunt the impact of the cavalry. This meant that the war fell into the hands of seasoned mercenaries, and that the need to pay them became increasingly important as the war dragged on. Commanders on both sides resorted to plundering villages and towns to feed and equip their soldiers and to pay their wages. The Thirty Years' War established a tradition of looting as an accepted act of warfare, a practice that laid waste the fragmented German states where much of the war was fought. The devastation caused by military conflict, looting, and the dislocation of crop production and distribution reduced the population by about one-third.

The peace treaties were hammered out in a five-year congress (1643–1648) in German towns of Westphalia. Since no armistice was arranged, fighting continued as negotiations proceeded and terms changed with success or failure on the battlefield. When the Treaties of Westphalia were finally issued in 1648, it was clear that the medieval organization of Europe had ended and that independent sovereign states, responsible only to themselves, had become the new order. After more than a century of religious wars, neither Catholic nor Protestant could claim victory. The principle that each prince had the right to choose the religion of his state, already proclaimed in the Peace of Augsburg in 1555, was reaffirmed. That Calvinism was among the choices ended the medieval concept of Western European unity. Papal condemnation of the treaties reflected the fact that the pope's representative at the conference was largely ignored

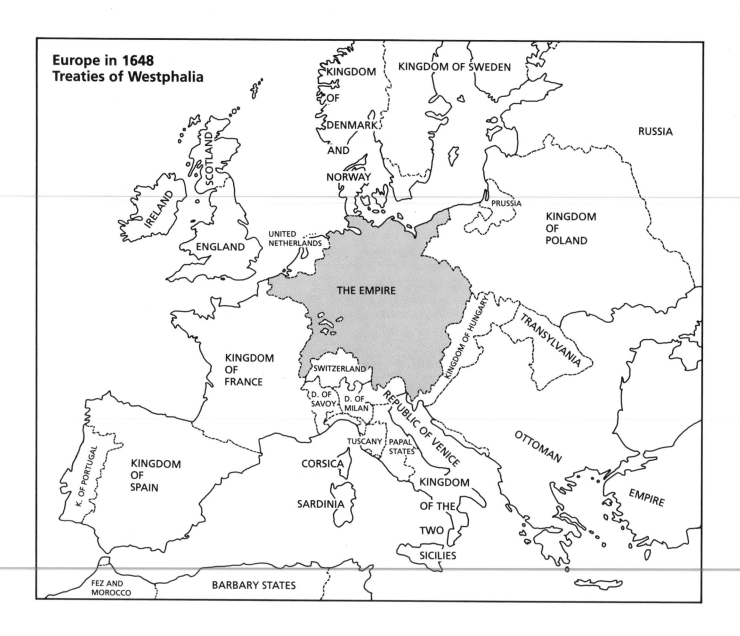

Europe in 1648
Treaties of Westphalia

KINGDOM OF SWEDEN

KINGDOM
OF
DENMARK
AND
NORWAY

RUSSIA

IRELAND

SCOTLAND

ENGLAND

UNITED
NETHERLANDS

PRUSSIA

KINGDOM
OF
POLAND

THE EMPIRE

KINGDOM OF HUNGARY

TRANSYLVANIA

KINGDOM
OF
FRANCE

SWITZERLAND

D. OF
SAVOY

D. OF
MILAN

REPUBLIC OF VENICE

OTTOMAN

K. OF PORTUGAL

KINGDOM
OF
SPAIN

TUSCANY

PAPAL
STATES

CORSICA

SARDINIA

KINGDOM
OF THE
TWO
SICILIES

EMPIRE

FEZ AND
MOROCCO

BARBARY STATES

and that the fragmentation of Christendom, begun during the Reformation, had gained official sanction by secular rulers. The authority of the princes, who had the right to make treaties and alliances with any other European state, also effectively ended the political power of the Holy Roman Empire.

By the Treaties of Westphalia, the Hapsburgs were forced to recognize the independence of the United Netherlands (Holland), the Swiss Confederation, and the small German states, including the important principality of Brandenburg-Prussia. The Hapsburgs retained control over Austria, Bohemia (now Czechoslovakia), and Hungary, which became the basis of a future monarchy on the Danube. Spain held on to the Spanish Netherlands, Franche-Comté, and its Italian territory, but remained at war with France until 1659, when the Treaty of the Pyrenees ended hostilities. France, with a foothold in the Rhineland, emerged from Westphalia as the strongest power in Europe, with opportunities for future expansion.

After centuries of evolution, the sovereign nation state became the accepted basis for political organization at Westphalia. Germany and Italy remained a collection of small, individual provinces until the nineteenth century, but the historical trend towards the nation state was increasingly clear. Medieval life had been dominated by feudal lords and the military contribution of armoured knights. As trade and commerce revived in the towns and cities, however, the new middle class of wealthy merchants often became civic office holders. Their interest in business usually aligned them with the king, who competed for power and prestige with the established nobility whose wealth was based on land. Through taxation of the urban middle class, the king gained a source of revenue independent of feudal dues, and the administration of these taxes helped to **centralize** the operation of the government and the power of the king.

Centralization was a key feature of the nation state and it developed first in England, through the role of the King-in-Parliament, then in France, with a more powerful monarch, during the medieval period. The arrangement of royal marriages for political purposes rather than love also consolidated territories throughout Europe.

As nation states came to blows over disputed territory, the scale, tactics, and technology of war changed and the knight was eclipsed as the cornerstone of battle. Only a prosperous king, rather than a feudal prince, could afford to outfit an army with the necessary weapons of the day.

ACCEPTANCE OF THE NATION STATE

Capitalism and the Commercial Revolution

The Renaissance and Reformation, in combination with the development of the nation state, had important effects on the changing nature of the European economy. The humanist focus on individual achievement emphasized the value of life on earth rather than rewards in heaven, and encouraged a belief in material advancement for everyone. Protestantism in general, and Calvinism in particular, stressed the moral value of thrift and hard work, but also gave religious

This scene from Friedrich Schiller's Mary Stuart, *performed at the Stratford Festival in 1982, shows the fashions that were popular during the Elizabethan period.*

THE INCREASE OF CAPITAL

THE COMMERCIAL REVOLUTION

approval to the collection of interest on borrowed money. For Calvin, an individual's economic success was a sign of favour from God. As strong monarchs brought increased stability and peace to their nation states, they also encouraged initiative by offering assistance and special privileges to aggressive merchants and traders. With large sums of money or **capital** available, individuals could invest in large-scale commercial or manufacturing enterprises with the intent of making a profit. This form of economic activity is known as **capitalism**, elements of which can be found in the ancient world and in the Italian cities of medieval Europe. Nevertheless, capitalism did not dominate Europe until after 1500 when the continent experienced a rapid commercial expansion that would last until the Thirty Years' War.

The great stimulus for this **commercial revolution** came from the discovery of the New World and new trade routes to Asia. After the fall of Constantinople to the Turks, Venice monopolized trade with the Orient and preserved the Mediterranean as the crossroad between East and West. As the voyages of Portugal and Spain opened new horizons, however, the economic power of Europe shifted northward to the developing nation states of the Atlantic seaboard. The careful planning and exploration of the Portuguese mariners paid off as they sailed to India, the Spice Islands, China, and even Japan. Throughout the sixteenth century, the Portuguese, along with the Spanish in Manila, controlled European trade within this vast domain and provided a steady stream of exotic spices, silks, cotton, tea, and coffee. Meanwhile, Spain gathered silver and gold bullion from mines in Mesoamerica and South America. Since Portugal and Spain manufactured few products, the riches of their high-sea voyages had to be exchanged for the goods produced in other European countries. As Spain paid for imports in silver and gold, capital for commercial development (and war) greatly increased in the major commercial cities of Europe. When other countries eventually entered overseas trade and the supply of precious metals shrank, Portugal and Spain fell by the wayside as major economic powers. Their contribution, however, paved the way for the economic prosperity that saw Europe's population grow from 65 million in 1475, to 90 million early in the seventeenth century.

During the first seventy-five years of the sixteenth century, Spanish and Portuguese goods from the Orient were brought north and distributed throughout Europe by the Dutch. As part of the Spanish Empire after 1516, Antwerp became one of the great trading cities on the continent. Home of Europe's first stock exchange and a centre for the diamond industry, Antwerp attracted merchants and bankers from all major trading nations and states. The arrival of overseas products was matched by a booming inland commerce drawn along the navigable Scheldt River. When Protestants in the Low Countries revolted against their Catholic Spanish masters in the 1560s however, Antwerp fell victim to the struggle. The city was sacked in 1576 and again in 1584. Eventually, at the Peace of Westphalia in 1648, Spain agreed to close the Scheldt River and much of the lost commerce went to the great Dutch port of Amsterdam.

As Holland fought for independence from Spain, access to Eastern products was cut off. At first, the Dutch pirated Spanish and Portuguese fleets, but when the latter developed convoys for protection, the Dutch sailed to the East for themselves. In 1602, the Dutch East India Company was formed and trading "factories" were established in Capetown, where Dutch and Huguenot farmers, known as (Boers), provided supplies for ships to India, Malaya, Indonesia, China, and Japan. In the seventeenth century, the Dutch replaced Portugal and Spain as the dominant force in trade with the East, and Amsterdam became the busiest commercial centre in Europe. The Dutch were also active in the New World through the efforts of the West India Company. Although colonies and bases were established from Brazil to New Amsterdam (later the English colony of New York), the Dutch lacked the population to maintain these territories in addition to their Far Eastern commitments.

The most serious rival to Dutch overseas trade was England, a country that had previously lagged behind in commercial expansion. England had little direct involvement in European affairs during the sixteenth and early to mid-seventeenth centuries, and had avoided the chaos and devastation suffered in the religious and political wars of the continent. Skilled and wealthy refugees periodically flocked to England to escape the trouble and persecution of their homeland, and a growing business middle class began to thrive under the Tudor monarchs. Yet, England was still a small and relatively poor country in comparison with the other European nations engaged in exploration and trade.

Moments in Time

The commercial success of the Dutch during the seventeenth century was paralleled by a golden age of artistic achievement symbolized by the gifted Rembrandt Harmenszoon Van Rign (1606–1669). One of the most skilled artists to ever pick up a brush, Rembrandt became famous for his portraits that were characterized by a sensitive use of light and shadow. Eventually his work covered a wide range of subjects including landscapes, the female form, studies of birds and animals, and scenes from history, mythology, and religion. Rembrandt's master work, *The Night Watch*, is a dramatic canvas that portrays a group of voluntary militia. It is now displayed in the Rijks Museum, Amsterdam.

THE MUSCOVY COMPANY

Indeed, the thrust to enter the commercial race depended on individual enterprise, which was encouraged by the Protestant Reformation.

The model for colonial development (and the forerunner of the modern corporation) was the Muscovy Company, established to trade with Russia during the reign of Henry VIII. English merchants pooled their resources to reduce the risk of loss by purchasing shares or stocks in the self-governing venture. In 1583, Sir Humphrey Gilbert died in an effort to establish a colony in Newfoundland and his half brother, Sir Walter Raleigh, failed in two attempts to settle on Roanoke Island in present-day North Carolina shortly afterwards. Raleigh had organized his second project as a joint-stock company, a precedent followed by Queen Elizabeth when she established the East India Company in 1600, with a monopoly on all English trade with the Orient. During the first half of the seventeenth century, however, the East India Company was overwhelmed by its great Dutch competitor. Although English ships continued to harass the Dutch and would eventually enjoy success, the English were driven out of what became known as the Netherlands East Indies. With 40 warships, 150 merchant ships, and 10 000 soldiers at its disposal, the Dutch East India Company was clearly the strongest European force on the high seas.

The first permanent English settlement in the New World was established in 1607 by a joint-stock company chartered by James I (1603–1625), first of the Stuart kings. Most of the one hundred adventurers who arrived were looking for the gold and silver so quickly found by the Spanish in their colonies. Instead, they discovered a land better suited to the less glamorous pursuits of farming, fishing, and trade. James was also indirectly responsible for England's second colony, largely because he was a less capable administrator than his Tudor predecessors. The moderate Protestant Reformation in England was not satisfactory to many people and a growing movement known as **Puritanism** wanted further purification of the Church of England. James rigidly informed them that they either accepted the Church as it was or they would be forced to leave. One radical group went to Holland, which proved to be equally disappointing. With the financial support of a group of London merchants, these Puritans and some of their English friends set sail for Virginia aboard the *Mayflower*. Poor navigation and fierce Atlantic storms, however, took them to Cape Cod, where they established a settlement at nearby Plymouth in 1620.

Where the Tudors had developed a strong monarchy working through Parliament, James believed in the divine right of kings in which the king was above the law and responsible only to God. Although this idea was popular on the continent, it led to a continual struggle with the wealthy squires and merchants who dominated the English Parliament. Charles I (1625–1649) shared his father's outlook, and made matters even worse by marrying a French Catholic princess and supporting a policy of persecution against all those who did not accept the Church of England. His attempt to establish absolute rule divided the country and resulted in the Civil War that lasted from 1642 to 1648. The success of the Puritan revolutionaries cost Charles his head the following year, and the Puritan leader Oliver Cromwell became lord protector of the republican Commonwealth that lasted eleven years.

Despite the turmoil of Charles's reign, English settlement of the New World continued to expand. By 1648, there were colonies in Virginia, Maryland, Massachusetts, Rhode Island, Connecticut and New Hampshire with a total population of about forty thousand. After 1630, several prosperous colonies were established in the West Indies that produced sugar, indigo, and cocoa. These colonies were considered more valuable than their English counterparts in North America. Charles, despite his shortcomings in domestic affairs, did have the foresight to build an English navy strong enough to protect the commerce generated by overseas trade. The stage was now set for England to challenge the commercial supremacy of the Dutch.

The Emergence of Bourbon France

When Henry IV (1589–1610) became the first Bourbon king to claim the French throne, the nation had been torn and divided by religion, the power of feudal nobles, and civil strife for three decades. To calm the fears of the majority, Henry converted to Catholicism claiming Paris was worth a Mass. In reality, he had little choice. By proclaiming the Edict of Nantes, Henry reassured his Huguenot supporters by giving them control of over two hundred walled towns, soldiers, local revenues, and the right to hold assemblies. In essence, Henry had created a type of republic within the French state. Backed tentatively by both religious camps, Henry attempted to increase the power of the monarch at the expense of the barons by starting a program of economic recovery including canal and harbour construction, road building, and new industries. Silkworms were illegally imported to break the oriental trade monopoly on this much sought-after cloth. French interests in the New World, left idle since Jacques Cartier entered the St. Lawrence in search of a route to Asia in 1534–1535, were revived. Samuel de Champlain founded the first permanent settlement at Québec in 1608 as part of an attempt to secure the region for France.

At the peak of his power, Henry was assassinated by a religious fanatic in 1610. The prestige of the monarchy had not yet been fully restored. When Henry was succeeded by nine-year-old Louis XIII, with his Italian mother, Maria de' Medici, as regent, the nobles and Protestants again challenged the authority of the crown. The nobility did not want to rule in place of the king, but hoped to keep authority decentralized to better serve their local interests. After Louis came of age, he turned to the talented Cardinal Richelieu as his most trusted adviser. Richelieu realized that the power of the Huguenots and the nobles would have to be broken if France was to become the greatest nation in Europe. He manipulated individual Huguenot towns into revolt and promptly defeated each in turn with a royal army. The Huguenots were allowed to retain their religious privileges but not the military rights granted by the Edict of

Nantes. At the same time, the nobility was relieved of its role in local affairs, while more authority was given to royal **intendants**, local adminstrators responsible to the king. When the nobility rebelled, as they did on five occasions, Richelieu organized the king's forces and crushed the opposition. Louis was a more capable king than many historians admit, but it was the work of Richelieu that engineered the foundation for the eventual triumph of royal authority.

The Sun King

CARDINAL MAZARIN

Richelieu knew that his work was unfinished and in the Italian-born Cardinal Mazarin he trained a worthy successor to fill his role as adviser and statesman. When Richelieu died in 1642 and Louis in 1643, the wisdom of this precaution became clear. The king's heir was his four-year-old son and namesake. With the approval of the queen mother, Mazarin guided French foreign policy and guarded royal power through another troubled regency. Mazarin's influence in shaping the Treaties of Westphalia weakened the Holy Roman Empire and opened the door for French domination of the Rhineland. Within France, the nobles attempted yet another series of uprisings known as the **Fronde** in a desperate attempt to curb royal authority. Mazarin cleverly kept his enemies divided and by 1653 had secured the position and control of the crown.

THE FRONDE

LOUIS XIV

Young Louis XIV, however, was terrorized by one plot in which the participants broke into his bedroom. Louis hid under the blankets as if he were asleep and escaped unharmed. From that day forth, Louis determined that no such affront to the king would be possible when he took over the reigns of government.

In 1659, Mazarin concluded the Peace of the Pyrenees, six years after the end of hostilities with Spain. Above and beyond the surrender of the provinces of Arois and Roussilon to France, a contract marriage was arranged between the Spanish king's daughter, Maria Theresa, and Louis XIV. Mazarin had made Richelieu's dream a reality as Hapsburg power was now eclipsed and Bourbon France became the foremost nation in Europe.

When Mazarin died in 1661, Louis assumed control of the government of France. There was no question that Louis owed a considerable debt to Mazarin and Richelieu for their skill in focussing power on the French monarchy. Yet, Louis went beyond what he inherited and left his personal stamp on an era in French history and Western civilization. Louis was the dominant personality of his age and he accepted the view, most eloquently expressed by Jacques-Benigne Bossuet, that kings were chosen by divine right as the natural order of worldly affairs. It was probable that the famous phrase, "The state, it is I" was uttered by his father, but Louis XIV embodied the spirit behind it and ruled accordingly. Europe had been riddled with forces of division that saw the Thirty Years' War, the English Civil War, and the Fronde create a condition of perpetual chaos. Absolute rule by a strong monarch responsible only to God appeared to be the best way to maintain order and stability, and Louis was determined to provide it.

N. Largillière pinx   J. Audran scul

Louis XIV.

FOUQUET

THE SUN KING

VERSAILLES

Louis fully intended to be the centre of attention for his people, a fact that his finance minister, Nicholas Fouquet, discovered the hard way. Fouquet had amassed a personal fortune by questionable means and used his wealth to build the splendid chateau of Vaux-le-Vicomte. A grand opening, in the presence of the king and his court, included fireworks and a specially commissioned play by Molière set against the beautifully manicured gardens and fountains of the estate. The glory that Fouquet drew upon himself as the owner of the chateau, however, made Louis extremely jealous since the chateau outshone any existing royal palace. Nineteen days later, Fouquet was arrested for embezzlement and imprisoned for life. All of Fouquet's property, including Vaux-le-Vicomte, was confiscated by the king.

Louis was a showman who needed a stage from which the royal will, like his chosen symbol, the sun, would radiate with a stunning magnificence for all to see and admire. Remembering the humiliation suffered in Paris during the Fronde, Louis selected Versailles, about 15 km outside the city, as the setting for his spectacle. His father had constructed a hunting lodge on the site, but Louis demanded a residence fit for the most powerful of kings. When Louis came to the throne, however, France was dependent upon other countries, particularly Italy, for the luxury products needed for such an enterprise. Louis and Colbert, the controller general of finance, commissioned the best foreign scientists, engineers, the most skilled artisans, artists, sculptors, and gardeners to work in France. Marble quarries in the Pyrenees, left idle since the days of the Roman Empire, were reopened while the Royal Manufacturers in France were reorganized to stimulate domestic production. Within two decades, France became Europe's leading producer and exporter of luxury goods that included marble, mirrors, velvet, and lace. After the labour of tens of thousands of workers and an estimated cost of half a billion dollars, Versailles became the official seat of government in 1682.

Versailles was designed to overwhelm the visitor and to proclaim the Sun King's dominance over the forces of nature. Individuals were dwarfed by the 415-m facade of the building, the wide avenues, and the gardens carefully trimmed in geometric patterns. Everywhere, water gushed from the mouths of statues and fountains in predetermined directions. It was as if nature had been controlled and made obedient to the will of the king who was universally present in statues and reliefs of the sungod, Apollo. A lesser man than Louis might have been lost amid such grandeur, but his charm and natural self-confidence exploited the setting to full advantage. Louis even wrote a guidebook and, on occasion, personally conducted tours of the grounds to impress the aristocracy of Europe as they gazed in awe at what the Sun King had created. Versailles, however, was freely open to everyone and it was not uncommon to find up to ten thousand people wandering its vast corridors hoping to catch a glimpse of the king and the social activities of the court.

Louis XIV's First Meal At Versailles, 1682

four plates of soup
six hard-boiled eggs
one whole pheasant
one whole partridge
mutton dressed with garlic
ham, salad
three breads
pastry, fruit
wine cut with water

Ludwig II's Hall of Mirrors at Herrenchiemsee is a replica of the Hall of Mirrors at Versailles. Kept in immaculate condition, the parquet floors are polished daily. The candles are never lit to protect the gilded trim and paintings from discolouration.

Louis kept himself at the centre of palace life. Even the smallest acts of his daily routine imposed a formal and rigid etiquette carefully observed by his court and over five hundred personal attendants. The *petite levée* marked the awakening of the king and was witnessed only by his closest aides and highest officials. Once Louis had washed and prayed, the *première entrée* began and more officials entered to discuss routine business. At the end of the morning ceremony, the *grande levée* permitted entrance of the remaining nobility who manoeuvred for the chance to give Louis a towel or help him with his coat. Personal recognition by the king might lead to personal favour. The king's bedchamber opened into the 72-m long Hall of Mirrors, which radiated light just as the Sun King radiated authority with his every move. Sunlight poured through arched windows to be reflected by seventeen mirrors that illuminated gilded decorations and the vaulted ceiling painted with scenes recalling the glories of Louis's reign. This was truly a regal setting for the most regal of kings.

PALACE ETIQUETTE

After working eight or nine hours on the affairs of state, Louis, even when exhausted, often insisted on his pleasures. In the late afternoon, he might play tennis or go on a hunt. The evening regularly featured a lavish dinner, a concert, a masquerade ball, or a comedy. This public and hectic pace had an important purpose. Louis required that the nobility maintain themselves in luxury at Versailles, that they followed the ceremonies of his daily routine, and be seen at his festive social events. This weakened the nobles financially, prevented them from developing a following in the provinces, and left them dependent on the

THE NOBLES AT VERSAILLES

The Sun King's Wars

Date	Initial Action	Opponents	Results
1667	Louis advanced questionable claims to the Franche-Comté and Spanish Netherlands.	France *versus* England, Holland, and Sweden	Treaty of Aix-la-Chapelle in 1668 was a compromise. Louis gave up his claims but kept a few towns in Flanders.
1672	Louis marched through the Spanish Netherlands to attack the Dutch.	France *versus* Holland, Denmark, Brandenburg, Austrian and Spanish Hapsburgs	Louis's forces were worn down. Peace was made at Nijmegen in 1678. Holland survived intact. Louis kept the Franche-Comté.
1681	Louis seized the independent republican city of Strasbourg.		
1683	Louis seized Luxembourg and financed a rebellion in Hungary.		The problems in Hungary encouraged the Turks to lay siege to Vienna. **Louis was now at the peak of his power.**
1688	Louis seized the Palatinate, a small German territory on the Rhine.	France *versus* the League of Augsburg: Holy Roman Empire, Spain, Sweden, Bavaria, Saxony, Palatinate, Holland, and England	English and Dutch fleets defeated the French. Louis won several battles but could not subdue the Dutch. A tired Louis was forced to accept the Peace of Ryswick in 1697. He lost all he had gained in the east but kept Strasbourg.
1700	Louis seized fortresses in the Spanish Netherlands thereby challenging Europe and beginning the War of the Spanish Succession.	France, Bavaria, and Spain *versus* the Grand Alliance: England, Holland, Brandenburg-Prussia, Holy Roman Empire, Duchy of Savoy	Treaties of Utrecht, 1713–1714. France remained a great nation but its threat to the balance of power had been checked. England emerged as a great colonial power.

king, who remained the focal point of all attention. In this way, Louis virtually eliminated the possibility of an uprising of nobles like the Fronde of his childhood. As additional insurance, he selected most of his advisors from the middle class to keep the nobles away from the reigns of power.

Versailles became the show-piece for Louis and French civilization. Above and beyond commissioning architects, like Le Vau and Hardouin-Mansart, and painters, like LeBrun, to build and decorate the palace, Louis gathered about him the most impressive court of artists in Europe. Royal financial support was given to the playwright of comedies Molière, the dramatists Racine and Corneille, the composer Jean Baptiste Lully, the poet La Fontaine, and painters such as Poussin, Lorraine, and Watteau. As more and more foreign visitors walked through the halls of Versailles, they were awed by the brilliant spectacle of entertainment and the excellence of French manufacturers and artistic achievement. France set the standards in fashion, dress, and manners that were copied by the aristocratic classes of the continent, while the French language became a badge of refinement, culture, and education.

French civilization during Louis's seventy-two-year reign was often likened to the Age of Augustus in ancient Rome, and Louis was compared in greatness to Caesar and Alexander. Were these comparisons merited or were Louis's courtiers merely echoing what the Sun King wanted to hear?

Louis had placed the Gobelins factory under state control to provide luxury items for his royal palaces. The craftsmanship was superb in the royal tapestries the factory produced, but Louis was always portrayed in a heroic military tradition even though he often fumbled on the battlefield. No doubt the advance of French civilization was enormous, but does the credit go to the Sun King or his able ministers? Modern historian John Wolf feels that Louis was responsible for much of what was achieved. The duke of Saint-Simon, who knew Louis well, was more critical, arguing that Louis was easily flattered in his pursuit of glory, petty in his suspicion of those at court, and dependent on talented subordinates for any success he enjoyed. Saint-Simon, however, was a member of the nobility that Louis excluded from high office which may have coloured his opinion. François Guizot, writing in the early nineteenth century, recognized that Louis had built the absolute government of France but went on to argue that it was too rigid to change and lacked popular support. Was it thus fair to claim that Louis steered the course that led to French greatness or that he was a passenger who stayed a little too long and who accepted the glory that rightly belonged to others?

THE GLORY OF LOUIS AND FRANCE

PROBLEM QUESTION

To what extent was Louis XIV responsible for the political, economic, military, and cultural predominance of French civilization during the Age of Absolutism?

ALTERNATIVE ONE

The Period of Brilliance–Based on *The Emergence of European Civilization* by John B. Wolf, 1962

Louis XIV had able associates, but this should not detract from his reputation as king. Cardinal Mazarin had told Louis that he could be a great king if he worked at it and Louis spent many hours each day doing just that. Although he listened to the advice of his ministers, he supervised their activities and was well aware of what they were doing.

Louis tried to bring order to the operation of his government. During the long period of warfare, lawlessness had spread throughout the countryside of France. No king could hope to gain respect if he could not keep the peace so Louis dealt with the problem directly. He sent his soldiers throughout the kingdom to catch the bandits and kidnappers who showed disrespect for the king's law and had the guilty hanged or beheaded to show that he was serious! Crime did not vanish from France but it was greatly reduced and more likely to be punished. Louis had also hoped to reorganize French law just as Justinian had done for Roman law under the Byzantine Empire. This proved to be too great a task, but the changes that Louis did make affected the administration of the treasury, the war office, the navy and other departments. Many of Louis's edicts lasted throughout the 18th century and became the basis of later French legal codes that still exist today. Certainly Louis had provided the basis for the modern bureaucratic state.

With Louis's approval, the skillful minister Colbert attempted to strengthen the French economy through close government regulation. Chartered companies were founded to trade overseas, foreign workers were imported to introduce their crafts to France, and legislation was passed to control the production of goods, including the conditions of apprenticeship. In the field of taxation, the major problem was that the two upper classes, the clergy and nobility, were largely exempt from the direct taxing power of the king. Colbert increased excise taxes on goods to share the tax burden more equitably, but little real progress was made. Nevertheless, his efficient offices collected more taxes with fewer losses than earlier governments which gave Louis an unprecedented source of wealth at his disposal.

One of the government's most successful efforts was the creation of Europe's first full-time or standing army organized by Le Tellier and Louvois. The threat of rebellion within France and Louis's ambition in Europe made such a force vital to French power and glory. Previously, European armies had been a loose collection of mercenaries whose loyalty was open to question. The new French army, a true descendent of the Roman legions, was clothed, fed, equipped and paid by the crown. Colbert equalled this achievement with the formation of the French navy, the foremost of its day. Seapower was critical to the development, protection and expansion of French commercial interests. Both the army and the navy were responsible to the king's ministers, controlled by the king's agents and were completely responsive to the king's authority.

European governments of the 17th century were only tolerant of their state religion and Louis was no exception. Dissent was considered to be treason. When Louis secured power after 1661, the question of religious uniformity was raised because French Huguenots (Protestants) had been left alone in Catholic France by previous governments who were either unable or unwilling to deal with them. The Huguenots had been associated with rebellion in the past, but by Louis's reign they were loyal to the king. Louis tried to get them to change their religion at first by bribery and later through quartering of soldiers in their homes. Many Huguenots began to emigrate to England, Holland, and Germany where they could practise their religion in peace. Louis was misled by his advisers into thinking that his policy of forced conversion was more of a success than it was. Believing that it would not affect many people, Louis revoked the Edict of Nantes, which had given the Huguenots the right to practise their beliefs, and banned the "Reformed religion" in 1685.

Although this move may have appealed to Catholic sensibilities, it was a mistake. The emigration already begun continued on an even larger scale. This meant that an enterprising and skillful segment of the French population was lost to other countries who benefitted from their talents. Much like those who left after the French Revolution of 1789 and the Nazi take-over of 1933, the refugees ousted by Louis went abroad and agitated against the hostile policies of their homeland.

It is true that Louis had mistresses, illegitimate children, and a costly court that could be summoned at his pleasure. But Louis had a purpose in this and that was to separate and elevate himself above the nobles and princes of the land. He lived life on a grand scale to keep himself apart from the masses. Just as his love affairs were exceptional, his sumptuous palaces and formal court etiquette focussed all attention and power on himself as the 'Sun King'. Versailles was the ultimate symbol of his personal magnificence. The palace was not protected by moats which showed Louis's personal confidence in his ability to rule and keep the peace. Palace life reduced the role of the nobles, who had been his rivals in power, to mere servants who reacted with submission to the king's every whim. Being forced to leave the court, away from the presence of the king, was now seen as a major disgrace.

At first Versailles was a challenge to the nobles to match the splendor of the king who no longer feared their power. It quickly became an announcement to Europe that France had replaced Spain as the leading power in the western world. Philip II had built the Escorial as a palatial symbol of Spanish glory. Louis built Versailles with salons, gardens, fountains and reflecting pools organized on an unprecedented scale, to proclaim that France now held the hegemony of Europe. Louis chose the emblem of the sun to underline the fact that all of France, indeed all of Europe had become satellites of his grandeur. In architecture, Versailles became the supreme symbol of the baroque age in which secular buildings became more important than religious ones. Its influence would eventually be felt in such distant locations as Washington and St. Petersburg (Leningrad). Versailles cast the shadow of French civilization under which half the princes of the world would live for the next century and a half.

When Louis's armies suffered defeat and swarms of tax collectors reminded the people of the cost of the king's policies, the early years of glory seemed to be forgotten. Louis's influence on the princes of Europe, however, continued throughout the 18th century. Louis was not the first 'enlightened despot' but he was a model for those who followed him. Even Napoleon looked to Louis for inspiration in the art of government. Just as Louis had defined 'kingship', the France he did so much to build defined the nature of the bureaucratic state for those that shaped the modern world in the succeeding decades.

Questions

1. How enthusiastic was Louis XIV about his job as king?
2. a) What did Louis hope to achieve in the operation of the French government and French law?
   b) Was he successful? Explain your answer.
3. What was the result of Jean Baptiste Colbert's attempt to strengthen the French economy?
4. a) Why could the new French army be compared with the legions of ancient Rome?
   b) Who controlled the new army and navy?
5. a) Did Louis oppose the French Huguenots because of their religious beliefs or because they did not bend to state authority? Give evidence to support your answer.
   b) Why was the revocation of the Edict of Nantes in 1685 a mistake?
6. a) According to Wolf, what was Louis XIV's main purpose in the formal, courtly life he lived at Versailles?
   b) What did the Escorial and Versailles represent to Europe?
7. What conclusions did Wolf draw about Louis XIV's importance in history?

ALTERNATIVE TWO

The Reign of Louis XIV—Based on *The Memoirs of the Duke of Saint-Simon*, translated by Bayle St. John in 1888

At 23 years of age he entered the great world as king under the most favourable conditions. His ministers were the most skillful in all Europe; his generals the best; his court was filled with illustrious and clever men.

Louis XIV was made for a brilliant court. In the midst of other men, his figure, his courage, his grace, his beauty, his grand manner, even the tone of his voice and the majestic and natural charm of all his person distinguished him till his death as the King Bee. He wished to reign by himself. His unceasing jealousy on this point became a weakness. The superior ability of his early ministers and his early generals soon wearied him. He liked nobody to be in any way superior to him. Thus he chose his ministers, not for their knowledge, but for their ignorance; not for their capacity, but for their want of it. His vanity, his unmeasured and unreasonable love of admiration, was his ruin. His ministers, his generals, his mistresses, his courtiers, soon perceived his weakness. They praised him with emulation and spoiled him. Praises, or to say truth, flattery, pleased him to such an extent, that the coarsest was well received, the vilest even better relished. It was the sole means by which you could approach him. Those whom he liked owed his affection for them to their untiring flatteries. This is what gave his ministers so much authority. They attributed everything to him and pretended to learn everything from him.

Though his intellect was beneath mediocrity, it was capable of being formed. God had sufficiently gifted him to enable him to be a good king; perhaps even a *tolerably great king*! He was by disposition good and just. All the evil came to him from elsewhere. His early education was neglected. He was scarcely taught how to read or write, and remained so ignorant that the most familiar historical and other facts were utterly unknown to him! He fell, accordingly, and sometimes even in public, into the grossest absurdities.

He was exceedingly jealous of the attention paid him. Not only did he notice the presence of the most distinguished courtiers, but those of inferior degree also. He looked to the right and to the left, not only in rising, but upon going to bed, at his meals, in passing through his apartments, or his gardens of Versailles, where alone the courtiers were allowed to follow him. He marked well all absentees from the court, found out the reason for their absence, and never lost an opportunity of acting towards them as the occasion might seem to justify. With the most distinguished, it was a demerit not to make the court their ordinary abode; with others 'twas a fault to come but rarely; for those who never or scarcely ever came it was certain disgrace. When their names were in any way mentioned, "I do not know them," the king would reply haughtily.

Louis XIV took great pains to be well informed of all that passed every-where; in the public places, in the private homes, in society and familiar intercourse. His spies and telltales were infinite. He had them of all species; many who were ignorant that their information reached him; others who knew it; others who wrote to him direct, sending their letters through chan-nels he indicated; and all these letters were seen by him alone; and always before everything else; others who sometimes spoke to him secretly in his cabinet, entering by the back stairs. These unknown means ruined an infinite number of people of all classes, who never could discover the cause; often ruined them unjustly; for the king, once prejudiced, rarely altered his opinion. He had an excellent memory; in this way, that if he saw a man who, 20 years before, perhaps, had in some way offended him, he did not forget the man, though he might forget the offense. This was enough to exclude the person from all favor. The representations of a minister, of a general, of his confessor even, could not move the king.

The most cruel means by which the king was informed of what was passing—for many years before anybody knew it—was that of opening letters. He saw extracts from all the letters in which there were passages that the chiefs of the post office, and then the minister who governed it, thought ought to go before him; entire letters, too, were sent to him, when their contents seemed to justify the sending. A word of contempt against the king or the government, a joke, a detached phrase, was enough. It is incredible how many people, justly or unjustly, were more or less ruined, always without recourse, without trial, and without knowing why. The chiefs of the post, nay, the principal clerks were in a position to suppose what they pleased and against whom they pleased.

It was his vanity, his desire for glory, that led him, soon after the death of the King of Spain, to make that event the pretext for war; in spite of the renunciations so recently made, so carefully stipulated in the marriage contract. He marched into Flanders; his conquests there were rapid; the passage of the Rhine was admirable; the triple alliance of England, Sweden, and Holland only animated him. In the midst of winter he took Franche-Comté, and then gave it back at the Peace of Aix-la-Chapelle, thus preserving his conquests in Flanders. All was flourishing then in the state. Riches everywhere. Colbert had placed the finances, the navy, commerce, manufacturers, letters even, upon the highest point; and his age, like that of Augustus, produced in abundance, illustrious men of all kinds.

With the success of one war, Louis was easily persuaded by his ministers to enter that famous Dutch War in which his love for Madame de Montespan reduced his glory and that of his kingdom. Everything being conquered, everything taken and Amsterdam ready to give up her keys, the king yielded to his impatience, quit the army, flew to Versailles, and destroyed in an instant all the success of arms! He repaired this disgrace by a second conquest, in person, of Franche-Comté, which this time was preserved by France. In 1676, with more victories in Flanders, the armies of the king suddenly approached those of the Prince of Orange near Heurtebise. According even to the admission of the enemy, our forces were so superior to those of the Prince of Orange, that we must have gained the victory if we had attacked. But the king, after listening to the opinions of his generals, decided against combat and turned tail. The army was much discontented. Everybody wished for battle. The fault therefore of the king made much impression upon the troops, and excited cruel railleries against us at home and in the foreign courts. The king stopped but little longer afterwards in the army, although we were only in the month of May. He returned to his mistress.

The power of France was acutely felt throughout Europe, America, Africa, and Sicily. The peak of Louis's reign, and the fullness of glory and prosperity declined after 1688. The great captains, the great ministers, were no more, but their pupils remained. The second epoch of the reign was very different from the first; but the third was even more sadly dissimilar.

More wars followed but France gained nothing. The king was obliged to acknowledge the Prince of Orange as King of England, after having so long shown hatred and contempt for him. Our fall, too, cost us Luxembourg; and the ignorance of our negotiators gave our enemies great advantages in forming their frontier. Such was the Peace of Ryswick concluded in September, 1697.

Shortly afterwards, by one of the most surprising and unheard-of pieces of good fortune, the crown of Spain fell into the hands of the Duc d'Anjou, grandson of the king. It seemed as though golden days had come back to France. Only for a little time, however, did it seem so. Nearly all Europe banded against France to dispute the Spanish crown. The king had lost all his good ministers, all his able generals, and had taken good pains they should leave no successors. When war came, then, we were utterly unable to prosecute it with success or honor. We were driven out of Germany, of Italy, of the Low Countries. We could not sustain the war, or resolve to make peace. Every day led us nearer and nearer to the brink, to the terrible depths of which were forever staring us in the face. A misunderstanding amongst our enemies, whereby England became detached from the grand alliance; the undue contempt of Prince Eugene for our generals, out of which arose the battle of Denain; saved us from the gulf. Peace came, and a peace, too, infinitely better than that we should have accepted if our enemies had agreed amongst themselves beforehand. Nevertheless, this peace cost dear to France, and cost Spain half its territory—Spain, of which the king had said not even a windmill would he yield! But this was another piece of folly he soon repented of.

Thus we see this monarch grand, rich, conquering, the arbiter of Europe; feared and admired as long as the ministers and captains existed who really deserved the name. When they were no more, the machine kept moving. But soon afterwards we saw beneath the surface; faults and errors were multiplied, and decay came on with giant strides; without, however, opening the eyes of that despotic master, so anxious to do everything and direct everything himself.

From William F. Church, ed., *The Greatness of Louis XIV*, pp. 32–42, by permission from D.C. Heath and Company.

Questions

1. a) According to Saint-Simon, what personal qualities did Louis XIV bring to the throne?
   b) How did Louis XIV's vanity affect his conduct?
2. a) Why do you think Louis XIV was so concerned about who was in attendance at court?

      b) How did Louis XIV use and misuse his network of spies?
3. a) According to Saint-Simon, why did Louis XIV take France into war?
      b) Are these reasons acceptable? Explain your answer with evidence.
4. a) How successful was France in the early wars of Louis XIV?
      b) What criticisms does Saint-Simon make of Louis XIV's conduct as the leader of the army?
      c) Are these criticisms believable? Explain your answer.
5. a) According to Saint-Simon, why did the fortunes of France decline in the second half of Louis XIV's reign?
      b) Is this a valid judgement of Louis XIV's career? Explain your answer with evidence.

ALTERNATIVE THREE

Architect of France—Based on *History of Civilization in Europe* by François Guizot, translated by William Hazlitt in 1900

When we occupy ourselves with the government of Louis XIV, when we try to appreciate the causes of his power and influence in Europe, we only think of his renown, his conquests, his magnificence, and the literary glory of his time. It is to external causes that we apply ourselves and attribute the European dominance of the French government. But I believe that this dominance had deeper and more serious foundations. We must not believe that it was simply by means of victories, lavish living or even masterworks of genius, that Louis XIV and his government played the part which it is impossible to deny them.

Recall to your memory the state into which France was fallen after the government of Cardinal Richelieu, and during the minority of Louis XIV: the Spanish armies always on the frontiers, sometimes in the interior; continual danger of an invasion; internal conflicts, urged to extremity, civil war, the government weak and discredited at home and abroad. It was from this state that the government of Louis XIV saved France. His first victories secured the country and retrieved the national honor. Unlike the wars that went before it, the wars of Louis XIV were not a personal whim; they were wars of regular government, fixed in the center of its states, and laboring to make conquests around it, to extend or consolidate its territory; in a word, they were political wars. No doubt personal ambition had a share in these wars; but examine one after another, particularly those of the first part of Louis's reign, and you will find that they had truly political motives; and that they were conceived for the interest of France, for obtaining power, and for the country's safety.

The results are proofs of the fact. France of the present day is still, in many respects, what the wars of Louis XIV have made it. The provinces which he conquered, French-Comté, Flanders and Alsace, remain yet incorporated with France. These were not senseless conquests, as others were up to Louis's time; a skillful, if not always just and wise policy, motivated Louis's expansionist ambition.

Leaving the wars of Louis XIV and turning to diplomacy, the results were similar. Diplomatic relations between countries had not been systematic prior to the 17th century. There had been no long alliances, or great and durable combinations, directed according to fixed principles, toward a constant aim, with that spirit of continuity which is the true character of established governments. During the course of the religious revolution, the external relations of states were almost completely under the power of the religious interest; the Protestant and Catholic leagues divided Europe. It was in the 17th century, after the Treaties of Westphalia, and under the influence of the government of Louis XIV, that diplomacy changed its character. It then escaped from the exclusive influences of the religious principle; alliances and political combinations were formed upon other considerations. It became systematic, with certain aims and principles. The regular origin of this system of balance in Europe belongs to this period. It was under the government of Louis XIV that the system, together with all the considerations attached to it, truly took possession of European policy.

It has often been said that the spread of absolute power was the main principle of the diplomacy of Louis XIV; but I do not believe it. This considera-tion played no very great part in his policy, until latterly, in his old age. The power of France, its dominance in Europe, the humbling of rival powers, in a word, the political interest and strength of the state, was the aim which Louis XIV constantly pursued, whether in fighting against Spain, the Emperor of Germany, or England; he acted far less with a view to the spread of absolute power than from a desire for the power and aggrandizement of France and of its government. For example, Louis tried to keep royal power in England weak–a move that would keep France in a strong position–by working to revive the republican party against Charles II. During the embassy of Barillon in England the same fact constantly appears. Whenever the authority of Charles seemed to obtain the advantage and the national party seemed on the point of being crushed, the French ambassador directed his influence to this side, gave money to the chiefs of the opposition, and fought, in a word, against absolute power, when that became the means of weakening a rival to France.

You will also be struck with the capacity and skill of French diplomacy at this period. The names of MM. de Torcy, d'Avaux, de Bonrepos, are known to all well-informed persons. When we compare the dispatches, the memoirs, the skill and conduct of these counsellors of Louis XIV with those of Spanish, Portuguese, and German negotiators, we must be struck with the superiority of the French ministers; not only as regards their earnest activity and the application to affairs, but also regards their liberty of spirit. There was no diplomacy in Europe in the 17th century which appears equal to the French, except the Dutch.

You see, then, that whether we consider the wars of Louis XIV, or his diplomatic relations, we arrive at the same results. We can easily conceive that a government, which conducted its wars and negotiations in this manner, should have assumed a high standing in Europe, and presented itself therein, not only as dreadworthy, but as skillful and imposing.

Let us now consider the administration and legislation of Louis XIV. Administration is the total means to propel the will of the central power through all parts of society, and to make the force of society, whether consisting of men or money, return again, under the same conditions, to the central power. It is the chief means of providing unity; and this was the work of the administration of Louis XIV. Up to this time there had been nothing so difficult, in France as in the rest of Europe, as to effect the penetration of the action of the central power into all parts of society. To this end Louis XIV labored, and succeeded, up to a certain point; incomparably better, at least, than preceding governments had done. Just run over, in thought, all kinds of public services, taxes, roads, industry, military administration, and others. There is scarcely one of which you do not find either the origin, development, or great improvement under Louis XIV. It was as administrators that the greatest men of his time, Colbert and Louvois, displayed their genius and exercised their ministry. It was by the excellence of its administration that his government acquired a generality, decision, and consistency which were wanting to all the European governments around him.

The legislative point of view gives the same fact. The great ordinances he issued, the criminal ordinances, the ordinances of procedure, commerce, the marine, waters, and woods are true codes that recast the laws just as our codes do today. Many of Louis XIV's laws were full of vices, but they were conceived in the interest of public order and for giving regularity and firmness to the laws. But even that was a great progress; and we cannot doubt that the ordinances of Louis XIV, so very superior to anything preceding them, powerfully contributed to advance French society in the career of civilization.

And now we inquire how it happened that a power, thus brilliant, thus well established, so rapidly fell into decline? How, after having played such a part in Europe, it became in the next century, so inconsistent, weak and inconsiderable? The fact is incontestable. In the 17th century the French government was at the head of European civilization; in the 18th century it disappeared; and it was French society, separated from its government, often even opposed to it, that now preceded and guided the European world in its progress.

Here we discover the evil and the infallible effect of absolute power. I will speak not of the faults of the government of Louis XIV; of the War of the Spanish Succession, of the Revocation of the Edict of Nantes, or of excessive expenses and other measures that compromised his fortunes. But, by the very fact that the government had no other principle than absolute power, its decline became sudden and well merited. The ancient French institutions, if they merited the name, no longer existed: Louis completed their ruin. He did not try to replace them. The absolute government of Louis XIV was a great fact, a fact powerful and splendid, but without roots.

It was not Louis XIV alone who was becoming aged and weak at the end of his reign: it was the whole absolute power. Pure monarchy was as much worn out in 1712 as was the monarch himself. This, then, is the state in which Louis XIV left France and power: a society in full development of riches, power and all kinds of intellectual activity; and side by side with this progressive society, a government that was stationary, having no means of renewing itself, of adapting itself to the movement of its people; devoted, after half a century of the greatest splendor, to immobility and weakness, and already, during the life of its founder, fallen into a decline which seemed like dissolution.

From William F. Church, ed., *The Greatness of Louis XIV*, pp. 88–97, by permission from D.C. Heath and Company.

Questions

1. a) According to Guizot, how did the government of Louis XIV change France?
   b) What evidence in war and diplomacy does Guizot offer to support his claim?
2. Why does Guizot rule out the possibility that Louis XIV was trying to spread absolute power?
3. How talented were the French ministers of state compared with those in the rest of Europe?
4. Why does Guizot feel that the administration and legislation of Louis XIV was more successful than that of other French governments?
5. Why did Louis XIV's government decline in the second half of his reign?
6. When considering the views of Wolf, Saint-Simon, and Guizot, can it be said that Louis XIV was a great leader? Explain your answer with evidence.

ANSWERING THE PROBLEM QUESTION

To ask if Louis XIV was responsible for or, in essence, caused the predominance of French civilization provides a different focus from problems previously studied. When the characteristics of Alexander, Hannibal, and Julius Caesar were examined, the emphasis was comparison against stated criteria to evaluate the quality of leadership. An analysis of Louis XIV will reveal the presence (and absence) of many of these same qualities, but the given question goes much further. Can an individual control the course of historical events to achieve a desired goal? Certainly, Louis dreamed of French hegemony in every field of human endeavour and midway through his reign it seemed as if his ambition was largely realized.

Several related questions must be considered, however, before a conclusion can be reached. Could Louis have completed the organization of the French bureaucracy without the groundwork laid by Richelieu and Mazarin? Colbert, Le Tellier, and Louvois were perhaps the most talented advisers in Europe. Does their success in improving economic efficiency, assembling artists at court, and creating a standing army detract from Louis's role or should the Sun King be given credit for their appointment in the first place? Louis's architects and artists established a triumph in the distinctive baroque style at Versailles, the Invalides (a magnificent home for disabled veterans in Paris), and in rebuilding the Louvre. But it was Louis who provided the driving spirit behind their construction and there is no doubt that the court life at Versailles was literally Louis's personal creation. Imitation has often been called the highest form of flattery and, during Louis's reign, French architecture and custom were copied throughout the civilized corners of the continent. Was this the result of Louis's style, or the quality of life that France would have produced with or without his guidance?

It has been said that Louis would have been a much greater king if he had died halfway through his reign! Without doubt, the glory of his early years was more than offset by a series of unsuccessful wars, climaxed by the disastrous War of the Spanish Succession. When Louis died of gangrene at age seventy-seven, he was as worn out as the tired rituals of court life at Versailles. The ministers of state who worked through the early years had died by the 1680s and their successors were much less able. Were Louis's military failures their responsibility? Was Louis simply unable to deal with the situation without his key people? Or was the elderly king simply not the leader he once was? His record is uneven. As a result of the Sun King's unprecedented construction projects and endless wars, France was deeply in debt and the burden of taxation still fell on the peasant class who was less able to pay. French military domination had been checked, but not surpassed on the continent, and French culture continued to be admired. What conclusion can be reached about the extent to which Louis XIV was responsible for the political, economic, military, and cultural predominance of French civilization during the Age of Absolutism?

THE STORY CONTINUES . . .

Absolutism in Europe After Westphalia

The attempt by the Sun King to bring order to France through absolute rule was mirrored in other European states. Out of the ashes of the Thirty Years' War emerged two new powers from the 360 German states who now held only a token allegiance to the weakened Holy Roman Empire. The heart of the empire had always been the Hapsburg family possessions centred in Vienna. It was the reorganization of these territories that marked the beginning of a new and smaller Hapsburg Empire on the Danube.

THE HAPSBURG EMPIRE

Humbled by the Treaties of Westphalia in 1648, the Hapsburgs were again pressed when the Turkish army, under Grand Vizier Kara Mustapha, besieged Vienna in 1683. The city held out until relieving armies of Poles and Germans, and the military brilliance of Prince Eugene of Savoy, forced the Turks to retreat.

Upper Belvedere, one of three royal residences of the Hapsburgs, is now used as an art gallery and for special state functions.

Highly decorated after his initial triumphs, Prince Eugene continued the campaign with a series of successful battles that eventually drove the Turks out of Hungary. He then played a major role in limiting the expansionist policies of Louis XIV with additional victories in the War of the Spanish Succession. The Hapsburg Empire gained a new lease on life, and by 1713 the family territories in Austria, Bohemia, and Hungary became indivisible under the leadership of Emperor Charles VI (1711–1740).

Although the Hapsburg, or Austrian, Empire had opposed the Sun King in battle, it chose to emulate his style of kingship. Baroque architecture, like Louis's Versailles, expressed the power and grandeur of the state and the aristocratic classes of Austria were quick to establish the same theme. Just beyond the gates of Vienna, Prince Eugene built the splendid palaces of Upper and Lower Belvedere as summer residences that were used by royalty for state occasions. Even more striking was the magnificence of Schönbrunn, rebuilt under Joseph I after its destruction by the Turks, and given its modern form by Maria Theresa in 1743. Here, the main chateau almost matched the scale and glory of Versailles and even boasted the same type of carefully patterned French gardens and beautiful fountains. As if this was not enough, within the city of Vienna, the twenty-six-hundred-room Imperial Palace, even larger than Schönbrunn, was the winter residence of the royal family and the main seat of government.

Less concerned about pomp and ceremony, but more concerned with power was Frederick William, the "Great Elector" of Brandenburg (1640–1688), who welded together the second major state that emerged from the Thirty

BELVEDERE

SCHÖNBRUNN

BRANDENBURG-PRUSSIA

Years' War. Frederick William brought together the scattered family possessions of the Hohenzollerns under one government to form, for the first time, the state of Brandenburg-Prussia. Like Louis XIV, Frederick William believed in absolutism, and since Brandenburg-Prussia was created as an act of state with no natural boundaries, centralized control was essential. This led to an emphasis on power and discipline focussed on the monarchy and supported by an efficient, national army and bureaucracy. Most of the feudal nobility, known as the Junkers, had been weakened by the Thirty Years' War and were only too glad to serve in the new army or as high-ranking government officials responsible to the state. As in France, Frederick William appointed royal supervisors to manage the provinces and he encouraged immigration, including the arrival of twenty thousand skilled and industrious French Huguenots. With a standing army of thirty thousand, and a strong civil service that grew out of the need to maintain it, Frederick William left Brandenburg-Prussia as the strongest state in Germany.

THE JUNKERS

As a result of the assistance given to the emperor against Louis XIV in the War of the Spanish Succession, the Great Elector's successor became the king of Prussia, a title recognized in the Treaty of Utrecht in 1713. Frederick William I (1713–1740) built upon the foundation of his grandfather, the Great Elector, by strengthening the economy, filling the treasury, and increasing the size of the army to eighty thousand. Indeed, about 70 percent of the national income was spent directly or indirectly on the army. Frederick William I set the Prussian nation into a military framework that stressed absolute obedience, duty, and personal sacrifice to the will of the state as the most desirable virtues. A Frenchman of the day aptly claimed that Prussia was not a state with an army but an army that possessed a state. Prussia had gradually increased its possessions on the Baltic and in Europe since the time of the Great Elector and it now possessed one of the largest and most efficient armies on the continent. There was no doubt that Frederick William I had completed the task of moulding Prussia into a major European power.

FREDERICK WILLIAM I

Far from the mainstream of European civilization, Russia had been left largely untouched by the classic civilization of Greece and Rome. Founded as a small state at Novgorod in the ninth century by the Norsemen, Russia was later converted by missionaries to Eastern Orthodox Christianity and adopted elements of Byzantine culture. Vast regions of open plains left Russia exposed to invasion by the Huns and the Mongols of Genghis Khan, but under Ivan the Great (1462–1505), the grand duke of Muscovy, foreign rule was ended and the foundations of imperial Russia were established. With Constantinople overrun by the Muslims, Ivan took up the cause of the Byzantine world and became the protector of the Greek Orthodox Church in the tradition of the Roman Caesars. Ivan IV (1533–1585), better known as "the Terrible," eventually took the title of tsar (from Caesar) and consolidated his absolute power by executing thousands of the nobility and taking their land. The tsars gradu-

RUSSIA

IVAN THE TERRIBLE

ally extended their control over more and more territory until, by the establishment of the Romanov dynasty in 1613, the Russian state held absolute rule over much of modern Russia.

Isolated by geography and frozen in the mould of Eastern culture, Russia was by-passed by the Renaissance and the discoveries and advances of the sixteenth and seventeenth centuries. Of more immediate concern was the fact that the quality of government service and the efficiency of the Russian army were inferior to their Western European counterparts. Peter the Great (1694–1725), at over 2 m in height the tallest and most able of the Romanov tsars, directed his considerable energy towards "opening windows to the West." By this remark, Peter meant that he would Westernize and modernize Russia. To this end, Peter travelled incognito mainly to Holland and England but also to the German states, France, Switzerland, Austria, and Prussia. A hulk of a man who could barely use a knife and fork, Peter had an unquenchable appetite for knowledge as he went into mills, shipyards, museums, hospitals, and artisan shops. He tried to absorb all aspects of Western life and showed a keen interest in architecture, printing, dentistry, and, of course, the preparations for war on land and sea. Peter arranged for five hundred European artisans to go to Russia to introduce new methods and for a select few Russian youths to study in the West to learn as much as they could.

As a result of Peter's travels, Western methods of administration were adopted in Russia and an imperial bureaucracy was created to carry out his policies. Opposition was not tolerated. When the nobility and Imperial Guard challenged his authority, Peter not only crushed the revolt but personally beheaded some of the rebels and saw to it that his own son was put to death. The power of the Russian state was more extensive than any nation in Western Europe. To signal his policy of Westernization, Peter taxed men who wore the long, oriental-style beards and stationed barbers at the entrance to towns to trim beards to a required length. He encouraged the use of tobacco, now a Western habit, and forced the nobility and town officials to wear clothes cut in a French or German style. Women were now encouraged to take part in social events and the Eastern custom of the harem was abolished. Although it was losing favour in the West, Russia even switched to the Julian calendar.

A key element in Peter's Western education was the modernization of Russia's military forces. Trained by Western officers, the army was reorganized and a shipbuilding industry was started to support the creation of a new navy. To end Russia's landlocked isolation, Peter wanted to secure a "window" or port on the Black Sea and the Baltic. Although only partially successful against the Turks in the south, the Northern War (1700–1721) against Sweden gave him his chance. Victory over Sweden brought the Baltic states under Russian control and enabled Peter to select a site for a new capital aptly named St. Petersburg. Just as Louis XIV had created a new seat of government at Versailles away from Paris, Peter compelled the members of the nobility to build residences in his new city away from the conservative influences of Moscow. The

PETER THE GREAT

WESTERNIZATION

THE NORTHERN WAR

Treaty of Nystad, in 1721, confirmed Russia's position as the dominant force in northern Europe and marked the beginning of a new period of expansion. Peter had given Russia a new direction by introducing elements of Western culture. The impact of these changes and the continuing adjustments they made necessary are still being felt today.

England: The Triumph of Limited Monarchy

Absolutism, the popular cornerstone of order in the nation states on the continent, was not the answer to the troubled politics of England. Despite the best of intentions, Cromwell could not secure a workable Parliament following the execution of Charles I and the real power of the state rested with the army and the lord protector himself. Cromwell's strict, Puritan rule became increasingly unpopular and after his death a freely elected Parliament invited the exiled Charles II to become king in 1660. The Restoration, as it was known, was marked by the growing power of Parliament at the expense of the Crown. Charles was denied the prerogative of special courts and taxation, given less income than he needed, and was forced to accept the return of the Anglican Church as the official Church of state. Both Puritans and Roman Catholics were excluded from politics. If the price of survival was to give in to Parliament on occasion, then Charles proved willing to pay. His flexibility in dealing with Parliament enabled Charles to realize his ambition of living out his reign in his homeland rather than in the callous climate of exile and humiliation.

In 1685, Charles was succeeded by his brother James who managed to bring the Stuart monarchy to an end in three short years! James II believed in a more extreme form of absolutism than that which had cost Charles I his head only thirty-six years earlier. He ignored the Test Act passed by Parliament and appointed Roman Catholics to public offices as magistrates and army officers, and to positions in universities. In attempting to impose Roman Catholicism on a country already drained by religious division in the past, James tactlessly alienated much of the political and public support usually given to the Crown. The birth of an heir to the throne raised the spectre of another Roman Catholic monarch and diverse opposition groups united to eliminate this possibility. In 1688, a parliamentary committee ruled that James had violated his oath to the people and the laws of the land, and that the throne was now vacant.

The king's daughter, Mary, raised as a Protestant before her father's conversion, and her husband, William of Orange, were asked to accept the throne of England. Abandoned by his generals, James rushed to France with no blood being spilled, save for the Battle of the Boyne in Ireland. The flight of the king became the Glorious Revolution that stamped the authority of Parliament on no less than an equal footing with the king. In 1689, the Bill of Rights outlined the limitations of royal power and, among other restrictions, declared that the king could not levy tax or raise an army without the approval of Parliament. At the very moment that absolutism reached its zenith under Louis XIV in France, England had become a limited monarchy bent in a direction that would allow the power of Parliament to grow at the expense of the Crown.

The Emergence of Mercantilism

The sudden influx of gold and silver from the Spanish colonies in the sixteenth century brought a new source of wealth to Europe, but it also dramatically increased prices. Governments, dependent on relatively stable incomes, often fell into debt because of the expense of wars and the chaos and destruction they brought. At the same time, there were no breakthroughs in industry or agriculture to increase production. The new nation states of Europe came to believe that real wealth depended on a large domestic supply of gold and silver.

As a practical method of controlling their supply of bullion, European nations introduced a set of policies that have become known as **mercantilism**. The goal was economic self-sufficiency. Since exports brought money (gold) into the kingdom, they were encouraged. Since imports had to be paid for in money that left the kingdom, they were kept to a minimum. If a nation could maintain a favourable balance of more exports than imports, in other words, sell more, buy less, the surplus paid for in bullion would increase national income.

Colonies were considered valuable if they contained gold or silver, or if they provided the raw materials and goods that could be traded for the precious metals. In addition, they served as protected markets for the manufactured goods produced by the mother country. Only the mother country could trade with its colonies and only the ships of the nation could carry its articles of trade, a precaution designed to prevent competitors from making a profit. In an age of frequent warfare, a healthy treasury enabled a government to hire large numbers of mercenaries, who fought for pay rather than for love of country. Mercantilism probably created as many problems as it solved. Nevertheless, at a time when accurate and readily available economic statistics were lacking, it offered a fitting approach to nation states that competed in economics as well as politics and war.

In 1651, England passed the first of a series of Navigation Acts in an attempt to limit Dutch trade. Collectively, the Navigation Acts and supporting legislation required that all trade to and from the English colonies must be carried in ships built, owned, and crewed by English subjects. They also declared that European goods imported into the colonies must go through England, where English merchants would benefit from increased trade or perhaps undersell the competition with British manufacturers. Since the Dutch were the great carriers of European trade, such legislation threatened their commercial supremacy and they did not stand idly by. Soon after the first of the Navigation Acts was passed, England and Holland were engaged in the first of three naval and commercial wars that broke out in just over two decades. Holland had the larger navy, but command was divided among provincial admiralties. The English fleet was administered through the more centralized agency of the lord admiral. Overall, the naval battles were fairly even, though the Dutch colony of New Amsterdam became the English colony of New York as a result of the conflict of 1665–1667. England, however, slowly regained control of its own trade from the Dutch, and London eclipsed Amsterdam as the leading port in Europe.

MERCANTILISM

THE NAVIGATION ACTS

THE GREAT FIRE OF LONDON

Such growth appeared to be nipped in the bud when a plague struck London in 1665, killing over seventy thousand. Within a year, the Great Fire burned for three days and levelled half the city. It had the unforeseen benefit, however, of wiping out the last remnants of the epidemic. London was quickly rebuilt as a city of stone and brick rather than of wood, and, by 1680, it had become Europe's largest city with a population of almost seven hundred thousand. By the end of the seventeenth century, with England in a dominant commercial position, England and Holland joined forces to face the might of Louis XIV whose attempt to subdue Europe threatened both countries.

JEAN BAPTISTE COLBERT

The greatest exponent of mercantilism in the seventeenth century was Jean Baptiste Colbert. Colbert was not only the Sun King's trusted controller general of finance, responsible for increasing revenue and reducing the debt, but also the minister of the marine, in charge of colonial administration. Just as absolute government had regulated domestic life in France, Colbert saw to it that the government should direct commercial development in overseas trade. His critics would later argue that the French bureaucratic state was too authoritarian and that its methods stifled initiative, but Colbert had inherited a difficult situation that required action. Development of Canada by land grants and chartered companies had become stagnant, while progress in the more valued sugar islands of the Antilles had been somewhat haphazard.

FRENCH COMMERCIAL EXPANSION

Under Colbert, a common pattern was established in each colony that included a French governor, the highest-ranking official, assisted by an intendant, and a sovereign council with powers akin to the parlements in France to dispense local justice. French commercial aims were greatly expanded when charters were given to the French Senegal Company to exploit the resources of Africa and to the French East India Company to challenge the monopoly of the Dutch and the English in the Orient. In a true mercantilist spirit, Colbert supported any cause that might strengthen the French economy and national self-sufficiency.

THE FRENCH NAVY

To improve the quality of the French navy, an essential step for a worldwide empire, Colbert rebuilt harbours and dockyards, established training schools, and even published an atlas that became the accepted manual for ship-building in France. The navy grew from less than two dozen vessels of various kinds in 1661, to 270 warships in 1677. French industries were protected by tariffs while roads, canals, and ports were constructed to improve internal transportation. Even the Académie des Sciences, a scholarly society, was commissioned with the noble goal of developing and using science for the benefit of humankind in general, but also for the benefit of France in particular. Efficiency increased in almost every venture Colbert organized, but the outbreak of wars and the late start by France into the race for colonial development limited the degree of success. Indeed, after Colbert much of the enthusiasm for administrative improvement and increased production either declined or fell into less capable hands.

Anglo-French Rivalry for Empire (1661–1740)

Mercantilism stressed the development of a self-contained economy between the mother country and her colonies. The competition that developed naturally between rival systems almost inevitably led to conflict. The nations of Europe were the focal point of power, the centre of civilization which colonies were intended to augment through material goods and prestige. But the responsibilities of colonial empires and the actual and potential wealth they represented pushed the conflicts of Europe to the frontiers of the world. Spain and Portugal clung to their colonies in South America, but were destined, as their wealth and strength declined, to play a secondary role as pawns in the European struggle. The Dutch, though skilled in trade, lacked the resources to dominate and increasingly found themselves forced to accommodate their great rival across the Channel. Competition for naval and colonial supremacy was to be settled by the policies of France and England, whose national resources greatly outdistanced their European rivals.

THE IMPORTANCE OF COLONIES

Much of French exploration in the New World had been motivated by a quest for riches, a need to convert the native people to Christianity, and a desire to find a passage through North America to the East. Colbert's plan, known as the Compact Colony policy, was designed to make New France a thriving enterprise with a diversified economy concentrated on the banks of the St. Lawrence River. With the development of agriculture, industries, and fisheries, Colbert hoped that the colony would become an important part of the mercantilist economy of France. The St. Lawrence, however, was linked to the Great Lakes, a natural system of waterways that stretched over 3200 km into the heart of the continent. Despite Colbert's plan and the opposition of colonial officials, the profits of the fur trade, a sense of adventure, and the need to contain the English enticed French explorers towards the interior. By 1673, Louis Jolliet and Father Jacques Marquette had explored the upper 900 km of the Ohio and Mississippi rivers and in 1682, Robert Cavelier de La Salle travelled the Mississippi to the Gulf of Mexico. Over the next half century, the French built a series of strategic posts along the Great Lakes-Ohio-Mississippi system to consolidate the frontier they had pioneered.

COLBERT'S COMPACT COLONY

FRENCH EXPLORATION

Meanwhile, on the eastern seaboard, hemmed in by the Appalachian Mountains, the English colonies had grown and prospered and boasted a population ten times that of New France. French-English rivalry had been evident in numerous coastal skirmishes early in the seventeenth century, but as the fur trade grew in importance, clashes became more frequent. The French, the Dutch, and their English successors gathered native allies and armed them in an attempt to secure an increasingly large hinterland for their furs. With France at the peak of its power, Louis XIV provoked the War of the League of Augsburg which only intensified the situation in North America. The colonial struggle, named King William's War, after the recently crowned English monarch who joined

COLONIAL CONFLICT

against Louis in 1689, saw several minor scuffles. The Treaty of Ryswick, that ended hostilities in 1697, restored all territories lost to either side in North America, except that France retained the trading posts it had won on Hudson Bay.

Europe again intruded on the history of North America a few short years later when the War of the Spanish Succession broke out in 1702 and spilled over into the colonies. Known as Queen Anne's War in North America, the fighting was more extensive and, this time, more advantageous for the British. In the Treaties of Utrecht, 1713–1714, France gave up Acadia and Newfoundland and returned the posts on Hudson Bay.

FRENCH COMMERCIAL PROSPERITY

With the peace that followed, France strengthened its position on a worldwide basis. Although Louis XIV's foreign policy of expansion had been frustrated by the combined might of Europe, France remained the strongest military power. The merchant marine was enlarged to eighteen hundred ships as France assumed control of much of the trade that flowed back and forth from the Middle East to Turkey to Western Europe. In India, the decaying rule of the Mogul Empire opened the door to the French East India Company and its English counterpart to manoeuvre for economic and political advantage. For the first time, France became a serious competitive threat to England's commerce in the East.

In the New World, a triangle of trade prospered for both England and France. The manufactured products of the mother country were traded mainly for the sugar and molasses of the Antilles that were converted into rum. Rum was then traded for what most Europeans regarded as commodities–the slaves of the Gold Coast. The slaves, valuable for their labour on the plantations, were then traded for additional sugar and molasses.

Between 1713 and 1740, the trade of France doubled, reflecting a newfound prosperity that spread throughout Europe. Protection of trade and commerce and the colonies that made them possible was regarded as a necessary function of the state. With the establishment of New Orleans, at the mouth of the Mississippi, as the capital of French Louisiana in 1718, and the construction of the great fortress of Louisbourg on Cape Breton after 1720, France staked-out the perimeter of the North American empire that it fully intended to defend. When Maria Theresa inherited the Hapsburg throne in 1740, the stage was set for another European war which would again have repercussions that followed the course of empire.

LOUISBOURG

Slavery and Empire

SLAVERY IN HISTORY

Slavery probably had its origin in prehistoric times, when conflicts between agricultural societies led to conquests for the victor and servitude for the loser. It is also possible that people sold themselves to pay their debts or became enslaved when they were punished for breaking local customs or laws. Certainly, in one form or another, slavery played an uncomfortably prominent role in every civilization on every continent throughout history. In the Age of

Discovery, much of the food, drink, and material prosperity provided by colonial empires came from the involuntary servitude of native peoples. Modern Europe might not have invented slavery, but it all too easily channelled the aboriginal societies it encountered into directions that satisfied European rather than native interests. The Portuguese exploration of Africa in the fifteenth century set the tone for the more than three centuries of slave trading that followed. Faced with a shortage of available labour at home, the Portuguese began to import African natives in 1444 at a rate that reached seven to eight hundred per year by 1460. It should be noted that while the Portuguese exploited the west coast of Africa, Arab traders were sending slaves from central Africa to the markets of the Middle East and the Orient. Both Christians and Muslims believed that they were bringing the benefits of civilization and religion to the people they enslaved. The fact that slavery was a common practice among African tribes and that native dealers were more than willing to trade captive warriors for manufactured goods simplified the task and lessened any moral burden the foreign buyer might have felt.

When the conquistadores arrived in the New World in the sixteenth century, they quickly realized that the Aztecs, Maya, and Inca utilized slave labour in working the fields and fighting in battles. The Spanish turned the tables on the native ruling classes and imposed the "civilizing influence" of the *encomienda*. This not only deprived Mesoamericans and South Americans of their freedom, but also their lives through disease and hard labour. To replace the rapidly dwindling number of natives available for exploitation, the Spanish joined the Portuguese in the quest for black African slaves. During the seventeenth century, as the Dutch, French, and English obtained Caribbean colonies, they also eagerly entered the slave trade that spread along the shore of the African coast.

It was believed that black Africans could better withstand forced labour in tropical climates than the West Indian natives. A black African worker, however, usually lasted only six to eight years in the field, which meant that the supply had to be constantly renewed and that the trade in human flesh flourished.

African slaves were first brought to the English colonies of North America when a Dutch trading ship arrived at Jamestown, Virginia in 1619. Throughout the first half of the seventeenth century, their status remained vague since there were no provisions in English law that allowed them to be treated differently from European servants. Almost half of the immigrants who came to the English colonies came in bond. That is, they exchanged the cost of the voyage in a written contract for two to seven years of labour for their sponsor. Known as **indentured servants**, they often worked and socialized with black Africans even though the European prejudice against blacks was always present. The black Africans did not have the benefit of a written contract to define their rights. In addition, there were few ways to resist an alien culture from which they were separated by language and colour. The children of black servants who were held for life became the property of their masters. When the profits of the plantation economy of the South grew in the second half of the seven-

SLAVERY IN THE AGE OF DISCOVERY

SLAVERY IN THE NEW WORLD

SLAVERY IN THE ENGLISH COLONIES

teenth century, legal codes were gradually changed to establish the relationship between master and slave. The English colonies gave religious freedom to European whites, but by the early eighteenth century, colour, custom, and law identified the black African slave as an exploitable resource with no sense of freedom.

COMMENT

Modern Europe began to take shape after 1350 with the aspirations and achievements of the Renaissance, the split of Christianity into competing Catholic and Protestant camps, and the assumption of power by the nation state and its secular rulers. Successful exploration and discovery enabled European civilization to spread and conquer distant lands throughout the world. Yet, despite these universal themes that immediately draw attention, there were other realities that were very much a part of European life.

Although the Black Death of 1348 was the most severe epidemic in European history, the plague continued to bring sudden outbreaks of horror and suffering on a significant scale for another four hundred years. The fear of recurring plague deeply affected the outlook of populations throughout the continent. Early in the sixteenth century, a bizarre set of drawings known as the "Dance of Death" began to appear on church walls and in woodcuts. Death became a preoccupation and reigned supreme in every sketch. It was often depicted as a scarred and twisted body or a smiling skeleton, with or without robes, leading the saint and sinner, emperor and subject, or pope and worshipper in a frightening celebration. Gradually, the importance of the dance declined and Death arrived as a surprise guest to take the king from the kingdom, the merchant from his money, or the farmer from his family. Death's grim warning played on such fears, "Once I was as you, soon you shall be as I."

As plagues came and went and the dead outnumbered the living in village after village, the causes of the epidemics were thought to be supernatural. Remedies were sought in potions that included fir, laurel, and oak leaves, or aromas of rue, roses, and cloves. It was also thought that protection from disease came from amulets of precious stones, bones from toads, and snake tongues. When people turned to the Church for practical preventatives and cures, they were not disappointed. The Church recommended wearing, folding, and/or eating paper inscribed with holy names or verses, and reciting certain prayers. Those who died were shown to have lack of faith. Not until the streets of cities were widened and the general level of public sanitation greatly improved, however, would periodic devastation by the plague be controlled.

During the Renaissance, as artists broke new ground in human expression and learned scholars examined the nature of the universe, the Church became rigid in protecting its faith against the influence of social change. When Church reform was ignored as the need for it grew, people became increasingly indifferent to ecclesiastical authority. Such secular attitudes were considered little short of heresy.

The cult of witchcraft enjoyed its greatest following since its shadowy beginnings in the folk religions of prehistoric time. Successfully ignored for centuries as a pagan fantasy, witchcraft received a stimulus when it was officially condemned by Pope Innocent VIII in a papal bull in 1484. By condemning witchcraft as heresy, Innocent probably felt that he could stamp out all opposition to the prestige and power of the Church.

Two inquisitors, Jacobus Sprenger and Henricus Kramer, were appointed to implement the pope's wishes. They produced a textbook, *Malleus Malleficarum* (Hammer of Witches) that became the legal source of authority for all Catholic witch hunters. In one of the great misrepresentations of history, it was claimed that women were inherently more wicked than men, that they were less likely to keep the faith, and therefore more prone to witchcraft. Men were not excluded as witches, but it was clearly women who were regarded as the main culprits. Many of the sick, elderly, and poverty-stricken females in local villages suffered severely from this prejudice in the wake of organized witch hunts.

Witches were supposed to possess special powers arranged in contracts with the devil. Among a host of other possibilities, witches could arouse or subdue love through spells and potions, control the weather, bring death at a glance (the evil eye), and induce sicknesses or cures. Witches were assisted by ointments, or salves, made from the powdered bones of hanged men, the blood of infants, and burnt toads that had been stuffed with stolen wafers. When the salves were properly applied, it was believed that a witch could become invisible and, with the aid of a broom, fly.

The problems of a community were usually blamed on a local witch who was, with few exceptions, a woman. A variety of methods were used to identify witches. Inquisitors and witch hunters, who were paid for each conviction, used torture, contrived evidence, encouraged family members to testify against each other, and bribed witnesses when none came forward. According to tradition, every witch had a ''devil's mark'' that was insensitive to pain and which was created when demons suckled their blood in return for blind obedience. If such a point was found (a bruise, bump, or scratch could be identified as such) a pin test was given to check the pain threshold. The ''pin'' that was thrust into the spot could be as large as a dagger and the victim often died no matter what result was produced. Even the medieval water test in which an innocent person sank to the bottom while a witch floated to the surface was considered reliable.

Witches convicted of a crime or, in some cases for just being witches, were either hanged or burnt at the stake. It is impossible to determine the number who died in the slaughter of witches because the inquisitors did not distinguish between witches and heretics. It is claimed that four hundred were burned at Toulouse during a single execution, that seven thousand died at Trier in the sixteenth century, and that Germany alone eliminated one hundred thousand in the next hundred years. Persecution of witches even spread to the New World.

In the notorious Salem witch trials of 1692, thirteen women and six men were hanged as witches even though they never confessed. From the eleventh to the eighteenth century, when the last legal sentences against witches were passed, a minimum of three hundred thousand perished in the name of the witchcraft they apparently practised. Superstition thus retained an enduring grip on people's imagination despite the modern trappings that graced other aspects of European society.

Perhaps the greatest sorcerer of modern Europe was Louis XIV! While the glories of his early years were tarnished by later failures, the presence of the Sun King cast a spell over his contemporaries and future generations. No matter what the occasion or place, from victory to defeat, politics to sport, or Paris to Versailles, Louis commanded the centre of attention. Better than anyone of his time, Louis understood that a king had to be *seen* performing his regal duties. Such an attitude would have made Louis a big hit in front of television cameras had he lived in the twentieth century. Great artists, architects, statesmen, and politicians came and went, but it was the grandeur of Louis that stamped his image on an entire historical era. His tastes and manners were copied during his lifetime and by several less worthy successors.

One intriguing footnote to history that stems partly from an admiration of Louis XIV is the story of Ludwig II of Bavaria. Known to Bavarians as "Mad King Ludwig," his past was already suspect when he came to the throne in 1864 at the age of eighteen. Ludwig's younger brother, Otto, had been insane since childhood, and his grandfather, Ludwig I, so indulged his mistress, the dancer Lola Montez, with riches and power that his sanity was also questioned. Ludwig II's attitude towards life could, at first, be described as delightfully unusual. Where many kings and politicians thought mainly about power, empire, and territory, Ludwig was obsessed with art and music! This got him into trouble almost immediately. Ludwig summoned the composer Richard Wagner to court, paid off his debts, and became his patron. Wagner, however, had been associated with the revolutionary movement of 1848 and lived a promiscuous private life that was not acceptable in royal circles. Although they remained friends, Ludwig had to force Wagner to leave after little more than a year. In 1867, Ludwig became engaged to Princess Sophie of Bavaria. A marriage coach was built, commemorative medals minted, and Sophie was fitted for a crown. Ludwig postponed the ceremony twice and then ended the engagement. This was the last time he contemplated marriage.

Frustrated in his patronage of Wagner and shaken by his romance with Sophie, Ludwig embarked on the course that his detractors claimed was sheer madness. He became the greatest castle builder of the last two centuries, even though he did not need a castle! Ludwig had no family or plans to start one and the royal palace of Residenz should have satisfied the ego of any reasonable ruler. Nevertheless, in 1869 he commissioned the building of Neuschwanstein on a cliff tucked into the beautiful Bavarian Alps. Indeed, the setting over-

Ludwig II's Castle Neuschwanstein in the Bavarian Alps was the inspiration for Walt Disney's Magic Kingdom.

looked lakes, valleys, and meadows creating a fairy-tale atmosphere that later inspired Walt Disney to use it as a model for his "magic castles" in the United States. Five years later, Ludwig began a second castle, Linderhof, and four years after that a third, Herrenchiemsee. Only Linderhof, Ludwig's favourite, was completed at the time of his mysterious death in 1886, yet Ludwig had plans for two or more and dreams for a dozen.

Within these castle walls, Ludwig indulged his childhood fascination with paintings of German legends, his devotion to Louis XIV and his successors, and secured his desire for total privacy. Unlike the Sun King he so admired, Ludwig became a virtual royal recluse. Normally, he slept during the day, had breakfast in the evening, lunch at 2:00 a.m., and dinner at dawn. At Linderhof and Herrenchiemsee he even had his meals raised on a "magic table" from the kitchen below so that he could eat alone. Here, Ludwig imagined the company of Louis XIV and had dinner talks with Marie Antoinette before going on a midnight ride in the forest. Ludwig was so inspired by Louis XIV that he had a bronze statue of the Sun King on a steed placed in the entrance of Linderhof, and, at Herrenchiemsee, a copy of the Hall of Mirrors that was longer than the original at Versailles.

Ludwig's castle-building ambitions, however, landed him in debt to the amount of 21 million marks by 1885. This was money owed to the state of Bavaria by Ludwig and his relatives, and it had to be repaid. The royal family feared that Ludwig might wipe out in a single generation a fortune that had taken eight hundred years to accumulate. At the government's request, four psychiatrists heard testimony from servants who apparently described Ludwig as a king who talked to trees, who saluted statues, and complained of pains in his head! On 8 June 1886, without actually examining Ludwig, the psychiatrists pronounced him insane. Ludwig was soon taken into custody to the small berg castle on Lake Starnberg near Munich. On 13 June 1886, Ludwig asked the psychiatrist Dr. von Gudden to accompany him on a walk. Two keepers began to follow but were motioned off by Dr. von Gudden. Several hours later, Ludwig, known to be a good swimmer, and Dr. von Gudden were both found floating in the lake in about 1 m of water. Von Gudden had marks of strangulation around his neck.

Several questions about these strange deaths have never been answered. Clearly, the family wanted to stop Ludwig from spending its money. Were the servants bribed to give damning testimony to the psychiatrists? Were the psychiatrists forced to give such an unprofessional report? Why was Dr. von Gudden insistent that he and Ludwig be left alone? The Bavarian papers printed stories, changed stories, and retracted stories as the government released conflicting information about the time and circumstance of the deaths. Did Ludwig strangle von Gudden and then commit suicide? Was the double murder set up by a third party? Or was it simply a very unusual accident?

Two things are now clear. Ludwig was prevented from building any more castles and the Bavarian government is sorry that he was! Up to eight thousand tourists a day visit each of the three castles that Ludwig left behind. Admission fees provide enough income to keep the 24-k gold trim on the castles gilded and to reward the government with a sizeable return on its investment. If only Ludwig had completed his dream!

It is a striking tribute to the lasting influence of Louis XIV that the glamour of his reign, as expressed in art and architecture, was copied 160 years after his death by his namesake (Ludwig translates to Louis) in another country. Despite the importance of the French Revolution and Napoleon and the declining glory of France, it was the Sun King's image that shone through the ages of history and captured the imagination.

Date A.D.	Event
1517	Luther nails his list of Ninety-five Theses to the door of Castle church in Wittenburg
1540	*The Age of Genius* (c.1540–1690) Ancients and moderns debate the nature of the physical world The sun is accepted as the centre of a universe that operates according to natural laws, including the force of gravity
1700	*The Enlightenment* (c.1690–1790) Course of human development is explained through reason Philosophers identify natural rights of humans and natural laws that govern human behaviour *Enlightened Despotism* Monarchs such as Catherine the Great of Russia (1762–1796), Frederick the Great of Prussia (1740–1786), and Joseph II of Austria (1765–1790) rule through progressive ideas to bring benefits to the people
1715	Louis XV becomes king of France
1740–1748	War of the Austrian Succession
1756–1763	The Seven Years' War–Britain emerges as the world's greatest colonial power, France is shaken financially and loses its North American empire, and Prussia becomes a great power
1769	James Watt improves the efficiency of the steam engine
1771	Richard Awkright organizes first cotton mill in Britain
1774	Louis XVI becomes king of France
1776	American Revolution–Thirteen British colonies declare their independence
1778	France enters an alliance with the United States against Britain Cost of the war pushes French debt to the breaking point
1784	Peter Onions and Henry Cort develop puddling process in iron production
1787	France's attempt at financial reform fails
1788	France experiences crop failure, drought, and economic depression
1789	The Estates General meets in France on 4 May The National Assembly forms on 17 June French Revolution–the Moderate Phase
1792	French Revolution–the Radical Phase
1795	The Directory
1799	Napoleon's coup d'état
1815	Napoleon is defeated at Waterloo Congress of Vienna–the triumph of reaction
1830–1848	Revolution and radical change fail

10

Europe and the French Revolution

BACKGROUND

The Idea of Progress in History

The idea that history is progress, which focusses on the conviction that society is constantly improving, had its origin about three hundred years ago. Earlier civilizations viewed the story of human development much differently. The Greeks and Romans assumed that history ran in cycles that led to decline and disaster after brief periods of success. Biblical writers of the medieval period regarded history as the unfolding of divine purpose in which one's time on earth was a preparation for ultimate fulfilment in the afterlife. A marked shift in attitude from the world beyond to life in the present dominated views of history during the Renaissance when people looked back to classical societies for inspiration and authority. The emphasis on human achievement, however, led scientific thinkers of the sixteenth and seventeenth centuries to debate whether the modern world could compete with an earlier age of glory. Did history in this life have a sense of direction?

The debate between the "Ancients" and the "Moderns" began tentatively with questions about the make up of the universe. The second-century Greek astronomer Ptolemy had assumed that the earth was the centre of the universe and his ideas were accepted with surprisingly few modifications throughout the medieval period. In 1543, however, Nicholas Copernicus (1473–1543) published his book, *On the Revolution of Heavenly Bodies*, in which he set forth the revolutionary theory that the sun, rather than the earth, was the centre of the solar system. There was no way to prove Copernicus's idea, but it posed some challenging problems for astronomers. How could the motion of the planets and other heavenly bodies be explained? What kept the planets from simply drifting off into endless space?

A half century later, William Gilbert (1540–1603) first suggested the role of a magnetic attraction, but it was the German, Johann Kepler (1571–1630),

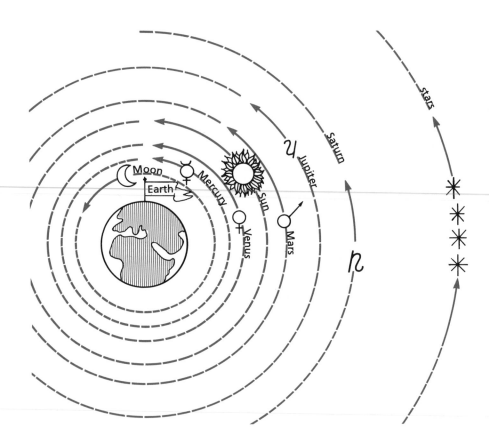

The Universe According to Ptolemy. The sun, moon, and planets circle the earth, the centre of the universe.

who created the next important link. Kepler demonstrated that the planets moved in elliptical orbits rather than circles, the "perfect" figures of God's work that were previously accepted. In addition, Kepler showed that mathematical laws applied to the speed, motion, and distance of a planet from the sun.

Galileo Galilei (1564–1642) made the next major breakthrough, in 1609, when he built a telescope and observed the heavens. He discovered that the moon's "perfect surface" was rough with mountains and plains, that there were other planets such as Jupiter with their own systems of moons, and that none of this made any sense unless the earth and the other planets revolved around the sun. The visual evidence and explanation that Galileo produced to confirm Copernicus's theory shook the foundation of the Church since all philosophy and theology was based on the Ptolemaic assumption that the earth was in a fixed position. Galileo was brought before the Roman Inquisition in 1633 and forced to deny his work, but Galileo knew that time and the evidence would prove his case. What was of key importance was that ancient learning had been questioned and, as a result of the publication (in lucid Italian) of

Galileo's research, that educated thinkers continued their inquiry into the operation of the universe.

The scientific breakthrough of what is sometimes called the "Age of Genius" was also concerned with identifying a scientific method of study. To eliminate past distortion, Francis Bacon (1561–1626), lord chancellor under James I of England, proposed the use of inductive reasoning based on close observation and analysis of evidence. In any study, each fact should be carefully examined to gradually build an idea before a final general statement is made. This, according to Bacon, would prevent people from jumping to conclusions that were not supported by observation and fact.

THE SCIENTIFIC METHOD

The philosopher René Descartes (1596–1650) took a more complicated approach in his landmark study, *A Discourse on Method*, published in 1637. For Descartes, doubt was the starting point of inquiry in the search for truth and ideas were acceptable only if they were based on systematic reasoning. He felt that the universe operated mechanically according to the uniform laws of nature and that deduction by mathematical reasoning based upon such rules gave absolute, logical conclusions. Descartes's understanding of the role of mathematics set him apart from Bacon, but both methods were necessary if science was to progress.

Certainly, the crowning achievement came in the seventeenth century when Cambridge professor Isaac Newton (1642–1727) closed the door on Ptolemy's conception of the universe through the use of techniques employed by his predecessors. Newton produced a synthesis of scientific knowledge that explained the theory of Copernicus, Gilbert's ideas about magnetism, Kepler's laws, and Galileo's study of movement. The key was Newton's realization that gravitation always worked the same way and that it was present everywhere. Newton convincingly demonstrated that gravity explained the motion of the planets, the moon, and the falling apple. The well-ordered, natural laws, first identified by Descartes, thus operated in a universe held together by the universal force of gravity.

NEWTON'S SYNTHESIS

In 1687, when Newton published his work, *Mathematical Principles of Natural Philosophy*, his synthesis convinced the educated world and was soon translated from the original Latin into the popular languages of Western Europe. Newton did more than anyone of his time to show that natural laws were universal and he was one of the few geniuses to receive due recognition for his accomplishments during his own lifetime. Even the Catholic Church eventually accepted Newton's conclusions, although it took more than a century for this to happen. Newton was a devout man who did not intend that his explanation of a rational universe be used to de-emphasize the central role of God and human beings. Nevertheless, believers in the existence of a universe run by mechanical laws began to drive a wedge between truth as defined by the faith of the Church, and truth as accepted by the reasoned evidence of the scientific method.

John Locke, born in Somersetshire in 1632, was the son of a strict but genial Puritan. The relationship between father and son was an ideal one that left its mark on Locke's educational theory. In his view, a good education attends to both the physical and the mental heeding exercise, play, and plentiful sleep, ''the great cordial of nature.''

The idea of progress, which seemed clearer with each scientific achievement, weighted the debate between the ''Ancients'' and the ''Moderns'' in favour of the latter. Among the first and most eloquent to express this view was Bernard le Bouvier de Fontenelle (1657–1757), secretary of the French Académie des Sciences, who interpreted and popularized the new learning. In his short but important pamphlet, *Digression on the Ancients and Moderns*, published in 1688, Fontenelle argued that human knowledge progressed through the build-up of experience, as if the educated mind of the present consisted of the minds of preceding ages. Fontenelle did not accept the full implications of the idea of progress. While he believed that the progress of knowledge was inevitable, he also felt that since humans were physically unchanged, their behaviour and moral character remained largely the same. It would be left to others to transfer the idea of progress in knowledge to a theory of progress for human society.

The Idea of Progress in the Enlightenment

The intellectual leaders of the eighteenth century felt that the breakthroughs of science had uncovered a blanket of ignorance and superstition, and that Europe was entering a more advanced period they termed the **Enlightenment**. In sharp contrast to the pessimism of the past, there was now an optimistic attitude about the course of human development. Just as the use of reason had yielded spectacular results to questions about the universe, there was an unrestrained confidence that reason applied to human problems would produce similar results and happiness for the individual. Humans were indeed perfectable. If natural laws explained the operation of the universe, there must be natural laws of human behaviour that could be applied to economic, social, and political institutions. For the great thinkers of the day, reason, rather than religion, had become the measuring stick of usefulness and progress. The Church was often seen as the source of superstition that had to be overcome. Although religious questions were still important, Europe was, for the first time since the early Roman Empire, under the control of secular rather than religious forces. Architects and artists now accepted royal palaces–the symbols of state authority –rather than churches as their major commissions. It was the power of the secular nation state and its potential for reform according to the dictates of the "Age of Reason" (a term often used for the Enlightenment) that intrigued many intellectuals. Ironically, they often pursued their faith in the use of reason to achieve progress with the enthusiasm of religious converts.

NATURAL LAWS AND HUMAN BEHAVIOUR

The impulse towards the Enlightenment, in the late seventeenth century, came from Newton's work in mathematics and physics. It was expanded with the studies of politics and human nature done by fellow Englishman John Locke (1632–1704), a physician by profession who was twice forced into exile because of his connection with the Whig party. Locke's writing was undoubtedly coloured by his participation in the English Revolution of 1688 and his personal friendship with William of Orange, but he attacked two established principles on purely rational grounds. The first was the Christian belief that all people were born evil, and the second was the popular notion of the "divine right of kings." Locke believed that the mind began as a "blank sheet" (tabula rasa) void of all characteristics, and acquired knowledge through observation and the experiences of the senses rather than by heredity. Once the information was gathered, the mind, through the use of reason, shaped this material into ideas. If a

JOHN LOCKE

society was faulty it was the result of the environment and this could be reformed to enhance progress and human happiness. Locke went on to argue that all individuals possess natural rights that are universal and cannot be taken away by a king or state. Should a king or state break this ''contract'' with the people and violate their natural rights, the people have a right to change the government, by force if necessary.

Locke's arguments were published in *Two Treatises on Civil Government*, written in 1688 to justify the removal of James II, and in *An Essay Concerning Human Understanding* completed two years later. Of critical importance was the influence of Locke on the French *philosophes*, a collection of writers whose concern about a wide range of social, moral, religious, and political issues made them the heart of the Enlightenment. Among the most famous were Montesquieu, Voltaire, and Diderot who spread Locke's ideas as well as their own throughout the educated élite of the continent. The importance of books had increased with every generation since the invention of the printing press and the publication of the writings of the *philosophes* quickly spread their ideas throughout the upper and middle classes of European society. It also became quite fashionable among French intellectual circles to discuss ideas characteristic of the Enlightenment in local coffee houses and the salons of socialites like Madame de Lambert and Madame Dupin. Fontenelle and the enthusiastic reformer Abbé de Saint-Pierre (1685–1743), who believed that social progress was inevitable, often attended such gatherings and public awareness of their ideas grew accordingly. The influence of Locke, however, was not limited to afternoon discussions, but became translated into revolution. That Thomas Jefferson owed an intellectual debt to Locke when he wrote the Declaration of Independence was clear in the following famous lines of the document:

> We hold these truths to be self-evident, that all men are created equal, that they are endowed by their Creator with certain unalienable rights, that among these are life, liberty, and the pursuit of happiness . . . That to secure these rights, governments are instituted among men, deriving their just powers from the consent of the governed, . . . That whenever any form of government becomes destructive of these ends, it is the right of the people to alter or to abolish it, and to institute new government, laying its foundation on such principles and organizing its powers in such form, as to them shall seem most likely to effect their safety and happiness.

The French aristocrat and *philosophe* Baron de Montesquieu (1689–1755) was influenced by the works of Locke and Newton, but developed considerable insight into political theory from his own travels and study. In his political classic, *The Spirit of the Laws*, published in 1748, Montesquieu argued that political institutions were determined by geographical, social, and historical circumstances. People developed different kinds of government because they lived under different conditions. It was the English constitution that provided Mon-

THE ENLIGHTENMENT IN ACTION

MONTESQUIEU

tesquieu with the model he most admired. He believed that Parliament, the monarch, and judges worked separately, each acting to limit the power of the other, to preserve individual liberty. Although Montesquieu actually misrepresented the operation of the English system, his idea of checks and balances through the separation of power greatly influenced the political leaders who drafted the United States Constitution of 1789.

Perhaps the guiding spirit and ultimate expression of the Enlightenment was found in the works of François-Maurice Arouet (1694–1778), better known by his pen name, Voltaire. Born into the upper middle class and possessed of a desire to improve his wealth and social standing, Voltaire asserted his independence from authority that demands blind obedience early in his career. He rejected the Catholicism of his Jesuit teachers and opportunities in the business world, intending instead to win fame as a literary figure. With the success of his classical tragedy *Henriade*, in 1723, Voltaire gained access to the small but influential literary élite of France which included the bourgeoisie and liberal-minded members of the clergy and aristocracy. It was among this group that the ideas of the Enlightenment flourished, ideas that left Voltaire with the conviction that the application of reason could solve most, if not all, of society's problems. Familiar as he was with the ideas of Locke and Newton, particularly after a two-year stay in England, Voltaire's skill lay in the devastating satire he hurled at the Church, the nobility, and the government. His pen became an intellectual sword that caused him to be feared and admired by the very classes he mocked.

The criticism Voltaire levelled against the existing political and social structures of France in the *Lettres philosophiques*, published in 1733, only served to enhance his reputation. He became a friend of Catherine of Russia and his correspondence with Frederick the Great led to an invitation to live and work at the Prussian court. Jealousy among those close to the king and Voltaire's insensitivity to criticism resulted in an early dismissal, but his friendship with Frederick endured. Voltaire's sharp wit and self-righteous manner often got him into trouble and he was twice sent to the Bastille, the famous and dreaded prison in Paris. Fortunately, as his fame increased so did his wealth and the four estates Voltaire purchased in the countryside of France and Switzerland usually provided sanctuary from offended critics. Concerned with the plight of wronged individuals, Voltaire worked tenaciously in a Catholic community for three years to reverse the verdict against an executed Protestant named Calas. This, and similar defences on behalf of victims of injustice, turned his fame into legend. In religious matters, Voltaire became involved in a crusade for toleration and, like other *philosophes*, personally endorsed the reasoned approach of **deism**. Deism accepted the Newtonian idea that God created the universe, that it operated according to natural law, and that it operated without God's interference. Since God could not alter these laws once they were set in motion, there was little need to pray or to follow the rituals of organized religion. What was important was to identify the natural laws and to live by their code. While royalty

VOLTAIRE

Voltaire–A Man of Wit and Wisdom

I have never made but one prayer to God, a very short one: ''O Lord, make my enemies ridiculous.'' And God granted it.

In general, the art of government consists in taking as much money as possible from one class of citizens to give it to the other.

All the reasoning of men is not worth one sentiment of women.

and aristocracy vied for Voltaire's attention in recognition of his skill and popularity, the Catholic Church never forgave his ''betrayal''–his constant criticism of Christian attitudes. For Voltaire, the Catholic Church (and intolerance of any kind) represented an obstacle to the idea of progress that he and other *philosophes* believed offered the key to a better society.

The spectrum of Voltaire's writing continued to expand throughout his career as he pioneered new techniques with a broadened scope in the writing of history, satire, and essays. His major contribution lay in the weaknesses and injustices of French society he exposed with barbed comments and reason. Yet Voltaire had no great love for the masses and he stopped well short of endorsing democracy as a form of government. In fact, he believed that society's welfare could only be entrusted to those monarchs who were enlightened with progressive ideas that they could bring to the people. Such a system became known as **enlightened despotism**. Although the Catholic Church denied Voltaire a Christian burial when he died in 1778, his body was later returned to Paris and paraded through the streets in triumph during the French Revolution.

The practices of enlightened despotism varied greatly according to the needs and circumstances of the monarch in question rather than strictly conforming to the ideas of reform-minded writers. Catherine the Great (1762–1796) of Russia recognized that the French *philosophes* shaped the direction of European thought so she courted their favour. Beginning with a genuine interest in intellectual ideas, Catherine developed a correspondence with Voltaire and his fellow *philosophes* Diderot and d'Alembert. She deliberately cultivated her image as an enlightened despot, described her policies in the most favourable manner, and became a public-relations success. As Catherine probably calculated, the *philosophes* discussed her ideas in the name-dropping circles of French society and her reputation grew accordingly.

The reality of Russia was much different. Although administrative reforms were made, their purpose and impact were to strengthen central authority. When an illiterate Cossack named Pugachev led an ill-fated peasant rebellion in 1773, the Russian army overwhelmed his disorganized forces and he was caged, drawn, and quartered. After this, Catherine entertained no thoughts of reform to improve life for the peasants. Catherine's efforts in industry, business, and education benefited the upper classes whose privileges were confirmed and symbolized in the Great Charter of the Nobility in 1785. As the strength of the nobles increased, the living conditions of the Russian serfs reached an unprecedented low.

Catherine pursued an expansionist policy to the south that resulted in the defeat of Turkey, the annexation of the Crimea, and, eventually, control over the north shore of the Black Sea. In the east, Poland was totally absorbed by Russia, Prussia, and Austria after the last of three partitions in 1795. Poland ceased to exist until it was resurrected after World War I in 1919. Catherine's approach was much more in the despotic, tsarist tradition than it was enlightened. Her intention was to improve the image and strength of Russia no matter what label was applied. Her success in achieving these goals earned Catherine a reputation as a ''great'' monarch.

Frederick the Great (1740–1786) was somewhat closer to the ideal of an enlightened despot, an ideal that became highly fashionable among royalty during the last half of the eighteenth century. Frederick was famed for his intellect and had a sincere interest in music, art, literature, and philosophy. Recognizing Voltaire's contribution to the mainstream of the Enlightenment, Frederick initiated a correspondence with the French scholar and invited him to Potsdam to live, work, and help him with his own writing. Although Voltaire's

ENLIGHTENED DESPOTISM

CATHERINE THE GREAT

FREDERICK THE GREAT

stay was short lived, the atmosphere of parties, plays, and philosophical discussions at court did much to advance Frederick's reputation as an enlightened monarch.

Frederick made himself the sole creator of Prussian policy. He spent long hours issuing his instructions through hand-written letters and rarely consulted his ministers. A network of spies was employed to weed out corruption in the bureaucracy, while a system of civil service examinations allowed promotion based on merit for talented administrators. In the spirit of the Enlightenment, Frederick pursued a policy of religious toleration, prevented landlords from expropriating peasant landholdings, and introduced practices that improved agricultural production. Reform in the legal system gave Prussia a deserved reputation for honesty throughout Europe.

Yet beyond the appearance of enlightened ideas, Frederick's major goal was the efficient operation of the Prussian state. In this he clearly sided with the Junker nobility by supporting their privileged position at the expense of the peasant serfs. Frederick believed that only the noble class possessed the natural leadership ability required to improve the Prussian economy and he did not interfere with the local administration of their estates. Mercantilist principles governed the economy as a whole with subsidies, monopolies, and tariffs applied where they were needed to encourage the growth of domestic industry. The end result was a diversified economy that strengthened the Prussian state but did little to improve the living conditions of the people. Like his predecessors, Frederick drained the wealth of the state to support the army which had now grown in size to about two hundred thousand soldiers. The victories Frederick won with the best-trained fighting force in Europe, rather than any of his enlightened reforms, established his reputation for greatness.

JOSEPH II

Perhaps the most sincere enlightened despot was Joseph II (1765–1790) of Austria who not only tried to rule according to the ideas of the *philosophes*, but really cared about his people. Similar to Frederick in some ways, Joseph felt it was his duty to provide good government for his people without their participation. Joseph shared power as co-regent with his mother, Maria Theresa, for the first fifteen years of his reign and her conservatism restrained his more extreme ideas. On his own after her death in 1780, Joseph began a major overhaul of the Hapsburg lands without recognizing that the collection of states in Hungary, Italy, the Netherlands, Bohemia, and Austria represented five different cultural traditions. With only minor exceptions, German was made the official language of every regional administration. As in Prussia, there was a secret police to watch over the operation of the bureaucracy. Joseph passed laws that recognized the legal equality of all classes, supported religious toleration, placed education and marriage under civil authority, and virtually abolished serfdom. He even revised some of the mercantilist practices in favour of the new ideas of economic freedom.

Unfortunately, Joseph moved too quickly with many well-intentioned reforms and often succeeded in offending those who were required to change without gaining the support of public opinion. When his agrarian reforms pushed the nobility to the brink of revolt in 1789, Joseph halted their implementation. This only served to alienate the very peasants he was trying to help and did not win the confidence of the nobles he had challenged. Joseph died a frustrated and disillusioned man in 1790, amid the woes of social turmoil and economic depression. His brother and successor, Leopold II (1790–1792), repealed most of Joseph's enlightened and revolutionary legislation. The nobles remained in control of their great estates and serfdom continued in practice until 1848. Nevertheless, the legal rights of the peasants with regard to occupation, marriage, and residence were preserved. Joseph's noble vision of reform from above was largely a failure, but it illustrated that the state had assumed responsibility for the welfare of its citizens. If faith in the perfectability of humans was going to lead to progress, as Joseph and the *philosophes* believed, meaningful reform had to have a broader base of support.

The *philosophes*, however, were not kings but creators of reasoned ideas. Certainly, the grandest project undertaken by the *philosophes* was the famous *Encyclopedia* (1751–1772), which eventually covered seventeen large volumes of text. Edited by Diderot and d'Alembert, the names of Montesquieu and Voltaire were among the 130 contributors who attempted to bring together in a single collection a summary of human knowledge. This included the scientific breakthroughs of the seventeenth century, the application of reason to social problems of the eighteenth century, and any useful information that might advance the cause of civilization. Implicit in this approach was the important belief that progress could be made through an enlightened education, and that an understanding of social and historical forces could lead to an improved quality in the conduct of human affairs. As the work on the *Encyclopedia* advanced, it became increasingly evident that any summary of existing knowledge, particularly when written with the moral perspective possessed by all of the *philosophes*, clearly illustrated the unfairness of living conditions in France. The importance of this picture was not lost on the intellectual bourgeois class that compiled it or on those who were ready to fight for change in 1789. Even though the *Encyclopedia* of the *philosophes* was not the first ever devised, it was the most comprehensive in scope and it became the model for those that followed.

The idea of progress through the application of reason to problems in the social and economic order was paralleled by new approaches in economics. Economic theory and practice in the seventeenth and eighteenth centuries were dominated by mercantilism in which the active intervention of the government through its legislation and taxing power was intended to achieve wealth and national self-sufficiency. In 1776, Adam Smith (1723–1790), professor of moral philosophy at the University of Glasgow, realigned this outlook with the ideas of the Enlightenment in his pioneering work, *An Inquiry into the Nature and Causes of the Wealth of Nations*. Just as Newton's concept of natural law in the universe had been translated into natural political rights, Smith argued that

THE PHILOSOPHES

ADAM SMITH

the natural law of economics was supply and demand. The emphasis was on individual economic freedom and free trade among nations. Restrictive government intervention in the form of tariffs, taxes, and related measures should be eliminated so that the natural law of economics could function without interference. *Philosophes* such as François Quesnay (1694–1774), who wrote articles for Diderot's *Encyclopedia*, had anticipated Smith's **laissez faire** ideas of free trade. Quesnay had been very critical of Colbert's mercantilist policies as obstacles to economic growth and progress. It was Smith, however, who laid out the theory of free trade which became widely discussed and which reigned supreme in Great Britain during the nineteenth century.

JEAN-JACQUES ROUSSEAU

As a cauldron of ideas, the Enlightenment did not always produce intellectual agreement. The most significant break from the focal point of reason came from the pen of philosopher Jean-Jacques Rousseau (1712–1778), whose ideas were among the most influential in later generations. Rousseau was the product of an unhappy childhood that left him with feelings of insecurity and alienation from society throughout his troubled and unconventional life. He agreed with Locke that humans originally lived in a state of nature and that they possessed certain rights. Rousseau set himself apart from the *philosophes*, however, by arguing that the good qualities of human nature sprang from emotions rather than reason. It was civilization and the growth of private property that produced evil, conflict, and bad government. However, he realized that civilization could not be abandoned to recapture the primitive state of nature. In his most important and famous work, *The Social Contract*, published in 1762, Rousseau tackled the problem of establishing a government that would secure natural equality for all. According to Rousseau, when people first left the state of nature they made a contract with each other to be governed by the **general will**. In its simplest form, the general will represents the real, unselfish desire of each individual and is, therefore, the purest wish of the people. Since the goal of the general will is the well-being of all members of society, freedom consists of total obedience to it. Any individual following a different path must be "forced to be free" or, in other words, compelled to accept the general will.

THE GENERAL WILL

Rousseau did not specify how the general will was to be determined, but it was the spirit of his writing, rather than the details, that became important. The significance of the general will strengthened the idea of democracy–the sovereignty of the people–but also became an instrument of dictatorship by implying that an élite group could define and enforce its meaning. For Rousseau, society did not operate mechanically according to rigid laws. It grew and changed according to the environment and the general will. Rousseau's work had a great impact on the emergence of nationalism and, with his stress on the importance of emotion, the romanticism that flowered during the nineteenth century.

The triumph of reason during the Enlightenment was geared to the interests of the educated élite in the bourgeois and aristocratic classes. Though sin-

Jean-Jacques Rousseau, born in Geneva in 1712, set out on his own at the age of sixteen, wandering first to Italy then to France. Rousseau gained sudden fame in 1750 when the Academy of Dijon awarded him a prize for his essay Discourse on the Arts and Sciences.

cere, their judgements on the course of human development were often incorrect. Voltaire and other deists speculated that the Christian Church might come to an end in the next generation. What they failed to see was that the vast majority of people continued to be impressed by the good works performed by both Protestant and Catholic clergy, and by the emotional comfort they provided. Indeed, there were a series of movements to free the churches from state control that greatly appealed to the local shopkeeper, peasant, and artisan. The Methodists in England, the Pietists in Germany, and the Jansenists in France attempted to revitalize religion through strict morality and manners, and an emphasis on personal contact with God. At the same time, enlightened despot-

Developments in Music

Musical Period	Purpose	Features	Composer(s)
Early Medieval (c.600–1200)	Religious	Gregorian chant encouraged the ritual use of music by the Church.	Gregory I (540–604)
Gothic (1200–1400)	Religious	Polyphonic period marked by the simultaneous performances of several equally important melodies.	Guillaume de Machaut (1300–1377)
Renaissance (1400–1575)	Religious/secular	Writing techniques were combined for the first time with attention to the musical idea and the beauty of the musical sound.	Guillaume Dufay (1400–1474)
Baroque (1575–1714)	Secular as entertainment for European upper classes	Grandiose effects were achieved; new forms of secular music such as the opera emerged; instrumental music assumed the same status as choral music; period was marked by a single emotional quality throughout composition.	Johann Sebastian Bach (1685–1750)
Classical (1715–1815)	Secular as entertainment for European upper classes	Homophonic style was achieved by combining a single melody with harmonic accompaniment; chamber music (one instrument played each part) and symphonic music (several instruments played each part) emerged; conductor led from the front of the orchestra; operas were perfected with every aspect of vocal and instrumental music contributing to plot development and characterization.	Joseph Haydn (1732–1809) Wolfgang Amadeus Mozart (1756–1791) Ludwig van Beethoven (1770–1827)
Early Romantic (1815–1850)	Entertainment for upper classes	Musical form is subordinated to theme; subjective qualities, emotions, are emphasized.	Frédéric Chopin (1810–1849)

ism, valued by the *philosophes* as an agent of progress, more often than not preserved the existing structure of privilege in society rather than acting as an agent for change.

Nevertheless, the Enlightenment inspired a lasting faith that reason and progress would ultimately prevail. The Marquis de Condorcet (1743–1794), in his *Sketch for a Historical Picture of the Progress of the Human Mind* (1793), reaffirmed in a brilliant synthesis the unfailing conviction that scientific methods applied to social problems would improve moral character. While the *philosophes* were essentially reformers, their ideas played a significant role in the American and French revolutions. The popularity of their work fostered a wider acceptance of toleration and freedom at the expense of established authority, and the need for education to combat superstition. Moving from the humanism of the Renaissance that glorified artistic achievement, the *philosophes* developed a humanitarian concern for individual well-being that became an entrenched feature of Western tradition. The individual gained a dignity that found full expression in nineteenth-century liberalism.

European Warfare in the Eighteenth Century

While the Enlightenment was gradually changing the way Europeans looked at their society, absolute monarchs considered themselves to be servants of the state and spoke of "state-interests" that could only be protected by force. What they really meant by "state-interests" were almost private, dynastic conflicts that were not the concern of the bulk of the population. No one wanted a return to the wholesale devastation wrought by the passion of the Thirty Years' War, and several factors combined to control the organization and scope of eighteenth-century warfare.

For all of their apparent power, absolute monarchs had difficulty increasing tax revenue, and this restricted the size of the army that could be raised. At the same time, officers became highly valued assets because there were never enough to meet military needs. By tradition, they were recruited from the "respectable" elements of society, but these groups were often exempt from duty. Only a sense of honour or an interest in a military career might induce enlistment from those that monarchs regarded as society's natural leaders. It was the officer's job to discipline the mercenaries, vagabonds, and prisoners who were either hired or kidnapped into service. Once in the army, soldiers were separated from the local community. The difference between the professional soldier and the civilian population was clearly recognized by prince and subject from state to state. It was not uncommon for a battle to rage in the countryside while the civilian population pursued its daily chores with little interest in the outcome. Wars were truly limited, as each side understood the rules of conduct, followed precise military drills, and restricted intent to victory on the battlefield rather than total destruction of the enemy. Even in bat-

STATE-INTERESTS

MILITARY ORGANIZATION

tle, dependence on supply lines maintained over poorly kept roads slowed mobility to a snail's pace and this inadvertently contained the evils of war to those trained to fight it.

Anglo-French Rivalry and the War of Europe 1740–1763

When Emperor Charles VI (1711–1740) died, he believed that a state paper, known as the Pragmatic Sanction, and a lifetime of hard work had secured recognition for his daughter Maria Theresa to succeed to the Austrian throne. Within weeks, however, newly crowned Frederick II ("the Great") of Prussia extended a questionable family claim to Austrian territory in Silesia, and Maria Theresa was immediately faced with the prospect of invasion. So began the War of the Austrian Succession (1740–1748) which soon engulfed most of the major European states.

WAR OF THE AUSTRIAN SUCCESSION

The continental struggle spilled over into the worldwide competition for colonies and economic supremacy between England and France. Most contemporaries agreed that there was only a fixed amount of trade and commerce and that every country should take steps to maximize its share of the market. Mercantilist policies attempted to monopolize trade within their own colonies and to trade as much as they could with the colonies of other countries. Economic expansion through increased trade became so important that nations justified war on behalf of commerce as a responsibility of the state. England and France confronted each other in the heart of North America, the West Indies, the Mediterranean, and India. Where local conditions failed to produce conflict, the trading interests of the mother country usually led to the outbreak of hostilities. Indeed, the European and colonial conflicts became so intertwined that a victory in one part of the world could be offset by defeat in another.

TREATY OF AIX-LA-CHAPELLE

The Treaty of Aix-la-Chapelle in 1748 marked the arrival of Prussia as a major European power. Under Frederick's skillful leadership, the army secured Silesia from Austria, which doubled Prussia's population and greatly increased its resources. Maria Theresa was forced to formally accept the loss of this territory in the treaty. In the colonial conflict, the most significant development was the British capture of the great French fortress of Louisbourg, which humbled French naval power in North American waters. In India, however, France captured the British city of Madras. Overall, the war had been indecisive and the peacemakers were forced to return to the unsatisfactory situation of 1713. Louisbourg was exchanged for Madras, but the major issues in Europe and the colonies were not resolved. Clearly, another round would have to be fought if stability was to be established in Europe and the struggle for colonies decided.

The breathing space provided by the peace of Aix-la-Chapelle encouraged another spurt of commercial activity by England and France as the volume of overseas trade reached an all-time high. The European thirst for coffee and tea, oriental art objects, fashionable fur hats, and tobacco for snuff and smoking could not be satisfied. To secure territory and increase trade at the expense of the competition, English and French colonies throughout the world engaged in intermittent conflict without a declaration of war. In India, the British and French East India Companies used existing native rivalries as an excuse to combat each other after 1750. French and English slave traders had several skirmishes off the coast of west Africa, while smuggling in the West Indies created confrontation and problems for both sides. The most serious situation developed in North America where the French built a chain of small forts to prevent the movement of Virginia land speculators and to stop native traders from securing more territory once they crossed the Appalachians. At Fort Duquesne (Pittsburgh), the French badly defeated the Virginia militia, led by Colonel George Washington, in 1754 and began the French and Indian War two years before hostilities broke out in Europe.

European wars had been based on the need to maintain a balance of power by preventing any one state from dominating the continent. Prior to the Thirty Years' War, several states opposed attempts by the Austrian and Spanish Hapsburgs to consolidate their domains. During the reign of Louis XIV, the powers of Europe united to limit French hegemony. With the success of Prussia in the War of the Austrian Succession, new alignments were needed to prevent the expansion of yet another major state. In the so-called "Diplomatic Revolution" of 1756, alliances were formed to match the new circumstances. France allied itself with its traditional enemy Austria, as well as with Russia, Saxony, and Sweden in opposition to Prussia, Great Britain, and the British kingdom of Hanover. Surrounded on several fronts with no natural frontiers, Frederick felt that bold action was required to save Prussia from its precarious position. The Prussian army marched into Saxony in August of 1756 and Europe was again plunged into a war that quickly became linked with the Anglo-French struggle over colonial empires.

Prussia appeared as if it would be overwhelmed throughout much of what came to be known as the Seven Years' War. With 4 million people, Prussia's population was only one-third that of Austria and one-fifth that of France and Russia, but Frederick's military genius and perserverance prevented collapse. Usually, the enemy forces were divided and Prussia could defeat them individually. When battles were lost, the coalition against Frederick did not know how to exploit its opportunity. Although France was successful at the start of the war, men and resources had to be diverted from its colonies. This gave Britain a major advantage in the struggle for empire. Under the brilliant leadership of William Pitt in 1757, Britain improved its organization and the supremacy of the British navy was used to ensure that colonial forces were well supplied. Britain was able to subsidize Frederick's war effort on the continent while it won a series of victories against France overseas. In 1758, the French fortress of Louisbourg was captured for the second time in as many wars. The climax of the imperial struggle came the next year, when General James Wolfe led a Brit-

THE SCOPE OF CONFLICT

THE DIPLOMATIC REVOLUTION

THE SEVEN YEARS' WAR

Rivalry for Empire Expansion

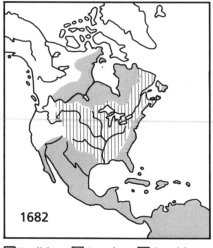

1682

☐ English   ☐ French   ☐ Spanish

1763

ish army against the French forces of General Louis Joseph de Montcalm and won a decisive victory on the Plains of Abraham outside Québec. This opened the door to the St. Lawrence and British control of North America. In India, the British navy and the military skill of Robert Clive overcame the superior forces of France and won the important victory at Plassey which gave Britain the province of Bengal. Total victory in India was assured when the British captured the French post of Pondicherry in 1761. Meanwhile, the British navy swept France from all but one of its island colonies in the West Indies.

By 1763, Russia and Sweden had already withdrawn from the war and the remaining participants were eager to make peace. The war in Europe had been a stalemate and this was reflected in the Treaty of Hubertusburg which returned conditions to those that existed prior to the conflict. Prussia gave up Saxony but received confirmation of its ownership of Silesia. The Treaty of Paris ended the imperial struggle between Britain and France in the colonies. Due to the skill of French negotiators, France did better at the bargaining table than it had done on the battlefield. All of North America was lost except for the two small islands of St. Pierre and Miquelon in the fishing grounds off the Atlantic coast, but Martinique, Guadeloupe, and San Domingo were retained in the West Indies. The British took control of the major slaving stations in Africa, and while France did maintain trading rights in a few towns, its power in India was crushed.

The treaties of 1763 stabilized the balance of power in Europe for a generation. Prussia was now firmly established as a great power as the dynastic struggle with Austria was now settled. Indeed, the centre of power began to shift towards the military states of central and eastern Europe. France, though still formidable, was badly shaken by the costs of the war and the loss of prestige that saw Britain triumph as the world's greatest colonial power. Little did anyone realize that the removal of the French threat in North America would stimulate a move towards independence that would separate Britain from a large part of its empire.

France and the Ancien Régime: Framework for Revolution

The **ancien régime** (old regime) in France was not as static as is often claimed. Rooted initially in the world of Louis XIV, several changes took place during the three-quarters of a century that separated the death of the Sun King from the French Revolution. These changes, however, revolved around the power exercised directly or indirectly by the monarch, the nobility, and the bourgeoisie. After the Sun King, the authority of the monarch was still considerable but seldom used in a constructive way, while the bourgeoisie fell from favour. The nobility, however, regained what they regarded as their natural position as members of a powerful and privileged group in society. Exempt from taxation despite their wealth, the nobility entertained no thought of relieving the lower classes from the burden of paying off the national debt established by Louis XIV and aggravated by a series of intermittent wars. Could a serious attempt at moderate reform have prevented the revolution of 1789? It is difficult to tell. Enlightened despotism had limited success wherever it was tried, and the maze of overlapping customs and jurisdictions in the tax structure of France defied a rational explanation. What was clear was that France was a rich nation with a poor government, and that those who could least afford it shouldered the greatest weight of taxation.

As previously outlined, the collapse of the Fronde after the Thirty Years' War severely weakened the French nobility and Louis XIV took full advantage of the situation. He elevated the bourgeois middle class to positions of favour as advisers and, led by Colbert, they did everything they could to glorify the reign of their grand monarch. The nobles had to stay at Versailles, which cost them dearly and prevented the development of a power base in the provinces to challenge royal authority. Louis's wars of expansion and the extravagance of his lifestyle were paid for by the labour of the lower classes, and attempts to adjust the tax structure were frustrated at every turn. Under a conscientious king like Louis, who had the charisma and style to dominate his realm, the system survived and enabled France to become the foremost power in Europe. The succession of lesser kings, however, removed the firm hand that was required if the huge national debt left by the Sun King was ever to be repaid.

A ruler with the character of Frederick the Great of Prussia might have made the changes necessary to prevent a crisis in France. The Sun King's great-grandson and successor, Louis XV, was no such man and his long reign from 1715 to 1774 was disastrous for his country. Louis came to the throne at the age of five and by the end of his regency developed a lazy and carefree attitude towards his responsibilities as king. Initially, he left the administration of the country to his officials. Under the able direction of his tutor, Cardinal Fleury, French prestige increased, the economy improved, and France began to recover from the human and material losses inflicted by the Sun King. When Fleury died in 1743, however, the indolent Louis decided to rule by himself even though he had little understanding of government. His secret style of conduct and diplomacy resulted in intrigue and contradiction as ministers came and went in rapid succession when they fell out of royal favour. An attempt was made to impose a universal 5 percent tax to finance the War of the Austrian Succession, but the nobility and clergy successfully resisted payment. The aura of the Sun King had always overwhelmed the provincial parlements that had previously been a source of power for the nobles against royal authority. Although Louis XV retained respect, his indifferent and confused leadership weakened the central government and encouraged the nobles to reassert their demands at the local level. The king had the final say, but the nobles were able to use the parlements to pressure the king and government to reverse their policy. When the Parlement of Paris engaged the support of the Church to oppose the 5 percent tax, the king and his ministers gave in to their demands.

Moments in Time

Elizabeth Vigée-Lebrun (1755–1842), a prolific and popular artist of her time, was a favourite of the aristocracy. Her popularity eventually extended to Versailles and she became court painter to Marie Antoinette.

On the eve of the Revolution, Vigée-Lebrun fled with her father and spent twelve years in exile. During that time she became a member of the academies of Rome, Florence, Bologna, St. Petersburg, and Berlin. She returned to France during the Napoleonic regime and spent the next twenty-two years painting over eight hundred portraits and landscapes. Elizabeth Vigée-Lebrun was one of the few successful women of the Napoleonic period.

With the Seven Years' War, the burden of the national debt continued to increase, but Louis became indifferent to the daily routines of kingship. Again, he abandoned the operation of state to ministers who were willing to tackle any problem except financial reform. Throughout his life, Louis preferred the diversion of the royal hunt or the company of his favourite mistress, Madame de Pompadour, who was unjustly credited as the real power behind the throne. Though Louis was, at times, blessed with good intentions, he lacked the ability and inclination to translate them into policy. His often-quoted prophetic words, "after me, the deluge," provide a fitting comment on the condition of France at the conclusion of his reign.

LOUIS XVI

Louis XVI (1774–1794) was no more suited to be king than was his grandfather. He shared the Bourbon enthusiasm for the hunt but also had such an interest in construction and physical labour that he often jumped in and helped workers move paving blocks and girders. It has been said that he would have been much happier as a locksmith or carpenter than a monarch at court. Louis was a simple, shy, and moral man who was dominated by a wife he adored and who never seemed certain about what to do next. He prided himself on being honest and frugal and the people of France seemed to respond to his humble dignity. No matter how much criticism was levelled at the government and the system of entrenched privilege, Louis himself was popular with his people until the end.

MARIE ANTOINETTE

His young wife, nineteen-year-old Marie Antoinette enjoyed no such honour. As one of Maria Theresa's sixteen children, Marie Antoinette's marriage to Louis was arranged to consolidate the alliance between France and Austria. Yet, it only served as a reminder of a foreign influence at court that was greatly resented. Marie Antoinette was irresponsible, frivolous, enjoyed parties, and lived an extravagant life. As a result, she was easy to dislike and, though falsely accused of buying a diamond necklace valued at 1.6 million livres, Marie Antoinette could not shake her reputation as "Madame Deficit." Her manipulation of the much-admired Louis only increased the outrage of peasant and courtier against her.

TURGOT

Louis began his reign intent on doing the best for his people by ruling as an enlightened despot. The choice of Turgot as controller of the treasury seemed like a good start. Turgot had already distinguished himself as an administrator and his unfinished outline, a *Discourse on Universal History*, set forth the idea of progress that influenced the writing of Condorcet. In keeping with the enlightened attitudes of the era, Turgot attempted to reduce the chaotic restrictions on trade and substitute a mild tax on all landowners in place of the traditional corvée or roadwork. By this time, however, the nobles had regained much of their formal political power and, along with the clergy, were in no mood to give up their exemption from taxation. Although Marie Antoinette wanted Turgot sent to the Bastille, Louis settled for his dismissal after only two years in office. Turgot left with this famous warning, "Never forget sire, that it was

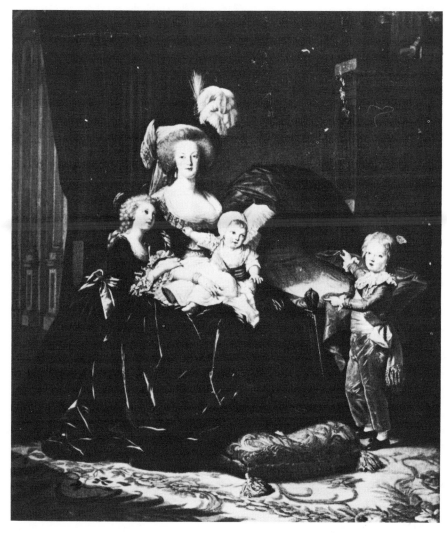

This portrait of Marie Antoinette with her children was painted by Elizabeth Vigée-Lebrun.

weakness that brought the head of Charles I to the block.'' He added that Louis was regarded as a weak king.

Louis's weakness, or at least his poor judgement, was clearly apparent when he could not resist the urging of Marie Antoinette and his advisers to enter the American Revolution on the side of the United States. France was still bitter about the losses suffered at British hands in the Seven Years' War and when the Thirteen Colonies proclaimed the Declaration of Independence in 1776, the opportunity for revenge was open. War supplies were sent almost immediately and, when success seemed possible after two years of struggle, a formal alliance between France and the United States was completed. The price of

THE AMERICAN REVOLUTION

British defeat, however, was 1 billion livres to a French economy already strained to the breaking point. Of equal importance was the democratic spirit that spread among French soldiers like the Marquis de Lafayette, who fought with the Americans and brought back their ideas to France. If the English colonies were willing to revolt because a tax *could* be applied, it seemed obvious that the oppressively taxed French lower classes had a much stronger case for either reform or rebellion against their central government. Enlightened ideas about the natural rights of humans were no longer just the pleasant fodder of discussion in a Paris salon. They were the rationale for a successful revolution.

THE FINANCIAL CRISIS

The financial condition of France was approaching the crisis point. To the people, the visible symbol of wealth and waste was the court at Versailles which included among expenses the care and maintenance of two hundred carriages and two thousand horses, and over five hundred personal servants for Marie Antoinette. Actually, the court of Louis XVI was trimmed down from those of his predecessors and accounted for only 6 to 8 percent of government revenues. The major culprit was the century of wars that pushed the total national debt to over 4 billion livres. It required over half the revenue collected each year just to pay the interest on the amount owing. After 1783, the skillful Charles Calonne became controller general and he approached the issue of financial reform with enlightened ideas similar to those of Turgot. The nobility and the clergy had to pay taxes if France was to avoid repudiation of the debt and a loss of confidence from foreign moneylenders. Louis took Calonne's proposals to a special Assembly of Notables, made up of the very privileged classes that Calonne wanted to tax. When the assembly rejected Calonne's plan, Louis soon dismissed him. The king then personally tried to gain acceptance of a uniform tax on landed property, but the Parlement of Paris, followed quickly by the parlements of the provinces that were dominated by the nobles, took up a common refrain. They demanded that Louis call the Estates General.

The Estates General and the Political Crisis

Louis had not supported any of his ministers against the increased power of the nobility. The nobles, through the parlements they controlled, pressed Louis to call the Estates General because they believed they would control the proceedings and preserve their traditional privileges. This seemed like a safe assumption. The Estates General consisted of three houses including the First Estate of the clergy, the Second Estate of the nobility, and the Third Estate which

VOTING IN THE ESTATES GENERAL

represented the rest of the population. Each estate met and voted separately, which meant that as long as the clergy and the nobility worked together, they could win a two to one majority. This would block any action proposed by the Third Estate that did not meet with their approval. Little serious thought was given to the fact that the Third Estate represented 98 percent of the people and that the system of voting by estate might be seen as unfair and unacceptable.

The Estates General had not been called since 1614 largely because the power of the king had been so dominant. It was almost impossible for the nobles to realize that the attempt to assert their influence over a weak king would mark the first important action of the French Revolution.

Many divisions existed within the First and Second Estates. The First Estate was made up of about one hundred thirty-five thousand members (.5 percent of the population) that reflected the hierarchy of the Church. Archbishops, bishops, and leaders of monastic orders, who often had ties with the nobility, were regarded as the upper clergy. They had a vested interest in protecting the wealth of the Church which, as the largest landowner in France, depended on tithes and endowments for revenue and exemption from taxation to keep it. The lower clergy included monks, friars, and parish priests who were often sympathetic to the people, but tied to the cause of their superiors. There were at least nine major distinctions of wealth and status within the nobility of the Second Estate, which numbered about four hundred thousand (1.5 percent of the population) in 1789. They, too, were exempt from taxation even though the nobles of the higher orders were the most able to pay. The bond that tied them to the clergy was the need to maintain the privileges that often sustained their wealth and social prestige.

The most diverse of the social orders in France was the Third Estate, which contained an unending list of occupations spread over 24.5 million people. Among its ranks were the peasants, who made up about 90 percent of the population, urban workers, and, most importantly, the bourgeoisie. Throughout the eighteenth century, the economic situation of the peasant gradually improved, although life for city workers was often appalling, and pockets of extreme poverty could be found in the countryside. Conditions generally took a turn for the worse in the 1780s. In times of bad harvests and increased prices, the nobility used its increased influence to reaffirm forgotten privileges and they collected their feudal dues with greater efficiency, as did the Church with its tithes. As customary dues increased along with direct taxation, the downtrodden members of the Third Estate came to resent the social superiority of the nobles and the arrogant political power they exercised through local parlements.

Perhaps the most significant element of the Third Estate was the bourgeoisie, a loosely fitted group of merchants, lawyers, writers, doctors, and manufacturers. The nobles slowly weeded them from the favoured positions they had held under Louis XIV. Although most members of the bourgeoisie enjoyed a relatively comfortable life, they did not enjoy the social status or political influence to which they believed their wealth and wit entitled them. It was among this group that the ideas of the Enlightenment, with its stress on knowledge, natural rights, and humanitarianism, firmly took hold. The application of reason to the social, economic, and political order of the ancien régime exposed the folly of ignorance, privilege, and callousness that the Enlightenment hoped to overcome.

THE FIRST ESTATE

THE SECOND ESTATE

THE THIRD ESTATE

THE BOURGEOISIE

The New System Demanded by the Third Estate

one vote for each *representative*

The Established System
one vote for each *estate*

Clergy 135 000   Nobility 400 000   Third Estate 25 000 000

□ = 100 000 people

The New and the Established Systems of Voting Power in France.

ABBÉ SIEYES

In 1788, Louis XVI announced that the Estates General would meet the following year according to the rules laid down in 1614. This caused an uproar from the Third Estate because the clergy and the nobility could always outvote them even though the Third Estate represented the overwhelming majority of the population. The most famous of the many pamphlets that were written in protest came from the hand of the philosopher and clergyman, Abbé Sieyes, who crystalized the feeling of the masses in the following words:

1. What is the Third Estate? Everything.
2. What has it been in the political order up to the present? Nothing.
3. What does it demand? To become something . . .

The Third Estate . . . includes everything that belongs to the nation; and everything that is not the Third Estate cannot be regarded as being the nation. What is the Third Estate? Everything.

In the spring of 1789, forty thousand local meetings were held and each was instructed by the government to elect deputies to the Estates General and to draw up a list of grievances known as *cahiers*. By the time the deputies were elected, the Third Estate had won the right to seat as many representatives as the combined total of the clergy and nobles. The elections produced 300 deputies from each of the First and Second Estates and 648 deputies, mostly from the bourgeoisie, to speak for the Third Estate. At the same time, the *cahiers* produced a host of demands that included a more equitable system of taxation, the abolition of feudal dues and customs, and a constitution. The Third Estate, in a desire to increase its influence and to eliminate the privileges of the clergy and nobles, wanted the three orders to sit together and vote by head. The clergy and the nobles understandably wanted to sit separately in the traditional manner to maintain their two to one majority over the Third Estate and therefore the privileges they had long enjoyed. All of the *cahiers* expressed what was probably a genuine feeling of loyalty to the king, but they were equally opposed to the exercise of his absolute power. At this point, no one in any class was thinking in terms of revolution, but everyone in the Third Estate was expecting change of some kind.

CAHIERS

An economic depression that paralleled the political crisis only served to stimulate the anticipation for reform. As if forewarning of events to come, nature wrought hail, wind, and drought upon France in 1788, which led to widespread crop failure and a shortage of bread. The coldest winter of the century froze the Seine River and prevented the proper distribution of what grain there was to Paris and the countryside. This doubled and sometimes quadrupled the price of bread and resulted in the poor spending up to 80 percent of their income on food. Hunger drove the destitute to food riots in Paris and other communities on several occasions. At the very moment that agriculture hit hard times, French manufacturers of textiles and hardware were faced by a flood of imports from England as a result of government policies that lowered tariffs. This increased unemployment to dangerous levels and produced a charged atmosphere receptive to reform that might improve the lot of the common people who suffered. Ideas for such reform sprang from the pamphlets and letters circulated by clubs that developed either from bourgeois literary societies in towns throughout France, or by groups created to meet the present crisis. A network of these political "cells" moulded public opinion on behalf of the Third Estate at the very moment the elections for the Estates General were being held. These clubs became the very fibre of the demand for change.

ECONOMIC DEPRESSION

POLITICAL CLUBS

The Estates General had no meeting place. It was finally decided to meet in a series of lesser rooms and salons at Versailles so that the king and queen could maintain their social routine. Would the voting take place by separate meetings of the First, Second, and Third Estates or by a single body voting by a head count of all deputies? That was the crucial question. When the controller general, Jacques Necker, failed to deliver reform in the direction of the already

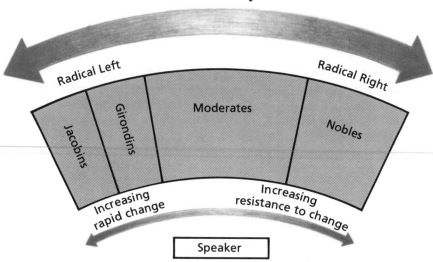

National Assembly 1789

Radical Left

Radical Right

Jacobins

Girondins

Moderates

Nobles

Increasing rapid change

Increasing resistance to change

Speaker

The National Assembly, 1789.

THE NATIONAL ASSEMBLY

THE TENNIS COURT OATH

popular slogans "equality and liberty" in his opening address to the Third Estate on 4 May 1789, the issue was hotly debated for over five weeks.

Instead of pressuring for further advantage, the nobles now perceived a greater threat to their influence and status from the widespread expectation of reform. They closed ranks with Louis to oppose the efforts of the Third Estate to create a single body of voting deputies. Finally joined by some of the minor clergy and liberal nobles sympathetic to reform, the Third Estate proclaimed itself the **National Assembly** on 17 June 1789, believing that it was the true representative of the nation. In response, Louis orderd the meeting hall used by the Third Estate closed for repairs. Under the leadership of Mirabeau, the National Assembly reconvened in an indoor tennis court at Versailles on 20 June and, after distress and division, swore the famous "Tennis Court Oath." They vowed never to separate until a constitution was established for the nation. By this time, the entire clergy had been won over to the National Assembly and more of the nobles were wavering. At first, Louis tried to veto the decision taken by the Third Estate and commanded the estates to meet separately as originally instructed. On 27 June, the irresolute Louis reversed his stand and officially blessed the merger of the three estates to form a National Assembly of twelve hundred deputies.

This seemed to mark the triumph of moderate reform that would make France a limited monarchy that operated in accordance with a written constitution. The political crisis had apparently been resolved in favour of the Third

Estate, led by the oratory of the bourgeoisie who made up the majority of its deputies. The first two weeks of July, however, would bring a decisive change to the direction of France and unleash forces that would eventually alter the fabric of Western civilization.

The French Revolution: Moderate Phase (1789–1792)

The joy that surrounded Louis's reluctant acceptance of the National Assembly proved short lived and the course of events soon got out of control. Louis ordered in troops from the provinces around Paris and Versailles, a move that has often been interpreted as royal preparation to force the submission of the Third Estate. Certainly rumours to that effect quickly spread among the crowds of the city, but it is not clear that this was Louis's intention. In any case, the hungry Paris mobs, with feelings running high against the nobility, were stirred by the flood of revolutionary pamphlets hitting the streets and by the rousing oratory of people like the duke of Orleans and Camille Desmoulins. Paris erupted almost daily during the first half of July, usually because people needed food. In their desperation they easily were moved to violence by the inflammatory words of any speaker.

THE PARIS MOB

One of the key elements in this charged atmosphere was the royal army. The foreign troops under the king's command, who were mostly Swiss, were trustworthy and could be relied upon to carry out their orders. The French troops, however, could not be shielded from the political pamphlets of the so-called patriots voicing the need for reform. Many soldiers mutineed and there was little that their aristocratic officers could do. Clearly, without the support of the army, the bourgeois leaders of the National Assembly could not impose their ideas for reform upon the king.

THE ROYAL ARMY

When the arrival of royal troops in Paris was followed by the dismissal of the popular controller, Necker, it appeared as if Louis was immediately going to roll back the gains made by the National Assembly. This indiscreet action welded together the divided elements of protest, and chaos in the common cause against arbitrary royal authority reigned throughout the city. On 14 July 1789, after seizing weapons from the Invalides, the Paris mob stormed the Bastille, the symbol of royal absolutism that caged the suffering victims of the lettres de cachet. Although the old feudal fortress surrendered without violence on the promise of safety for its guards, the mob went wild and only after several hours of fury, two hundred deaths, and the mutilation of several corpses did the passion of the people subside. Surprisingly, only four forgers, two mad-men, and a common criminal were actually found in the prison, but the event was hailed as a heroic triumph for freedom over the evil forces of tyranny throughout France and all of Europe. The French still celebrate their national holiday on 14 July.

STORMING OF THE BASTILLE

The French Revolution–Moderate Phase (1789–1792)

1788	August 8	Louis XVI summons a meeting of the Estates General
1789	January	Abbé Sieyes leads demand for reform of voting procedure of the Estates General
	February–March	Lists of grievances known as *cahiers* are drawn up by the three estates
	May 5	Estates General assembles at Versailles
	June 17	The Third Estate proclaims itself the National Assembly
	June 20	The National Assembly takes the Tennis Court Oath
	July 14	Paris mob storms the Bastille
	July 17	Louis XVI returns to Paris with the National Guard and accepts a cockade of red, white, and blue–the tricolour of the Revolution
	July–August	Peasants experience the ''Great Fear''
	August 4	National Assembly abolishes feudalism
	August 26	The Assembly passes the Declaration of the Rights of Man and Citizen
	October 5	Women march on Versailles
	October 6	Louis XVI agrees to move the royal family to the Tuileries Palace in Paris
	October 20	National Assembly moves to Paris
	November 2	National Assembly confiscates Church lands
1790	June 19	National Assembly abolishes the practice of hereditary nobility and respective titles
	July 12	Civil Constitution of the Clergy is proclaimed
1791	June 20	Royal family's flight to Varennes fails
	August 27	Emperor of Austria and the king of Prussia issue the Declaration of Pillnitz
	September 3	The National Constituent Assembly proclaims the Constitution of 1791
	October 1	Legislative Assembly holds first meeting under the new constitution
1792	April 20	Legislative Assembly declares war on Austria; Prussia joins Austria against France
	July 25	Manifesto of the duke of Brunswick is issued
	August 10	Paris Commune seizes power by killing the king's Swiss guards at the Tuileries
	September 2–7	The ''September Massacres'' occur
	September 21	The National Convention abolishes the monarchy; France is declared a Republic

With the rebels in control of Paris, a new government, the **Commune**, was established at the Hôtel de Ville (the town hall) and a new citizen army was created. Known as the **National Guard**, it was commanded by the liberal noble the Marquis de Lafayette, veteran of the American Revolution and friend of George Washington. After some hesitation, Louis returned to Paris on 17 July 1789 with the National Guard. Standing in front of a large crowd, Louis accepted a cockade of the blue and red colours of Paris to which Lafayette added the white of the king. The *tricolore* became the emblem of the French Revolution and Louis wore this badge on his hat as he visited the National Assembly at Versailles to demonstrate his acceptance of the new order.

THE PARIS COMMUNE

Just as the stones of the Bastille would eventually be scattered over the French countryside, the Revolution spread to the provinces. Paris was used as a model for the creation of thousands of local republics that overthrew the bastilles of the nobility in their towns. Real and imagined threats of royal troops and hired bands of thugs spread rapidly by rumour. This created the "Great Fear" of late July in which peasants, armed with pitchforks and scythes, ransacked country houses, seized food, destroyed records of their feudal dues, and brought government to a standstill. News of violence in the provinces quickly reached Versailles and the National Assembly realized that the grievances of the peasants had to be redressed if order was to be restored. On 4 August 1789, amid frenzied enthusiasm, the privileged classes rose and renounced their traditional rights with such thoroughness that feudalism and the ancien régime were abolished. There were no longer any lords and serfs but only French citizens and the nation of France. In a statement of intent for shaping the constitution that was to follow, the Assembly issued the Declaration of the Rights of Man and the Citizen on 26 August 1789. Based on English and American precedents, the bourgeois document captured the ideals of the Enlightenment in the stirring words, "Men are born, and always continue, free and equal in respect of their rights." Among these natural rights were the rights of "Liberty, Property, Security, and Resistance of Oppression." Law was defined as "the expression of the will of the community" while the nation, above any individual, was "the source of all sovereignty." Among other rights proclaimed, the equality of taxation, equality before the law, freedom of speech and the press, and religious toleration embodied the highest aspirations of moderate reform.

END OF THE ANCIEN RÉGIME

DECLARATION OF THE RIGHTS OF MAN AND THE CITIZEN

The August decrees catered to two different interests in French society. Sacred to the peasants was the abolition of feudalism which represented everything they hoped to gain and created a willingness to turn to any group or anyone who could preserve their rights in the new order. The Declaration of Rights reflected the idealistic, even naive outlook of the bourgeoisie who seemed to believe that proclamations alone could solve the problems of France. Such expectations were raised that disappointment was bound to follow.

MARCH OF THE WOMEN

By September, order had been restored to the countryside, but Louis fumbled his way into another upsurge of violence before the year was out. Characteristically, he hesitated in accepting the abolition of feudal privilege and the Declaration of Rights. He also held a royal military banquet at Versailles at the very moment that hunger again ruled the streets of Paris, and by 5 October another crisis had been reached. Parisians organized a **March of Women** so their cries of hunger could be heard at Versailles, but it turned into an unruly mob of men, women, and children by the time it reached the palace. Lafayette and the National Guard followed them in an attempt to maintain order, but all promises were broken the following day when the mob rushed into the palace. Peace was restored only when Louis agreed to move from Versailles to the palace of the Tuileries. The Parisians chanted that they had brought ''the baker, the baker's wife, and the baker's child'' home to roost. The National Assembly returned to Paris ten days later. Lafayette and the National Guard could not control the voice of protest that often erupted into violence with little notice. Now the National Assembly was under the critical eye of Parisian crowds who regularly attended the public sessions cheering when the most extreme revolutionary ideas were introduced and jeering anything that smacked of moderation.

ASSIGNATS

During the next two years of relative calm, the National Assembly hammered out a new constitution. In the meantime, it had to deal with the pressing issue of financial chaos that became even worse when the direct and indirect taxes of the ancien régime were swept aside. The single tax on land and income issued by the Assembly fell well short of the required revenue. Under the direction of Mirabeau, the Assembly nationalized the extensive landholdings of the Church and used them to back the printing of paper money known as **assignats**. Though successful in the short term, the temptation of government to print more money than its collateral warranted gradually prevailed and the value of the assignats fell sharply.

CIVIL CONSTITUTION OF THE CLERGY

Of even greater consequence was the passage of the Civil Constitution of the Clergy by the Assembly in July of 1790. With Church lands now confiscated, the Civil Constitution brought the Church under state control and provided for the payment of the clergy from public funds. Bishops and priests were to be elected by the people rather than appointed by Rome, and the clergy was required to take an oath of loyalty to uphold the new constitution and the Civil Constitution of the Clergy. Most of the bishops and priests refused to swear loyalty to the new order while Pope Pius VI condemned the whole process and the stripping of papal authority. Although the binding of Church and state was in line with the thinking of the Enlightenment, the common people, driven more by emotion than reason, were seriously divided. With grave misgivings, Louis reluctantly accepted the Civil Constitution and then determined to leave France and seek foreign assistance to check the increasing excess of the Revolution.

Since July of 1789, many nobles, known as **émigrés**, had left France to seek aid from foreign rulers to work against the Revolution. Louis resolved to do the same and on 20 June 1791, he and Marie Antoinette slipped by the guards at the Tuileries and fled by stagecoach disguised as a valet and governess. Almost within sight of his goal, Louis was recognized at Varrennes and brought back as a prisoner to Paris. Unfortunately, Louis had left a letter proclaiming his belief in absolute rule and his intention of leading a loyal army of émigrés back to France to destroy the Revolution and reestablish the ancien régime. The flight to Varrennes discredited Louis in the eyes of the people, but he was kept on because the majority still believed that a constitutional monarchy was the only acceptable form of government.

FLIGHT TO VARRENNES

Meanwhile, the National Assembly had been working on a new constitution and had become known as the **Constituent Assembly** in honour of this purpose. Most of the reforms proposed reflected the bourgeois interests of the deputies. To replace the Estates General, a new, elected body known as the **Legislative Assembly** was to be created. Although the need for equality was proclaimed in the Declaration of Rights, the franchise was restricted to those who paid a certain amount of tax. Clearly, the bourgeois deputies wanted only those changes that would ensure their political leadership rather than that of the lower classes of society they originally claimed to represent. The minimum tax qualification limited the vote to about fifty thousand men–equality made no pretence about women–which meant that wealth rather than the ancestry of the ancien régime became the measure of political power. To offset the charge of centralization made against absolute monarchy, France was divided into eighty-three departments subdivided into communes and cantons that were run by elected officials. In fact, too much power was given to local government which hindered the operation of the entire political system.

THE CONSTITUENT ASSEMBLY

The new constitution was issued in September of 1791 and, with its task complete, the Constituent Assembly dissolved itself. In an unselfish gesture, the members of the Assembly made themselves ineligible for reelection. This eliminated those with the experience needed to run the Legislative Assembly that, in effect, was thrown into the shifting and difficult tides of the Revolution. Although Louis vowed to uphold the new constitution, his attempt to flee the country clearly showed that he could not be trusted. France now had a constitutional monarchy with a monarch who did not believe in its principles. This greatly reduced any chance of success.

THE NEW CONSTITUTION

Once the euphoria of 1789 subsided, each change in the Revolution created new problems. In that emotional year, hundreds of political clubs were organized throughout France to discuss the course of the Revolution. The most famous, as well as the most important, was the Friends of the Constitution, later changed to Friends of Equality and Liberty, and better known as the **Jacobin Club**, after the former Jacobin monastery where it met in Paris. Initially embracing a wide spectrum of reforming opinion from the Parisian middle class, the

THE JACOBIN CLUB

Jacobin Club became more extreme when membership widened in 1792 to include the poorer classes. Over four hundred affiliated branches sprang up in the provinces including the French-controlled island of Corsica, where Napoleon Bonaparte became a founding member.

THE GIRONDINS

Within the National Assembly, a faction of the Jacobin Club, known as the **Girondins** (after the department of Gironde near Bordeaux), became a powerful voice. The Girondins genuinely wanted to preserve the progress of the Revolution and became convinced that the country could only be united by a successful war that exposed the enemies of their cause. Following Louis's attempted escape, Emperor Leopold II of Austria, brother of Marie Antoinette, and the king of Prussia issued the Declaration of Pillnitz which threatened intervention against the Revolution if the powers of Europe could act in unison. This and related agitation by the émigré nobles drove the Girondins to argue that the Revolution in France was not safe until similar ideas had triumphed across Europe. On a less honourable level, the bourgeois Girondins were supported by wealthy business and shipping interests who felt that such a war would yield increased production, commerce, and profit. When Leopold's sudden death placed his more conservative brother, Francis, on the Austrian throne, the Girondins won the day. In April of 1792, the Assembly declared

REVOLUTIONARY FRANCE AT WAR

war against Austria and proclaimed it a "war against kings, peace with all peoples." Prussia joined in against France soon afterward.

The inadequately prepared French army, weakened by the disappearance of its émigré officers, suffered a series of defeats in the early going. It appeared that Louis might be saved by his foreign friends as enemy troops were soon on French soil heading towards the capital. Pandemonium ruled in Paris. Gripped by an upsurge of nationalism and marching to the stirring words of the "Marseillaise"–later to become the national anthem–French patriots pushed on against the foreign invaders and turned against their king. It was believed that monarchists of any stripe were plotting to overthrow the Revolution. The Paris mob broke into the Tuileries on 20 June, ridiculed Louis and forced him to wear the red cap of liberty. Hearing of the insult, the Austrian duke of Brunswick issued a manifesto warning that if the king and his family were harmed the people of Paris would suffer a terrible punishment. Instead of helping the royal

THE BRUNSWICK MANIFESTO

cause, however, the Brunswick Manifesto led directly to the fall of constitutional monarchy.

The anger of the Paris mob, which had been quiet since Lafayette and the National Guard fired on a mass demonstration the previous year, reached a new peak as patriotic feelings swelled and food prices again became extremely high. Crowds of angry **sans-culottes**, so-called because they wore the long, loose pants of the Parisian worker, poured through the streets around the palace on the night of 9 August 1792. Convinced that Louis had given the army's

DANTON

battle plans to the enemy, the extremists, led by Georges-Jacques Danton, engineered a military coup the following morning. When the Tuileries palace was

This monument in Luzern, Switzerland was commissioned by the French government to honour the Swiss guards who died defending Louis XVI.

invaded on this occasion, the Swiss guards were all killed. Louis and the royal family sought refuge in the Legislative Assembly, but arrived only to be taken prisoner. With constitutional monarchy at an end, the Assembly, in desperation, declared an election for a **National Convention** to draw up yet another constitution. As the Prussian army neared Paris, chaos and fear guided the mob. For six days in the "September Massacres," Jean-Paul Marat led the extremists in a raid of prisons and jails where upwards of two thousand people, including nobles, priests, prostitutes, and criminals were accused of counter-revolutionary activity and were indiscriminantly murdered. On 20 September 1792, the same day that the Prussians were halted at Valmy, the National Convention held its first meeting, and the following day France was declared a Republic.

THE NATIONAL CONVENTION

THE SEPTEMBER MASSACRES

The French Revolution: Radical Phase (1792–1794)

The summer chaos of 1792 converted the Revolution from moderate change, represented by constitutional monarchy, to radical ambition, as defined by the new Republic. Genoa, Venice, the Dutch Republic, and the Swiss Confederation were the only other republics in Europe and they were in a state of decline or stagnation. The American experiment, though inspirational, was still ironing out its own problems. But France was the greatest nation in Europe. It stamped the very word "republic" as a signal for revolution in the name of "liberty, equality, and fraternity" that easily could be turned against the absolute monarchies of other European states. French victories in the fall of 1792, due more to the enemies' mistrust of each other than French military genius, made the spread of the Revolution a believable idea.

The French Revolution–Radical Phase (1792–1794)

1792	September 21	The National Convention abolishes the monarchy; France is declared a Republic
1793	January 21	Louis XVI is executed
	February 23	Food riots break out in Paris
	March 10	Revolutionary Tribunal is established to try enemies of the Revolution
	April 6	Committee of Public Safety is established
	May 21	Jacobins begin attack on the National Convention
	June 2	Jacobins demand expulsion of Girondins at the Convention
	June	The Reign of Terror begins
	July 27	Robespierre joins the Committee of Public Safety
	August 23	Conscription is introduced in an effort to mobilize the people to defend the Republic and the Revolution; the *Levée en Masse* is called
	September 17	The Law of Suspects is introduced
	September 29	The Law of General Maximum is introduced
	October 16	Marie Antoinette is executed
	October 31	Girondins are executed
1794	April 5	Danton and his supporters are executed
	July 28–29	Robespierre and his followers are executed; the Republic of Virtue ends

The Jacobin Club, which controlled the hastily elected National Convention, had become divided. Although the Girondins had pushed for war, they were horrified at the senseless killings of the September Massacres. Their efforts to place the Revolution on a more moderate course resulted in their expulsion from the Jacobin Club and left momentum and power with more radical elements. The critical question centred on the fate of the king. There was no doubt of Louis's treason, but, by delaying the trial, the Girondins wanted to avoid an execution that might stir additional foreign hostility against France.

THE "MOUNTAIN"

The more radical Jacobins, known as "the Mountain" because they sat in the highest seats of the National Convention's amphitheatre, demanded the king's head. Following months of debate, a trial was held in which the final vote in favour of execution was won by the Mountain by 387 to 344. On 21 January 1793, at what is now the Place de la Concorde, "Citizen Louis Capet," as the king came to be called, stepped up to the guillotine. With a dignity reminiscent of Charles I of England, Louis proclaimed, "I die innocent of all crimes imputed to me. I pardon the authors of my death, and pray God that the blood you are about to shed will never fall upon France." His head was raised to the cries of a cheering crowd seconds later.

With the death of Louis, the tide temporarily turned against the young Republic. Eager to extend earlier victories, the National Convention declared war against Holland and England in February of 1793, and the coalition against France was joined by Spain soon after. France was not ready to take on the combined powers of Europe, and the situation was made worse by a monarchical rebellion in La Vendée and food riots in Paris that resulted from yet another round of high prices and low supply. At this difficult moment, the crowds that engulfed the Convention hall were turned in favour of the Jacobin Mountain by the politicians of Paris. When they could be found the Girondin leaders were arrested and guillotined in what amounted to a continuation of the September Massacres. Faced with danger from within and without, the Convention authorized a twelve-member Committee of Public Safety that was to rule with almost dictatorial power until the emergency passed. A democratic constitution that was drafted by the Mountain was never put into practice. Policing powers were given to the Committee of General Security while the Revolutionary Tribunal tried counter-revolutionaries according to the "law of suspects" with little regard for legal procedures.

The committees and the Tribunal were the administration and instrument of what came to be known as the **Reign of Terror**. From June 1793 to July 1794 hundreds of thousands of people were imprisoned and upwards of forty thousand guillotined in the name of saving the Revolution from traitors. Although victims ranged from Marie Antoinette to the peasants and workers of the street, only 15 percent came from the nobility and clergy. The leading spirit, whose name became synonymous with the Terror, was Maximilien Robespierre, a member of the Committee of Public Safety who had led the Mountain in the earlier attack on the Girondins. For Robespierre, the purpose of the Terror was clear and desperate:

> . . . To establish and consolidate democracy, to achieve the peaceful rule of constitutional laws, we must finish the war of liberty against tyranny . . . We must annihilate the enemies of the Republic at home and abroad or else we shall perish. . . .

Simply put, the Terror was justice, "swift, severe, and inflexible" and, while its methods were despotic, Robespierre believed that the "government of the Revolution is the despotism of liberty against tyranny."

The real threat to the Revolution came from the armies amassing on the borders of France. To deal with that situation, the Committee of Public Safety took decisive action that had a lasting impact on the nature of modern warfare. The entire nation of France was mobilized behind the war effort in the *Levée en*

EXECUTION OF LOUIS XVI

THE COMMITTEE OF PUBLIC SAFETY

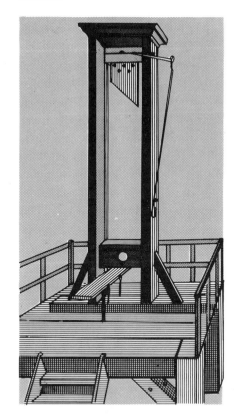

"Madame Guillotine."

Masse of 23 August 1793. Able-bodied, single men between eighteen and twenty-five years of age had to serve in combat; married men had to "forge arms and transport provisions;" women had to "make tents and clothing and . . . serve in hospitals;" while children had to "turn old linen into lint." Even the elderly were ordered to go to public places and preach the virtues of the Republic to encourage enthusiasm for the war. The ranks of the army swelled to eight hundred fifty thousand by the spring of 1794, which made it the largest in European history. A young soldier and supporter of the Jacobins, Napoleon Bonaparte, displayed his talent for organization and rose to the rank of brigadier-general by the age of twenty-four, but it was the older commanders who led the attack against the divided European coalition. By late 1793, France had pushed back the enemy and was on the march to its "natural frontiers" of the Rhine, the Alps, and the Pyrenees, a territory that exceeded the conquests of the Sun King, Louis XIV. The success of the *Levée en Masse* meant that the nations of Europe would eventually be forced to either respond in kind or suffer defeat on the battlefield. As nation mobilized against nation, the scale of warfare was greatly augmented and the tidy conflicts of the eighteenth century, where soldiers fought soldiers while civilians went about their business, would be changed forever. Although it served the Revolution, the *Levée en masse* was the first step towards the horrible, total war of the twentieth century.

With the guillotine greatly reducing the number of outspoken opponents of the Revolution, and the success of French armies on the battlefield, Robespierre attempted to establish the **Republic of Virtue**. This was a sincere but misguided attempt to reshape life in France. Robespierre believed that the Terror was necessary to enforce Rousseau's idea of the general will–the expression of the wishes of the people. Since Rousseau did not explain how the general will was to be determined, in practice it became the judgements and moral values of Robespierre and a few key advisers on the Committee of Public Safety. The public executions organized for the bloodthirsty crowds of Paris were meant to convey the seriousness of his purpose. In place of Christianity, which was regarded as counter-revolutionary, Robespierre launched and encouraged belief in the "Supreme Being of Nature" in a formal ceremony in June of 1794. Virtue was seen in the replacement of *Citoyen* and *Citoyenne* (citizen) for *Monsieur* and *Madame* as forms of social address. The king, queen, and jack of spades were replaced with figures of the sans-culottes, soldiers, Rousseau, and famous personalities from Republican Rome. Of more lasting impact was the introduction of the metric system of weights and measures, based on the rational organization of the decimal system, and worked out by a commission headed by Joseph Lagrange. Another creative twist was the adoption of a revolutionary calendar that eliminated saints' days and Sundays and declared national holidays commemorating events of the Revolution: 14 July (1789)–the storming of the Bastille; 10 August (1792)–the overthrow of the monarchy; 21 January (1793)–the execution of Louis; and 21 May (1793)–the seizing of control of the National Convention by the Jacobins and Paris Commune.

Thermidorian Reaction and the Directory (1794–1799)

1794	August	Machinery of the Terror is dismantled; the Convention follows a middle path between radicals and moderates
1795	April–July	Peace is made with Prussia, Holland, and Spain
	May	Sans-culottes march on the National Convention demanding "bread and the Constitution of 1793"
	August 22	Constitution of 1795 is proclaimed
	October 6	Napoleon suppresses royalist riots in Paris with "whiff of grapeshot" The Directory governs France until 1799
1799	November 9	Napoleon overthrows French government in coup d'état

The fear generated by the machinery of the Terror, however, eventually overtook its creator. As a symbol of the end of the ancien régime, the execution of Marie Antoinette had at least been understood. When the same fate befell first the Girondin leaders, then the radical sans-culotte Jacques Herbert and his Commune followers, and finally the more conservative Jacobin Georges-Jacques Danton, it was clear that no one was safe. One of the few brave enough to take action against the Terror was a former supporter of the Revolution, Charlotte Corday. Believing that Marat was a key figure in the Terror, she sneaked into his room and stabbed him to death while he was bathing in mineral water! Yet Robespierre was not overthrown by popular protest. His attempt to control food prices and the ruthless approach used by commissioners to requisition supplies from the countryside were resented, but most people remained silent in case they became the victims of "Madame Guillotine." The turning point came when the other members of the Committee of Public Safety became convinced that *they* were soon to be executed. In a carefully designed plot on the ninth of Thermidor (27 July 1794), Robespierre was denounced at a meeting of the National Convention and, in the next two days, the "tyrant" and ninety-two of his followers were beheaded. So ended the Republic of Virtue.

CHARLOTTE CORDAY

OVERTHROW OF ROBESPIERRE

Thermidorian Reaction and the Directory (1794–1799)

With the death of Robespierre, opposition from all walks of life now voiced its disapproval of the year of bloodshed. Former revolutionary zealots now denied any connection with the Republic of Virtue, but many Jacobins were murdered by those who had suffered from the crimes committed in the name of the Revolution. In what has been termed the **Thermidorian Reaction**, the machinery of the Terror, including the Committee of Public Safety, the Tribunal, and the Jacobin clubs were dismantled. A surge of freedom was felt in the press and the arts, as knee breeches returned and several Catholic churches were reopened. Many of those imprisoned by the Jacobins were released while

THERMIDORIAN REACTION

émigrés flocked to their homeland by the thousands. The withdrawal of price controls, however, increased prices and precipitated a march by the sans-culottes on the National Convention in May 1795. Now out of favour, their protests were muted by the Convention, while the Paris Commune, so much a part of the unpredictable nature of the Revolution, was finally dissolved.

The National Convention drew up another constitution that was proclaimed on 22 August 1795. It reflected the interests of the bourgeois middle class by making property qualifications so high that only twenty thousand men–less than half the number of the 1791 constitution–were enfranchised. Clearly, democracy and the chaos of the mob were viewed with suspicion. Legislative power was given to a Council of Ancients and a Council of Five Hundred who appointed an executive **Directory** of five men to serve for five years. Royalists, as well as city workers, were opposed to this plan because the bourgeois leaders decreed that two-thirds of the new councils had to come from members of the existing Convention. Plans among royalist sympathizers in the provinces to place Louis XVI's son on the throne ended prematurely with the boy's death at the age of ten in June of 1795. Then, Louis XVI's brother, exiled in Italy, issued a declaration stating his intention to regain the throne and reestablish the ancien régime. The Directory, buoyed by popular opinion, resolved to prevent the return of the monarchy at all costs. In October of 1795, royalist riots in Paris that involved twenty-five thousand protesters were broken up by four thousand troops led by the former Jacobin, Napoleon Bonaparte, who knew how to organize troops and use artillery. His famous "whiff of grapeshot" dispersed the Parisian mob and showed that the army was now the key to political power. With the royalist "right" in temporary abeyance, the Directory was now faced with a challenge from the working class "left." In 1796, François Babeuf, known as "Gracchus" after the populist leaders of ancient Rome, organized a "Conspiracy of Equals" on behalf of the labourers and poor craftsmen of Paris. Often regarded as the first class-conscious socialist, Babeuf wanted to abolish private property and introduce a planned economy. When he was betrayed and guillotined, the uprising was easily defeated and the Paris mob finally disarmed. Nevertheless, it clearly showed the precarious position of the Directory and its narrow base of support among the propertied middle class.

With France's finances in chaos and its political position unstable, the fate of the Directory became increasingly involved with the career of Napoleon. There was no question that the people of France wanted peace as part of a return to normal life after the Terror. The war to liberate freedom-loving peoples from oppression had become a more traditional conflict to advance the prospects of the French nation. Peace was made with Spain, Prussia, three other German states, and Holland during 1795, on terms that were generally favourable to France. Only England and Austria remained at war. In 1796, Napoleon was given command of the French army in Italy as a reward for saving the

THE DIRECTORY

"WHIFF OF GRAPESHOT"

NAPOLEON IN ITALY

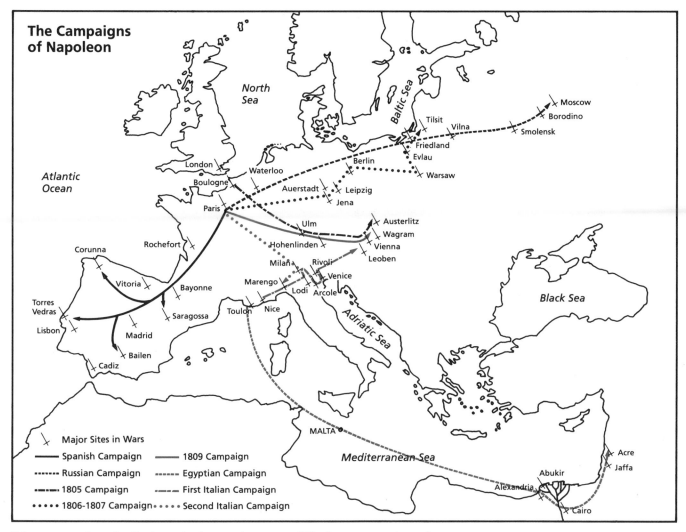

The Campaigns of Napoleon

North Sea

Baltic Sea

Atlantic Ocean

Moscow
Borodino
Tilsit
Vilna
Smolensk
Friedland
Berlin
Evlau
London
Waterloo
Warsaw
Boulogne
Auerstadt
Leipzig
Paris
Jena
Ulm
Austerlitz
Hohenlinden
Wagram
Vienna
Milan
Rivoli
Leoben
Marengo
Venice
Lodi
Arcole
Black Sea
Corunna
Rochefort
Bayonne
Vitoria
Nice
Toulon
Adriatic Sea
Torres Vedras
Saragossa
Lisbon
Madrid
Bailen
Cadiz
MALTA
Mediterranean Sea
Acre
Jaffa
Abukir
Alexandria
Cairo

Major Sites in Wars
— Spanish Campaign
······· Russian Campaign
–·–·– 1805 Campaign
•••• 1806-1807 Campaign
— 1809 Campaign
- - - - Egyptian Campaign
- - - - First Italian Campaign
• • • • Second Italian Campaign

Directory against the Paris mob the previous year. His famous words at the start of the campaign stirred his troops:

> You are badly fed and nearly naked—I am going to take you to the most fertile plains in the world. You will find there great cities and rich provinces. You will find there honour, glory, and wealth.

Though ill-equipped and usually outnumbered, Napoleon's brilliant military strategy led to a series of victories over Austria and its Sardinian allies. In the harsh Treaty of Campio Formio of 1797, Austria was compelled to recognize the French annexations of Belgium, the left bank of the Rhine, and Lombardy. Northern Italy was reorganized into the Cisalpine Republic, which was

THE TREATY OF CAMPIO FORMIO

nominally independent, but, in fact, merely a French satellite territory. In return, Austria was allowed to annex Venice, a republic that had been independent for over a thousand years. Tribute in cash and art poured over the Alps into France and Napoleon became a national hero.

As Napoleon's popularity soared, the Directory ran aground. A majority of royalists had been returned to the councils in the elections of 1797. This threatened the political power of the middle-class directors. Only by annulling the elections, with the support of a military force commanded by an aide of Napoleon, did the Directory hang on. Partly as another reward and partly to keep him occupied away from the centre of power, Napoleon was given command of an army that was to invade England. This was the one country that stood between France and peace or, perhaps more importantly, between Napoleon and his dreams of additional conquest and glory. Recognizing that England's strength depended on overseas commerce, Napoleon decided to cripple England's trade in the Mediterranean by invading Egypt and then campaigning overland as far as India. At the Battle of the Pyramids, in July 1798, the French forces massacred the Turkish Mamelukes and easily took control of Egypt. The following week, however, the British fleet, under Admiral Horatio Nelson, destroyed the French navy at Abukir Bay, near the mouth of the Nile River. Napoleon had suffered his first defeat and was now stranded with his army in Egypt.

Trapped by the British navy, though in control of Egypt, Napoleon decided to advance upon Syria. Along the way he captured Constantinople and crushed the Ottoman Empire. Recognizing the danger of French expansion in the Mediterranean, Europe formed a Second Coalition against France in 1799 that included England, Austria, Russia, Turkey, Naples, Portugal, and the papacy. As these powers began to challenge the European territories recently occupied by France, the Directory became increasingly unpopular. Another election returned an overwhelming majority for the opposition and rumours of royalist plots to overthrow the government abounded. Amid this confusion, Napoleon saw his chance. Forced to return to Egypt to subdue a Turkish attempt to retake it, Napoleon abandoned his troops to certain surrender, slipped through the British fleet, and returned to France. He immediately allied himself with a plot organized by one of the directors and executed a successful coup d'état on the 18 Brumaire (9 November 1799). During this coup, Napoleon almost fainted at a critical moment and it was his brother Lucien who sent in the troops to end the life of the Directory. A new government of three consuls, with Napoleon as first consul, hailed a new era. Shortly afterwards, Napoleon and his fellow consuls proclaimed, "Citizens, the Revolution is established on the principles upon which it was founded: it is over."

Freedom, Authority, and the People

The relationship between individual freedom and the authority by which individuals are governed is central to civilized life. Just what this relationship should

---

Moments in Time

Mary Wollstonecraft (1759–1797), a British novelist and feminist, was outraged by the failure of the events in France to emancipate women. In her book, *A Vindication of the Rights of Woman*, she argued that the progress of human knowledge and virtue would be halted until women were given equal status with men, and that both sexes should receive identical education. Her belief that women should be free to determine their own destinies would be a long time in becoming a reality.

NAPOLEON'S COUP D'ÉTAT

be was a major theme of the Enlightenment and a practical matter for the leaders of the French Revolution. Specific grievances, which are the chief concern of the vast majority of the population, usually reflect the problems that exist in a particular historical setting. The questions of principle that underlie these problems, however, are often as relevant today as they were to the historical period from which they emerged.

THOMAS HOBBES

When Thomas Hobbes (1588–1679) published his *Leviathan* in 1651, he anticipated the discussion of principles later penned by the French *philosophes*. Hobbes was thoroughly critical of the chaos brought by religious disputes and the English Civil War, symbolized by the execution of Charles I. What was needed was an authority with supreme, absolute power to preserve peace and order. Hobbes believed that the state of nature was characterized by a "war of each against all" in which people would destroy themselves much as they did through the years of civil war in his own time. Through the use of reason, people gave up their freedom to create a sovereign state that could not be challenged. This would ensure the safety of all. Although the sovereign state had unlimited power, which was all the justification it needed, its goal was to satisfy the needs of its subjects so that it, too, could survive. The ancien régime had many of the elements of the sovereign state pictured by Hobbes despite the weaknesses of Louis XVI. Were the interests of the people of France better served by the absolute rule of Louis XVI or by the chaos and bloodshed of the Revolution that followed over the next decade?

As previously mentioned, John Locke believed that human beings possessed natural rights to life, liberty, and property and that societies were formed to protect these rights. In contrast to Hobbes, Locke argued that citizens were justified in changing or overthrowing their government if these natural rights were violated. Locke used this argument to explain and defend the Glorious Revolution of 1688 in England. Could his concept of natural rights be applied to the moderate phase of the French Revolution? Were the people of France better off as a result of the changes that occurred?

Jean-Jacques Rousseau also agreed that humans first lived in a state of nature and had certain rights. Unlike Hobbes, who argued that humans in a state of nature could not be trusted, Rousseau believed that they were basically good and that the general will of the communities they formed represented the best intentions of the people. Since the general will was always right, any opposition must be wrong and therefore had to be changed for the benefit of the community. Rousseau's ideas are often associated with the radical phase of the Revolution, and there is no doubt that under Robespierre his ideas were taken to a bloody extreme. There were, however, some positive accomplishments during the radical phase as well as an unleashing of forces that greatly affected the subsequent history of France and Europe. Was France a better place in which to live as a result of these changes? What was the relationship between abstract ideas and the reality of the French Revolution?

> ## Moments in Time
>
> The Declaration of the Rights of Man and the Citizen totally ignored the rights of women and children. In response, Olympe de Gouges (1745–1793) wrote the *Declaration of the Rights of Woman* in which she demanded equal rights in public and private life and before the law. For her condemnation of the revolutionaries and their new government, she was sentenced to death by Robespierre and guillotined.

JEAN-JACQUES ROUSSEAU

PROBLEM QUESTION

To what extent did the course of the French Revolution indicate that the political, economic, and social interests of the people were best served by the theory of absolute rule held by Hobbes, the concept of natural right explained by Locke, or the theory of Social Contract presented by Rousseau?

ALTERNATIVE ONE

Leviathan—Based on *Leviathan* by Thomas Hobbes, 1651

Origin of the State

The final cause, end, or design of men, who naturally love liberty, and dominion over others, in the introduction of that restraint upon themselves, in which we see them live in commonwealths, is the foresight of their own preservation, and of a more contented life thereby; that is to say, of getting themselves out from that miserable condition of war, which is necessarily consequent, to the natural passions of men, when there is no visible power to keep them in awe, and tie them by fear of punishment to the performance of their covenants, and observation of the laws of nature.

For the laws of nature, as "justice," "modesty," "mercy," and, in sum, "doing to others as we would be done to," of themselves, without the terror of some power to cause them to be observed, are contrary to our natural passions, that carry us to partiality, pride, revenge, and the like. And covenants, without the sword, are but words, and of no strength to secure a man at all. Therefore notwithstanding the laws of nature, which everyone hath then kept, when he has the will to keep them, when he can do it safely, if there be no power erected, or not great enough for our security, every man will and may lawfully rely on his own strength and art, for caution against all other men.

The only way to erect such a common power as may be able to defend them from the invasion of foreigners and the injuries of one another, and thereby to secure them in such sort as that by their own industry, and by the fruits of the earth, they may nourish themselves and live contentedly, is to confer all their power and strength upon one man, or upon one assembly of men, to bear their person; and everyone to own and acknowledge himself to be the author of whatsoever he that so beareth their person shall act, or cause to be acted, in those things which concern the common peace and safety: and therein to submit their wills, every one to his will, and their judgements to his judgement. This is more than consent, or concord; it is a real unity of them all in one and the same person, made by covenant of every man with every man, in such manner as if every man should say to every man, "I authorize and give up my right of governing myself, to this man or to this assembly of men, on this condition, that thou give up thy right to him and authorize all his actions in like manner." This done, the multitude so united in one person is called a "commonwealth," in Latin *civitas*. This is the generation of that great leviathan, or rather, to speak more reverently, of that mortal god, to which we owe under the immortal God, our peace and defense. For by this authority, given him by every particular man in the commonwealth, he hath the use of so much power and strength conferred on him, that by terror thereof, he is enabled to perform the wills of them all, to peace at home, and mutual aid against their enemies abroad. And in him consisteth the essence of the commonwealth; which, to define it, is "one person, of whose acts a great multitude, by mutual covenants one with another, have made themselves every one the author, to the end he may use the strength and means of them all, as he shall think expedient, for their places and common defense."

And he that carrieth this person is called sovereign, and said to have sovereign power; and everyone besides, his subject.

The attaining to this sovereign power is by two ways. One by natural force; as when a man maketh his children to submit to themselves, and their children, to his government, as being able to destroy them if they refuse; or by war subdueth his enemies to his will, giving them their lives on that condition. The other is when men agree among themselves to submit to some man, or assembly of men, voluntarily, on confidence to be protected by him against all others. This latter may be called a political commonwealth, or commonwealth by institution; and the former, a commonwealth by acquisition. Now, I shall speak of a commonwealth by institution.

The Nature of Sovereignty

A commonwealth is said to be instituted when a multitude of men do agree and covenant, everyone with everyone, that to whatsoever man or assembly of men shall be given by the major part the right to present the person of them all, that is to say to be their representative; everyone, as well he that voted for it as he that voted against it, shall authorize all the actions and judgements of that man or assembly of men in the same manner as if they were his own, to the end to live peaceably among themselves and be protected against other men.

From this institution of a commonwealth are derived all the rights and faculties of him, or them, on whom sovereign power is conferred by the consent of the people assembled.

And as the power, so also the honour of the sovereign, ought to be greater than that of any or all the subjects. For in the sovereignty is the fountain of honour. The dignities of lord, earl, duke, and prince are his creatures. As in the presence of the master the servants are equal, and without any honour at all; so are the subjects in the presence of the sovereign. And though they shine some more, some less, when they are out of his sight; yet in his presence, they shine no more than the stars in the presence of the sun.

Questions

1. a) Why do freemen willingly live in a commonwealth?
   b) Did the ancien régime serve this purpose? Explain your answer.
2. a) What were the laws of nature?
   b) Will men follow these laws of their own accord? Explain your answer.
3. a) How much authority does the commonwealth possess?
   b) Did Louis XVI and the government of France have this much power? Explain your answer with evidence.
4. Describe the formation and characteristics of a ''commonwealth by institution.''
5. a) What degree of honour is given to the sovereign power?
   b) Did Louis XVI receive this kind of honour as the absolute monarch of France?
6. To what extent was the ancien régime the ''Leviathan'' described by Hobbes?

ALTERNATIVE TWO

Civil Government—Based on *Second Treatise on Government* by John Locke, 1690

Chapter II: Of the State of Nature

To understand political power, we must consider the natural condition of all men, and that is a state of perfect freedom to do as they please and dispose of their possessions and persons as they think fit, within the bounds of the law of nature, without asking leave or depending upon the will of any other man.

A state also of equality, wherein no one has more power or authority than another. . . .

The state of nature, which has the law of reason to govern it, teaches all mankind who will but consult it, that being equal and independent, no one ought to harm another in his life, health, liberty or possessions; for men being all the workmanship of one omnipotent and infinitely wise Maker; all the servant of one sovereign Master, sent into the world by His order and about His business; they are His property, whose workmanship they are, made to last during His, not one another's pleasure. Such is the natural condition of all men, until they consent to become a member of a political society.

Chapter VIII: Of the Beginning of Political Society

When any number of men have, by the consent of every individual, made a community, they have thereby made that community one body, with a power to act as one body, which is only by the will and determination of the majority. . . .

Chapter IX: Of the Ends of Political Society and Government

If man in the state of nature is free, why will he part with his freedom and subject himself to the dominion and control of any other power? To which it is obvious to answer, that though in the state of nature he had such a right, the enjoyment of it is uncertain and constantly exposed to the invasion of others. This makes him willing to quit this condition which, however free, is full of fears and continued dangers; and it is not without reason that he seeks out and is willing to join in society with others who are already united, or have a mind to unite for the mutual preservation of their lives, liberties and estates, which I will call by the general name—property.

The great and chief end, therefore of men uniting into commonwealths, and putting themselves under government, is the preservation of their property; to which in the state of nature there are many things wanting. . . .

And so, whosoever has the legislative or supreme power of any commonwealth, is bound to govern by established standing laws, issued to the people; and to employ the force of the community at home only in the execution of such laws, or abroad to prevent or redress foreign injuries and secure the community from inroads and invasion. And all this to be directed to no other end but the peace, safety and public good of the people.

Chapter XVIII: Of Tyranny

Where law ends, tyranny begins, if the law be transgressed to another's harm; and whosoever in authority exceeds the power given him by the law, and makes use of the force he has under his command to break the law, ceases in that to be a magistrate, and may be opposed as any other man who by force invades the right of another. Exceeding the bounds of authority is no more right in a greater than a petty officer, no more justifiable in a king than a constable. But so much the worse in him, since he has more trust put in him, is supposed, from the advantage of education and counsellors, to have better knowledge and less reason to do it, having already a greater share than the rest of his brethren.

Chapter XIX: Of the Dissolution of Government

When legislatures and rulers break the trust given to them, and either by ambition, fear, folly, or corruption try to grasp for themselves, or put into the hands of others, an absolute power over the lives, liberties and estates of the people, by this breach of trust they forfeit the power the people had put into their hands for quite contrary ends. The people now have a right to resume their original liberty, and by the establishment of a new legislature (such as they shall think fit), provide for their own safety and security.

Questions

1. a) Compare Locke's view of the state of nature with the ideas expressed by Hobbes.
   b) How does the "law of reason" affect the state of nature according to Locke?
2. a) Why does man give up his freedom to become part of a community?

b) What is the main objective of government?

3. In what way must the supreme power of any community try to govern?

4. a) What condition results when the laws of a community are broken?

   b) What can be done when government breaks the trust given to it by the people?

5. a) When the Estates General met in 1789, what classes of French society felt that Louis XVI had violated the trust given to him?

   b) What motivated the attempt to reform France into a constitutional monarchy during the moderate phase of the Revolution?

   c) Were living conditions in France better during the moderate phase of the Revolution than they were during the ancien régime? Explain your answer.

ALTERNATIVE THREE

The Social Contract–Based on *The Social Contract* by Jean-Jacques Rousseau, 1762

Man is born free, and everywhere he is in chains. Many a man believes himself to be master of others who is, no less than they, a slave. How did this change take place? I do not know. What can make it legitimate? To this question I hope to be able to furnish an answer.

I assume that mankind reached a point when there were more disadvantages than advantages in remaining in a state of nature. The original state of nature could not last under such conditions and the human race would have perished unless it changed.

Men cannot create new powers, but they can unite and control those they already possess. Only by coming together and pooling their strength could men meet the challenges exerted upon them. They had to develop a central direction and work together. Such a focus of power can happen only when agreement is reached among several individuals. But the self-preservation of each individual comes from his own strength and freedom. How can he limit these without harming himself and neglecting his duty to his own concerns?

Some form of association had to be found in which the strength of the whole community will be enlisted for the protection of the person and property of every citizen in such a way that when united to his fellows, he renders obedience to his own will, and remains as free as he was before. This is the basic problem solved by the Social Contract.

The clauses of this Contract are determined by the Act of Association in such a way that the least modification will render them null and void. Although the terms of the association may never have been formally accepted, they must be the same everywhere and universally recognized. Should the Social Contract be broken, each associated individual would regain the rights that were his in a state of nature.

In the Social Contract, each individual voluntarily gives up all his rights to the community. Since each man has made the same sacrifice without reservation, the conditions are equal for everyone. And because conditions are equal, it is in everyone's interest to make life pleasant for all.

Moreover, since all rights have been surrendered to the community, the union is as perfect as it can be and no one has any claim against the community. If individuals retained certain rights, with no superior authority to choose between them and the public good, then each would attempt to expand his personal rights. A state of nature would still exist. And the association would become ineffective or despotic.

The Social Contract can be reduced to the following terms: "Each of us puts his person and all his power in common under the supreme direction of the general will, and we receive into the body politic, each individual as an indivisible part of the whole. . . .

For the Social Contract to work, everyone must realize that any individual who does not obey the general will must be forced to do so. Thus, a man must be forced to be free since freedom is now defined as obedience to the will of all.

Questions

1. What did Rousseau mean when he said "Man is born free, and everywhere he is in chains"?
2. What basic problem is solved by the Social Contract?
3. Why did Rousseau feel that men have no right to revolt?
4. a) What is the "general will"?
   b) Rousseau did not explain how the general will was to be determined. Why could this become a problem in practice?
5. a) Robespierre admired Rousseau's philosophy. Did the Reign of Terror accurately reflect the ideas put forward? Explain your answer.
   b) Did the Republic of Virtue contribute anything positive to France that could be attributed to Rousseau's philosophy? Again, explain your answer.

ANSWERING THE PROBLEM QUESTION

To apply abstract ideas to the churning developments of the French Revolution is indeed a difficult task. The dynamic momentum of the Revolution, which began with a demand for moderate reform, pushed ideas and solutions increasingly towards the radical left. Open debates in the Assembly, the Convention, political clubs, and even on street corners often intimidated the voices of limited change. Spectators repeatedly hurled jibes at anyone who failed to support the most extreme measures of the moment. Anything else was considered counter-revolutionary. No one seemed to be in control of events for more than a brief period of time before either quickly falling to the background or becoming a victim of the guillotine.

The principles of social organization presented by Hobbes, Locke, and Rousseau were issued in contrasting historical settings. Hobbes, of course, was no friend of revolution, but while the ideas of Locke and Rousseau made for fascinating parlour discussion, it was difficult to apply them with any sense of direction. Usually, the lofty principles of reform, first proclaimed with sincerity, became public slogans that were bandied about so that particular groups or classes might advance their own interests. Yet, all too often, it was the hunger-driven, at times bloodthirsty mob and the radical municipal government of the Paris Commune that steered the direction of change. Principles had little meaning unless they resulted in the immediate redress of specific concerns.

The theory of absolute rule, advocated by Hobbes, supported the stability of the ancien régime and all its imperfections rather than the chaos and violence of revolution. When the nobles forced the calling of the Estates General, they hoped to solidify their position within society and enhance their existing political power and privilege. Would French society as a whole have benefited if the nobles had achieved their objectives? The members of the bourgeoisie were thoroughly soaked in the ideas of the Enlightenment. Their commitment to them was genuine, perhaps to the point of naivety. Nevertheless, the self-appointed leaders of the Third Estate used the rhetoric of the Enlightenment to achieve moderate reforms that would give them a degree of political power in the new order, in line with their economic strength. Would the reforms advocated by the bourgeoisie have benefited anyone but themselves? The various elements of the Third Estate, from the peasant to the urban worker, knew the ideas of the Enlightenment mainly from public pronouncements, gossip, and political slogans. Their lot was clearly the most desperate, particularly during the economic and financial crisis of the 1780s. Would they have been better off with reform legislation passed by Louis XVI and the central government rather than changing the very nature of the political system? Did they have any reason to believe that any such changes were forthcoming?

If the conclusion was reached that reform of some kind had to occur in the ancien régime, it becomes a question of how much change was needed to best serve the people. John Locke's concept of natural rights justified a wide range of actions, including complete overthrow, if a government violated the sacred trust of power given to it by the people. During the moderate phase of the Revolution, the middle class settled for a more modest approach that sought to change the absolute power of the French king into a constitutional monarchy that limited his authority. As Louis XVI's untimely and unwise attempt to flee the country strengthened antimonarchist sentiment and the Girondins carried the nation into a war to save the Revolution, France was more divided than ever. Was this a failure of moderate reform? Should steps to abolish the monarchy have been taken sooner as Locke might have argued? Or was the pace of change simply out of the hands of any responsible group that might have implemented successful reform?

Certainly the Terror, as administered by Robespierre, and the Committee of Public Safety moved with unrivalled swiftness to change the face of France in the name of the Revolution. Was this decisiveness and authoritarian action needed to bring order to France? Robespierre sincerely equated the policies of the Committee of Public Safety with the general will described by Rousseau. Yet the widespread carnage, particularly among the lower classes, could easily be seen as an attempt to establish and maintain power at any cost rather than a campaign to uphold revolutionary ideals in a "Republic of Virtue." Would the people of France have agreed with the latter assessment or with the views expressed by Robespierre? The Committee rallied the emotion and resources of the nation to defend France with the *Levée en Masse*. The result was the greatest army that Europe had ever seen and its success in expanding the frontiers of France fuelled people's pride and nationalism. In saving France from foreign invasion, did the new army justify the tactics of the Terror? Robespierre attempted to reform even the smallest aspect of French life in terms that would have been acceptable to enlightened thinkers. The revolutionary calendar, stripped as it was of religious overtones, was but one example. The Committee's effort to regulate prices, although unpopular when introduced, was soon looked upon with favour by the middle class when inflation grew much worse under the Directory. Would the Terror have brought lasting benefits to the people of France if the Committee had not turned on Robespierre? Or would the senseless killing have continued in the hands of a government more dangerous than Louis XVI could have imagined?

One of the most intriguing careers of the revolutionary era was that of Abbé Sieyes, famous for his inspirational document on behalf of the Third Estate in 1789. With considerable skill, Sieyes adapted to each major shift in political power, emerging as one of the five directors in 1795. Sieyes was also the director who decided to "use" Napoleon to carry out the coup of 1799 without realizing how quickly the young general would consolidate the situation in his own favour.

The advantage of hindsight allows us to know how the French Revolution and Napoleon's quest for power turned out. At each moment of change, however, there were several options that might have altered the pattern of developments. Had the National Guard been able to control the Paris mob, had Louis accepted his fate, had Robespierre concentrated less on execution and more on finding a common ground for additional reform, or had Sieyes turned to someone other than Napoleon in 1799, the Revolution would have taken a different shape. As it was, the people of France experienced a decade of unprecedented turmoil and change, and under Napoleon emerged, once again, as the predominant power in Europe. Was this what the reasoned approach to the problems of society had promised? Were the people better served by the absolute rule advocated by Hobbes, the concept of natural rights expressed by Locke, or the terms of the Social Contract described by Rousseau?

THE STORY CONTINUES . . .

Napoleon Bonaparte

Napoleon's career had been truly remarkable and would never have been predicted at his birth in 1769 on the rugged and backward island of Corsica. His attractive and forceful mother was permissive enough to allow the young Napoleon to play in a bare room where he apparently painted the walls with rows of soldiers in battle formation. Yet she was consistently strict and birched Napoleon when he misbehaved. Napoleon's father, a poor lawyer, recognized that when France acquired Corsica in 1768, its grip would be permanent. He was able to secure a scholarship for one of his sons–Napoleon–and sent him to French military colleges at Autun in 1779 and then Brienne. From the age of ten, Napoleon was on his own and his Corsican accent, uncouth dress, temper tantrums, and intense seriousness set him apart from his classmates. Upon his father's death, when Napoleon was only fifteen years old, he assumed a sense of responsibility for his family. His elder brother Joseph was far too irresponsible.

Though good at mathematics, Napoleon was only an average student. If something interested him, however, he could easily absorb vast amounts of material. Usually this was information that was not taught in school. In 1784, Napoleon obtained an appointment to the École Militaire in Paris and earned a commission as a second lieutenant in southern France the following year. Assigned to a regiment in Louis XVI's army, Napoleon received practical training as an artillery officer, but it was during this period that he became deeply impressed with the writing of Rousseau.

With the outbreak of the Revolution in 1789 and the emigration of many nobles from the officer corps, there were undreamed-of opportunities for ambitious young officers who stayed in France. Napoleon embraced the Revolution with enthusiasm, but spent much of the first four hectic years organizing revolutionary political clubs in Corsica. Forced to leave his homeland when an attempt to seize power went awry, Napoleon, now a captain, joined a military detachment of the Revolution commanded by General Carteaux. Adoption of Napoleon's plan and his personal direction of the artillery led to the recapture of the port of Toulon from the British in late 1793, after months of limited success. With the ranks of skilled officers already depleted, Napoleon emerged as a brigadier-general for his efforts.

Such rapid progress was sidetracked when Napoleon, a former Jacobin, was jailed as a terrorist for a brief period following the execution of Robespierre and then released. It appeared as though his military career was finished until Director Barras had Napoleon appointed to discharge the threat to the Republic in 1795. Napoleon had been in Paris for a short time in 1792 and witnessed the storming of the Tuileries. He was struck by the weakness of Louis XVI in the face of mob violence. When given his own chance he fired without hesitation into the rebel columns and killed over five hundred people on the steps of

---

Moments in Time

When Napoleon came to power, Ludwig van Beethoven's reputation as a composer and performer had already spread beyond the musical élite of Vienna. He was an enthusiastic supporter of the French Revolution and his opposition to tyranny was symbolized by a bust of Brutus that always adorned his desk. Napoleon's decision to be crowned emperor so provoked Beethoven that he withdrew his dedication of the *Eroica* Symphony to the French leader. Following Napoleon's defeat, Beethoven insisted on conducting a public performance of "Wellington's Victory," one of his weakest compositions, at the Congress of Vienna.

the Church of St. Roch. Napoleon's sense of order had replaced the revolutionary principles he once held so dear.

Prior to receiving command of the Italian expedition, Napoleon married a former mistress of Barras named Josephine Beauharnais, six years his senior. Josephine, though alarmed by Napoleon's impetuous courtship, believed he could repay her debts. Napoleon was genuinely in love, or at least as close to love as he would ever allow himself, and realized that Josephine's aristocratic connections would elevate his social status to that of his military rank. Having watched the political manoeuvring for power in the Revolution, the ever-practical Napoleon carefully built his own image with a skill that matched his military talent. Napoleon later revealed that his victory at Lodi, near Milan, first stirred his ambition to great accomplishment: "From that moment, I foresaw what I might be. Already I felt the earth flee from beneath me, as if I were being carried into the sky."

Returning from Italy as a triumphant general earning unrivalled prestige, Napoleon now pressed the epic quality of his struggle, particularly in Egypt. Choosing to call his most famous encounter the "Battle of the Pyramids," his name became linked to what seemed like a great victory when the margin of battle was slight, contrary to his own lie that the French were vastly outnumbered. In Europe and the New World, the vision of Egypt opened up an awareness and interest in the history of the mysterious pharaohs. Indeed, the study of Egyptology dates from Napoleon's arrival and the stories of ancient grandeur that followed him home. It also overshadowed his subsequent defeats and the ruthless slaughter of almost three thousand Turkish prisoners who surrendered at Jaffa on a promise that their lives would be saved.

Although Napoleon was careful to preserve the trappings of democracy with four assemblies of state, there was no doubt that he intended to centralize power in his own hands as first consul. Napoleon went to the people for approval in a popular vote known as a **plebiscite**, but only *after* the new constitution was declared to be in effect and his own position was secure. This was a shrewd move. It gave meaning to the basic principle of the French Revolution that sovereignty rested with the people. At the same time, it by-passed the elected representatives of government and aligned Napoleon with the wishes of the nation as expressed through a democratic vote. That Napoleon judged the mood of the people correctly was clearly revealed on 7 February 1800 when the vote for the constitution showed a staggering 3 011 007 in favour and only 1 562 opposed! Napoleon used the plebiscite with equal effectiveness on several other occasions.

By 1800, Napoleon had demonstrated many of the qualities that made him perhaps the most extraordinary personality of the modern age. Although only 1.57 m tall, his unique combination of charisma, ego, and intensity enabled him to dominate any individual or group assembled in his presence. He inspired loyalty and devotion among his generals, support staff, and soldiers even in times of defeat. His military genius, characterized by decisiveness,

THE CHURCH OF ST. ROCH

JOSEPHINE BEAUHARNAIS

BIRTH OF AMBITION

FIRST CONSUL

LEADERSHIP QUALITIES

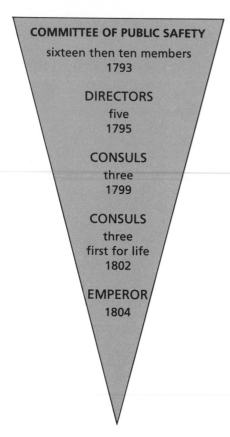

COMMITTEE OF PUBLIC SAFETY

sixteen then ten members
1793

DIRECTORS

five
1795

CONSULS

three
1799

CONSULS

three
first for life
1802

EMPEROR

1804

The Government of France, 1793–1804. The base of power was increasingly limited, so that by 1804 Napoleon, as emperor, was in sole control of France.

TREATY OF LUNEVILLE

TREATY OF AMIENS

CONSUL FOR LIFE

resourcefulness, and the instinctive ability to make the right move at the right time, was admired by all and feared by his enemies. The duke of Wellington claimed that Napoleon's presence on the battlefield was worth forty thousand troops. Napoleon was one of the few generals in history who understood every detail of organization down to the position of the last rifle as well as the overall picture of the tactics required for victory. Once he set his sights on a particular objective, Napoleon worked with fearsome energy consuming any idea that might be useful, and pushed his men to their limits until his goal was achieved. Yet this natural leader who so motivated others and claimed devotion to them, would remorselessly sacrifice thousands of soldiers for limited gain if the situation demanded it. Pursuit of victory resulted in a nightmare of wasted deaths as the scale of battle increased from tens of thousands to hundreds of thousands of men. If soldiers eventually became pawns, Napoleon's family always remained dear to him. Three of his brothers and two of his sisters were given thrones in French satellite states as Napoleon's empire expanded. His mother, frugal to the end, was laden with wealth. Despite awesome ability, Napoleon's vision of empire exceeded even his talent and he plunged Europe into a fateful struggle without admitting the limits of what he could achieve.

From First Consul to Emperor

Despite the cry for freedom heard during the decade of revolution, it was clear that the people preferred peace and order. Napoleon perceived this and he was the man to meet these needs. At home, Napoleon moved quickly to crush the royalist rebellion in the Vendée which had been waged intermittently since 1793 and often terrorized the countryside. In foreign affairs, France was confronted by the Second Coalition. Overtures by Napoleon helped to separate Russia from the coalition and withdraw from active participation in the war. At the same time, Napoleon wrote letters proclaiming his desire for peace to Austria and England, knowing full well that the offer would be rejected while France dominated Belgium, the Rhine, and knocked on the doorstep of Italy. In a two-pronged attack, aided by the fortunate arrival of a support division, Napoleon defeated Austria at Marengo in Italy, while the French general Moreau earned the more important victory at Hohenlinden. The Treaty of Luneville, in 1801, slightly enlarged the concessions made by Austria four years earlier at Campo Formio. Once again, this left only Britain to oppose France and the war between the two great powers was becoming stalemated. Britain was supreme at sea while France dominated the continent, and the Treaty of Amiens, signed in 1802, though generally favourable to France, reflected that situation. Napoleon took full credit for the peace and the victories that preceded it. Although the British public was disappointed by the treaty, it was greeted with joyous enthusiasm in France. Napoleon used the euphoria of the moment to hold another plebiscite to amend the constitution and make himself consul for life. Again, the vote was overwhelming, with 3 568 885 in favour and only 8 374 against. Napoleon, however, realized that the break in hostilities was only a truce and that the war would soon be resumed.

As a domestic reformer during the Consulate, Napoleon was at his creative and energetic peak. He gave France many institutions which have endured to the present in one form or another. The task of centralizing the administration, begun by Richelieu and interrupted by the Revolution, was completed. France was divided into departments, *arrondissements*, and communes (towns) with a corresponding set of officials, the prefect, subprefect, and mayor appointed directly or indirectly by the central government. In practice, Napoleon recruited the most able ministers and officials he could find to make sure that his intended reforms were properly implemented and France was better off for the choices he made. Napoleon also introduced an effective system to collect and audit taxes, a reform that reduced corruption and shared the tax burden on the most equitable basis yet experienced. The Bank of France, created to stabilize currency, became an important agent of the government in controlling national finance and, in 1803, acquired a monopoly on the right to issue banknotes.

Hand in hand with administrative and financial reform was the need for the codification of laws. The task of making sense out of the confused tangle of Roman, feudal, national, and local customs had already begun under the Sun King, Louis XIV, but it was Napoleon who pushed it through to completion. Napoleon knew little about legal technicalities and, despite keen interest, his presence at meetings often hindered rather than helped the proceedings. Yet the end result of the effort, the **Code Napoléon**, gave French civilization a solid legal foundation that became the hallmark of domestic peace. The code was issued in five parts as the work was completed, including the civil code of 1804 governing marriage and family, and subsequent codes relating to procedure, commerce, and criminal and penal justice. There was no doubt that the great virtue of the code was that it clarified people and property relationships in one unified legal system rather than by the principles of any particular law that was registered. The bourgeoisie applauded the protection given to property, the declaration that all men were equal before the law, the supremacy of the state, and the freedom of conscience. However, critics later pointed out that Napoleon tried to freeze France forever while the process of social change continued. For example, the power of the husband in the family was entrenched as he was given control over all his wife's property while the status of labourers was fixed with a provision that outlawed collective action. The rigid implications of these and similar provisions shackled future attempts to reform. Nevertheless, the impact of the code was immediate and efficient, and despite the amendments and additions of the modern age, it remains in force to this day.

Napoleon probably lacked even a trace of religious conviction, but he understood the emotional importance of religion to society. The Revolution had been at odds with the Roman Catholic Church, which only served to divide the loyalty of the nation in crisis after crisis. Napoleon intended to heal the

ADMINISTRATIVE CENTRALIZATION

CODE NAPOLÉON

THE CONCORDAT

domestic breach and to appear as a good Catholic in Italy where Church opposition could be a major obstacle to French rule in the states he planned to conquer. The Concordat of 1801, forced through by Napoleon over the objections of his deist and sceptical advisers, was an agreement with the Roman Catholic Church on terms favourable to France. While France agreed to maintain churches and pay the clergy, the pope gave up all claims to Church land sold during the revolutionary decade. The French government was given the right to nominate bishops, while the pope retained the right to install them. Although Roman Catholicism was recognized as the religion of the majority, other religions were allowed.

The Concordat, which lasted until 1905, did not rest easy with the Church. Further irritants were the passage of strict regulations for public worship and the so-called "Organic Articles" that proclaimed the supremacy of the state over the Church and were withheld from the pope until the Concordat was approved. Of equal concern were the reforms that Napoleon brought to education. Revolutionary governments had been too preoccupied to implement changes in education, which remained the preserve of the Church. Napoleon, however, introduced a national system of education in 1802 that featured select secondary schools known as lycées to be run by the government. They emphasized state indoctrination, military training, science, and mathematics. In 1808, the process of centralization was completed with the establishment of the University of France to supervise higher education in regional centres throughout the nation. From this system, Napoleon expected to groom the skilled personnel needed to run the country. At the same time, the financing of elementary education was largely neglected and usually left to the whim of local interests. Napoleon saw no reason to educate the common people. His attitude towards the education of women, which would be considered outrageous today, was a major step backward even for the time:

UNIVERSITY OF FRANCE

> I do not think that we need trouble ourselves with any plan of instruction for young females; they cannot be better brought up than by their mothers. Public education is not suitable for them, because they are never called upon to act in public. Manners are all in all to them, and marriage is all they look to.

LEGION OF HONOUR

Nevertheless, Napoleon had risen to the top by means of his own instinct and superior ability and he appreciated the need to recognize men of special talent to enlist their efforts for the nation. To reward such meritorious individuals, Napoleon created another institution, the Legion of Honour, which has survived to the present. Those who witnessed and applauded the abolition of all titles of the nobility in 1790 were concerned about the apparent return of distinction. For Napoleon, such honours, given at his own discretion to achievers regardless of their birth, was another means to encourage loyalty and harness the service of the capable. Though membership was initially limited to six thousand and was usually given to the military, those who demonstrated talent in any field were eligible. Soon, the Legion of Honour became an ''army'' in size, but the honour remained highly valued.

The reforms introduced by Napoleon were a mixture of original ideas and the completion of projects begun or conceived by earlier governments. Although he skillfully focussed credit upon himself even when it was not earned, Napoleon deserved praise for the sheer energy required to bring so many important changes into effect. In the public's eye, his accomplishments ensured **equality** and stirred the consciousness of **fraternity** among all French citizens. Napoleon not only realized that people would sacrifice **liberty** for order, but believed that an enlightened absolute ruler of strength was best for France. He had already begun his march in that direction by using the police to arrest political opponents and closing newspapers critical of the Consulate.

Following the plebiscite that confirmed the fact of Napoleon's appointment as consul for life, the touches of royalty began to emerge as his image appeared on coins and only his first name was used on official documents. Long inspired by the power of the Caesars, Napoleon expanded a public works plan to develop a modern network of canals and roads to include construction of classical arches and columns that beautified Paris with a Roman flavour. But despite his eminence, Napoleon had to wait for the right occasion to consolidate absolute power. A royalist conspiracy engineered by envious generals who looked upon Napoleon as a mere usurper who took power through a military coup, gave him his chance to act. Although the plot was afoot for almost a year, the conspirators implicated an unknown member of the Bourbon family as the central figure but no one could identify him. Napoleon's first move was to arrest the generals. He then determined, without evidence, that the missing Bourbon was the young duke d'Enghien. The unfortunate duke, who knew nothing of the scheme, was arrested in his hunting clothes, tried after Napoleon had instructed the judges to render a verdict of guilty, and then shot within ninety minutes after the farce began. Although some were highly suspicious of the official story and abhored the incident, the press printed what it was told and the public believed the charges levelled against the duke. In the tense atmosphere of the trials of the generals, most of whom were also executed, Napoleon secured his confirmation as a hereditary emperor from the legislative bodies of the Consulate in May of 1804. Napoleon again appealed to the people with a plebiscite in a token gesture for approval, and the results were similar to the others: 3 572 329 in favour with only 2 579 opposed.

HEREDITARY EMPEROR

Napoleon turned the appointment to full advantage with an extravagant coronation worthy of Roman pageantry. It was held within the sacred tradition of the Cathedral of Notre Dame in Paris in December of 1804 and Napoleon invited the pope to consecrate the empire and the crowning of the new Charlemagne. In the prearranged ceremony, Napoleon took the crown–a duplicate of Charlemagne's original–after it was lifted by the pope and he crowned himself. In a way, the concentration of absolute power in the hands of one person was the logical conclusion of revolutionary government. Twelve mem-

CORONATION IN NOTRE DAME

The Coronation of Napoleon *(detail)* by Jacques Louis David. The painting shows Napoleon crowning his wife, Josephine, as empress. Napoleon's mother is shown seated in the gallery (top left). In fact she did not attend the ceremony.

bers of the Committee of Public Safety had been replaced by five directors, then three consuls were eclipsed by a consul for life. As hereditary emperor, Napoleon dearly wanted to leave his empire to his offspring, but he never lost sight of the fact that power alone was the real justification for his throne. Following the coronation, memberships in the Legion of Honour were given to the loyal and to those whose loyalty could be bought. Nevertheless, Napoleon's rise to the pinnacle of power in five years was a remarkable achievement and it only whet his appetite for greater worlds to conquer.

War and Empire

With Britain holding Malta, while France ruled south Italy in violation of the Treaty of Amiens, the uneasy peace lasted little more than a year. Anticipating the outbreak of hostilities, Napoleon sold the Louisiana territory recently acquired from Spain to the United States in 1803, doubling the size of the republic and strengthening an overseas rival to Britain. Already upset with the continued French occupation of the Austrian Netherlands (Belgium) and with French trade restrictions, Britain declared war on France three weeks later.

BRITAIN AND FRANCE AT WAR

Napoleon responded with a planned invasion of Britain with a flotilla of fifteen hundred flat-bottomed barges and boats. Over the next two years, he assembled the Grand Army of one hundred thousand at Boulogne, opposite Dover, and another eighty thousand at Brest and Holland. The success of the plan depended on temporary control of the English Channel. To achieve this, Napoleon devised a manoeuvre in which the French admiral Villeneuve would decoy the British fleet to the West Indies, leaving the English Channel safe for an invasion by his rafted army, and then return before the British recognized the scheme. Napoleon was so confident of victory that a column was raised at Boulogne to celebrate the occasion. Meanwhile, although the Treaty of Luneville had given Napoleon the right to reorganize the territories of the German states, the changes were drastic and geared to suit his own interests. This caused alarm in several states. Though concerned, Prussia decided to remain neutral, but Austria and Russia joined Britain in a Third Coalition against Napoleon by April of 1805.

THE THIRD COALITION

Napoleon hastened to implement his deception against Britain, and Villeneuve successfully lured away the British fleet. The plan was quickly found out, however, and Napoleon only discovered his admiral's return by reading a British newspaper almost two weeks after Villeneuve had reached Spain! With the invasion foiled, Napoleon marched the Grand Army across the continent at the breakneck speed that only he could muster and overwhelmed a surprised Austrian force at Ulm on 20 October 1805. The following day, French and Spanish fleets encountered the British navy at the Battle of Trafalgar, one of the most significant battles ever fought. Admiral Horatio Nelson split the French and Spanish line of thirty-three ships and engaged each half on his own terms. After five hours of fighting, twenty of the French and Spanish vessels were out of action while Nelson's fleet of twenty-seven survived without a loss. Nelson was fatally wounded by a French sailor but died aboard his flagship, the H.M.S. *Victory* knowing the day was won.

NELSON AT TRAFALGAR

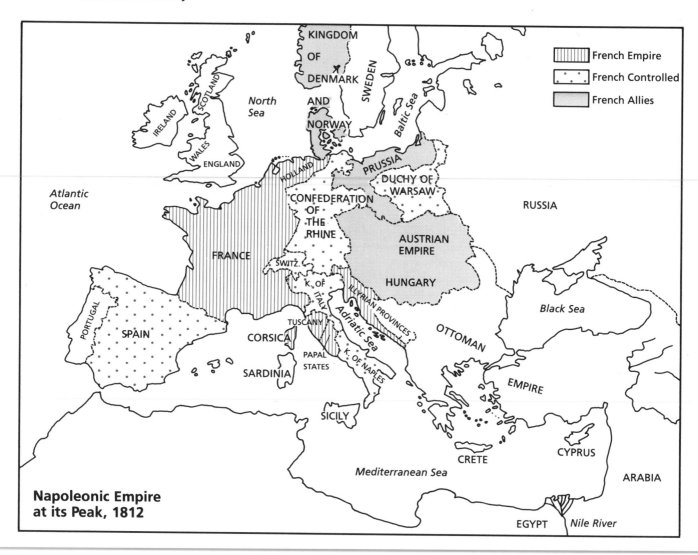

Napoleonic Empire at its Peak, 1812

Legend:
- French Empire
- French Controlled
- French Allies

Map labels: KINGDOM OF DENMARK AND NORWAY, SWEDEN, Baltic Sea, PRUSSIA, DUCHY OF WARSAW, RUSSIA, North Sea, IRELAND, SCOTLAND, WALES, ENGLAND, Atlantic Ocean, HOLLAND, CONFEDERATION OF THE RHINE, AUSTRIAN EMPIRE, HUNGARY, Black Sea, FRANCE, SWITZ., K. OF ITALY, ILLYRIAN PROVINCES, OTTOMAN EMPIRE, PORTUGAL, SPAIN, CORSICA, TUSCANY, Adriatic Sea, PAPAL STATES, K. OF NAPLES, SARDINIA, SICILY, CRETE, CYPRUS, Mediterranean Sea, ARABIA, EGYPT, Nile River

AUSTERLITZ

Trafalgar crushed Napoleon's dream of invading England and marked the beginning of a century of British naval supremacy. Upon hearing the shattering news from Trafalgar, Napoleon tried to open peace negotiations with Austria and Russia, but was refused. The emperor then marched his army from Vienna to the town of Austerlitz, where on 2 December 1805, he destroyed an Austro-Russian force in what he later described as his most brilliant military victory.

Humiliated for a third time by Napoleon, Francis II of Austria left the coalition and sued for peace. With most central European states now satellites of France following the Treaty of Pressburg, Napoleon officially dissolved the

END OF THE HOLY ROMAN EMPIRE

Holy Roman Empire in 1806 after it had staggered on in dwindling forms since the days of Charlemagne. At the same time, Napoleon reorganized French client states in Germany to form the Confederation of the Rhine. In so doing, however, Napoleon ignored the interests of Prussia, whose continued neutrality had been bought with the gift of Hanover after Austria's defeat. Concerned by the expanding French hegemony, isolated Prussia ill-advisedly declared war on France, only to be humbled by Napoleon at Jena and Auerstadt. It would have made more sense to have joined the coalition the previous year when victory was possible, rather than to go it alone with an army whose efficiency had crumbled since the days of Frederick the Great.

JENA

After occupying Berlin, Napoleon marched his army eastward to face the Russians who entered the war too late to alter the outcome. Following the bloody but indecisive battle at Eylau, Napoleon won a major victory over the Russians in June of 1807 at Friedland in east Prussia. Tsar Alexander I met Napoleon aboard a raft in the Niemen River to discuss peace terms, while the Prussian king, Frederick William III, paced anxiously along the river bank waiting for the results. Alexander was spellbound by Napoleon who, in the Treaty of Tilsit, took half of Prussia's territory, imposed an indemnity, limited the size of the Prussian army, and forced the acceptance of a French army of occupation. Napoleon agreed to help Alexander against the Turks, but in return Alexander had to recognize all French conquests in Europe and to assist France against Britain if the war continued.

FRIEDLAND

The Treaty of Tilsit represented the apex of Napoleon's power. His Grand Empire and satellite kingdoms extended from Belgium and Holland in the north to Spain in the west, Naples in the south, and the Grand Duchy of Warsaw in the east. With the Austrians, Prussians, and Russians forced into military alliance, Napoleon's Grand Empire exceeded the realm of Charlemagne and the Rome of the Caesars. As Napoleon rolled over Europe, he always presented himself as a "liberator" relieving the people he conquered from their oppressors while his troops spread the ideals and accomplishments of the revolutionary era. Upon first impression these claims could be believed, but could Napoleon's dominance stand the test of time?

TREATY OF TILSIT

NAPOLEON'S GRAND EMPIRE

The Continental System and Nationalist Backlash

Officially, Napoleon only acknowledged Trafalgar as an unwise skirmish followed by a storm that cost France some ships. Recognizing in practice that Britain was now safe from invasion, Napoleon attempted to conquer his most stubborn adversary through a more efficient version of the economic warfare first used on an occasional basis by revolutionary governments. If Britain was master of the sea, it was equally clear that Napoleon ruled much of the land, and he determined to use his military power to cut off Britain's export trade with Europe. Napoleon reasoned that with a severely reduced export market, British manufacturing would rapidly decline, mass unemployment would result, and the havoc of the moment would force Britain to beg for peace. At the same time, the continent would rationalize its own production and trade, focussing

ECONOMIC WAR

on France, to attain a high degree of economic independence. Though not allowed to sell, Britain would be allowed to buy certain French manufactures which would drain British gold reserves and hasten economic collapse.

THE CONTINENTAL SYSTEM

From Berlin, following the defeat of the Prussians at Jena, Napoleon issued a decree in 1806 that launched the **Continental System**, which forbade all states controlled or allied with France to trade with Britain. The drawback was that Napoleon lacked the navy to enforce a blockade. This meant that the trade of neutral countries was beyond his control unless neutral ships trading with Britain were actually seized.

ORDERS IN COUNCIL

The British responded in 1807 with the **Orders in Council** which required neutral ships to harbour in Britain before going to ports on the continent and turned the tables on Napoleon by blockading any ports that followed the Berlin decree. Since Britain did have a strong navy, its blockade was to prove more effective than the paper proclamations issued by the emperor. Napoleon claimed that the British violated the rights of neutral countries and, in December of 1807, he decreed from Milan that neutral ships complying with the British Orders in Council would be treated as enemy ships.

MILAN DECREE

If Britain was to be subdued by the Berlin and Milan decrees, it meant that all of Europe had to be manipulated by Napoleon. This was a tall order, but Napoleon attempted to enforce it through the satellite kingdoms and client states of France, and the treaty obligations he imposed on Austria, Prussia, and Russia.

The Continental System became the focal point of the Napoleonic Empire, but it had to be enforced with ruthless efficiency to achieve its goal. Beyond the problems of smuggling and the British navy, however, there was a serious flaw. As Napoleon tightened his grip on the continent, it was the neutral countries and French allies that were hardest hit. The British economy was inconvenienced rather than threatened, while French manufacturers enjoyed increasing prosperity in continental markets even though overseas trade suffered. Britain's control of the sea lanes not only limited the selection of goods, but forced Europe to use overland transport, which greatly increased prices. Added to this were the troops requisitioned for Napoleon's army, the cost of supplies, the natural resentment of the conqueror, and the intangible but important fact of the claims to liberty originally planted by the emperor and French troops. Unwittingly, Napoleon's attempt to cripple Britain served mainly to stimulate nationalist opposition to the Grand Empire.

THE "SPANISH ULCER"

The Iberian Peninsula was the first to revolt against the Continental System and was the crucial source that triggered Napoleon's ultimate defeat. Portuguese opposition was quickly brought into line, but it was the "Spanish ulcer" that proved to be his undoing. Although allied with France since 1796, Spain was a country led by clergymen and aristocrats who had little sympathy for the French Revolution. When Napoleon occupied the country to enforce his economic warfare against Britain, he forced the abdication of the king and placed his brother Joseph on the throne. The aristocrats and clergy led a mass insurrection against the French. Napoleon's military success in Europe was facilitated by forced marches with few supplies which enabled him to strike with surprise and to live off the rich agricultural produce of whatever community he occupied. The mountainous and barren terrain of Spain offered no such opportunity and was more suited to the hit-and-run tactics of the Spanish guerillas who challenged him. While the emperor himself might win an encounter he personally directed, the poorly armed Spanish guerilla force was able to tie up an enormous French army at great expense to the French treasury. When Napoleon overran the Papal States in 1808 to align Italy with the Continental System, the pope excommunicated him for his actions. This motivated the pious Spanish to fight even harder. Aided by the future duke of Wellington, who landed a British force in support of the Spanish cause, the six-year Peninsular War gradually eroded the military and psychological hold that Napoleon had exercised over the Grand Empire.

Though poor communications in Spain compounded military problems, it did not take long for news of the Spanish rebellion to spread across Europe. With France in difficulty, Austria declared war in 1809, intent on breaking free from the French yoke. Napoleon realized that the Grand Empire and the Continental System depended on the use as well as the threat of force. He hastily returned from Spain to take command of another French army, this one relatively inexperienced. In central Europe, where Napoleon's tactics were ideal, he carried the day against an Austrian force at Wagram. The margin of victory was much less decisive than the earlier battle at Austerlitz, but it was clear that Austria could not defeat France by itself. The Treaty of Schönbrunn compelled Austria to cede territory, enter another alliance with France, and to submit to the Continental System. Following the treaty, Napoleon attempted to soothe Austrian feelings by blending politics with his dynastic ambition. He secured an annulment of his marriage to Josephine, who had failed to provide an heir, and as his new bride took Marie Louise, daughter of Francis II of Austria and niece of Marie Antoinette. The arrangement did not abate Austrian hatred of Napoleon or make for a warm marriage, but Marie Louise did bear the emperor a son.

By 1810, the Grand Empire seemed secure, particularly after Sweden was forced to accept the Continental System and Holland, which had offered stubborn resistance, was incorporated into France. But the bitter struggle in Spain, characterized by savage atrocities on both sides, and an improved showing of the Austrian army, encouraged growing opposition from Tsar Alexander. No longer awed by Napoleon, Alexander was upset with the lack of French assistance against the Turks, Napoleon's choice of an Austrian rather than a Russian bride, expansion of the Grand Duchy of Warsaw, and the drying up of British manufactured goods. Anti-French sentiment was widespread at the Russian court and to ignore it was to invite assassination. Alexander broke from the restrictive Continental System by opening Russian ports to British ships and prepared for war.

WAGRAM

MARIE LOUISE

THE OPPOSITION OF TSAR ALEXANDER

This was a difficult moment for Napoleon, although the importance seemed to have escaped him. Bloated and pale, his physical deterioration was obvious and was accompanied by disturbing periods of drowsiness, a lack of concentration, and a refusal to accept advice. Growing opposition to the Continental System in Europe was paralleled by the opposition of the French business community which, despite previous prosperity, began to feel that more profits could be made with a different economic approach. The emperor ignored the problem. Though burdened with a ruinous war in Spain, Napoleon's hope to make the Grand Empire "the metropolis of all sovereigns" and to personally become "something fabulous, something colossal and unprecedented" drove him further from reality. After his coronation as emperor, the wars of France had become Napoleon's wars, and Napoleon's will, he truly believed, was that of the people of France. Napoleon felt that one more victory would fulfill his dream and, with an awareness of the difficulties involved, organized a military force of over six hundred thousand men to invade Russia in June of 1812.

Although the Grand Army of unprecedented size was made up of reluctant conscripts from seven states of the empire, Napoleon was supremely confident that he could squash Alexander's resistance once and for all. At first by confusion, then by design, however, Alexander withdrew into the vastness of Russia, avoiding major conflict, destroying supplies, and burning the countryside in a "scorched earth" policy of retreat. As Napoleon pursued, he overextended his supply lines and, as in Spain, he found nothing to replace them in the Russian wasteland. Napoleon pushed on, against his own better judgement, in the hope of fighting a decisive battle, but the reality of starvation led to the death or desertion of almost half a million men.

The Russians finally dug in at Borodino, 110 km from Moscow. Napoleon's depleted army won a narrow victory in one of the bloodiest battles in history when fifty thousand died and twenty thousand were wounded. Anxious to reach Moscow to witness its legendary grandeur and obtain fresh supplies, Napoleon trudged onward. Much to his surprise and frustration, Napoleon found Moscow practically deserted and the city soon in flames when he entered it in September. Forced to retreat within a month, Napoleon's weakened army straggled home in subzero temperatures, contending with almost daily attacks from the well-supplied Russian army that now advanced in its wake. Fewer than thirty thousand men crossed the Niemen River. The Grand Empire appeared to be finished.

The decimation of the French forces in the disastrous retreat from Moscow provided clear evidence that Napoleon was not invincible. Indeed, with internal reform and resentment against the foreign conqueror building, it now seemed that the French Empire could be rolled back. In Prussia, the emancipation of the serfs had opened a spectrum of opportunity for work and political power that coincided with the spread of patriotic literature and a surge of nationalist sentiment. A revised system of military service created a reserve army of one hundred and twenty thousand men and signalled the arrival of Prussia,

THE INVASION OF RUSSIA

First Coalition (1792–1793)

France *versus* Austria, Prussia, French émigrés, Spain, England, the United Netherlands, Sardinia, Naples, Sicily, and Portugal.

Second Coalition (1799)

France *versus* England, Austria, Russia, Turkey, Naples, Portugal, and the papacy.

Third Coalition (1805–1806)

France, Spain, and Napoleonic satellite states *versus* England, Russia, Austria, Sweden, Naples, and Prussia.

Fourth Coalition (1813)

France and Napoleonic satellite states *versus* England, Russia, Austria, Prussia, and Sweden.

now thoroughly regrouped after the defeat at Jena, as a modern state. The Napoleonic policies that brought civil equality and domestic improvement to the Italian states now served to inspire riots aimed at ending French dominance. Wellington pushed French armies across the Pyrenees from Spain into southern France at the very moment that the Confederation of the Rhine began to crumble.

Out of this backlash against the Grand Empire arose the Fourth Coalition of Prussia, Russia, Austria, and Britain which embarked on a "War of Liberation" to remove the French harness from Europe. Even the northern power, Sweden, agreed to send troops to assist the cause. It was as if the rights of nationality, equality, and liberty that first rallied the French Revolution were now turned on Napoleon.

THE FOURTH COALITION

Meanwhile, Napoleon had rushed back from the Moscow campaign to deal with the spread of opposition. It was a tribute to his organizational genius and personal magnetism that he raised an army of two hundred and fifty thousand men in four months, but, like the Grand Army of the previous year, it was critically inexperienced. Napoleon's tactical skill secured three minor victories in the early going, but with either his energy drained or his judgement impaired, he failed to pursue the defeated Prussian forces.

At the Battle of the Nations near Leipzig in 1813, Napoleon was overwhelmed by the combined forces of Prussia, Austria, Russia, and Sweden. Now on the run at the very moment that Wellington penetrated southern France, Napoleon rejected generous peace terms and recruited another army of about one hundred thousand largely untrained youths. Though greatly outnumbered, Napoleon staged a brilliant defence until the coalition armies left him alone and marched on Paris. With the capital in foreign hands, Napoleon's own marshals forced him to abdicate. By the Treaty of Fontainebleau in 1814, Napoleon relinquished the throne, but kept his title of emperor for the tiny Mediterranean island-kingdom of Elba, where he had already been sent, and received a substantial income. Humbled and divided after almost a quarter century of war, paid for by the blood of the common people, the citizens of France breathed a sigh of relief now that Napoleon was apparently gone forever.

LEIPZIG

THE TREATY OF FONTAINEBLEAU

From his confinement in Elba, Napoleon watched and waited as the victorious nations gathered first at Versailles, then at Vienna, to thrash out a general peace agreement for Europe. The Bourbon Louis XVIII returned to rule France with a parliament in accordance with a written constitution. Many of the émigré nobles also returned and immediately demanded reforms that would return them to political office, military rank, and their old social privileges. By comparison, Napoleon's régime seemed much more appealing.

LOUIS XVIII

The Hundred Days

Napoleon escaped from Elba and landed in France on 1 March 1815 with a few hundred soldiers, so beginning "the Hundred Days" between the first exile and final banishment. His charisma and bravery quickly won over the troops sent to arrest him. The general discontent with the Bourbon government that threatened to reverse the gains of the Revolution enabled Napoleon to regain Paris in three weeks without firing a shot. The crowds cheered wildly upon his return and Napoleon proclaimed his intention to establish a liberal régime.

WATERLOO

The allies at Vienna promptly stopped their squabbling, condemned Napoleon, and prepared for war. Napoleon had no chance despite another valiant attempt. At Waterloo in Belgium, the better-equipped armies of Prussia, Holland, and Britain greatly outnumbered the French force that was, on this critical occasion, not so skillfully handled by Napoleon. In addition, the Austrian and Russian armies waited in the wings to finish off any French survivors. Napoleon was decisively defeated on 18 June 1815 after a three-day battle by the combined forces of Europe, and he was compelled to abdicate for a second time.

ST. HELENA

He was sent to the distant British island of St. Helena, over 7200 km away in the South Atlantic. Here, Napoleon spent the last six years of his life writing his memoirs to project the most favourable interpretation of his career into the myth he had created.

Napoleon inherited the ideals and the wars of the French Revolution. The ideals were preserved in institutions and social changes and were exported to Europe in the emperor's own wars of expansion. By introducing and encouraging equality and fraternity wherever his armies marched, Napoleon inadvertently stirred a nationalist sentiment throughout the continent that undermined the Grand Empire at the very moment it seemed secure. As Napoleon's experienced officers and troops became depleted in the endless campaigns of his heroic ambition, as Spain and Russia drained his resources and maligned his reputation, and as European generals began to work in concert and master the very tactics that Napoleon had employed, the emperor's defeat could not be avoided.

THE EMPEROR'S CAREER

History lived and history recorded are never the same, but Napoleon's impact on both has few equals. His career cannot be crystalized in a single passage, but the force and contradictions of Napoleon are perhaps appropriately reflected in the words of Alfred de Musset:

> The life of Europe was centred on one man; all were trying to fill their lungs with the air he breathed. . . .
> Never had there been so many sleepless nights as in the time of that man; never had there been seen . . . such a nation of desolate mothers; never was there such a silence about those who spoke of death. And yet there was never such joy, such life, such fanfares of war in all hearts. Never was there such pure sunlight as that which dried all this blood.

The Emergence of Industrialism to 1850

The sweeping changes brought to the Western world by political revolution were accompanied by major developments in industry. Although often referred to as the **Industrial Revolution**, the term is somewhat misleading. There was no precise beginning; much of the impact was gradual; the changes continue to affect our lives today; and the process is still spreading to the developing nations of the Americas, Africa, and Asia. Whatever the label applied to these changes, the key ingredient was the substitution of machinery and mechanical power for manual and animal labour in the production of materials and goods.

THE NATURE OF INDUSTRIAL DEVELOPMENT

The earliest appearance of such machinery came in England after the middle of the eighteenth century for reasons that we will examine. Prior to these technological improvements, however, was the equally dramatic breakthrough during the seventeenth century in the production of weaponry that historians are only now starting to appreciate. This was the period when England became a commercial and military leader, and it marked the arrival of muskets and artillery as permanent replacements for the sword and pike on the battlefield. Only the introduction of the removable bayonet in 1680 provided a cruel reminder of a previous age of hand-to-hand combat. The reliance on bigger, bulkier, and more efficient weapons was also reflected in naval warfare. In 1632, the Royal Navy listed only 81 brass and 147 iron pieces in its arsenal. By 1683, English warships were armed with 8 396 cannons and over 350 000 cannon balls. The increase in quantity and improvements in quality of firearms of all types required increased knowledge about the combustion of gunpowder and better construction of gun chambers, barrels, and carriages. These technical advances either anticipated the inventiveness of the machine age or provided technology that could be directly applied in various stages of production.

THE ROLE OF WEAPONRY

The conditions necessary for industrial development came together in Britain after 1760. Britain was the world's leading commercial nation blessed with an excellent location for overseas trade. The need for finished goods to export to the colonies and the Orient stimulated domestic production. Institutions like the Bank of England that originally provided credit for trade and commerce were also available to back larger industrial enterprises and government financial needs as they arose. Provincial banks, which numbered four hundred in 1790, provided credit to merchants and manufacturers on a local scale. Many of Britain's advantages sprang from the fact that it was a small, relatively flat island. Long safe from foreign invasion and free from internal strife since the Glorious Revolution of 1688, Britain escaped the dislocation and damage of war that plagued the continent during the eighteenth century. In a country that was stable and united, the British government was able to pursue policies favourable to commerce and industry that were not possible in the divided German states or amid the web of tariffs and tolls that fragmented the French economy. The island had many natural harbours and an abundance of navigable streams that provided good communication and cheap transportation over the short, cross-country distances. Overland transportation on the continent was more expensive and much less efficient on unimproved roads. As industry grew in the later eighteenth and early nineteenth centuries, hundreds of miles of canals and turnpikes were constructed that gave Britain better transporta-

THE SETTING FOR BRITISH INDUSTRIAL DEVELOPMENT

tion than any other country in Europe. At the very moment when wood, a much-used, traditional resource, was in short supply because of depleted forests, Britain was fortunate to have large reserves of coal and iron that were essential for the new technologies.

CHANGES IN AGRICULTURE

Changes in agricultural production greatly assisted industrial development and again Britain had a major advantage. Traditionally, village farmlands looked like patchwork quilts of rectangular furlong fields, subdivided into half-hectare strips. Farmers employed the three-field system in which one field was always fallow. Ploughing was done co-operatively and, since farmers usually owned a strip in each furlong, every farmer had at least some land under cultivation. Farmers also had the right to pasture grazing animals on the common land of the village. From the sixteenth century onward, however, English landlords began the **enclosure movement** which eventually sectioned off both the furlong and common pasture. Farmers received lots equal to the total area owned in individual strips with an occasional extra allotment as the common land disappeared. The impact of private ownership gradually introduced by enclosure was to improve the efficiency of owners who now had one large farm and to squeeze out the farmers who had less land and could not survive without access to common pasture. As owners of large farms gobbled up the smaller, less productive lots, Britain developed a class of wealthy landlords who owned huge estates that were rented to tenant farmers in holdings of 40 to 200 ha. At the same time, French farms averaged only 5 ha in size, while German farms, save for the estates of the Junker class, were even smaller. Higher production on British farms led to the sale of agricultural surpluses and the increased commercialization of agriculture. By the eighteenth century, it also meant that less labour was required to produce more food. Many peasant farmers who could not find work on large farms began to emigrate to the cities and even to America to find jobs and a new way of life.

ENCLOSURE

As the basis of landownership changed, improved methods of agriculture also helped to increase yields while new breeding practices resulted in more food from livestock. During the early eighteenth century there was a new interest in scientific experiment and innovation that produced techniques as revolutionary as the "enlightened" ideas about social progress. Lord Townshend introduced the turnip, a crop that could grow on marginal land and which could be used with clover to provide forage for livestock while adding nitrogen to the soil. When used on fallow fields in the traditional crop rotation cycle, Townshend discovered that the subsequent yields of wheat and barley increased significantly. After watching vineyard workers in France maximize yields by hoeing and aerating the soil, Jethro Tull developed animal-drawn machinery, including his famous drill-plough, to plant seeds in rows, break the ground, and keep weeds under control. Robert Bakewell was equally successful in new selective breeding methods that represented a turning point in animal husbandry. His work paved the way for the introduction of new breeds, including Hereford cattle, Berkshire hogs, and Leicester sheep. Aided by the increased availability

"TURNIP" TOWNSHEND

JETHRO TULL

ROBERT BAKEWELL

of animal feed, the weight and quantity of sheep and cattle doubled by the end of the century and the animals had a higher proportion of meat.

With meat now a regular part of people's diet and with improvements in sanitation and medicine, the death rate declined and population growth skyrocketed. Britain's population grew by less than .5 million between 1700 and 1750, but between 1750 and 1800 it jumped by 4 million and between 1800 and 1850 by an astounding 10 million people. As more children survived to adulthood, had larger families, and lived longer, they chose or were forced to go into the cities. London grew from nine hundred and fifty-nine thousand in 1800 to two million six hundred and eighty-one thousand by 1850. This was typical of the increase experienced in the five largest cities. By 1850, more people lived in the city than in the country and it was the urban population that provided most of the cheap labour demanded by the new technologies of the industrial age.

POPULATION GROWTH

The dynamic thrust that produced the industrial age came from innovations in three key areas, the first of which came in cotton textiles. Indeed, it was the rapid progress made in the British textile industry that gave rise to the term "Industrial Revolution." At the turn of the eighteenth century, guilds were in decline and most manufacturing was done in the so-called domestic system. Merchants or capitalists would purchase material and distribute it to people who produced the finished products by hand in their own homes. The cotton textile industry depended on the importation of cotton fibre that was turned into cloth by thousands of spinners and weavers across the countryside. Textile manufacturers had successfully lobbied the government to pass the Calico Acts of 1700 and 1720 that prohibited the importation of finished cotton cloth from India. This gave the domestic industry in Britain a chance to develop.

COTTON TEXTILES

THE DOMESTIC SYSTEM

A series of inventions, each related to the other, resulted in spectacular growth during the last half of the eighteenth century. The first step came in 1733, when John Kay invented the flying shuttle that allowed one weaver to do the work of two and increased the demand for yarn. This demand was met in 1765, when James Hargreaves developed his "spinning jenny," which turned four spindles at the same time and produced a fine cotton thread. Four years later, Richard Awkright built (though Thomas Highs invented) the water frame that produced a much stronger thread at even cheaper prices. In 1771, Awkright organized the first cotton mill in which he brought together a large number of spinning machines and employed workers from the local villages to run them so that cotton could be produced on a large scale. The idea caught on and, by 1788, there were 119 cotton mills in Britain. Perhaps the most significant breakthrough, perfected in 1779, was Samuel Compton's "mule," which combined elements of the spinning jenny and the water frame. The mule produced a fine *and* strong thread, and by 1812, 80 percent of Britain's cotton was produced using this machine. Mechanical weaving began when Edmund Cartwright secured a patent for a power loom in 1785. The savings from power spinning and weaving were such that cotton cloth could now be exported to India where it

THE FLYING SHUTTLE

SPINNING JENNY

THE WATER FRAME

THE MULE

THE POWER LOOM

THE FACTORY SYSTEM

THE IRON INDUSTRY

THE PUDDLING PROCESS

THE ROLLING MILL

THE STEAM ENGINE

JAMES WATT

undersold the local market! The demand for cotton cloth could not be satisfied. Following Eli Whitney's invention of the "cotton gin" in 1793, which cheaply separated the seeds from American short-staple cotton fibres, the United States became the major supplier of raw cotton for British mills. British imports of cotton fibre rose from about 2 000 000 kg annually in the 1770s to over 400 000 000 kg in 1860. The methods that saw cotton replace wool as Britain's leading industry were soon adapted to sugar refineries, rope factories, distilleries, and a host of other manufacturers that witnessed the value of **mechanization** and the factory system in the production process.

The second major impetus towards industrial development came from the iron industry which had existed since the medieval period. Wood, in the form of charcoal, had traditionally been used to heat the iron ore, but it was now in short supply as forests became depleted satisfying the demands for ships, houses, furniture, and heat. Although Britain had abundant reserves of coal, it added impurities that reduced the quality of iron. In 1709, Abraham Darby discovered how to make an improved grade of iron by using burnt coal or coke with limestone to smelt iron ore. It was still inferior to the iron produced in other countries even after it was hammered by a blacksmith or ironworker to remove the impurities that remained. In 1760, Britain imported over twice the amount of iron it produced, mostly from Sweden and Russia. During the 1770s, the application of steam to operate bellows and hammers improved the quality of British iron. The turning point, however, came in 1783 and 1784 when Peter Onions and Henry Cort independently perfected the puddling process in which molten iron was stirred in puddles to cleanse the iron of impurities. Cort, who was intent on making better guns for the British navy, also developed the rolling mill. White-hot iron was sandwiched between massive rollers that manipulated the iron into the sheets, rods, beams, or rails that were required. Production in iron took off in a fashion that paralleled the growth of the textile industry. Britain's iron output rose from 18 288 t in 1757 to about 127 000 t in 1796 to 2 286 000 t by 1850. In the same period, Britain had changed from a net importer to become the world's leading producer and exporter of iron and its associated products.

The third critical advance was the fundamental improvement in the steam engine. Like the Egyptians at the dawn of history, eighteenth-century industrialists had to rely on wind, water, and human and animal labour for power. Better windmills and water wheels were built, but they were dependent upon the seasons and the whim of the weather. In 1709, Thomas Newcomen built a cumbersome steam engine with a low efficiency that could only be used to pump water out of a mine. The problem was that the cylinder had to be heated and cooled with each stroke of the piston. In 1769, after years of experimentation, James Watt, an instrument maker at the University of Glasgow, developed an external condenser that solved the problem by removing the steam from the cylinder. Watt teamed up with a successful businessman named Matthew Boulton and, by hiring skilled watchmakers, they were able to build an engine that could drive the vertical movement of the piston into a rotary action capable of driving industrial machinery. Watt and Boulton received a twenty-five-year patent for their steam engine in 1775 and agreed to install their engine in return for a rental fee. All of the 481 steam engines operating in Britain in 1800 came from the Boulton-Watt factory. The engine was first employed as an efficient water pump but soon found use as a power source for industrial bellows in iron production, the manufacture of cotton, milling, and brewing, among several others.

MATTHEW BOULTON

As the benefits of the factory system became apparent, the quality of iron improved, and the steam engine unleashed a new and usable source of power, industrial development became self-perpetuating. In factories, workers concentrated on one particular task in the manufacturing process rather than trying to make the entire finished product themselves. This division of labour greatly increased production, as it was gradually applied in industry after industry. Demands for high-quality iron in factory machinery, guns, ships' hardware, and agricultural equipment created a corresponding demand for coal to produce the iron. Iron and coal had to be transported and the solution in the industrial era was the railroad. British coal carts had been run on wooden rails built by German miners since the sixteenth century. Wooden rails were gradually replaced by iron, but only gravity, human, and horsepower moved the carts. In 1804, Richard Trevithick built a rather inefficient steam locomotive to ease the task. It was not until 1825, however, that George Stephenson's locomotive, the *Rocket*, made a successful run over the Stockton and Darlington railroad and demonstrated new possibilities. The railroad era was launched in 1830 when Stephenson's engine opened the Liverpool and Manchester line, the first specifically built for steam locomotives. The railroad not only became essential for transportation, but increased the demand for iron and coal. By 1850, Britain had constructed 10 560 km of track, far more than any country in Europe and second only to the United States, where distances were much greater.

DIVISION OF LABOUR

STEPHENSON'S ROCKET

The short-term and long-term benefits derived from higher production were rivalled by the misery of those who endured the living and working conditions of the early industrial city. People flocked into urban areas that were ill-equipped to provide the necessities of life for such a rapid influx. Tenement buildings and rows of decrepit cottages that housed up to twelve people per room closed in city streets strewn with rotting refuse that produced foul odours and disease. Construction was so shoddy that entire blocks were known to crumble and sanitation facilities were virtually nonexistent. The squalor often equalled the worst conditions of the preindustrial era. Over it all hung the blanket of black smoke that left grit on every brick. Although the death rate for Britain dropped dramatically, it actually made a significant increase in the five largest cities during the 1830s and 1840s when industrialism became firmly

URBAN SQUALOR

Gustave Doré's Over London by Rail *shows English city life during the Industrial Revolution. Construction of row and tenement housing was often so shoddy that walls simply collapsed.*

entrenched. Death always came earlier to the labouring classes, and it was not uncommon to find industrial cities where a labourer's average age at death was twenty-one years or less. With the congestion of people increasing the danger of crime, and few outlets in the form of parks or recreation, the industrial city was a place to which people were driven when they had nowhere else to go.

THE CAPITALIST CLASS

Working conditions were a product of the rapid pace of industrial development and a reflection of employer attitudes. Employers were usually members of the new middle class of capitalists who owned the banks, factories, businesses, and railroads. They grew up in a laissez faire atmosphere where the government allowed economic development without interfering in a negative way. Their economic strength was translated into political power when the First Reform Bill of 1832 began to concentrate parliamentary representation in the cities and enfranchised the middle class by introducing new voting regulations. From this point onward, the landed aristocracy of inherited wealth–unless it took advantage of the new opportunities–began to give way to the influence of those who made their money in the business of industrial development.

INDUSTRIAL WORKERS

Equally new and far more numerous were the industrial workers, a loosely knit class that included a wide range of occupations and interests. It was this group in all its variety that had to suffer its employers' attempts to keep costs down and production up to compete successfully with other manufacturers.

Women were treated with less respect than men, and children with less than either parent. This meant lower wages and docile workers for employers who willingly exploited thousands of children in an effort to pay for the costs of the new machinery and other overhead. In the textile industry, the working day was lengthened from twelve to fourteen to sixteen hours with few stoppages for meals or rest. Children were awakened at five o'clock in the morning to begin a long day and often had to be whipped just to avoid falling asleep. The luckiest ones were simply pale, sickly, and poorly clothed. Many others were deformed through injury and overwork which attested to their employers' lack of concern for safety standards and the dangers of the new industrial machinery. To keep humidity high and prevent the breakage of thread, cotton mills kept windows closed. This left workers no choice but to breathe the hot, dusty air filled with cotton fibres throughout their working lives. Most men were between the ages of sixteen and twenty-four and appeared stunted and enfeebled after experiencing years in such adverse conditions.

The situation was no better in the mines that supplied industries with raw materials. All employees faced the dangers of rock slides, caveins, and flooding that were common to the industry. Women and children crawled on hands and bare knees pulling and pushing loaded carts in dimly lit, poorly ventilated, narrow tunnels. Miners were often tied to the company through the "truck system" in which they were paid in goods, services, and company script that was only redeemable at the company store. Conversion of surplus script into real money was difficult and often discouraged by the company.

THE "TRUCK SYSTEM"

And yet the age was not without conscience. As humanitarian reformers from all political parties tried to catch up to the abuses imposed by rapid change, legislation began to reverse the damage that was done. The specifics of reform suggest how extreme the problems had become. By the Factory Act of 1833, children under the age of nine could not be employed in textile factories; children between nine and thirteen were limited to nine working hours a day and forty-eight hours in a week; while children from thirteen to eighteen could work twelve hours a day and sixty-nine hours in a week. The Mines Act of 1842 prohibited boys under the age of ten and all women from working in the mines. In 1847, the twelve-hour day was introduced for men in most industries while children under eighteen and all females were restricted to ten hours a day.

THE BEGINNING OF REFORM

Other attempts to improve the lot of workers were less successful prior to 1850. Robert Owen, humanitarian owner of England's largest cotton mill, did what he could to provide decent conditions for his own workers. Owen's efforts to organize workers into one big union in 1834, however, ended in failure as a result of government repression and division within the ranks. Workers then tried another approach. With only one male in eight eligible to vote after the First Reform Bill, an attempt was made to extend democracy to the industrial working class. The People's Charter, drawn up in 1838, called for universal male suffrage, the annual election of Parliament, the secret ballot, equal elec-

ROBERT OWEN

THE CHARTISTS

toral districts, and the payment of and removal of property qualifications for members of Parliament. With Parliament controlled by the middle class, petitions presented on behalf of the **Chartists** were turned down in 1839 and 1842. In the strikes and riots that followed in protest, the government jailed many of the Chartist leaders and even sent some to the penal colony in Australia. A final petition of 2 million signatures, many of which were falsified, was prepared for presentation to Parliament in a great demonstration calling for five hundred thousand supporters. Alarmed by the possibility of revolution, the government hired one hundred and seventy-six thousand constables to disperse the crowd and again rejected the petition. This left significant reform for the working class to succeeding generations.

THE LUDDITES

The problems associated with industrial development were not always approached through legal reforms. Rapid technological change created new jobs and made others obsolete. With the introduction of the power loom, the livelihood of weavers using the hand-loom was doomed to extinction and, between 1811 and 1830, they turned to violent protest. They called themselves the **Luddites** in honour of Ned Ludd, who had protested against the use of stocking-knitting machines during the 1780s. Secret meetings were held, military drills practised, and notices were circulated invoking factory workers and the communities to destroy the new machinery until its use was banned by Parliament. Riots and protests in Stockport, Middleton, and Manchester, among several other places resulted in hundreds of deaths and injuries, but the power of the middle-class factory owners through the local militia was not to be denied. It was as if the violent protests of blacksmiths in another generation could have stopped the arrival of the automobile. Yet, the dislocation was real and symbolized the problems people had to face in adapting to changing times.

THE END OF MERCANTILISM

The demand for British products after 1815 stimulated continued industrialization and, between 1830 and 1850, the process was completed. Britain was the world's financial, commercial, and industrial leader. With the repeals of the Corn Laws, which had placed a tax on imported grain in 1846, and the Navigation Acts in 1849, Britain had virtually abandoned the old colonial (mercantilist) system and turned to free trade. British production could compete favourably with any nation. Since most European countries were only in the earliest stages of industrialization, they usually followed policies of protection to encourage development of their domestic industries.

THE SLOW SPREAD OF INDUSTRIALISM

In the decade after the Napoleonic wars, British methods first spread to Belgium, a country blessed with newly won independence, proximity to Britain, and large reserves of coal. By 1830, Belgium's coal production tripled that of France, steam power began to change Belgium's textile industry and, as in France, coal began to replace charcoal in the production of iron. In 1835, Belgium inaugurated an efficient railroad system to win the carrying trade of northwestern Europe. French trade and production had declined with the collapse of Napoleon's Continental System, but by the 1830s France ranked second on

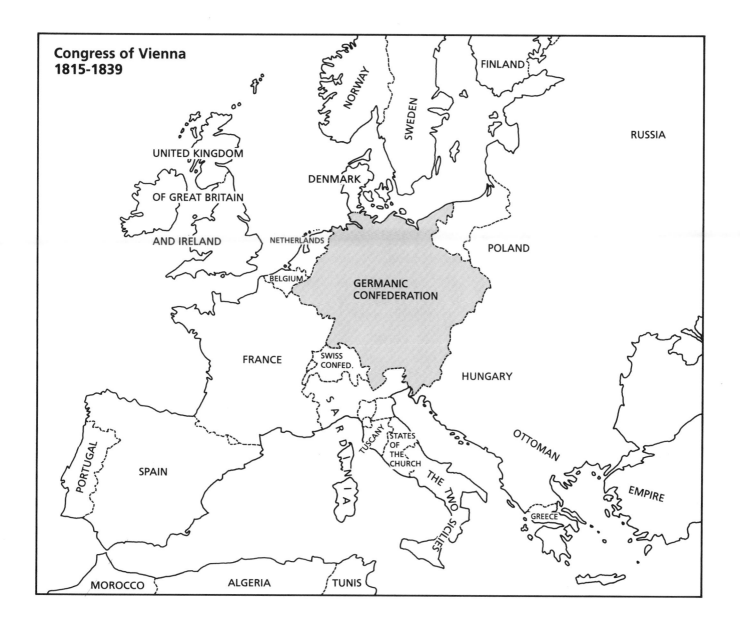

**Congress of Vienna
1815–1839**

NORWAY

FINLAND

SWEDEN

RUSSIA

UNITED KINGDOM

OF GREAT BRITAIN

DENMARK

AND IRELAND

POLAND

NETHERLANDS

BELGIUM

GERMANIC
CONFEDERATION

FRANCE

SWISS
CONFED.

HUNGARY

PORTUGAL

SPAIN

SARDINIA

TUSCANY

STATES
OF
THE
CHURCH

THE TWO SICILIES

OTTOMAN

EMPIRE

GREECE

MOROCCO

ALGERIA

TUNIS

the continent to Belgium in industrialization. Although it was possible to travel from Paris to Warsaw by rail in 1848, the new techniques of production were slow to be employed. In the rest of Europe, industrialization was not completed until the second half of the nineteenth century.

Despite its impressive beginning, the United States, like most of Europe, did not produce a mature industrial society until after 1850. Railroad construction was paralleled by the introduction of labour-saving devices like the sewing machine and the mechanical reaper, but these were used only on a small scale. Eli Whitney, whose invention of the cotton gin greatly increased the productive value of the southern slave, also created a method of musket production using standardized, interchangeable parts. Combined with the idea of the division of labour, the use of interchangeable parts eventually became a cornerstone of industrial America in the twentieth century.

COMMENT

As the war against Napoleon wound down, the allies began the peace process that was to shape Europe for succeeding generations. In March 1814, Austria, Prussia, Russia, and Britain agreed to continue their alliance for twenty years to maintain the settlement they were about to draw up. To their credit, a distinction was made between Napoleon and the French nation in the First Treaty of Paris, signed in May by the restored Bourbon monarch Louis XVIII. The lenient terms recognized the French boundaries of 1792, demanded no indemnity, and even allowed France to keep the art treasures that Napoleon had plundered from Europe. Napoleon's irresponsible, last-ditch attempt to rally the French people and regain power in the Hundred Days, however, forced the allies to impose a harsher settlement. In the Second Treaty of Paris in November, 1815, France was reduced to the more restrictive boundaries of 1790, required to pay an indemnity of 700 million francs, subjected to an army of occupation for five years, and had to return its stolen art treasures.

Meanwhile, at the **Congress of Vienna**, assembled between September of 1814 and June of 1815 to iron out a general settlement for Europe, the delegates of the victors had to deal with the forces set in motion by the French Revolution and Napoleon. The seriousness of this pivotal conference was set against a lavish spectacle of entertainment. Dinners and dances, attended by the crowned heads of state and the aristocratic élite in their striking uniforms, alternated with, and often became part of, the business meetings and intrigues where the future of Europe was to be decided. The talented negotiators, however, worked as hard as they played and never lost sight of their purpose. Their main objective was to prevent French domination of the continent and the catastrophe of endless war by reestablishing a balance of power among the nations of Europe. The chief architect and manipulator of the settlement was Austria's outstanding chancellor, Clemens Wenceslas Lothar von Metternich (1773–1859), whose family had been forced to flee its castle during the Napoleonic wars. Lord Castlereagh of Britain, though not an admirer of Metternich, was also influential in bringing a measure of stability to Europe. This would enable Britain to sell its burgeoning supply of goods unhindered by war. At the same time, the victors wanted to secure compensation for the losses incurred during the years of conflict. Disagreements, squabbling, and even diplomatic confrontation resulted as negotiators manoeuvred for advantage before a final settlement was achieved. Nevertheless, the Congress of Vienna was imbued with the conservative philosophy of Edmund Burke whose *Reflections on the Revolution in France*, published in 1790, condemned the Revolution and, therefore, now suited aristocratic intentions. Burke had argued that a small minority had wrongly severed the country from its past. The congress now attempted to revive the virtue of the old order that existed before the Revolution. Wherever it was possible, this meant reestablishing "legitimate" governments of absolute monarchy with a supportive nobility to replace the governments that Napoleon had left behind.

The balance of power created to contain France was the greatest achievement of the Congress of Vienna. Although isolated struggles occurred, there was no general war in which all of the great powers were involved until after 1850, largely because the balance of 1815 gave no reason for conflict. When the congress had redrawn the map of Europe, Holland received the Austrian Netherlands (Belgium and Luxembourg) while Austria was compensated with Venice and Lombardy in Italy. Prussia received territory from Saxony (an ally of Napoleon) and the left bank of the Rhine, thereby becoming the protector of German interests. There was no desire to return to the three hundred states of the Holy Roman Empire, so Napoleon's Confederation of the Rhine was replaced by the loose German Confederation of thirty-nine states that included Prussia, but which was under the leadership of Austria. Denmark, another supporter of Napoleon, was penalized with the loss of Norway to Sweden, a nation that had sent troops to ensure the emperor's defeat. The unstable Tsar Alexander retained his conquests of Finland and Bessarabia won earlier in the war and had to abandon his dream of an expanded kingdom of Poland. This would have cost Prussia the territory it controlled in Poland and given Alexander a springboard for further expansion into Eastern Europe. Britain, which had financed much of the war with generous subsidies to the allies, retained strategic posts taken by the British navy for the benefit of a worldwide empire. This included Heligoland, Malta, the Cape of Good Hope, Singapore, Ceylon, Trinidad, and Tobago.

With the conclusion of the Treaty of Vienna in June of 1815, the unpredictable Tsar Alexander entered a religious phase of personal development. He believed that the treaty should be underscored by a "Holy Alliance" in which sovereigns were to regard each other as brothers and rule according to Christian principles. The high-blown rhetoric was ridiculed by many but signed by all so that Alexander would not be offended. Of greater importance was the Quadruple Alliance of Russia, Austria, Prussia, and Britain concluded the same day as the Second Treaty of Paris. Here, the great powers agreed to defend the

Vienna agreement, by force if required, and to hold conferences to discuss action to maintain peace as the need developed. The Congress System, which was expanded to readmit France to the European community at the Congress of Aix-la-Chapelle in 1818, foreshadowed elements of the League of Nations formed in 1919 after World War I. Even though the Congress System was whittled away through self-interest by 1828, it marked an important and serious attempt to maintain peace and stability following a quarter century of constant warfare.

As the royal influence of the Bourbons and the Hapsburgs resurrected itself on the decaying thrones of Europe, it became clear that the real danger to peace and order came from within each nation. The allies had made war on Napoleon because he was a tyrant who treated the nationalities of Europe like pawns in the game of empire. Now that the emperor was gone, they proceeded to make the same mistake. People of all ethnic backgrounds were placed under governments they disliked and had no voice in choosing. The aristocratic Metternich, whose name became associated with restored monarchy and the balance of power, had good reason to be concerned. The nationalism spawned by the French Revolution, and carried to the corners of Europe by Napoleon, spelled trouble for a state like Austria with such a variety of peoples within its jurisdiction. As the Poles, Czechs, Croats, Slovaks, Ruthenes, Magyars, Serbs, and Italians under Austrian rule began to appreciate their separate languages and cultures, each group began to think of the day when it might establish its own country. Nationalism often became aligned with liberalism, which stressed freedom and equality for the individual. And liberalism found expression in the democratic notion of choosing one's own government, a notion that could threaten the hierarchy of nobles and kings arbitrarily established by the Congress of Vienna. Metternich equated democracy with revolution and he believed that the French Revolution was the ''hydra with jaws open to swallow up the social order.''

A series of uprisings, motivated by varying degrees of nationalism, liberalism, and democracy, broke out after 1819. Revolts in Italy and Spain gave Metternich his chance to call congresses at Troppau, Laibach, and Verona (1820–1822). Most of the allied powers agreed to intervene militarily and were successful in subduing the revolutions. Britain remained aloof, partly for domestic reasons and partly because it did not wish to intervene in a revolt on the continent unless British interests were directly involved. The situation in Spain was complicated by revolt in the Spanish colonies of the New World with which Britain was enjoying a prosperous trade. While Britain accepted the restoration of Ferdinand VII to the Spanish throne, the other allied powers were warned to keep their hands off the Spanish colonies. At this juncture, Britain received somewhat overblown support from the United States. Concerned about Russian advances on the Pacific coast, the United States granted recognition to the South American republics and proclaimed the Monroe Doctrine, warning European nations against any interference in the American hemisphere. The United

States lacked the power to enforce such a bold declaration, but the British, with the world's strongest navy, embraced the doctrine and also gave recognition to the South American colonies. Such a rebuke staggered the Congress System.

The Greek rebellion against the Ottoman Empire, which began in 1820, provided the final knockout. The Greeks were compared with the Athenians of the past and caught the imagination of the public, while the Turks were likened to the dreaded Persians. In 1828, the British, French, and Russian navies, hoping to share in the benefits of intervention, destroyed the Turkish and Egyptian fleets at Navarino Bay. This gave the Greeks the push they needed to achieve independence, which was finally recognized by the sultan in 1830. It also undermined Metternich's hope of co-operation among the great powers by placing Britain, France, and Russia in support of a new national state, while Prussia and Austria protested against the whole enterprise.

Although collective action by the great powers eventually broke down, the conservative elements in each nation remained intent on preserving order. In Germany, the universities had been hotbeds of nationalist agitation and were riddled with secret societies pushing liberal ideas. When a university student assassinated an unpopular, reactionary journalist in 1819, Metternich saw his chance and secured passage of the repressive Carlsbad Decrees. The decrees set up a strict censorship of the press, prohibited meetings, and established a special inquiry to investigate student activity. Metternich's victory was so complete that there were few nationalist disturbances for almost three decades. The year of the Carlsbad Decrees in Germany also saw a British crowd assemble on St. Peter's Field, Manchester to listen to a speech advocating government reform. The gathering was peaceful, but local authorities panicked and had the speaker arrested. They ordered first the local militia, then a group of Waterloo veterans to disperse the crowd. In the confusion that followed, known as the Peterloo Massacre, eleven people were killed, while over four hundred were injured. The government responded with the Six Acts of 1819 that placed restrictions on the press, public meetings, and the right to bear arms.

It became increasingly difficult to keep a lid on change as commerce expanded and Europe began to industrialize after 1815. The number and influence of middle-class capitalists, industrialists, merchants, bankers, teachers, and lawyers grew significantly. They wanted the last vestiges of feudalism removed and to achieve political power equivalent to their economic strength. Usually, this meant a demand for liberal reform to change the degree of representation. In the early stages of this process, the demands for change won the support of the industrial workers, who became the largest class as factories gradually infiltrated the cities. Once the middle class entrenched itself in power, however, it began to oppose further reform that might shift control in the direction of the workers. In Britain, where the political and social structure bent in accordance with the liberal trend, the middle class secured their political goals without violence in the First Reform Bill of 1832. Across the English Channel in France,

Moments in Time

Charles Maurice Talleyrand-Perigord (1754–1838) was a skilled diplomat and political chameleon who enjoyed a truly remarkable career in ever changing times. Ordained as a priest, he was excommunicated for accepting the Civil Constitution of the Clergy in 1790. Following the execution of Louis XVI, Talleyrand was listed as an émigré and fled to the United States. Allowed to return in 1796, he served as foreign minister for the Directory and later for Napoleon after working for the successful coup of 1799. Talleyrand reemerged at the Congress of Vienna where he attempted to secure the return of the Bourbon monarchy and advantageous peace terms for France. In the July Revolution of 1830, it was Talleyrand who advised Louis Phillipe to accept the French crown. He finished his extraordinary career as the French ambassador to Great Britain.

the rising ambition of the middle class came into conflict with the entrenched aristocracy and turned to revolution.

The Bourbon Restoration in France did not turn back the clock to 1789 thanks to the good sense and realistic attitude of Louis XVIII (1815–1824). Louis accepted the will of the allied powers and gave his subjects a Constitutional Charter. The basic equality and freedom of all Frenchmen was guaranteed and an elected Chamber of Deputies instituted, although the electorate was limited to one hundred thousand of the wealthiest citizens in a population of 29 million. Despite the political turmoil in the early years, Louis's government paid the war indemnity and passed some liberal reforms, including voluntary enlistment, rather than conscription, for recruitment in the army. More repressive measures came after 1820 following the murder of the duke of Berry, thought to be the only Bourbon likely to produce a male heir to the throne.

Upon Louis's death in 1824, his brother became Charles X (1824–1830) and he immediately and unwisely determined to reverse the progress made by the Revolution. Through financial manipulation of the national debt, Charles saved 1 billion francs and then gave it to the nobility to pay for losses suffered after 1789. This alienated the middle-class holders of government bonds, who now had to accept lower interest rates to make the saving possible. An attempt by Charles to reintroduce elements of feudalism was stopped in the legislature. When elections in 1830 gave strong representation to the middle class, Charles dissolved the government, called another election, and found himself faced with more middle-class opposition than before. On 26 July 1830, Charles issued the Ordinances of St. Cloud which suspended the freedom of the press, dissolved the Chamber of Deputies, and reduced the size of the electorate to weaken the voting strength of the opposition. Two days later, "La Marseillaise" could be heard in Paris and the streets were barricaded with paving stones, furniture, wagons, and any other available material to heights of 20 m! A revolution had begun and Charles, who had left for a brief hunting trip, now fled the country for Scotland.

The July Revolution, though supported by students and workers who voiced radical demands, quickly came under the control of more moderate, middle-class reformers. Louis Phillippe (1830–1848), the duke of Orleans, was invited to be the king, through God's grace and the "will of the nation." When Tsar Nicholas I (1825–1855) heard about the July Revolution, he exclaimed, "Saddle your horses, gentlemen, France is in revolution again." And France did ignite a series of revolts across Europe. Uprisings in Germany and Italy enjoyed initial success only to see Austria firmly establish conservative rule. Belgium won its independence from Holland, while Britain, which avoided revolt, was spurred to parliamentary reform. Meanwhile, Tsar Nicholas squashed an ill-managed Polish plot of aristocrats and university students by imprisoning and executing thousands, while as many more intellectuals fled to the safety of London and Paris. In essence, the forces of change had succeeded in Britain, France, and Belgium, where industrialism was most advanced, the middle class large, and their determination intense. Revolutions in Germany, Italy, and Poland failed because industrialism was least developed, and the fledgling middle class was overpowered by the organized force of the conservative governments.

After 1830, the nationalism and liberalism that owed their origins to the French Revolution and the crosscurrents of industrial development intensified throughout Europe. The middle classes became more determined to achieve or extend their power as circumstances warranted. For the industrial workers, the goal was either to gain a share of what the middle classes had won or to unite with them to improve the lot of all.

Meanwhile, radical intellectuals began to prepare new ground with theories of socialism in which the government owned and administered the means of production and distribution. Among the most prominent was the "Utopian socialist" Henri de Saint Simon, who dreamed of a society governed by intelligent leaders in which people worked according to their talents and were rewarded according to their contributions. Louis Blanc shifted the emphasis in his phrase "From each according to his abilities, to each according to his needs." For Blanc, the role of the government was to assist in building national workshops, which he believed would become so efficient that they would run the capitalists out of business.

In January of 1848, the *Communist Manifesto*, written by twenty-eight-year-old Karl Marx and Frederick Engels as a proclamation of principles for the small, extremist group, the League of the Just, was published in German. It had no effect on the events of that year and remained a little-known work until later triumphs made the authors famous. Although the call for revolutionary action to the workers of the world was stirring, there was no one listening, or at least reading. What set the framework for the revolutions of 1848 were the economic slump in England, high unemployment throughout the continent, and the failure of the potato and grain crop in 1845 and 1846 that forced up food prices. Starvation threatened.

Again, the spark that set the continent ablaze with revolution came from Paris. A shot, fired to quell a demonstration leading to a reform banquet, turned complaint into revolution and the barricades were resurrected in the streets. As in 1830, government troops lacked the will to fight and Louis abdicated to Britain. News of revolution in France spread quickly. In Vienna, workers and students stormed the palace and forced Metternich into exile. First the Hungarians, then the Czechs proclaimed the existence of autonomous parliaments within the empire, while Austrian troops were driven from Milan and Venice. Although a barrage of liberal promises was issued from Berlin, a minor incident led to hostilities. The Prussian troops, untrained in back-alley warfare, suffered the humiliation of bricks, boiling water, and chimney pots dropped on their persons from the rooftops. Frederick William IV gave in and summoned a parliament.

In little more than a year, the forces of reaction had regrouped, rolled back the wave of revolution, and reasserted their control. When the new government in France held elections, Louis Napoleon Bonaparte, nephew of the emperor, became the president of the Second French Republic. He soon took steps to rule in the same fashion as his namesake. Within the Austrian Empire, the imperial army crushed resistance in Venice, Milan, and Prague, and, with the assistance of one hundred and forty thousand Russian troops, subdued the Hungarians. In Prussia, the army remained loyal to Frederick William IV, who retook Berlin, recovered his crown, and implemented a new conservative constitution that gave limited voting rights to the wealthiest classes.

By 1850, conservatism appeared triumphant. The Hapsburgs in Austria, the Romanovs in Russia, and the Bourbons in Naples had power and prestige. The political success of the middle class in Britain was denied to the workers whose political progress had been sidetracked by the Chartists. And yet conservative governments had been challenged on several occasions by uprisings of nationalism, liberalism, and class struggle, which became increasingly clear as the process of industrialization continued. At midcentury, these elements were too divided in practice, if not in theory, and too poorly organized to achieve success. Liberalism and socialism had temporarily been discredited, but nationalism was regarded as a force with which to be reckoned. For Austria, it had the potential to break up an empire. For Italy and for Germany, it had the potential to build a nation. The revolutions of 1848 had been generated in towns and cities by middle-class intellectuals, when most of the people worked in the factories or lived in the country. Though the revolutions failed, their impact was sobering. The political power of the conservative élite could face the demands of the masses through reform, intransigence, or suppression. Whatever the response, the masses could no longer be ignored.

Bibliography

THE ORIGIN OF HUMANS

Aiello, Leslie. *The Concise Book of the Origins of Man*. Scarborough: Prentice-Hall Canada Inc., 1982.

Allen, Frederick Lewis. *Only Yesterday*. New York: Harper and Row, 1964.

Claiborne, Robert. *The First Americans*. New York: Time-Life Books, 1974.

Constable, George. *The Neanderthals*. New York: Time-Life Books, 1973.

Darwin, Charles. *The Origin of Species*. New York: Penguin Books, 1982.

Edey, Maitland. *The Missing Link*. New York: Time-Life Books, 1977.

Fisher, Helen E. "Richard Leakey's Time Machine." *Omni*, March 1983.

Hitching, Francis. "Was Darwin Wrong?" *Life*, April 1982.

Howells, William. "Homo Sapiens: 20 Million Years in the Making." *UNESCO Courier*. New York: 1972.

Johanson, Donald, and Maitland Edey. *Lucy*. New York: Simon and Schuster, 1981.

Kern, Edward P.H. "Battle of the Bones." *Life*, December 1981.

Leakey, Louis S.B. "Our African Ancestors." *UNESCO Courier*. New York: August/September 1972.

Leakey, Richard. *The Making of Mankind*. New York: E.P. Dutton, 1982.

Leakey, Richard, and Roger Lewin. *Origins*. New York: E.P. Dutton, 1977.

Morrell, Virginia. "My Brother, the Ape." *Equinox*, September/October 1983.

Napier, John. "The Evolution of the Hand." In *Human Ancestors: Readings from Scientific American*. San Francisco: W.H. Freeman and Co., 1979.

Prideaux, Tom. *Cro-Magnon Man*. New York: Time-Life Books, 1979.

Resenberger, Boyce. "Ancestors." *Science Digest*, April 1981.

Simons, Elwyn. "The Early Relatives of Man." In *Human Ancestors: Readings from Scientific American*. San Francisco: W.H. Freeman and Co., 1979.

_____. "Ramapithecus." In *Human Ancestors: Readings from Scientific American*. San Francisco: W.H. Freeman and Co., 1979.

Stoler, Peter. "Puzzling Out Man's Ascent." *Time*, 7 November 1977.

Walker, Alan, and Richard Leakey. "Hominids of East Turkana." In *Human Ancestors: Readings from Scientific American*. San Francisco: W.H. Freeman and Co., 1979.

Ward, Olivia. "Darwin Scholars Gear Up for Fight." *The Toronto Star*, 14 March 1983.

Washburn, Sherwood. "Tools and Human Evolution." In *Human Ancestors: Readings from Scientific American*. San Francisco: W.H. Freeman and Co., 1979.

White, Edmund, and Dale M. Brown. *The First Men*. New York: Time-Life Books, 1973.

York, Derek. "Ape-Like Creature Walked Upright–Counting to 4 Million B.C." *The Globe and Mail*, 10 June 1982.

_____. "Man, Ape Parting May have Been Late." *The Globe and Mail*, 22 September 1983.

NOAH'S ARK

Balsiger, David, and Charles Sellier. *In Search of Noah's Ark*. Los Angeles: Sun Classic Books, 1976.

"The Birth of Civilization." *Science Digest*, April 1981.

Claiborne, Robert. *The Birth of Writing*. Alexandria: Time-Life Books, 1977.

Fell, Barry. *America B.C.* New York: Simon and Schuster, 1976.

Furneaux, Rupert. *Ancient Mysteries*. London: Futura Publications, 1976.

Hamblin, Dora Jane. *The First Cities*. New York: Time-Life Books, 1973.

Hawkins, Gerald. *Stonehenge Decoded*. New York: Doubleday and Co. Inc., 1965.

Hitching, Francis. *The World Atlas of Mysteries*. Toronto: William Collins Sons and Co. Ltd., 1978.

McDonald, Robert. "Soviet Bear Snorts at Ark Hunt." *The Toronto Star*. 23 July 1983.

McGowan, Chris. *In The Beginning . . .* Toronto: Macmillan of Canada, 1983.

Morris, H.M. *Scientific Creationism*. Toronto: Macmillan of Canada, 1974.

_____. Interview in *In Search of Noah's Ark*, Sun Classic Pictures Inc., 1976. Film.

Ricker, John, and John Saywell. *The Emergence of Europe*. Toronto: Clarke Irwin and Co., 1968.

Stover, Leon E., and Bruce Kraig. *Stonehenge*. Chicago: Nelson-Hall, 1978.

Thom, A. *Megalithic Sites in Britain*. London: Oxford University Press, 1967.

Wernick, Robert. *The Monument Builders*. New York: Time-Life Books, 1979.

PUZZLE OF THE PYRAMIDS

Casson, Lionel. *Ancient Egypt*. Alexandria: Time-Life Books, 1978.

Cottrell, Leonard. *Lost Civilizations*. New York: Collins, Franklin Watts Inc., 1974.

Dunan, Marcel, and John Bowle, eds. *Ancient and Medieval History*. New York: Crown Publishers, 1972.

Edwards, I.E.S. *The Pyramids of Egypt*. Baltimore: Cardinal, Sphere Books Ltd., 1961.

Hitching, Francis. *The World Atlas of Mysteries*. Toronto: William Collins Sons and Company Limited, 1978.

Mendelssohn, Kurt. *The Riddle of the Pyramids*. London: Cardinal, Sphere Books Ltd., 1976.

Starr, Douglas. "Plastic Megaliths." *Omni*, 5:50, February 1983.

Trueman, John H., and Dawn C. Trueman. *The Enduring Past*. Toronto: McGraw-Hill Ryerson Limited, 1982.

Van Däniken, Erich. *Chariots of the Gods*. New York: Bantam Books, 1968.
Wilson, Clifford. *The Chariots Still Crash*. Scarborough: Signet Books, 1975.

ATLANTIS

Bacon, Edward. "Atlantis." In *Man, Myth and Magic*, part 6. Hicksville: Marshall Cavendish USA Ltd., 1974.
Casson, Lionel. "Where did Homer's Heroes Come From?" In *Mysteries of the Past*, edited by Joseph J. Thorndike. New York: American Heritage Publishing Company, 1977.
Cottrell, Leonard. *Lost Civilizations*. New York: Collins, Franklin Watts Inc., 1974.
Edey, Maitland. *Lost World of the Aegean*. New York: Time-Life Books, 1975.
Hitching, Francis. *The World Atlas of Mysteries*. Toronto: William Collins Sons and Company Ltd., 1978.
Muck, Otto. *The Secret of Atlantis*. Toronto: William Collins Sons and Company Ltd., 1976.
Plato, *Timaeus and Critias*. Translated by Desmond Lee. New York: Penguin Books Ltd., 1977.
Sakellarakis, Yannis, and Efi Sapouna-Sakellarakis. "Drama of Death in a Minoan Temple." *National Geographic*, February 1981.

THE IDEALS OF SPARTA AND ATHENS

Agard, W.R. "What Democracy Meant to the Greeks." In *Civilization in Perspective*, edited by John Patton. Toronto: Macmillan of Canada, 1972.
Andronicos, Manolis. "Athenian Democracy's Grand Design." *UNESCO Courier*. New York: October 1977.
Canby, Courtland. *Archaeology of the World*. Amsterdam: Chancellor Press, 1980.
Dunan, Marcel, and John Bowle, eds. *Ancient and Medieval History*. New York: Crown Publishers, 1972.
Eadie, John, and Ivan Krakowsky. *Athens: The Parthenon*. Study Print no. 10-6010. Encyclopedia Britannica Educational Corp., 1968.
Greece, the Golden Age. Life Educational Reprint, no. 66. 1963.
Greece, Pride and Fall. Life Educational Reprint, no. 67. 1962.
Hicks, Jim. *The Persians*. Alexandria: Time-Life Books, 1978.
Parry, Hugh. *The Individual and His Society: Alcibiades–Greek Patriot or Traitor?* Toronto: Macmillan of Canada, 1969.
———. *Ideals of Education: Spartan Warrior and Athenian All-Round Man*. Toronto: Macmillan of Canada, 1969.
Ricker, John, and John Saywell. *The Emergence of Europe*. Toronto: Clarke, Irwin and Co., 1968.
Thucydides. "History of the Peloponnesian War." Translated by Rex Warner. In *32 Problems in World History*, edited by Edwin Fenton. Glenview: Scott Foresman and Company, 1969.
Toynbee, Arnold. *A Study of History*. New York: Weathervane Books, 1972.
Trueman, John H., and Dawn C. Trueman. *The Enduring Past*. Toronto: McGraw-Hill Ryerson Ltd., 1982.
Warner, Rex. *World Mythology*. London: Royce Publications, 1983.

ALEXANDER, HANNIBAL, AND JULIUS CAESAR

Barzini, Luigi. "The Enigma of Caesar." In *Caesar: Flawed Genius*. Life Educational Reprint, no. 70. 1966.
Bowra, C.M. *Classical Greece*. New York: Time-Life Books, 1965.
Connolly, Peter. *Hannibal and the Enemies of Rome*. Morristown: Silver Burdett Co., 1979.
Dal Maso, Leonardo B. *Rome of the Caesars*. Rome: Bonechi-Edizione, 1976.
Dunan, Marcel, and John Bowle, eds. *Ancient and Medieval History*. New York: Crown Publishers, 1972.
Edey, Maitland. *The Sea Traders*. New York: Time-Life Books, 1974.
Hamblin, Dora Jane. *The Etruscans*. New York: Time-Life Books, 1976.
Lloyd, Alan. *Destroy Carthage*. London: Souvenir Press, 1977.
Parry, Hugh. *Julius Caesar: The Legend and the Man*. Toronto: Macmillan of Canada, 1972.
———. *People as Possessions: Master and Slave in the Roman World*. Toronto: Macmillan of Canada, 1972.
Porter, R.L. *Alexander the Great and His Partnership with the Persians*. Labyrinth Classical Studies, no. 28. University of Waterloo, January 1984.
Ricker, John, and John Saywell. *The Emergence of Europe*. Toronto: Clarke Irwin and Co., 1968.
Trueman, John H., and Dawn C. Trueman. *The Enduring Past*. Toronto: McGraw-Hill Ryerson Limited, 1982.
Vickers, Michael. *The Roman World*. Oxford: Elsevier-Phaidon, 1977.
Wells, H.G. *The Outline of History*. New York: Garden City Books, 1961.

THE TRIUMPH AND DECLINE OF ROME

Balsdon, J.V.D. "Life and Leisure." In *Civilization in Perspective*, edited by John Patton. Toronto: Macmillan Company of Canada, 1972.
Brooks, P.S., and N.Z. Walworth, *When the World Was Rome*. New York: J.B. Lippincott Company, 1972.
Buchanan, David. *Roman Sport and Entertainment*. Hong Kong: Longman, 1980.
Bury, J.B. "History of the Later Roman Empire." In *The Fall of Rome*, edited by Mortimer Chambers. Toronto: Holt, Rinehart and Winston, 1963.
Connolly, Peter. *Pompeii*. London: Macdonald Educational Ltd., 1979.
Dal Maso, Leonardo B. *Rome of the Caesars*. Rome: Bonechi-Edizione, 1976.
Dudley, Donald R. *The Civilization of Rome*. New York: New American Library, 1962.
Fenton, Edwin. *32 Problems in World History*. Glenview: Scott, Foresman and Company, 1964.
Forsyth, P.Y. *Setting The Record Straight: The Ancients and Mt. Vesuvius*. Labyrinth Classical Studies, no. 28, January 1984.
Gascoigne, Bamber. *The Christians*. London: Jonathan Cape Ltd., 1977.
Hadas, Moses. *Imperial Rome*. New York: Time-Life Books, 1971.
Kern, Edward. *Rome, Lively Hub of the Empire*. Life Educational Reprint, no. 16. 1966.
Magi, Giovanna. *All Pompeii*. Naples: Bonechi Editore, 1977.

Mathews, Kenneth D. *The Early Romans*. Toronto: McGraw-Hill Ryerson.

Parry, Hugh. *People as Possessions: Master and Slave in the Roman World*. Toronto: Macmillan of Canada, 1972.

Quennell, Peter. *The Colosseum*. New York: The Reader's Digest Association Ltd. with Newsweek Book Division, 1971.

Ricker, John, and John Saywell. *The Emergence of Europe*. Toronto: Clarke, Irwin and Company, 1968.

Salmon, E.Togo. "The Roman Army and the Disintegration of the Empire." In *The Fall of Rome*, edited by Mortimer Chambers. Toronto: Holt, Rinehart and Winston, 1963.

Trueman, John H., and Dawn C. Trueman. *The Enduring Past*. Toronto: McGraw-Hill Ryerson Ltd., 1982.

Wells, H.G. *The Outline of History*. New York: Garden City Books, 1961.

EUROPE AND THE PRE-COLUMBIAN DISCOVERY OF AMERICA

Ayyildiz, Ugur. *Istanbul*. Istanbul: NET

Bray, W.M.; E.H. Swanson; and I.S. Farrington. *The New World*. Belgium: Elsevier-Phaidon, 1975.

Brown, R. Allen; Michael Prestwich; and Charles Coulson. *Castles*. New York: Greenwich House, Blanford Press, 1982.

Burland, C.A. "Aztecs." In *Man, Myth and Magic*. London: BPC Publishing Ltd., 1970.

Canby, Courtland. *Archaeology of the World*. London: Chancellor Press, 1980.

Cantor, Norman F. *Medieval History*. London: The Macmillan Company, 1969.

Casson, Lionel. "Who First Crossed The Oceans?" In *Mysteries of the Past*, edited by Joseph C. Thorndike. New York: American Heritage Publishing Company, 1977.

Dunan, Marcel, and John Bowle, eds. *Ancient and Medieval History*. New York: Crown Publishers, 1972.

Eliade, M. "Patterns in Comparative Religion." In *Man, Myth and Magic*. London: BPC Publishing, 1970.

Fitzgerald, M.P., and D.R. Rayburn. *Eratosthenes of Cyrene*. In *Labyrinth Classical Studies*. January 1981.

Furneaux, Rupert. *Ancient Mysteries*. London: Futura Publications, 1976.

Gimpel, Jean. *The Cathedral Builders*. In *32 Problems in World History* edited by Edwin Fenton. Glenview: Scott, Foresman and Company, 1969.

Hale, John R. *Age of Exploration*. New York: Time Inc., 1966.

Hartt, Frederick. *Art*. vol. 1. New York: Harry N. Abrams Inc., 1976.

Heyerdahl, Thor. *The Ra Expeditions*. New York: The New American Heritage Library Inc., 1971.

Hitching, Francis. *The World Atlas of Mysteries*. Toronto: William Collins Sons and Company Ltd., 1978.

Major, J.R.; R. Scranton; and G.P. Cuttino. *Civilization in the Western World*. Toronto: J.B. Lippincott Company, 1971.

Mariott, J.A.R. *The Eastern Question*. London: Oxford At The Clarendon Press, 1969.

Mendelssohn, Kurt. *The Riddle of the Pyramids*. London: Cardinal, 1974.

McDowell, Bart. "The Aztecs." *National Geographic*, December 1980.

Reid, Richard. *Buildings*. London: Michael Joseph, 1980.

Ricker, John, and John Saywell. *The Emergence of Europe*. Clarke, Irwin and Company, 1968.

Sellman, R.R. *The Crusades*. New York: Roy Publishing Inc., 1955.

Setton, Kenneth M. "The Norman Conquest." *National Geographic*, August 1966.

Sherrard, Philip. *Byzantium*. New York: Time-Life Books, 1966.

Simons, Gerald. *Barbarian Europe*. New York: Time-Life Books, 1968.

Stuart, Gene S. *The Mighty Aztecs*. Washington, D.C.: The National Geographic Society, 1981.

Trueman, John H., and Dawn C. Trueman. *The Enduring Past*. Toronto: McGraw-Hill Ryerson Limited, 1982.

Wells, H.G. *The Outline of History*. New York: Garden City Books, 1961.

Wolf, John B. *The Emergence of European Civilization*. New York: Harper and Row, 1962.

EUROPE AND THE SUN KING

Bayer, K. *Vienna Imperial Palace*. Vienna: Burghauptmannschaft.

Bertelli, Carlo. "The Last Supper." *National Geographic*, November 1983.

Blitzer, Charles. *Age of Kings*. New York: Time Incorporated, 1967.

Brons, Martin. *Albrecht Dürer*. Königstein in Taunus: Karl Robert Langewiesche Nachfolger Hans Koster, 1970.

Chamberlin, E.R. *Renaissance Times*. New York: Perigee Books, 1980.

Cruickshank, J.E. *The Modern Age 1500–1763*. Toronto: Longmans Canada Limited, 1963.

Desing, Julius. *King Ludwig II*. Lechbruck: Verlag Kienberger, 1976.

Filipovsky, Kurt. *The Belvedere Palace*. Vienna: Österreichische Staatsdruckerei.

Guizot, François. "History of Civilization in Europe." Translated by William Hazlitt in 1900. In *The Greatness of Louis XIV*, edited by William F. Church. Toronto: D.C. Heath and Company, 1972.

Hale, John R. *Renaissance*. New York: Time-Life Inc., 1965.

Hartt, Frederick. *Art*. vol. 2. New York: Harry N. Abrams, 1976.

Hemming, John. *The Search for El Dorado*. London: Michael Joseph, 1978.

Hojer, Gerhard. *Herrenchiemsee*. Munich: Bayerische Verwaltung der staatlichen Schlösser, Gärten und Seen, 1981.

———. *Linderhof Palace*. Munich: Bayerische Verwaltung der staatlichen Schlösser, Gärten und Seen, 1981.

Lavender, E.F.B. Lewis, and N. Sheffe. *A Thousand Ages*. Toronto: McGraw-Hill Company of Canada, 1961.

Lemoine, Pierre. *Versailles*. National Museum of Castle of Versailles.

Mackirdy, K.A.; J.S. Moir; and Y.F. Zoltvany. *Changing Perspectives in Canadian History*. Don Mills, Ontario: J.M. Dent & Sons, 1971.

Moseley, Ray. "Was this King of the Castles Really Mad?" *Toronto Star*, 14 January 1984.

Ricker, John, and John Saywell. *Europe and the Modern World*. Toronto: Clarke, Irwin & Company Ltd., 1976.

Ripley, Elizabeth. *Michelangelo*. New York: Oxford University Press, 1953.

Schwarz, Lurt. *Schönbrunn*. Schlosshauptmannschaft Schönbrunn, 1963.

Seller, Charles, and Henry May. *A Synopsis of American History*. Chicago: Rand McNally and Company, 1969.

Saint-Simon, Duc de. *The Memoirs of the Duke of Saint-Simon of Louis XIV and the Regency*. Translated by Bayle St. John in 1881. In *The Greatness of Louis XIV*, edited by William F. Church. Toronto: D.C. Heath and Company, 1972.

Stamp, Kenneth M. *The Peculiar Institution*. New York: Vintage Books, 1956.

Trueman, John, and Dawn C. Trueman. *The Enduring Past*. Toronto: McGraw-Hill Ryerson Ltd., 1982.

Wells, H.G. *The Outline of History*. Revised edition. New York: Garden City Books, 1961.

"Witchcraft Hysteria Still Haunts Salem." *Toronto Star*. 10 November 1984.

Wolf, John B. *The Emergence of European Civilization*. New York: Harper & Row, 1962.

EUROPE AND THE FRENCH REVOLUTION

Blum, Jerome; Rondo Cameron; and Thomas G. Barnes. *The European World*. Boston: Little, Brown, and Company, 1970.

Bury, J.B. *The Idea of Progress*. New York: Dover Publications Inc., 1960.

Craig, Gordon A., *Europe Since 1815*. Toronto: Holt, Rinehart and Winston, 1966.

Creal, Michael. *The Idea of Progress: The Origins of Modern Optimism*. Toronto: Macmillan of Canada, 1970.

_____. *The Dynamics of Revolution: France 1789–94*. Toronto: Macmillan of Canada, 1970.

_____. *Voltaire: Passionate Fighter for Liberty*. Toronto: Macmillan of Canada, 1970.

Cruickshank, J.E. *The Modern Age*. Toronto: Longmans Canada Ltd., 1963.

Curtis, Michael, ed. *The Great Political Theories*. New York: Avon Books, 1973.

Fenton, Edwin. *32 Problems in World History*. Chicago: Scott, Foresman and Company, 1969.

Fessenden, Nicholas B. *The Impact of the Industrial Revolution*. New York: Harcourt Brace Jovanovich, 1978.

Gingerich, Owen. "The Foundation of Modern Science." *UNESCO Courier*, April 1973.

Herold, Christopher J. *The Age of Napoleon*. New York: American Heritage Publishing Co. Inc., 1983.

Hux, Allan D., and Frederick E. Jarman. *The French Revolution*. Toronto: Academic Press Canada, 1982.

Kick, H.W. *The Rise of Modern Warfare*. New York: Crescent Books, 1982.

Mendenhall, Thomas; Basil D. Henning; and Archibald S. Foord. *The Quest for a Principle of Authority in Europe 1715–Present*. Toronto: Holt, Rinehart and Winston, 1965.

Merton, Robert K. *Science, Technology and Society in Seventeenth Century England*. New York: Harper and Row, 1970.

Ricker, John, and John Saywell. *Europe and the Modern World*. Toronto: Clarke, Irwin and Company, 1976.

Spencer, Robert. *The West and a Wider World*. Toronto: Clarke, Irwin and Company, 1966.

Wells, H.G. *The Outline of History*. New York: Garden City Books, 1961.

Wolf, John B. *The Emergence of European Civilization*. New York: Harper and Row, 1962.

Photo Credits

Adespoten Photo Service 11; The Bettman Archive 210, 260, 333, 368; Bodleian Library, Oxford 204 (Ms. Gough Liturg. 2, fol. 30^r), 382; Harvey Booth 12, 56; The British Museum 176, 192; C. Coulter 61, 150 (right), 243; Calligraphy-Ann Checchia, 282; *Country Life* 271; Dale Davis 14, 56 (bottom), 59 (top and bottom), 60, 73, 77, 80, 86, 147, 150 (left), 151, 152, 153 (top and bottom), 178 (top and bottom), 179, 182, 201, 227 (bottom), 228, 230, 231, 253, 254, 283, 297, 309; Susan Hider 146; Alan Hirsch 51, 236, 237; Mas Kikuta, 13, 58; Joe Matiasek 41, 102, 252; Olivetti, Milan 248-249; Public Archives of Canada 281 (C-34183); *Punch* magazine 29; La Réunion des musées nationaux, Paris 316 (79 DN 7252), 320 (77 DN 3870), 325 (79 EN 8886); Matthew J. Richmond 227, 229; Royal Library, Windsor Castle 250 (bottom); Royal Ontario Museum 36, 42 (neg. no. 910.10), 49, 93 (cat. no. 962.228.28), 95 (cat. no. 962,244a-b), 101 (cat. no. 919.5.18), 106 (cat. no. 925.2.28), 139 (cat. no. 906.31), 257 (cat. no. 925.48.28), 270 (cat. no. 960.218.10); Stratford Festival 276 (play directed by John Hirsch, designed by Tanya Moiseiwitsch, L-R: Graeme Campbell as Burleigh, Pat Galloway as Queen Elizabeth I, Stephen Russell as Leicester, Colin Feore as Davison, William Needles as Shrewsbury, Joel Kenyon as Kent. Photograph by Robert C. Ragsdale, F.R.P.S.); Bob Thaves © 1984 Newspaper Enterprise Assn. Inc. 100; Jack Townsend 345; Uffizi Gallery, Florence: Scala 116; U.S. Naval Historical Center 24; Vatican Museum (Musei Vaticani) 250, 251; Victoria and Albert Museum 194.

Index